Pete,
Thanx for all
your hard work,
hopefully this is
not the end? from Georgia

for.
...

EMINENT BAI
IN THE TIME OF BA

CW00829124

To Pete
with love and thanks
for all your hard work
on "The Seven Valleys"
Project. Becky

George Fixsen

Pete
Thank at lot
for all your
hard work
we could not
have done it
with out you
Thank you
from Roxy

...I will always remember
you - pete meguir!!!
Pete
Daryl
Thank you very
much for all
your herd worke
We appreciate it
very much.
Jenny

Pete, You are simply
The Best!!
Thank you for everything.
Love Samia
x x

Dear Pete sorry
for writing all over
your new book but
we had to say thanks
for all your help. All
the best for the future
Luv Purina

By the same author

BAHÁ'U'LLÁH
The King of Glory

BAHÁ'U'LLÁH
A brief life, followed by an essay entitled
THE WORD MADE FLESH

THE BÁB
The Herald of the Day of Days

'ABDU'L-BAHÁ
The Centre of the Covenant of Bahá'u'lláh

KHADÍJIH BAGUM
The Wife of the Báb

EDWARD GRANVILLE BROWNE AND THE BAHÁ'Í FAITH

MUHAMMAD AND THE COURSE OF ISLÁM

Dear Peter,
You have awakened
and enthused a generation
of our precious junior youth.
We will miss you and your dear family
so much! With much love, Nike and Jita

Your
dedication,
enthusiasm +
persistence are
an inspiration.
Your efforts + hard
work are really
appreciated. And
the sacrifice of your
time by your family
as well. Thank you
so much. When is
the CD available?
With love + hugs,
Zari xxx

Peter, the CD is
great, you did
a grand job, thanks
Valerie

Mírzá Muḥammad-Taqí, known as Ibn-i-Abhar

'Nothing daunted them, no blow ever swerved them from their straight path, no rancour embittered their lives. Serving the Faith of Bahá'u'lláh was the only goal they knew.'

EMINENT BAHÁ'ÍS
in the Time of Bahá'u'lláh

with
Some Historical Background

by

H. M. Balyuzi

GR
GEORGE RONALD
OXFORD

GEORGE RONALD, Publisher
46 High Street, Kidlington, Oxford OX5 2DN

Grateful acknowledgement is made for extracts taken from the following works:

Baron, S. W. *A Social and Religious History of the Jews* (Vol. III), © 1957, Columbia University Press. By permission. Koestler, Arthur. *The Thirteenth Tribe: The Khazar Empire and Its Heritage*, ©1976. Reprinted by permission of A. D. Peters & Co Ltd. Zaehner, R. C. *Zurvan, A Zoroastrian Dilemma,* 1955, Clarendon Press, Oxford. *The Dawn-Breakers: Nabíl's Narrative of the Early Days of the Bahá'í Revelation:* Copyright 1932, 1953, 1962 © 1970, 1974 Reprinted with permission of the National Spiritual Assembly of the Bahá'ís of the United States.

British Library Cataloguing in Publication Data

Balyuzi, H. M.
Eminent Bahá'ís in the time of Bahá'u'lláh with some historical background.
1. Bahai Faith—Biography
I. Title
297'.89'0922 BP390

ISBN 0-85398-151-5
ISBN 0-85398-152-3 Pbk

Phototypeset by Sunrise Setting, Torquay, Devon
set in Times Roman 11 on 13 point
Printed and bound in Great Britain at
The Camelot Press Ltd, Southampton

Contents

PART II

Illustrations and maps are indexed under the relevant headings.

Foreword

THE PASSING of the Hand of the Cause of God Hasan M. Balyuzi was a great blow to the many people around the world who were admirers of his writings. At the time of his death, he was half-way through a monumental four-volume study of the life and times of the Founder of the Bahá'í Faith, Bahá'u'lláh. He had intended the first volume in this series to contain the basic biography of Bahá'u'lláh, together with some chapters on the history of nineteenth-century Írán as a background for the events of Bahá'í history. As this volume grew in size, it was decided to transfer most of the historical chapters to a later one. The first volume, with the title *Bahá'u'lláh, The King of Glory*, was published shortly after Mr Balyuzi's passing and contained three of the historical chapters (10, 14 and Appendix).

Mr Balyuzi had planned the second volume to consist principally of biographies of a selection of the most important disciples of Bahá'u'lláh. By the time of his death, he had completed fourteen of these, with a further four partially written. Shoghi Effendi, the Guardian of the Bahá'í Faith, had included in *The Bahá'í World*, Vol. III (pp. 80–81), the names of nineteen Bahá'ís whom he designated as 'Apostles of Bahá'u'lláh'. Mr Balyuzi intended to include all of these among his biographies. 'The Story of Badí'', one of these, was told in the first volume (Chapter 33). The life of Mírzá Músá, Áqáy-i-Kalím, the brother of Bahá'u'lláh, another of the Apostles, was so inextricably bound up with that of Bahá'u'lláh Himself that it was, in effect, also covered in the first volume. The life of yet another, Mírzá Abu'l-Faḍl-i-Gulpáygání, Mr Balyuzi considered so momentous that he felt he could not confine it to a mere chapter, and he asked the present writer to prepare a separate book entirely on the life of this notable figure. For the remaining sixteen Apostles, Mr Balyuzi had, at the time of his passing, completed only three biographies and partially written three more. In the last four months of his life, however, he had come to realize that to include biographies of all of the Apostles of Bahá'u'lláh, his second volume would itself have to become two separate volumes. But his death supervened and the projected chapters remained unwritten. As a token of Mr Balyuzi's intentions, the present writer has contributed short accounts of the remaining Apostles of Bahá'u'lláh in Chapter 20, including Mírzá Abu'l-Faḍl, and has briefly completed the three unfinished biographies, as well as two other chapters. These additions are clearly indicated in the text for Chapters 9, 13, 14, 17 and 18, where the added material follows a line of asterisks.

It had also been Mr Balyuzi's intention to write a brief account of Mírzá Ḥasan, Mírzáy-i-Shírází, the greatest of the Shí'ih mujtahids of his age, who, as would appear from the account in this volume, bore secret allegiance to the Faith of Bahá'u'lláh. Since most of the text of this chapter was to have been a translation of Mírzá Ḥabíbu'lláh Afnán's account of his father's meeting with this famous cleric, a curtailed version is included as Chapter 19. It is clear from statements made in some of the existing chapters, as well as from notes left among his papers, that a number of other chapters had been contemplated, such as one on the Seven Martyrs of Yazd and another on the Ṭihrán persecutions of 1882–3.

For the third volume of this series, Mr Balyuzi had envisaged an ambitious project. He would set Bahá'u'lláh's Tablets to the Kings and Rulers of the World against the history of nineteenth-century Europe. And he would demonstrate how the three 'false gods', of which Shoghi Effendi had written in *The Promised Day is Come* (pp. 113–14), had led to the destruction of the once-mighty continent of Europe. To this end, Mr Balyuzi had already completed some exhaustive research, had written an introduction, and had translated those parts of the *Súriy-i-Mulúk* (Tablets to the Kings) as yet untranslated. But this is as far as he had reached at the time of his death.

The fourth volume of the series was to have been a collection of documents, principally from non-Bahá'í sources, relating to the life of Bahá'u'lláh. Mr Balyuzi had asked the present writer to take responsibility for the collection of the material for this volume, and shortly before his passing I had presented him with a provisional list of contents which he had approved.

Thus, while the third volume must remain forever unwritten, it is hoped that the material for the fourth volume may eventually be gathered, translated and published. The historical chapters omitted from the first volume also remain to be published.

MOOJAN MOMEN

Preface

MY FATHER'S DEATH was announced to the Bahá'í community, on 12 February 1980, by a cable from the Universal House of Justice, the text of which was later chosen by the House of Justice to be inscribed upon the stone erected over his grave. He lies now within yards of the resting-place of the Guardian of the Bahá'í Faith, Shoghi Effendi; and visitors to that revered and beautiful spot who chance upon his grave may read these lines: ' . . . his outstanding scholarly pursuits will inspire many devoted workers among rising generations follow his glorious footsteps . . . '

In her memorial article to my father, soon to be published in *The Bahá'í World*, Vol. XVIII, Mrs Marion Hofman writes of him: 'A student from his youth, he became in the last decade of his life and in the sight of all the Bahá'í world its pre-eminent scholar, yielding place only to Mírzá Abu'l-Faḍl, by whose learning Mr. Balyuzi was himself astonished.'

For all those who knew him, whether as friend, colleague, mentor, teacher, Bahá'í co-worker, or as member of his family, each will have his own personal memory of him. Removed now in time by five years from his physical presence, my own strongest memory is of his gentleness. Yet I fancy that had I ever asked him how he would himself best wish to be remembered, then I think that it would have been his hope that his scholarship might endure. His respect for learning was central to his faith; and although he was rarely given to anger, he could never accept calmly any abuse of scholarship, whether from deliberate falsification or from careless ignorance, whenever he encountered it.

The time will come, no doubt, when my father's writings will require revision. The study of history is not a static discipline; continuing research in any field of enquiry is likely to continue to bring to light new information, and these hitherto hidden facts may lead in time to fresh interpretation and different perspectives. Yet I believe that his books will abide; for nothing false will ever be found in them, no half-truths, no distortions of available information carefully tailored to lend support to his conclusions. Every fact that they contain, every source of information, every reference, will have been painstakingly and exhaustively checked and researched, either by himself or by those whom he entrusted to assist him. When a book was finally committed to print and publication, it left my father's pen with his absolute conviction that he had served truth to the fullest of his ability: for anything less would have been a denial of the strength and power of the Covenant of Bahá'u'lláh, in which his belief was absolute and his faith never failed him.

In *The Passing of Shoghi Effendi*, written soon after his death in 1957, his widow, Amatu'l-Bahá Rúḥíyyih Khánum, opens with these words: 'All those who were privileged to know the beloved Guardian Shoghi Effendi from the time of his childhood until his passing remember him as being incarnate with life; a dynamic, almost electric force seemed to radiate from him.'

In November 1925, as a boy of seventeen, brought up in a Bahá'í family but not yet with any commitment to the Faith, my father arrived to stay for one night in Haifa, *en route* to start his University life in Beirut. He arrived there at a time of great preoccupation and personal sorrow for the Guardian, as Dr John Ebenezer Esslemont lay dying in the old Pilgrim House. Yet despite his troubled mind – and my father has written how he sat up with Dr Esslemont through that night – Shoghi Effendi took time to greet this youth with great kindness, and stayed to talk with him and answer his questions for over an hour. In my father's words: 'It was that bounty of meeting Shoghi Effendi and all that I saw in him, which confirmed me in the Faith of Bahá'u'lláh. The course of my life was changed.'

After that, my father was to meet Shoghi Effendi on various occasions during his student days, when holidays were spent in Haifa with other young Bahá'í students, the last being in February 1932 before he left for England to continue his education there. This proved to be his last ever meeting with the Guardian. The nearly fifty years that remained of his life would be spent in the service of the Bahá'í Cause: a service which was an eloquent testament to the 'dynamic, almost electric force' of the Guardian which had so charged and enthused his soul.

In 1938 my father wrote a short biography of Bahá'u'lláh, the

Prophet Founder of the Bahá'í Faith, and Shoghi Effendi acknowledged its publication by expressing the hope that he would complete the companion essays which he intended writing on the lives of the Báb, Who preceded Bahá'u'lláh and heralded His coming, and of Bahá'u'lláh's son, 'Abdu'l-Bahá, as these, the Guardian felt, would be of valuable help in the teaching of the Cause. It was to be another thirty-three years, through circumstances described in its Foreword, before *'Abdu'l-Bahá, The Centre of the Covenant of Bahá'u'lláh*, was published, with its dedication 'To the ever present spirit of the Guardian of the Cause of God'; and nine years later his book *Bahá'u'lláh, The King of Glory* was also dedicated to Shoghi Effendi.

I can still recall vividly that day in November 1957 when, as a child of thirteen, I stood on the graveside as Shoghi Effendi's coffin was lowered into the ground. In that charged moment I can remember looking up at my father and marking how rigid and motionless he stood, his face almost devoid of expression. When he came to speak the final prayer, the one of Bahá'u'lláh's which begins 'Glory be to Thee, O God, for Thy manifestation of love to mankind!', he did so almost in a monotone, his voice sounding to me drained of emotion. I could not properly understand then, but believe now, in the knowledge of all that happened after, that at that moment his heart was broken. The depth of his grieving was such that he was in a state of profound shock, in which his feelings were numbed so that emotion could find little outlet.

For six years after that he kept going, borne along by the force of events during a time of great crisis and momentous decisions, when the duties imposed upon him by his station as a Hand of the Cause had to be met. But after the culminating events of this period, the election of the first Universal House of Justice and the Bahá'í World Congress in London in 1963, the increasingly fragile prop of physical health finally collapsed, and he plunged into a dark and despairing retreat, punished by illness of the body and near mental breakdown.

In her memorial article Mrs Hofman has written of how his mind was filled with 'forebodings of guilt for his wasted days and abdication of his responsibilities as a Hand', but also she tells how, 'all unrecognized, another path was to open before him, another way of service as a Hand which the Will and Testament of 'Abdu'l-Bahá had delineated: to promote learning'. For it was to his historical researches that he turned for a lifeline, and although he was to suffer from continually deteriorating health for the remainder of his days, he managed to summon together the spiritual strength and mental energy to embark upon a decade of writing that saw the publication of five major works of history: his biographies of the lives of the three Central Figures of the Bahá'í Faith, his work entitled *Edward Granville Browne and The Bahá'í Faith*, and *Muḥammad and the Course of Islám*, this last book written out of his conviction that an objective evaluation of Islám is an essential prerequisite to an understanding of the origins of the Bahá'í religion.

In his Foreword to this present volume, Dr Momen has explained how it came to be written, and how it fits into my father's plan for a four-volume study of the life and times of Bahá'u'lláh. Those readers previously unfamiliar with Bahá'í history will certainly encounter some difficulties, and for them some acquaintance with my father's earlier books will be found to be of assistance, particularly *The Báb*, which gives the background events to some of the biographies contained in Part I, and also, of course, *Bahá'u'lláh, The King of Glory*, intended as volume one of the four-part work. Reference to *Muḥammad and the Course of Islám* could be helpful for certain chapters of Part II. The following brief explanation of the distinction between Bábís and Bahá'ís may also assist the reader, since this was not generally understood in Írán during most of the period covered by this volume.

Bábí is the name given to the followers of the Báb, the young merchant of Shíráz, Siyyid 'Alí-Muḥammad, who in May 1844, at the age of 25 years, declared Himself to be the Báb, the Gate of God, the return of the hidden Imám-Mahdí, the Deliverer eagerly awaited by the world of Shí'ih Islám. His Ministry was to last but six years, though in that short time He attracted thousands to accept His Cause, and in doing so inevitably provoked the most bitter enmity amongst those who did not believe in Him. Supported by the State, the orthodox Persian clergy instigated a period of brutal and fanatical persecution, which not only brought the Báb before a firing-squad to meet His death in July 1850, but almost succeeded in obliterating the followers of the new religion.

During the few years of His Ministry, the Báb wrote frequently of the coming of another, 'Him Whom God shall make manifest'. In 1863, thirteen years after the martyrdom of the Báb, a nobleman of Mázindarán and a Bábí, Mírzá Ḥusayn-'Alí, declared Himself to be that One foretold by the Báb, the return of Christ to Earth to lead mankind into a new epoch of spiritual development. He took the title Bahá'u'lláh – the Glory of God – a designation first mentioned by the Báb. Before long the greater part of the surviving Bábí community had accepted the leadership and the Message of Bahá'u'lláh, and they became known as Bahá'ís. Some never did, however, and they remained Bábís.

Bahá'u'lláh gave strength and courage back to the beleaguered and persecuted community of the Báb but, as will be learned from this volume, He was not able to put an end to the opposition of the Muslim clergy, and the hounding and sporadic butchering of His followers was to continue throughout His lifetime. This book tells the stories of some of those followers.

Although references are given for quotations, and published books and documents are listed in the bibliography, it seems fitting to mention the names of those Iranian Bahá'ís whose writings were important sources for my father: 'Abdu'lláh-i-Ṣaḥíḥ-Furúsh, Ḥájí Mírzá; Abu'l-Faḍl, Mírzá; 'Azízu'lláh-i-Jadhdháb, Áqá; Ḥabíbu'lláh Afnán, Ḥájí Mírzá; Ḥaydar-'Alí, Ḥájí Mírzá; Ḥusayn-i-Zanjání, Mírzá; Ibn-i-Aṣdaq (Mírzá 'Alí-Muḥammad); Maḥmúd-i-Furúghí, Mírzá; Malik-Khusraví, Muḥammad-'Alí; Nabíl-i-Akbar (Áqá Muḥammad-i-Qá'iní); Nabíl-i-A'ẓam (Muḥammad-i-Zarandí); Na'ím (Mírzá Muḥammad); Náẓimu'l-Ḥukamá (Mírzá Siyyid Muḥammad); Samandar, Shaykh Káẓim; Síná, Siyyid Ismá'íl; Sulaymání, 'Azízu'lláh; Valíyu'lláh Khán, Mírzá.

On behalf of my father, most grateful thanks are extended to those who published several of these historic documents or made available others as yet unpublished, amongst whom he would have surely mentioned, as he had done in his previous books, his cousin, Abu'l-Qásim Afnán. Finally, my father's own words intended for 'Azízu'lláh Sulaymání should be quoted: 'The present writer is much indebted to the author of those eight volumes [*Maṣábiḥ-i-Hidáyat*], from which he has gleaned many of his facts.'

All translations from Persian and Arabic, unless otherwise attributed, were made by my father, including the many important Tablets by Bahá'u'lláh, the Báb and 'Abdu'l-Bahá, whose translations have been approved at the Bahá'í World Centre. The unsparing assistance extended by the Research Department in connection with these Tablets, as well as that of the Audio-Visual Department in seeking out and reproducing the invaluable photographs of early believers, is acknowledged with deep gratitude.

I have left until last to write about the two people without whose efforts the publication of this book would not have been possible, Mrs Marion Hofman and Dr Moojan Momen, not because their contributions demote them to be considered after others, but because proper recognition of their extraordinary service to my father makes a most fitting postlude at this ending of the road: the publication of his last major Bahá'í history.

Dr Momen was first introduced to my father in January 1972 by his uncle, Dr Iraj Ayman. He was at that time completing his medical studies in London, and in such free time as he had available was pursuing his interest in the history of the Faith by researches in the Public Record Office. Dr Ayman was aware that my father was in great need of an assistant to aid him with research, and so effected the introduction. There very quickly developed a bond between them, and a recognition on my father's part of Dr Momen's considerable ability as an historian, which allowed him to trust completely Dr Momen's judgement and correctness of method.

Although, at first, still heavily engaged in his studies and later having to cope with the demands on him as a full-time medical practitioner, Dr Momen gave unselfishly of his time in carrying out research for my father in the preparation of *The Báb* and, most importantly, *Bahá'u'lláh, The King of Glory*; in the Preface to this latter book my father expresses his profound gratitude to Dr Momen for his help 'of inestimable value'. Not, however, until 1981 with the publication of Dr Momen's massive work, *The Bábí and Bahá'í Religions, 1844–1944*, could the true measure of Moojan's help to my father be realized. For anyone familiar with that work will not fail to recognize the enormous volume of research that must have gone into its preparation. Yet, it was while engaged upon that preparation, and also pursuing his career in medicine, that Dr Momen found the time to help my father to the degree and with the effect that he did.

My father loved Moojan as though he had been of his own family, and he was amongst the first that I telephoned with the news on the morning of my father's death. He came at once to be with us and share in our grief. On that same day we opened letters that my father had left to be read after his passing. In these he appointed Dr Momen to be one of his three literary executors, together with my mother and myself; and he entrusted to his safekeeping the diaries and letter books of his father, Muvaqqari'd-Dawlih, which he treasured highly amongst his collected library. Some time before he had spoken to Moojan of his dear wish to write a biography of his father, but he greatly doubted whether he had sufficient time left to him on earth to accomplish this task. So instead, he enjoined Moojan to give thought to writing this book, that he himself would never write.

Mrs Marion Hofman first met my father on her wedding day, in October 1945, from when began a close friendship that endured to the end of his days, and has continued beyond the grave with her most moving and beautifully written memorial article for *The Bahá'í World*, from which I have earlier quoted.

For my part, I must limit myself here to the bare statement that Marion has personally edited and prepared all of the seven books of my father published since 1970, including the present volume; that she prepared the indexes for *Edward Granville Browne and The Bahá'í Faith*, for *'Abdu'l-Bahá*, for *Bahá'u'lláh, The King of Glory* and for this present book; and that in so doing she enjoyed his complete trust and confidence and, since his death, that of his family too.

When in August 1970 Marion sent to my father copies of the published *Edward Granville Browne and The Bahá'í Faith*, after extensive correspondence and many meetings between them on its editing and production, he wrote to her: 'The production is excellent . . . With warmest love . . . and much grateful thanks'; and, three months earlier, when he saw the typescript of the Index, he had written to her: 'I am sure this index will serve as a model for future Bahá'í books'.

He did not live to see a published copy of *Bahá'u'lláh, The King of Glory*, but, had he done so, how delighted he would have been with it, and how much he would have appreciated the efforts of Marion to produce a book so fitting in its presentation to its subject-matter.

Now, for this present volume, with no one to confirm their decisions but themselves, Mrs Hofman and Dr Momen have taken the incomplete manuscript left by my father, and by their determination and consummate skills, and encouraged by their love for him, have given life to his book.

I, and my family, are deeply grateful to them both.

London ROBERT BALYUZI
1 February 1985

Part I

Thou hast made mention of the loved ones in those regions. Praised be God, each one of them attained the honour of being remembered by the True One – exalted is His glory – and the names of them, one and all, flowed from the Tongue of Grandeur in the kingdom of utterance. Great indeed is their blessedness and happiness, inasmuch as they have drunk the choice wine of revelation and inspiration from the hand of their Lord, the Compassionate, the Merciful.

Bahá'u'lláh

Prologue

MANY, MANY YEARS AGO, 'Abdu'l-Bahá wrote in a Tablet, addressed to a Bahá'í of Írán, of an incident belonging to the days when Sulṭán Muḥammad-i-Fátiḥ (the Conqueror), the celebrated Ottoman ruler, had laid siege to the proud Constantinople; and that great centre of learning, the world-famed metropolis of the Eastern Roman Empire (once overwhelmingly rich, but shamelessly despoiled as early as 1205 by uncouth, greedy Crusaders) was, at last, about to fall before the mighty arms of Islám. At such a moment of destiny a Byzantine nobleman, convinced that fate had brought Byzantium to its end, went to visit a prelate, and found that worthy divine busy in his sanctum, scribbling fast.

'What are you composing so hurriedly, at a time so precarious?' the nobleman asked.

'Oh, I'm writing a treatise against Muḥammad,' replied the prelate.

Hearing that, the sorely-tried and desperate nobleman exploded.

'You utter, utter fool,' he exclaimed. 'Can you not see that you are late, by far too late! The time for writing a refutation of the Prophet of Arabia is long, long past. Look out there, over the ramparts of our city. What do you see? There, look well. There are rank upon rank of the soldiers of Islám. There are the waving banners of Islám triumphant. When the Faith of Muḥammad was confined to the wastelands of Arabia, that was the time to write your silly refutations; not today, not today. We shall very soon be the vassals of the Great Turk!'

From its inception the Faith of the Báb and Bahá'u'lláh has had its traducers. Fierce persecutions – merciless and relentless – apart, many there have been, fanatic and shallow, unprincipled and vain, both in the East and the West, who have taken up their pens, oftentimes vicious and vitriolic, at times licentious, to refute that which the Lord of creation has purposed for this age, which is that Age of Fulfilment promised to Man from the dawn of historical times.

But none of these outbursts of human ingratitude have had the slightest effect on the onward march of the Faith of the Báb and

Bahá'u'lláh from victory to victory. These traducers, not having learned their lesson, are still writing tome after tome packed with falsehood to (as they imagine) besmirch the reputation of the Cause of God. They are far too late. The Faith of Bahá'u'lláh has encircled the globe.

Many they were who gave the most precious of all they possessed – their lives – that the Cause of God should live and flourish. Their blood watered the plant which the hand of the Almighty had fashioned into existence; their constancy buttressed it against tempestuous winds; their unbreakable faith shielded it from the onrush of malice and evil intent.

And many they were, too, who toiled and laboured all their lives, to share with their fellow-men the inestimable bounty which was theirs: the recognition of Him Who shall lead Man to peace – peace with himself and his Creator. Nothing daunted them, no blow ever swerved them from their straight path, no rancour embittered their lives. Serving the Faith of Bahá'u'lláh was the only goal they knew.

This book is their story.

MAP OF IRAN

(See map of Northern Iran, page 289.)

I

Ismu'lláhu'l-Aṣdaq
A Notable Survivor of Shaykh Ṭabarsí

MULLÁ ṢÁDIQ-I-MUQADDAS-I-KHURÁSÁNÍ, whom Bahá'u'lláh honoured with the designation Ismu'lláhu'l-Aṣdaq – The Name of God the Most Truthful – was a disciple of the Shaykhí leader, Ḥájí Siyyid Káẓim-i-Rashtí. His master laid on him the mandate to reside in Iṣfahán, and pave the way, in that renowned city of 'Abbás the Great, for the Advent of the Qá'im. Mullá Ḥusayn-i-Bushrú'í, the Bábu'l-Báb, on his way with his unique and wondrous mission to Bahá'u'lláh in Ṭihrán, met Mullá Ṣádiq, a fellow-disciple and friend of old, in Iṣfahán, where he had been living for a while as directed by Siyyid Káẓim, and gave him the tidings of the Advent of the Báb.* However, Mullá Ḥusayn was not allowed to divulge the identity of the Heavenly Being, the near approach of Whose appearance had been emphatically asserted by Ḥájí Siyyid Káẓim.

Mullá Ṣádiq himself has told the story of how he came to know and recognize the Báb – and here it is:

I asked Mullá Ḥusayn to divulge the name of Him who claimed to be the promised Manifestation. He replied: 'To enquire about that name and to divulge it are alike forbidden.' 'Would it, then, be possible,' I asked, 'for me, even as the Letters of the Living, to seek independently the grace of the All-Merciful and, through prayer, to discover His identity?' 'The door of His grace,' he replied, 'is never closed before the face of him who seeks to find Him.' I immediately retired from his presence, and requested his host to allow me the privacy of a room in his house where, alone and undisturbed, I could commune with God. In the midst of my contemplation, I suddenly remembered the face of a Youth whom I had often observed while in Karbilá, standing in an attitude of prayer, with His face bathed in tears at the entrance of the shrine of the Imám Ḥusayn. That same countenance now reappeared before my eyes. In my vision I seemed to behold that same face,

* The Báb declared His Mission to Mullá Ḥusayn on the night of 22 May 1844.

those same features, expressive of such joy as I could never describe. He smiled as He gazed at me. I went towards Him, ready to throw myself at His feet. I was bending towards the ground, when, lo! that radiant figure vanished from before me. Overpowered with joy and gladness, I ran out to meet Mullá Ḥusayn, who with transport received me and assured me that I had, at last, attained the object of my desire. He bade me, however, repress my feelings. 'Declare not your vision to anyone,' he urged me; 'the time for it has not yet arrived. You have reaped the fruit of your patient waiting in Iṣfáhán. You should now proceed to Kirmán, and there acquaint Ḥájí Mírzá Karím Khán with this Message. From that place you should travel to Shíráz and endeavour to rouse the people of that city from their heedlessness. I hope to join you in Shíráz and share with you the blessings of a joyous reunion with our Beloved.' (Nabíl-i-A'ẓam, *The Dawn-Breakers*, pp. 100–101)

Mullá Ṣádiq, enamoured as he was of the mien and the bearing of that young Siyyid, Whom he had encountered facing the Shrine of the Third Imám [Ḥusayn], had, one day, ventured to speak to Him and invite Him to visit his house, where Siyyid Káẓim was expected to attend a *Rawḍih-Khání*, an assemblage devoted to the recital of the sufferings of the House of the Prophet, and particularly the martyrdom of the Third Imám. The young Siyyid had readily and graciously accepted the invitation. When Mírzá 'Alí-Muḥammad, that young Siyyid of Shíráz, arrived at Mullá Ṣádiq's house, Siyyid Káẓim and his disciples were already there and seated. On seeing the young Shírází make His entrance, Siyyid Káẓim immediately rose and asked Him to take a seat much higher in the room. Those present were amazed and speechless because of the marked respect shown by Siyyid Káẓim to this very young Siyyid, Who was unknown in their circles in Karbilá. And the preacher who occupied the pulpit was momentarily struck dumb. He could not utter a word. This preacher was none other than Mullá Ḥusayn-i-Bushrú'í, destined to be the first believer in the new Theophany, that faithful soul who had apprised Mullá Ṣádiq of the Advent of the Qá'im of the House of Muḥammad.

Now, complete silence settled over that gathering, until Siyyid Káẓim's voice was heard directing Mullá Ḥusayn to recite some lines of a poem of Shaykh Aḥmad-i-Aḥsá'í, recalling the sufferings of the Third Imám. The words which Mullá Ḥusayn uttered caused the young Shírází to weep so disconsolately and so bitterly that the entire congregation was deeply affected. Later, when sherbet was served, Siyyid 'Alí-Muḥammad did not partake of it.

A few days later, Siyyid 'Alí-Muḥammad once again encountered Mullá Ṣádiq in the compound of the Shrine of the Third Imám. He told him that His uncle had arrived from Shíráz and asked whether Mullá Ṣádiq wished to meet him. That afternoon Mullá Ṣádiq visited the house where Siyyid 'Alí-Muḥammad lodged. He found that His uncle had many visitors: Persians of high rank, divines and merchants. Siyyid 'Alí-Muḥammad Himself was busy dispensing tea and other refreshments. Mullá Ṣádiq was soon expressing to the Shírází merchant the unbounded admiration which he cherished for his Nephew, so unique in every way. Ḥájí Mírzá Siyyid 'Alí was glad to hear a total stranger speak in such glowing terms of his Nephew and replied: 'In Shíráz all the members of our family are well known for their outstanding qualities, but my young Nephew *is* unique and excels them all. But despite His high qualities, He falls short in one way. He neglects His studies.' Mullá Ṣádiq responded that should the young man be kept in Karbilá, he himself would undertake to supervise His studies, to which offer Ḥájí Mírzá Siyyid 'Alí readily agreed. However, soon after, both he and his remarkable Nephew returned to Shíráz.

Mullá Ṣádiq was the son of a well-known man of Khurásán named Mírzá Ismá'íl. He had two brothers, one of whom, the twenty-two-year-old Mírzá Muḥammad-Ḥasan, on hearing in 1848 that a number of Bábís were on their way to Mázindarán, forwent his marriage on the eve of his wedding day and took the road with his fellow-believers to follow the standard raised by Mullá Ḥusayn. On the way to Shaykh Ṭabarsí he met martyrdom at the hands of the horsemen of Khusraw-i-Qádíkalá'í. Mullá Ṣádiq was the eldest of the brothers. He had sat at the feet of Ḥájí Siyyid Káẓim-i-Rashtí and had risen high in the circle of his disciples. But when his teacher had directed his steps to Iṣfahán he had accepted the great responsibility laid upon him.

The Báb had told Mullá Ḥusayn that Mullá Ṣádiq would unhesitatingly respond to His call and enrol himself under His banner, and it happened exactly as the Báb had foretold. As soon as Mullá Ṣádiq realized that He, the tidings of Whose advent Mullá Ḥusayn had given him, was none other than the same young Shírází Siyyid Whom he had met, some years before, in Karbilá, and Whom he had exceedingly admired, he threw all caution to the winds and rose up with all his vigour to serve Him and His Cause. On the very morning after the night when the full light of truth dawned upon him, he left Iṣfahán on

The Masjid-i-Vakíl in Shíráz in which the Báb was invited to clarify His position (Dieulafoy, La Perse*)*

The Bazar of Vakíl in Shíráz (Dieulafoy, La Perse*)*

foot to walk all the way to Shíráz. He took a path from which there could be no turning, a path which led away from pomp and power, from the fruits of worldly success. He well knew what price he was paying for his devotion. It took Mullá Ṣádiq twelve days to reach the abode of his Beloved. But the Báb was not in Shíráz. He had gone on pilgrimage to Mecca, accompanied by Quddús, who, before long, returned bearing a Tablet of the Báb. Mullá Ṣádiq had, in the meantime, become a *Píshnamáz* (the cleric who leads the congregation in prayer in the mosque).

Reading in the Tablet of the Báb, with which Quddús had entrusted him, the instruction to add to the usual words of the *adhán* (call to prayer) the following: 'I bear witness that He whose name is 'Alí-Qabl-i-Muḥammad [a reference to the name of the Báb*] is the servant of the Baqíyyatu'lláh [the Remnant of God, referring to Bahá'u'lláh]', Mullá Ṣádiq set out to give effect to that unmistakable command. Let Nabíl-i-A'ẓam describe that event and its aftermath:

> . . . he, one day as he was leading his congregation in prayer in the Masjid-i-Naw [New Mosque], suddenly proclaimed, as he was sounding the adhán, the additional words prescribed by the Báb. The multitude that heard him was astounded by his cry. Dismay and consternation seized the entire congregation. The distinguished divines, who occupied the front seats and who were greatly revered for their pious orthodoxy, raised a clamour, loudly protesting: 'Woe betide us, the guardians and protectors of the Faith of God! Behold, this man has hoisted the standard of heresy. Down with this infamous traitor! He has spoken blasphemy. Arrest him, for he is a disgrace to our Faith.' 'Who,' they angrily exclaimed, 'dared authorise such grave departure from the established precepts of Islám? Who has presumed to arrogate to himself this supreme prerogative?'
>
> The populace re-echoed the protestations of these divines, and arose to reinforce their clamour. The whole city had been aroused, and public order was, as a result, seriously threatened. The governor of the province of Fárs, Ḥusayn Khán-i-Íravání, surnamed Ájúdán-Báshí, . . . found it necessary to intervene and to enquire into the cause of this sudden commotion. He was informed that a disciple [Quddús] of a young man named Siyyid-i-Báb, who had just returned from His pilgrimage to Mecca and Medina and was now living in Búshihr, had arrived in Shíráz and was propagating the teachings of his Master. 'This disciple,' Ḥusayn Khán was further informed, 'claims that his teacher is the author of a new revelation and is the revealer of a book which he asserts is divinely inspired. Mullá Ṣádiq-i-Khurásání has embraced that faith, and is fearlessly summoning the multitude to the acceptance of that message. He declares its recognition to be the first obligation of every loyal and pious follower of shí'ah Islám.'

* 'Qabl' means 'before'.

Ḥusayn Khán-i-Íraváni, surnamed Ájúdán-Báshí
Governor of the Province of Fars

Ḥusayn Khán ordered the arrest of both Quddús and Mullá Ṣádiq. The police authorities, to whom they were delivered, were instructed to bring them handcuffed into the presence of the governor. The police also delivered into the hands of Ḥusayn Khán the copy of the Qayyúmu'l-Asmá', which they had seized from Mullá Ṣádiq while he was reading aloud its passages to an excited congregation. Quddús, owing to his youthful appearance and unconventional dress, was at first ignored by Ḥusayn Khán, who preferred to direct his remarks to his more dignified and elderly companion. 'Tell me,' angrily asked the governor, as he turned to Mullá Ṣádiq, 'if you are aware of the opening passage of the Qayyúmu'l-Asmá' wherein the Siyyid-i-Báb addresses the rulers and kings of the earth in these terms: "Divest yourselves of the robe of sovereignty, for He who is the King in truth, hath been made manifest! The Kingdom is God's, the Most Exalted. Thus hath the Pen of the Most High decreed!" If this be true, it must necessarily apply to my sovereign, Muḥammad Sháh, of the Qájár dynasty, whom I represent as the chief magistrate of this province. Must Muḥammad Sháh, according to this behest, lay down his crown and abandon his sovereignty? Must I, too, abdicate my power and relinquish my position?' Mullá Ṣádiq unhesitatingly replied: 'When once the truth of the Revelation announced by the Author of these words shall have been definitely established, the truth of whatsoever has fallen from His lips will likewise be vindicated. If these words be the Word of God, the abdication of Muḥammad Sháh and his like can matter but little. It can in no wise turn aside the Divine purpose, nor alter the sovereignty of the almighty and eternal King.'

That cruel and impious ruler was sorely displeased with such an answer. He reviled and cursed him, ordered his attendants to strip him of his garments and to scourge him with a thousand lashes. He then commanded that the beards of both Quddús and Mullá Ṣádiq should be burned, their noses be pierced, that through this incision a cord should be passed, and with this halter they should be led through the streets of the city. 'It will be an object lesson to the people of Shíráz,' Ḥusayn Khán declared, 'who will know what the penalty of heresy will be.' Mullá Ṣádiq, calm and self-possessed and with eyes upraised to heaven, was heard reciting this prayer: 'O Lord, our God! We have indeed heard the voice of One that called. He called us to the Faith – "Believe ye on the Lord your God!" – and we have believed. O God, our God! Forgive us, then, our sins, and hide away from us our evil deeds, and cause us to die with the righteous.'* With magnificent fortitude both resigned themselves to their fate. Those who had been instructed to inflict this savage punishment performed their task with alacrity and vigour . . .

An eye-witness of this revolting episode, an unbeliever residing in Shíráz, related to me the following: 'I was present when Mullá Ṣádiq was being scourged. I watched his persecutors each in turn apply the lash to his bleeding shoulders, and continue the strokes until he became exhausted. No one believed that Mullá Ṣádiq, so advanced in age and so frail in body, could possibly survive fifty such savage strokes. We marvelled at his fortitude when we found that, although the number of the strokes of the scourge he had received had already exceeded nine hundred, his face still retained its original serenity and calm. A smile was upon his face, as he held his hand before his mouth. He seemed utterly indifferent to the blows that were being showered upon him. When he was being expelled from the city, I succeeded in approaching him, and asked him why he held his hand before his mouth. I expressed surprise at the smile upon his countenance. He emphatically replied: "The first seven strokes were severely painful; to the rest I seemed to

* Qur'án 3: 190–91.

have grown indifferent. I was wondering whether the strokes that followed were being actually applied to my own body. A feeling of joyous exultation had invaded my soul. I was trying to repress my feelings and to restrain my laughter. I can now realise how the almighty Deliverer is able, in the twinkling of an eye, to turn pain into ease, and sorrow into gladness. Immensely exalted is His power above and beyond the idle fancy of His mortal creatures."' Mullá Ṣádiq, whom I met years after, confirmed every detail of this moving episode. (ibid. pp. 144–8)

Another Bábí who shared the sufferings of Mullá Ṣádiq and Quddús was Mullá 'Alí-Akbar-i-Ardistání. The *farráshes* who were perpetrating these abominations were crying out to the populace: 'O Muslims! These men have not committed murder, they are not thieves, they have not cheated anyone, they have not gone beyond the limits of the law; but they are clever and eloquent men of learning who want to rob you of your Faith. Since we are parading these enemies of Religion, now captive and vanquished, before you to behold, you must be most generous with your offerings and gifts to us.' A merchant, by whose place of business they were passing, stopped them in their tracks and told them: 'That being so, let me have a share of this righteous deed and inflict more pain on these men.' Having said this, he brought a long and stout piece of timber and put one end on the shoulder of Quddús and the other on the shoulder of Mullá Ṣádiq. Next he attached a measuring device to the pole and had eighty bales of sugar weighed and placed on it. It was a hot day. Whenever Quddús and Mullá Ṣádiq, overcome by the heaviness of the load and the heat of the day, tried to shift their feet, their tormentors lashed them mercilessly. At the end of this fiendish method of torture, the *farráshes* were suitably rewarded. When these minions of the governor had done their worst, the three Bábís, covered with wounds and sores, were led out of the city and told to take to the open road and never come back.*

Mullá Ṣádiq-i-Muqaddas wended his way to Yazd. Along the route, whenever he came across anyone ready to listen, he told them of the advent of the Báb. He stayed two months in Yazd and openly made his announcement. Then he sent a herald to call out throughout the town: 'Whoever has not met the emissary of Bábu'lláhu'l-A'ẓam [the Most

* As I write these lines I have before me an account of the recent persecutions and terrible sufferings of the Bahá'ís of the tribe of Buwayr-Aḥmadí in the province of Fárs. The heroism of these men and women of the present day matches the heroism of Quddús and Muqaddas and Mullá 'Alí-Akbar-i-Ardistání. The power of sacrifice and steadfastness conferred on them by Bahá'u'lláh was well evinced.

Great Báb] and has not heard him, let him come on Friday to the mosque of Muṣallá and listen to the tidings which he brings you.' On that Friday a huge crowd gathered at the mosque. Mullá Ṣádiq ascended the pulpit and told the people, in no uncertain terms, that He Whose coming had been promised to them had indeed come. He read them 'one of the best-known and most exquisitely written homilies of the Báb,' and then spoke to them:

'Render thanks to God, O people of learning, for, behold, the Gate of Divine Knowledge, which you deem to have been closed, is now wide open. The River of everlasting life has streamed forth from the city of Shíráz, and is conferring untold blessings upon the people of this land. Whoever has partaken of one drop from this Ocean of heavenly grace, no matter how humble and unlettered, has discovered in himself the power to unravel the profoundest mysteries, and has felt capable of expounding the most abstruse themes of ancient wisdom. And whoever, though he be the most learned expounder of the Faith of Islám, has chosen to rely upon his own competence and power and has disdained the Message of God, has condemned himself to irretrievable degradation and loss.' (ibid. p. 186)

At first no one made any retort, no one raised objections or disputed with Mullá Ṣádiq. But before long there arose a murmur of dissent. Gradually it rose to a crescendo. The fickle crowd rushed to the pulpit, intending to drag Mullá Ṣádiq down and murder him. Let Nabíl tell us what happened next:

. . . The masjid rang with cries of 'Blasphemy!' which an infuriated congregation shouted in horror against the speaker. 'Descend from the pulpit,' rose the voice of Siyyid Ḥusayn* amid the clamour and tumult of the people, as he motioned to Mullá Ṣádiq to hold his peace and to retire. No sooner had he regained the floor of the masjid than the whole company of the assembled worshippers rushed upon him and overwhelmed him with blows. Siyyid Ḥusayn immediately intervened, vigorously dispersed the crowd, and, seizing the hand of Mullá Ṣádiq, forcibly drew him to his side. 'Withhold your hands,' he appealed to the multitude; 'leave him in my custody. I will take him to my home, and will closely investigate the matter. A sudden fit of madness may have caused him to utter these words. I will myself examine him. If I find that his utterances are premeditated and that he himself firmly believes in the things which he has declared, I will, with my own hands, inflict upon him the punishment imposed by the law of Islám.'

By this solemn assurance, Mullá Ṣádiq was delivered from the savage attacks of his assailants. Divested of his 'abá and turban, deprived of his

* Siyyid Ḥusayn-i-Azghandí, a very influential divine of Yazd, whose nephew, Mírzá Aḥmad-i-Azghandí, had embraced the Faith of the Báb and was also in Yazd at the time. His uncle wished him to stay in that town and help him parry the pretences of the followers of Ḥájí Karím Khán, the Shaykhí leader. (HMB)

sandals and staff, bruised and shaken by the injuries he had received, he was entrusted to the care of Siyyid Ḥusayn's attendants, who, as they forced their passage among the crowd, succeeded eventually in conducting him to the home of their master.

Mullá Yúsuf-i-Ardibílí,* likewise, was subjected in those days to a persecution fiercer and more determined than the savage onslaught which the people of Yazd had directed against Mullá Ṣádiq. But for the intervention of Mírzá Aḥmad and the assistance of his uncle, he would have fallen a victim to the wrath of a ferocious enemy.

When Mullá Ṣádiq and Mullá Yúsuf-i-Ardibílí arrived at Kirmán, they again had to submit to similar indignities and to suffer similar afflictions at the hands of Ḥájí Mírzá Karím Khán and his associates. Ḥájí Siyyid Javád's† persistent exertions freed them eventually from the grasp of their persecutors, and enabled them to proceed to Khurásán. (ibid. pp. 186–7)

The governor of Kirmán gave them an escort of horsemen to see them safely out of the province. Everywhere, on his way to Khurásán, Mullá Ṣádiq gave all whom he met the tidings of the advent of the Báb. Fear knew him not and nothing daunted him. Eventually he reached the camp of Mullá Ḥusayn, the Bábu'l-Báb, who, on a memorable day in Iṣfahán, had told him that the New Day had dawned. The destination of Mullá Ḥusayn was Mázindarán. Mullá Ṣádiq joined the small band of his fellow-believers, whose number increased as they went on.

In the heart of the forests of Mázindarán, within the fortress which they raised around the shrine of Shaykh Ṭabarsí, these God-intoxicated men defied their adversaries for several months. Their number was just over three hundred. Apart from a few like Riḍá Khán-i-Turkamán (whose father was a courtier of high rank), the overwhelming majority of these Bábís were clerics, students of theology, tradesmen, who had never wielded a sword in their lives. Yet they put armies to flight. Mullá Ḥusayn led sortie after sortie until he was mortally wounded. Finally, promises and vows that proved to be false caused the famished Bábís to lay down their arms and abandon their fortress which harboured the remains of the Bábu'l-Báb. They were massacred treacherously, sanctifying with their blood the soil of Mázindarán, already honoured to have been the ancestral home of Bahá'u'lláh. Only a few survived the holocaust, one of whom was Mullá Ṣádiq-i-Muqaddas of Khurásán.

* One of the Ḥurúf-i-Ḥayy (the Báb's Letters of the Living). (HMB)

† The Imám-i-Jum'ih of Kirmán. He was a distant cousin of the Báb, and like another celebrated cousin, Ḥájí Muḥammad-Ḥasan, known as Mírzáy-i-Shírází (see chap. 19), was secretly a believer in Him. Ḥájí Siyyid Javád rescued Quddús, as well, from his adversaries. (HMB)

Prince Mihdí-Qulí Mírzá, who commanded the royal troops, handed over Mullá Ṣádiq and Luṭf-'Alí Mírzá of Shíráz (an Afshárid prince) to a certain Ḥusayn Khán who was a well-known person in Mázindarán, and whose father had met his death while fighting the besieged Bábís of Shaykh Ṭabarsí, to take them home and kill them in the presence of his mother and sister to help assuage their grief. It was agreed that should he fail to put them to death he would pay a thousand *túmáns* to the prince. Ḥusayn Khán must have paid an equally large sum of money to Mihdí-Qulí Mírzá, to have the two Bábís released to him. As the Mázindarání grandee and his captives, chained and bound, went on their way towards his home, at every village and town he would call the divines to come and examine the Bábís. The divines everywhere, seated and with Mullá Ṣádiq in chains standing before them, put every question to him and were answered politely, clearly, convincingly, based on evidence culled from the Qur'án and Traditions. And everywhere the divines gave the same answer to the grandee's question, who asked them time and again: 'Does this man merit death?' To which the answer came: 'No, never; we have never before met a man so learned, nor heard such masterly exposition. Even if he be an infidel, he should not be put to death.' Thus they progressed through the province of Mázindarán. Ḥusayn Khán was captivated by the serenity and certitude of Mullá Ṣádiq, and came to the decision to spare their lives. When he reached home he called in the members of his family and told them all that had happened. 'Everywhere the divines unitedly gave the verdict', he said, 'that these men do not merit death.' His relatives were also united in the same answer. Ḥusayn Khán, true to his word, informed Mihdí-Qulí Mírzá that he and his relatives would not be a party to the execution of the two Bábís.

The prince wanted them to be sent to Ṭihrán, there to be put to death. During the time of their detention in the home of Ḥusayn Khán, Mullá Ṣádiq and Luṭf-'Alí Mírzá had helped a shepherd of that neighbourhood named 'Avaḍ-Muḥammad to embrace the Faith of the Báb. Being apprised of the prince's wish, he told the prisoners that their only hope lay in escaping. Mullá Ṣádiq, enfeebled by the privations he had endured, was unwilling to undergo the hazards entailed. But the insistence of the shepherd, who was willing to be privy to any scheme that would give them their freedom, overcame the reluctance of Mullá Ṣádiq. 'Avaḍ-Muḥammad helped them leave that neighbourhood through paths not usually frequented. He also provided them with food. They walked throughout the night in the thick forests that cover Mázindarán and sought refuge during the day in the dense parts of the forest. After two weeks they reached Míyámí with their feet sore and bruised. There they recounted to the relatives of those heroic men the story of the thirty-three Bábís of that locality who had fallen at Shaykh Ṭabarsí. They had to rest for a while at Míyámí to recuperate before taking the road to Mashhad.

Luṭf-'Alí eventually reached Ṭihrán where he was caught up by the upheavals of 1852 and lost his life. For Mullá Ṣádiq life in Mashhad became impossible. Around the year 1861 he said farewell to that city of renown and with a number of persons accompanying him travelled to Baghdád. There he went into the presence of Bahá'u'lláh and recognized Him as the One in Whose path the Báb had sacrificed Himself – the Promised One of the *Bayán*. For fourteen months he basked in the sunshine of the presence of Bahá'u'lláh, and then as directed by Him he returned to his native province of Khurásán.

Again he met bitter opposition from all sides. Particularly vehement were the assaults made upon him by the followers of Ḥájí Muḥammad-Karím Khán-i-Kirmání.* But Mullá Ṣádiq held his ground, despite all the machinations of his adversaries. Then, the headstrong governor-general of Khurásán, Sulṭán-Murád Mírzá, the Ḥisámu's-Salṭanih (an uncle of Náṣiri'd-Dín Sháh), fell in with the opponents of Mullá Ṣádiq and had him arrested. A week later Mullá Ṣádiq was sent to Ṭihrán, in the company of a large number of Turkamán prisoners. In Ṭihrán he was lodged in Síyáh-Chál, the same prison where Bahá'u'lláh had been immured in 1852. Even there Mullá Ṣádiq could not be silenced. He brought a number of his fellow-prisoners to accept the Faith of the Báb and Bahá'u'lláh. Among those he converted was Ḥakím Masíḥ, a Jewish physician who was attending the prisoners. He was the first Bahá'í of Jewish background in Ṭihrán and was the grandfather of Luṭfu'lláh Ḥakím who was in recent years elected to the first Universal House of Justice. Many well-known men who were acquainted with him visited him in Síyáh-Chál and tried hard to induce him to write a few lines which they could show to Náṣiri'd-Dín Sháh and obtain his release. But he consistently refused to comply with their wishes and make any appeal. He wrote:

* He considered himself the successor to Siyyid Káẓim, and fostered opposition to the Báb amongst the Shaykhís.

Sulṭán-Murád Mírzá, the Ḥisámu's-Salṭanih
Governor-General of Khurásán

'It is shameful that a man in need should appeal to another one in need.' Thus he stayed for twenty-eight months in that prison. Then Náṣiri'd-Dín Sháh, of his own accord, ordered his release. Mullá Ṣádiq refused to leave the dungeon without his fellow-prisoners. He had pledged his word to them, he said, that they would leave Síyáh-Chál together. When the Sháh learned of Mullá Ṣádiq's stand he was amazed, but asked for a list of all the inmates of Síyáh-Chál. Besides Mullá Ṣádiq, there were forty-three names in that list. All but three were pardoned, and those three had been arrested only recently and were guilty men.

Mullá Ṣádiq's son, Ibn-i-Aṣdaq, who was named and appointed by Bahá'u'lláh a Hand of the Cause of God, states in a short biography of his father: 'Twice he was taken to the Inspectorate which was in the charge of 'Aynu'l-Mulk. There he said: "Some of these men have been in this prison for seven years. They have no clothing left, are bare

Ḥájí Mullá 'Alíy-i-Kaní, the influential divine to whom the Tablet of Bahá'u'lláh to Náṣiri'd-Dín Sháh was referred for reply (left), *and Siyyid Ṣádiq-i-Sanglají (1812–83), one of the foremost 'ulamá of Ṭihrán* (right)

and in utter misery. They ought to be clad and allowed to go home in peace. The authorities should provide them with suitable clothes and money and send them home, bring some joy into their miserable lives." His praiseworthy initiative led to the introduction of the Faith of God in all the areas where these people lived. Its abiding results will endure for ever. The descendants and the clans of those men are within the fold of this Faith, ever ready to be of service to others.'

After departing from the house of 'Aynu'l-Mulk, Mullá Ṣádiq stayed for three days in the mosque of Sipahsálár. From there he moved to the house of Muḥammad-Válí Mírzá (a son of Fatḥ-'Alí Sháh), who was greatly attached to him. His sojourn there lasted nineteen days, and there he came face to face with a number of very influential divines of Ṭihrán, such as Ḥájí Mullá 'Alíy-i-Kaní and Siyyid Ṣádiq-i-Sanglají. These men had heard of the vast learning of Mullá Ṣádiq. One after the other, in rapid succession, they asked him intricate questions and posed him many problems to resolve. It must be said that none of those divines was favourably inclined towards the

Faith of Bahá'u'lláh. Indeed, the two already named were bitterly hostile. Ḥájí Mullá 'Alíy-i-Kaní was the man who, when given Bahá'u'lláh's Tablet to Náṣiri'd-Dín Sháh so that he might write an answer to it, treated the matter with great disdain. Now, they all fell under the spell of the speech of Mullá Ṣádiq. None of them, however hard he tried, could match, let alone surpass his deep knowledge, his eloquence, his logic and measured speech. When these proceedings in the home of his relative were reported to Náṣiri'd-Dín Sháh, he, of all the people, upbraided Ḥisámu's-Salṭanih (his own uncle) for condemning such a man as Mullá Ṣádiq to imprisonment. He ordered two of his best horses, richly saddled, to be given to Mullá Ṣádiq, as well as a gift of money. The mother of Náṣiri'd-Dín Sháh, who was present that day in the house of Muḥammad-Válí Mírzá and sitting with a number of other ladies of high rank behind a curtain, was listening to the trial of strength between Mullá Ṣádiq and the divines of Ṭihrán; she presented him with rich, valuable clothes befitting his rank. Mullá Ṣádiq courteously returned all the royal gifts and wrote a letter to the Sháh expressing his gratitude. Then he borrowed a sum of money from a fellow-believer in Ṭihrán and took the road to Khurásán. It was then that he helped Ḥájí Mírzá Muḥammad-Riḍá, the Mu'taminu's-Salṭanih, the future Vazír of Khurásán, to embrace the Faith of Bahá'u'lláh. (See chap. 5.)

Three years later, Mullá Ṣádiq returned to Ṭihrán and helped in changing the secret hiding-place of the remains of the Báb. Having performed that service, urgently required, he left the capital once again and visited Káshán, Iṣfahán and Yazd. Everywhere he went he fearlessly and energetically taught and propagated the Faith of Bahá'u'lláh. But his most outstanding service was that which he rendered in Yazd. There, some of the Afnáns (relatives of the Báb) were still hesitant and uncommitted; Mullá Ṣádiq made them see and totally accept the truth of the new Theophany. After this remarkable achievement, he returned to his native province of Khurásán where, for six years, he travelled throughout that province teaching, continuously teaching. During that time he was constantly attacked, reviled and denounced by adversaries. But he never faltered, although his sufferings as well as old age were telling upon him. Finally, physical disabilities forced him to retire from the field.

Ill and exhausted, his dearest wish now was to attain, once again, the presence of Bahá'u'lláh. Before long that wish was realized.

Bahá'u'lláh summoned him to 'Akká. When that call reached him he was revived. He sent word that he desired the people to come and visit him. They came, and to them, Bahá'í or non-Bahá'í alike, he gave such advice as would serve them well in days to come. His visitors were greatly moved. His words came from a heart pure and unsullied, from a soul brave and constant, leaving a deep impression on all who were privileged to hear him, and evoking a response commensurate with his earnestness. A good many wished to accompany and serve him in his pilgrimage. Bahá'u'lláh had, however, directed him to bring only one person with him, and those who wished to be with him vied for that honour. Mirza Ja'far was the man who secured it. His son, the future Hand of the Cause Ibn-i-Aṣdaq, accompanied them until they reached Sabzivár. There he offered his father a small sum of money which he did not accept. The route which Mullá Ṣádiq took was through Caucasia. It was a long and tiring journey, but he stood up to its hardships. And, at long last, he found himself in the presence of Bahá'u'lláh. He had lived expectantly for that moment. All his toils, his sufferings, spread over so many years were forgotten at that supreme moment, and for four months he had the bounty of living close to his Lord. At the end of that period of untold bliss the Tongue of Grandeur thus addressed him:

> O My name, the Aṣdaq!* Render thanks unto God that We called thee to appear before the Seat of Glory, to hear Us and to witness the Light of the Countenance of thy Lord, the Exalted, the Mighty, the Single, the Supreme; and We sent thee back to inform the people of what thou hast seen and understood, and to call them to the utmost constancy, lest their steps falter at the clamour of any corrupt pretender. O My name! recall every day Our counsel to thee in Our Presence. Verily, thy Lord is the All-Knowing, the All-Informed. (Quoted in Sulaymání, *Maṣábiḥ-i-Hidáyat*, vol. 7, p. 408)

The time had come for parting from the presence of Bahá'u'lláh and he turned homewards by way of Mosul and Baghdád. All along that route he gave the people he met the tidings of the advent of the Day of God. Physically he was exhausted, but his spirit shone as bright as ever. His dedicated soul knew no repose except in obeying the command of his Lord. When he reached Hamadán, his physical strength had touched its nadir, but not the bravery of his soul. He stayed for twelve days in Hamadán, never resting. On the last day he told his servitors to bring him his best, his most costly clothes. He put

* the most truthful

them on, using a good deal of rose-water and perfume. Then he asked those who were with him to leave him alone for an hour. At the end of that hour he called them back, and asked one of them to help him undress. He had only one arm out of his sleeve when he said to the man who was helping him, 'That is enough'; the next moment he was gone – gone from this world. Thus, calmly and serenely, death brought release to Mullá Ṣádiq, Ismu'lláhu'l-Aṣdaq, from untold tribulations which would have broken a lesser man, but were endured by him with radiant acquiescence in the path of his Lord. His death occurred in the year 1889.

Some thirty years later, one evening in Haifa, 'Abdu'l-Bahá, the Centre of the Covenant of Bahá'u'lláh, spoke of Ismu'lláhu'l-Aṣdaq, describing him as a Hand of the Cause of God and 'truly a servant of the Lord from the beginning of life till his last breath'. And then He recalled an incident of which He Himself was a witness, an incident of the far-off days of Baghdád:

> . . . he [Mullá Ṣádiq] was seated one day in the courtyard of the men's apartments . . . I was in one of the rooms just above . . . At that moment . . . a grandson of Fatḥ-'Alí Sháh, arrived at the house. The prince said to him, 'Who are you?' Ismu'lláh answered, 'I am a servant of this Threshhold. I am one of the keepers of this door.' And as I listened from above, he began to teach the Faith. The prince at first objected violently; and yet, in a quarter of an hour, gently and benignly, Jináb-i-Ismu'lláh had quieted him down. After the prince had so sharply denied what was said, and his face had so clearly reflected his fury, now his wrath was changed to smiles and he expressed the greatest satisfaction at having encountered Ismu'lláh and heard what he had to say.
>
> He always taught cheerfully and with gaiety, and would respond gently and with good humor, no matter how much passionate anger might be turned against him by the one with whom he spoke. His way of teaching was excellent . . . He was a great personage, perfect in all things . . .
>
> He was truly Ismu'lláh, the Name of God. Fortunate is the one who circumambulates that tomb, who blesses himself with the dust of that grave . . . (*Memorials of the Faithful*, pp. 5, 6, 8)

2

The Story of Two Ashrafs

IN THE LONG and glory-studded roll of the Bábí-Bahá'í martyrs of Persia one encounters the names of two Ashrafs: the first hailed from Zanján, the city of the heroic Ḥujjat; the second was a native of Bushrúyih who resided in Najafábád – townships from both of which many an intrepid martyr has stepped into the arena of history to mark the unshakeable resolve of the faithful and the eternal infamy of the persecutor. Two eventful decades intervene between the immolation of the two Ashrafs. The first – Ashraf of Zanján – was a siyyid of noble birth in the full prime of his vigorous youth; the second was an eloquent and erudite guide and mentor of middle age.

The father of Ashraf of Zanján had stood valiantly under the banner of Ḥujjat and had died in the ensuing holocaust. So comely, so engaging, so handsome was his son that the adversaries were loth to hand him over to the executioner. They led his mother to the prison-house that she might persuade him to deny his faith and thus obtain his freedom. But that brave woman, who had but this one accomplished son of dazzling beauty, told him: 'Ashraf, my son! Shouldst thou abjure thy faith, I shall renounce thee for ever.' Such was the mettle of those who had given their allegiance to Bahá'u'lláh.

Ashraf, whose full name was Siyyid 'Alí-Ashraf, and who came to be known as Ashrafu'sh-Shuhadá' – the Noblest of Martyrs – had attained the presence of Bahá'u'lláh in Adrianople, the renowned city of Hadrian which had fallen into disrepute, and which Bahá'u'lláh had termed the 'Remote Prison'. That encounter and attainment had set his faith doubly ablaze. On his return from Rumelia, in an orchard outside the city gates that belonged to him, he had a room built in which to praise his Lord and to transcribe the verses flowing from the Most Exalted Pen. His fellow-believers would foregather there to benefit by his company. The enemy was alert and watchful. The young siyyid was seized and cast into prison. With him into prison went another heroic youth, whose father had also died under the banner of Ḥujjat. Naqd-'Alí was blind, but the Most Exalted Pen honoured him with the designation of Abú-Baṣír – the Father of Insight. He too was determined to take the same road as his father, the road to martyrdom.

The resolve of these two young men could not be shaken, and the day came when they were led to the scaffold. The Imám-Jum'ih of Zanján, related as he was to Ashraf, was there to make a last effort to save him from death. The mother of Ashraf was also there to see her son drink of the same cup as her glorious husband. As the Imám-Jum'ih's importunities increased, urging Ashraf not to throw away his life, the plea and the injunction of Ashraf's mother was heard: 'Remember, my son: shouldst thou deny thy faith, the faith of thy father, I shall renounce thee for ever and ever!'

Such were the circumstances of the death of two heroic men of Zanján of imperishable memory, one of them in the very bloom of his youth. When Ashraf was beheaded, in the presence of his implacable mother, he was holding in his embrace the decapitated corpse of his companion. And as Ashraf's mother saw her son die, she held back her tears and would not let a single one well from her eyes. Her soul was agonized but happy, for her son's death was in the path of Bahá'u'lláh.*

The other Ashraf, who hailed from Bushrúyih, the home of the Bábu'l-Báb, but resided in Najafábád, and who quaffed the cup of martyrdom two decades later in 1888, was a man who once commanded a pulpit. People were attracted to him despite their waywardness, because he was kind and wise and learned. When he heard the call of the Lord of Hosts, the Master of the Day of Judgement, his pure soul responded to it. Then, as it became known that he had embraced the new Faith, he had to leave Najafábád and seek refuge in a hamlet near the township of Ábádih, where he spent his solitary days in communion with his Lord. In those far-off days Ábádih and its environs had no Bahá'ís.

It was to Ábádih that the desecrated heads of the Bábí martyrs of the second episode of Nayríz (1853), together with Bábí prisoners in chains, had been brought on the way to Ṭihrán. The incident was highly reminiscent of what had occurred more than a millennium

* See *Gleanings from the Writings of Bahá'u'lláh*, LXIX, for Bahá'u'lláh's account of Ashraf's death. (Ed.)

before, in the wake of the tragic deaths, on the bank of the river Euphrates, of the Imám Ḥusayn, the Sayyidu'sh-Shuhadá' – the Prince of Martyrs – and those courageous souls who fearlessly stood by him, faithful to the House of the Prophet. Then, too, the wicked of this world had raised the severed heads of the martyrs on their lances and had herded prisoners – women and children – together, to parade them in the streets of Kúfih and Damascus. Amongst those remnants of the House of Muḥammad there was one solitary youth – 'Alí, now the Fourth Imám – who was too ill to raise himself from his couch on the day that his father and brother and cousins, together with the faithful, fell on the plains of 'Iráq. He was the only male survivor of that dastardly massacre, and though still stricken by enervating fevers, was then the sole silver-tongued spokesman of his House. To the unthinking, beguiled and jeering mob who had hurled their wild imprecations at them, accusing them of being seceders and traducers of the law, 'Alí II had replied: 'Nay, indeed, we are the preservers of the law, the trustees and the Guardian of the Faith of the Apostle of God'.

Now, in mid-nineteenth century, when the implacable enemy once again brought severed heads hoisted on lances and tortured prisoners to display before the mob, orders reached Ábádih from higher authorities not to proceed further with the desecrated heads but to bury them in that township. On a lonesome piece of barren earth, the heads of the martyrs of Nayríz were thrown into a pit. (Decades later, 'Abdu'l-Bahá honoured that piece of wasteland, then turned into a garden, with the designation of Ḥadíqatu'r-Raḥmán – the Orchard of the Merciful.) A notable of the town of Ábádih, Siyyid Muḥammad-'Alí, known as Siyyid Mullá Áqá Ján, noticed amongst the prisoners who were to be taken to Ṭihrán a young siyyid, twenty years old, named Siyyid Ghulám-'Alí. He was of arresting beauty, but was desperately ill, hardly able to move. His heart touched by the plight of this young man, Siyyid Muḥammad-'Alí appealed to the commander of the troops in the name of their illustrious Ancestor, the Holy Prophet, to allow him to keep Siyyid Ghulám-'Alí in Ábádih and have him nursed to health. Luṭf-'Alí Khán-i-Qashqá'í, a brigadier in charge of the prisoners, requested from the benevolent notable of Ábádih the sum of ten *túmáns*, before he would release Siyyid Ghulám-'Alí. That kind-hearted man went about procuring the cash, and caught up with the troops, already on the move, at Shúlgistán.

Luṭf-ʿAlí K͟hán, commander of the Qashqáʾí Regiment in the second upheaval of Nayríz (1853), whose son embraced the Faith of Baháʾuʾlláh

Having at last obtained the release of that sick, emaciated youth, Siyyid Muḥammad-ʿAlí put him on his own horse and himself led the animal and walked all the way back to Ábádih. There he called in Áqá Muḥammad-Ḥusayn, the Ḥakím-Báshí (Chief Physician), to restore that ailing youth to health. But Siyyid G͟hulám-ʿAlí had suffered much and did not recover. He was buried in the cemetery of Ábádih where his grave is unknown; only his memory remains and the memory of Siyyid Muḥammad-ʿAlí, whose generous heart guided him to rescue that maltreated youth from the grasp of the foe, and afford him a few days of rest and peace before death took him away.

The son of Luṭf-ʿAlí K͟hán, the Qashqáʾí commandant who had maimed and murdered the Bábís of Nayríz, in the course of time embraced the Faith of Baháʾuʾlláh. He was Ḥájí Muḥammad-Ṣádiq K͟hán, and he became a devoted Baháʾí, so conscious of the enormity of the cruelties of his father that he was certain their evil consequences would be visited on him. Qábil, the celebrated Baháʾí poet and teacher of Ábádih, who, on Ḥájí Muḥammad-Ṣádiq K͟hán's own request, had retailed to him the story of his father's rapacity, was so greatly moved by the son's sense of shame and remorse that he wrote of it to 'Abdu'l-Bahá. Here is 'Abdu'l-Bahá's response, which He wished to be conveyed to Ḥájí Muḥammad-Ṣádiq Khán:

The true morn dawneth from the depths of a darksome night, and the world-illuminating light of day poureth forth from the canopy of a night of gloom. The enchanting flower bloometh on a branch of thorns, and multitudinous plants grow out of the sad, sodden earth. The delightful fruit sprouteth upon a piece of wood. Thus is seen the truth of the words: 'Thou bringest the living out of the dead, and Thou bringest the dead out of the living.' [Qur'án 3: 27] The Commander of the Faithful* was wont to say to Muḥammad the son of Abú-Bakr: 'Thou art my child.' Clear it is that physical fatherhood and sonship are not factors of true import. Canaan was the son of Noah and Abraham was the son of Ádhar. One father was a Prophet, but His son was disowned and cut off. Another father was an idolator, yet his Son was the great and exalted Friend† . . . Therefore be not saddened. Pray thou and supplicate at the threshold of the One True God, begging forgiveness for thine earthly father. 'Abdu'l-Bahá will also, with utmost lowliness, implore at the threshold of God that perchance the musk-laden breeze of His forgiveness may waft over the Khán‡ and from the billowing sea of His grace a wave may pass over him and cleanse him of the defilement of sin and transgression. This is not far removed from the ocean of the grace of Bahá, His mercy, and His pardon . . . (Unpublished)

Here, history repeats itself. Luṭf-'Alí Khán, the Qashqá'í commandant, comes to Ábádih triumphant after the massacre of the innocent, with severed heads which he is told to part with, and a host of suffering captives whom he drives on to Shíráz. His son, Ḥájí Muḥammad-Ṣádiq Khán, embraces the Faith of Bahá'u'lláh and makes donations to have an edifice raised at the place where the heads of his father's victims are consigned to earth. This is what followed the second blood-stained episode of Nayríz. While subsequent to the first episode of Nayríz (1850), when the valiant Vaḥíd met a martyr's death, a grandson of one of the Núrí chiefs, responsible for much of the barbarities there, gave his allegiance to Bahá'u'lláh. He was a colonel of artillery named Faraju'lláh Khán who, in 1888, related to Edward Granville Browne in the city of Yazd the story of how his own elders had behaved at Nayríz and how they had received their meed.§

But now, once more to the story of Ábádih and the second Ashraf,

* 'Alí Ibn Abú-Ṭalib, the first Imám.
† A sincere friend. Abraham is known as Khalílu'lláh – the Friend of God.
‡ The father of Ḥájí Muḥammad-Ṣádiq Khán.
§ The Núrí chief was Mihr-'Alí Khán, the Shujá'u'l-Mulk. The account is given by Browne in *A Year Amongst the Persians*, pp. 440–42. (This passage will be included in a forthcoming compilation of the works of E. G. Browne on the Bahá'í Faith.)

who, as soon as that township became peopled with the followers of Bahá'u'lláh, abandoned his retreat in the village of Dih-Daq and established his residence in the town. During the years that Mírzá Ashraf had lived in the village, because of the fierce opposition he had encountered in Najafábád he had concealed his true allegiance from the notables of Ábádih with whom he consorted. So when he came out into the open in Ábádih, the fanatics of that town were shocked and dismayed, shocked because they had known Áqá Mírzá Ashraf as an erudite Shí'ih divine, and dismayed because they were well aware of his powers of speech and exposition.

In that year (1861) when the intrigues and agitations of Mírzá Buzurg Khán-i-Qazvíní, the Persian consul-general in Baghdád, and Shaykh 'Abdu'l-Ḥusayn-i-Ṭihrání, the Shaykhu'l-'Iráqayn, were nearing the end desired by them, the fame of the One so bitterly opposed by those two plotters was resounding all over Írán. Three young men of Ábádih, two of whom were sons of the Ḥakím-Báshí, the same physician who years before had attended Siyyid Ghulám-'Alí, were studying in Iṣfahán. They heard of Mírzá Ḥusayn-'Alí (Bahá'u'lláh), Son of the Vazír-i-Núrí, and His achievements within the Bábí community. One of the sons, Mírzá 'Aṭá'u'lláh (later entitled Siráju'l-Ḥukamá' – the Light of the Physicians), and his brother Mírzá Isḥáq, together with their compatriot, Mullá Muḥammad-Ḥusayn, became particularly interested in what had reached their hearing and in the rumours current amongst the *habitués* of the theological seminaries of Iṣfahán. They told Mírzá Asadu'lláh (known in Iṣfahán as Ḥakím-Iláhí – the Divine Philosopher), who was a close friend of Mírzá 'Aṭá'u'lláh, of their newly-found interest. Mírzá Asadu'lláh was a Bábí and he, in his turn, informed Mírzá Ḥasan (Sulṭánu'sh-Shuhadá' – King of the Martyrs) of the interest aroused in the minds and hearts of the three young men of Ábádih. A meeting was arranged between them, and before long Mírzá 'Aṭá'u'lláh, his brother and their companion gladly gave their allegiance to the New Theophany. This Siráju'l-Ḥukamá' of future years, who eventually became the leading physician of the town, proved to be a tower of strength in the Bahá'í community which was emerging in Ábádih. Several decades later his uncle, Ḥájí Muḥammad-Ṣádiq, left the Shaykhí fold at the age of eighty-five and embraced the Faith of Bahá'u'lláh, which he served devotedly till his death at the age of ninety.

Mírzá 'Aṭá'u'lláh, later entitled Siráju'l-Ḥukamá' (the Light of the Physicians), a Bahá'í who became the leading physician of Ábádih

At the same time that Bahá'u'lláh was on the point of departing from Baghdád to Constantinople (1863), a number of notables of Ábádih were in 'Iráq on pilgrimage to the holy shrines of the Imáms, including Dá'í Ḥusayn, who was to become one of the most stalwart Bahá'ís of Ábádih. Hearing that Bahá'u'lláh was in the Najíbíyyih Garden, just outside Baghdád, he thought seriously of going there himself, as many were doing, to discover what all that commotion was about, but fearing the consequences he did not venture out. He was a friend of Mírzá 'Atá'u'lláh, the son of the Ḥakím-Báshí, and on his way back to his home town discovered at Iṣfahán that his friends there were nurturing a secret which surprised him. They asked him: 'What is going on in Dáru's-Salám? [Baghdád]' He told them all he knew. His friends expressed great surprise but kept their secret to themselves. Then, all together, they left Iṣfahán for Ábádih. Ensconced in their home town they divulged their secret: they had embraced the Faith of the Báb. So did Dá'í Ḥusayn with a devotion fortified by all that he had heard and witnessed in Baghdád, to be followed by others including his son, Karbilá'í Ḥasan Khán.

It was then that Áqá Mírzá Ashraf let it be known that he was a Bahá'í. Soon Ábádih became a stronghold of the Faith of Bahá'u'lláh, and a number of its leading citizens came into the Bahá'í fold. Of course, as everywhere else in the storm-tossed Cradle of their Faith, these steadfast Bahá'ís had, from time to time, to face the venom and fury of their adversaries. One such was Sulṭán-Mas'úd Mírzá, the Ẓillu's-Sulṭán, who was always alert to inflict some fresh injury upon them. He stretched out his hand, already stained with the blood of the innocent, snatched Mírzá Ashraf, and had him delivered to the executioner.

A letter written by the father of the present writer to Edward Granville Browne, on 3 July 1889, gives the full story of the martyrdom of the second Ashraf – Ashraf of Ábádih. Browne published a partial translation of the letter in the Journal of the Royal Asiatic Society for October 1889 (pp. 998–9), prefaced by these lines:

Those who were present at the Meeting of the Society on April 15th, 1889, at which my first paper was read, will remember that in the discussion which followed it, General Houtum-Schindler stated that a Bábí had been put to death at Isfahán in October, 1888. In reply to inquiries which I made of my friends in Persia, I received a little time ago a letter containing an account of this event, of a portion of which I here give the translation:

'You wrote that you had heard from General Schindler of the martyrdom of one of this sect [the Persian word '*Ṭáyifih*' used in the letter means 'a people', 'nation', 'tribe']. The details are these. A child, who was one of the servants of the andarún (women's apartments) of the Prince Ẓill-es-Sulṭán, had become acquainted with several individuals of "the friends" (aḥbáb), and Áḳá Mírzá Ashraf of Ábádé had apprized him of this Matter ['*Amr*': 'Cause'] (*i.e.* had converted him to Bábíism). News of this reaches the Prince Ẓill-es-Sulṭán. They torment the child to make him tell the truth, but he in no wise discloses the matter. Guile enters the hearts of the Prince's servants. One of them goes and inquires of several of "the friends", "Where is Áḳá Mírzá Ashraf? I have a wife in Ábádé, and I desire to send her a letter and some money. Since Áḳá Mírzá Ashraf has acquaintances in Ábádé, I wish to send them by means of him." These, believing this representation, point out to him the abode of Áḳá Mírzá Ashraf. When they recognize Áḳá Mírzá Ashraf, they seize him and bring him into the presence of the Prince. The Prince inquires of Áḳá Mírzá Ashraf, "Art thou of this sect?" He answers, "I am not." He says, "If thou art not, curse" (them, or the Báb or Behá). He replies, "Since their wickedness has not been made apparent to me, I will not curse" (them). ['I have not seen anything bad from them, I will not curse.']

Eventually the Prince obtains a decision from several of the *'Ulamá*, and telegraphs to Teherán, "If this person be not killed, the *'Ulamá* and the populace will raise disturbance: the 'Ulamá, moreover, have pronounced sentence: he himself, also, has confessed that he is of this sect, and it is necessary to kill him to quiet the people." The order comes from Teherán, "Do whatever appears desirable." Then the Prince orders the execution of Áḳá Mírzá Ashraf. According to the accounts I have heard, they cut off his head and then gibbet him. Afterwards they set fire to his body. I myself was acquainted with Áḳá Mírzá Ashraf. [Not translated by Browne: 'I met him in Bombay in the year 1884. We oftentimes met each other there.'] His age seemed to be about sixty. He was a man of understanding and education; a good calligraphist; and extremely courteous and amiable. [Not translated by Browne: 'In the year 1886, when I was coming from Ṭihrán to Shíráz, I met him again in Ábádih.'] In every way he was a most excellent man.'

Edward Browne inserted the Persian text of this letter in Note Y of the Appendices to his translation of *A Traveller's Narrative*, and followed it by these lines:

On August 4th, the day after I received the above letter, I wrote to a friend at Isfahán, on whose kindness I felt sure I might rely, for information which no one was better qualified than himself to give. On October 8th, just a year after Mírzá Ashraf's martyrdom, I received his answer, which bore the date September 6th, 1889. 'Yes,' he wrote, 'it is quite true that Aga Mirza Ashraf of Ábâdé was put to death for his religion in the most barbarous manner in Ispahan about October last. The hatred of the Mullas was not satisfied with his murder, but they mutilated the poor body publicly in the *maidan* in the most savage manner, and then burnt what was left of it.'

Thus died Áqá Mírzá Ashraf of Ábádih, and that was what the rapacious enemy did to the 'mutilated' body of that 'most excellent man'.

3

Núrayn-i-Nayyirayn
The Twin Shining Lights

'THE TWIN SHINING LIGHTS', or 'The Twin Luminous Orbs', were two stalwart brothers, natives of Iṣfahán, whom the Pen of Bahá'u'lláh – the Most Sublime Pen – extolled as Sulṭánu'sh-Shuhadá' (the King of Martyrs) and Maḥbúbu'sh-Shuhadá' (the Beloved of Martyrs). Mírzá Muḥammad-Ḥasan, the King of Martyrs, was two years younger than his brother, Mírzá Muḥammad-Ḥusayn, the Beloved of Martyrs. They were beheaded in the city of 'Abbás the Great in the year 1879. Their deaths were planned, decreed and encompassed by three persons: Mír Muḥammad-Ḥusayn, the Imám-Jum'ih of Iṣfahán, stigmatized by Bahá'u'lláh as Raqshá' – the She-Serpent; Shaykh Muḥammad-Báqir, another influential divine of that city whom the Most Sublime Pen singled out as Dhi'b – the Wolf; and Sulṭán-Mas'úd Mírzá, the Ẓillu's-Sulṭán, the avaricious, tyrannical son of Náṣiri'd-Dín Sháh who governed that city of immortal memory. It was the rapacity and the innate viciousness of those divines, combined with the greed and corruption of the Prince-Governor, which delivered those noble souls, whom all the inhabitants of Iṣfahán knew as selfless, upright and kindly men, into the hands of the executioner. Decades later, in Paris, the Prince begged 'Abdu'l-Bahá to believe that he was only carrying out the orders of his father, the monarch, who was goaded by those rascally men, Mír Muḥammad-Ḥusayn and Shaykh Muḥammad-Báqir, and that he himself was innocent of complicity in that crime. But he was lying blatantly. It is true that the murders of those two brothers were envisaged and planned at the beginning by the two divines, but the Prince-Governor's interest was aroused by the discovery that a large sum of money was involved.

Mírzá Ḥasan and Mírzá Ḥusayn were both rich and highly endowed

Shaykh Muḥammad-Báqir, an influential divine of Iṣfahán whom Bahá'u'lláh stigmatized as Dhi'b – the Wolf

Sulṭán-Mas'úd Mírzá, Ẓillu's-Sulṭán (1850–1918) Governor of Iṣfahán

with trading acumen. Following in the footsteps of their father, Mírzá Ibráhím, a brother of Mírzá Muḥammad-'Alíy-i-Nahrí and Mírzá Hádíy-i-Nahrí,* they had for years acted for the Imám-Jum'ih in the management of his property. Due to their assiduous attention to the interests of the Imám-Jum'ih the estate of that unscrupulous divine prospered, but because of the payments they had to make on his behalf, Mír Muḥammad-Ḥusayn came to owe them the sum of eighteen thousand *túmáns*, which was quite a substantial amount in those days. The two brothers were merchants and as such always, naturally, had a number of creditors and debtors. At a time when the Afnáns (the relatives of the Báb) had vast and exceedingly profitable trading concerns stretching from Hong Kong to Tiflís (Tbilisi) in the Caucasus,† Mírzá Ḥasan and Mírzá Ḥusayn, in Iṣfahán, acted commercially in concert with them. And now, when the two brothers asked the Imám-Jum'ih for the money owed to them, he stalled, and made the payment dependent on a careful scrutiny of the books. Even then he jibbed at clearing his debt and set about finding a way to evade payment. One day in the public bath he happened to meet Shaykh Muḥammad-Báqir, who was a divine more influential than himself. He told the latter of his plight (which was anything but sorrowful), his huge debt to Mírzá Ḥasan and Mírzá Ḥusayn, and spoke at length of the riches of the two brothers. Shaykh Muḥammad-Báqir, enticed by the wealth involved, promised the perfidious Imám-Jum'ih his support and the two of them concocted a plan to destroy the two honest and upright merchants. Next, they went to the Prince-Governor with their nefarious design. As soon as he was apprised of considerable riches, he unhesitatingly agreed to have Mírzá Ḥasan and Mírzá Ḥusayn detained.

On the 17th day of Rabí'u'l-Avval, which the Shí'ihs consider to have been the day of the Birth of the Prophet, those two intrepid men with a younger brother, Mírzá Ismá'íl, called on the Imám-Jum'ih to offer him their felicitations. Áqá Muḥammad-Báqir-i-Mudarrís, who was a father-in-law of Ẓillu's-Sulṭán and a man free of guile and fanaticism, well aware of the intentions of the two plotting divines, advised

* The reader is referred to *Bahá'u'lláh, The King of Glory*, pp. 339–42. (Ed.)

† Ḥájí Mírzá Muḥammad-'Alí, cousin of the Báb (a son of His maternal uncle, Ḥájí Mírzá Siyyid Muḥammad), had the virtual monopoly of trading in Chinese porcelain ware, and these goods were manufactured to his specifications for the nobility of Írán, even for Náṣiri'd-Dín Sháh, with the names of the clients inscribed on them. His own name: 'Muḥammad-'Alí al-Ḥusayní', was inscribed on some pieces which were ordered for himself or for members of his family and relatives. Photographs exist of Náṣiri'd-Dín Sháh sitting at his meal with such Chinese porcelain plates, bowls and dishes on his table.

Mírzá Ḥasan to take himself away from that hostile assemblage as soon as he could. Mírzá Ḥasan left the house of the Imám-Jum'ih silently and quietly and repaired to the house of the man who had given him a friendly warning. Shortly after, Mírzá Ḥusayn and the youthful Mírzá Ismá'íl went to the Imám-Jum'ih, as it was customary to ask his permission to leave. The Imám-Jum'ih told them to stay for a while longer, because he had some business to transact with them, and then, noticing that the other brother was not with them, enquired where Mírzá Ḥasan was. He became much agitated when he learned that Mírzá Ḥasan had left, and immediately dispatched his men to seek him and bring him back. They went in search of him to his house, only to be told that he was still with the Imám-Jum'ih and had not returned. Infuriated, the minions of that unscrupulous divine broke brutally into the house of Mírzá Ḥasan, even into rooms and apartments – the *andarúní* – where the ladies of the household lodged. Neither in his house nor anywhere else could they find any trace of Mírzá Ḥasan. Then, a mischief-maker informed the Imám-Jum'ih that the man he was seeking was in the house of Áqá Muḥammad-Báqir-i-Mudarrís and they, the two scheming divines, sent word to Ẓillu's-Sulṭán that Mírzá Ḥasan had taken refuge there. When the Prince-Governor, himself well involved in that diabolical plot, learned that his own father-in-law had given protection to Mírzá Ḥasan, he demanded an explanation. Áqá Muḥammad-Báqir was angered, informed Mírzá Ḥasan of Ẓillu's-Sulṭán's high-handed action and together they rode to the residence of the Prince. In the meantime Mírzá Ḥusayn and Mírzá Ismá'íl had both been put under arrest. And Ẓillu's-Sulṭán, as soon as he set eyes on Mírzá Ḥasan, began to upbraid him. He grew violent in his denunciation, and seeing that Mírzá Ḥasan would not yield an inch in renouncing his Faith, took that noble siyyid's firmness as a personal insult and struck Mírzá Ḥasan's head and face with his cane, drawing blood.

Let the able and creative pen of Mírzá Abu'l-Faḍl of Gulpáygán tell the rest of the story of the Núrayn-i-Nayyirayn – the Twin Luminous Orbs:

During the days of their imprisonment, he [the Prince] sent for Jináb-i-Mírzá [Mírzá Ḥasan] several times and held parleys with him. One day, he told Jináb-i-Mírzá that the Imám-Jum'ih and others of the 'ulamá of Iṣfahán were complaining that he had become a believer in this novel Cause. The Mírzá replied: 'That is true, but the reason that the Imám-Jum'ih is inimical towards me is this: I have for several years defrayed all the expenses of his household, what they ate and what they wore. He owes me a sum of money, and because I have lately asked him to settle his debt he has turned against me.' The Prince said: 'That is true, but now come and renounce this Faith, and curse its leaders.' Jináb-i-Mírzá remained silent. Ẓillu's-Sulṭán continued to press him, saying: 'I swear by the salt of His Majesty the monarch, and the pure soul of the Commander of the Faithful ['Alí, the First Imám] that should you curse them, I would always give you help and support, get from the Imám-Jum'ih all that he owes you and make your enemies disappointed, make them abandon their hostility.' Again that manifestation of constancy said nothing. In the end the Prince said: 'Come, by my life, and curse them.' But his insistence was of no avail. Seeing that, the Prince was infuriated and shouted: 'Why don't you curse them?' Jináb-i-Mírzá, at last, spoke: 'If Your Highness knew what I know, you would not order me to do any cursing.' Hearing this, the Prince became totally a changed man, enraged, bestial, burning with fury, completely beside himself, his face alarmingly darkening, and his hand went several times to his sword, half unsheathing it. Finally he took up his walking-stick and so pounded the head and face of that Rock of Constancy that the blessed visage was covered with wounds. Then, before an examining body, Mírzá Muḥammad-Ḥusayn, too, refused to renounce his Faith. But being very young and tender in years, Mírzá Ismá'íl did not follow the example of his two glorious brothers and took himself apart from the true Faith. Thus he was freed.* However, the Imám-Jum'ih and others thought that the noble descent and the wealth of the Mírzá might bring about his freedom and so, once again, they took counsel together. There in that gathering they decided to present the case to the sovereign and obtain permission to have the Mírzá executed. Whereupon, they sent a telegram to Ḥájí Mullá 'Alíy-i-Kaní, who is today the Chief of the jurists of Ṭihrán, and asked him to inform His Majesty the monarch that the 'ulamá of Iṣfahán had, in their concern for the security of the sovereign, detained and imprisoned two Bábís, and now requested his permission to have them put to death, so that rendering him this service they should be considered as truly well-wishers of the State. Having received that telegram, the Sháh ordered Ẓillu's-Sulṭán to dispatch the two brothers in chains to Ṭihrán. Being thus commanded, Ẓillu's-Sulṭán paused and did not go ahead with the execution of the Mírzá. But the Imám-Jum'ih and Shaykh Báqir came to realize that the Sháh would not involve himself in the death of those two innocent men, and their journey to Ṭihrán would undoubtedly result in their release.

So the two divines took counsel together a third time and decided to carry out their design through public rioting. Therefore, on the 23rd day of Rabí'u'l-Avval 1296 [17 March 1879], they first ordered the tradesmen and the shopkeepers in the bazar to shut their shops. Next, the 'ulamá, such as the

* It is said that the Imám-Jum'ih, for purposes of his own, gave out that Mírzá Ismá'íl had renounced his Faith. In any case, we find Mírzá Ismá'íl, in later years, back in the Bahá'í fold. (HMB)

Imám-Jum'ih; Shaykh Báqir; Ḥájí Mírzá Háshim, who was a son of the previous Imám-Jum'ih; Mírzá 'Abdu'l-Javád, son of Áqá Muḥammad-Mihdíy-i-Kabbásí; Áqá Siyyid 'Alíy-i-Burújirdí, and others of the jurists of Iṣfahán, numbering more than fifty – each one accompanied by a huge crowd of rascals and rioters, tradesmen and people of the bazar – rode in the direction of the residence of the governor. With shouts of 'Oh for our Religion! Oh for our Faith!' they threw the whole city into uproar. As related by a reliable man, their barbarous yells were heard as far away as Qal'iy-i-Gaz, which lies at a distance of nine miles from Iṣfahán.

While this tumult was going on Ẓillu's-Sulṭán was in his bath. He was greatly alarmed by the shouts of the populace and enquired the reason for this gathering of the masses. He was told that the host of the 'ulamá and their followers had turned out, wishing to make it known that there should no longer be any delay in dealing with the case of the Mírzá and demanding that His Highness put him to death; otherwise they themselves with the force at their command would have him executed. Ẓillu's-Sulṭán, leaving his bath, called the 'ulamá to his presence, and they made their demand. The Prince told them that the two siyyids were not guilty of any treasonable act and had done nothing hostile to the State; that the quarrel of the 'ulamá with them was totally of a religious and sectarian nature, and he himself could not intervene in matters of faith and belief; moreover, 'His Majesty, our sovereign Lord, has expressly commanded me to send them to the capital; therefore I cannot order their execution.' The 'ulamá said: 'We will order their execution and will shoulder the responsibility, as far as His Majesty is concerned.' The Prince replied: 'But I shall not give orders to the executioner to carry out this deed.' Several of the 'ulamá in that assemblage, one of whom was Shaykh Muḥammad-Taqí, a son of Shaykh Muḥammad-Báqir and known as Shaykh Najafí, rolled up their sleeves, declaring: 'With our own hands we shall slay them.' As the Prince noticed that those hard-hearted men were thus daring and emboldened in their wish to spill innocent blood, he told them: 'Write me an edict and state the necessity of putting them to death. This is a document that I shall require.' The 'ulamá, some sixty of them who were present, had such a document written, signed and witnessed, and then sent it to the Prince. And as soon as he set eyes on that piece of paper, the Prince issued orders for the demolition of the edifice of sublimity and honour with the hatchet of tyranny, the cutting down of the spreading tree of generosity and beneficence with the axe of enmity and rebelliousness. Thus, as orders were given for the downing of those twin resplendent stars of the firmament of noble descent, satanic brutes dragged them out of the prison-house, and by the side of Ṭálár-i-Ṭavílih (one of the renowned buildings of Iṣfahán, reared by the Ṣafavid kings) spilled their precious blood, which was the very essence of purity, the repository of humaneness. After they had quaffed the cup of martyrdom, ropes were fastened to their legs and their sanctified bodies were dragged to the foot of the gallows, where they lay throughout the day. The Prince had sent a number of his footmen to keep watch around them and stop the people from throwing stones and heaping insults.

A street in Iṣfahán in the time of Ẓillu's-Sulṭán (Dieulafoy, La Perse*)*

The pavilion of Ẓillu's-Sulṭán in Iṣfahán (Dieulafoy, La Perse*)*

At the close of the day, Shaykh Báqir ordered his own men to take the corpses to a place near the rivulet 'Níyasarm', where an archway was standing, place them under that arch, and bring it down over them. Later, Ẓillu's-Sulṭán sent for Mírzá Ismá'íl and told him to give a proper burial to those two sanctified bodies, and he committed them to earth in the Takht-i-Fúlád cemetery. (Quoted in Ishráq-i-Khávarí, *Kitáb-i-Núrayn-i-Nayyirayn*, pp. 260–65)

Exactly nine years later, early in 1888, Edward Granville Browne was in Iṣfahán. He has told us in his immortal work, *A Year Amongst the Persians*, how in that city of 'Abbás the Great, after months of search and waiting, he met the followers of Bahá'u'lláh. There it was that he had the privilege to converse, for an hour or two, with that celebrated veteran of the Faith, Ḥájí Mírzá Ḥaydar-'Alí, himself a native of Iṣfahán. And he visited what was known to be the graves of the Núrayn-i-Nayyirayn in the vast cemetery of Takht-i-Fúlád.

Let Browne himself, in his own inimitable way, tell us the story of his visit to that sacrosanct spot:

. . . I asked the *dallál** whether he knew where the two Seyyids who suffered martyrdom for the Bábí faith about the year 1879 were buried.

'Yes,' he replied, 'I know the spot well, and will take you there if you wish it; but surely, Ṣáḥib, you who are so eager to obtain our books, who desire to visit the graves of our martyrs, must be prompted by some motive beyond mere curiosity. You have been to Acre, you have been honoured by beholding the Blessed Countenance, you are yourself a Bábí. Say, is it not so? There is no need to conceal anything from me.'

'My friend,' I answered, 'I am neither a Bábí, nor have I been to Acre; yet I confess that I am actuated by something more than mere curiosity. I cannot but feel that a religion which has produced examples of such heroic courage and fortitude as yours, merits a careful examination, since that must needs contain noble thoughts which can prompt to noble deeds. In visiting the graves of your martyrs I would fain pay a tribute of respect to those who gave up wealth, ease, and consideration, nay, even life itself, for the faith which they held dearer than all else.' . . .

Next day, early in the afternoon, my friend the *dallál* came to conduct me to the tombs of the martyrs. After a walk of more than an hour in a blazing sun, we arrived at the vast cemetery called *Takht-i-Fúlád* ('the Throne of Steel'). Threading our way through the wilderness of tombstones, my companion presently espied, and summoned to us, a poor grave-digger, also belonging to the persecuted sect, who accompanied us to a spot marked by two small mounds of stones and pebbles. Here we halted, and the *dallál*,

* E. G. Browne does not give the name of this tradesman in his book. However, in a diary in English, parts of which are in Persian and even Sanskrit characters, he has recorded his name. It was Áqá Javád.

turning to me, said, 'These are the graves of the martyrs. No stone marks the spot, because the Musulmáns destroyed those which we placed here, and, indeed, it is perhaps as well that they have almost forgotten the resting-places of those they slew, lest, in their fanaticism, they should yet further desecrate them. And now we will sit down for a while in this place, and I will tell you how the death of these men was brought about. But first it is well that our friend should read the prayer appointed for the visitation of this holy spot.'

The other thereupon produced a little book from under his cloak, and proceeded to read a prayer, partly in Arabic, partly in Persian. When this was concluded, we seated ourselves by the graves, and the *dallál* commenced his narrative.

'This,' said he, pointing to the mound nearest to us, 'is the tomb of Ḥájí Mírzá Ḥasan, whom we call *Sulṭánu'sh-Shuhadá*, "the King of Martyrs", and that yonder is the resting-place of his elder brother, Ḥájí Mírzá Ḥuseyn, called *Maḥbúbu'sh-Shuhadá*, "the Beloved of Martyrs". They were Seyyids by birth, and merchants by profession; yet neither their descent from the Prophet, nor their rare integrity in business transactions and liberality to the poor, which were universally acknowledged, served to protect them from the wicked schemes of their enemies' . . . (pp. 227–8, 231–2)

Edward Browne then proceeds to relate the circumstances of the martyrdom of the Núrayn-i-Nayyirayn, as he heard them that afternoon from Áqá Javád, the *dallál* of Iṣfahán, and later from the Bahá'ís of Shíráz. Continuing with the narration of Áqá Javád, he records:

. . . 'But we cannot mark the spot where they are buried with a stone, for when one was put up, the Musulmáns, whose malignity towards us is unbounded, and who know very well that we pay visits to these graves in secret, overthrew it. Our friend here' (pointing to his companion) 'was brought to believe by means of these martyrs. Was it not so?'

'Yes,' answered the other, 'some time after their death I saw in a dream vast crowds of people visiting a certain spot in the cemetery. I asked in my dream, "Whose are these graves?" An answer came, "Those of the 'King of Martyrs' and the 'Beloved of Martyrs'." Then I believed in that faith for which they had witnessed with their blood, seeing that it was accepted of God; and since then I visit them continually, and strive to keep them neat and orderly, and preserve the spot from oblivion by renewing the border of bricks and the heap of stones which is all that marks it.'

'He is a good man,' rejoined the *dallál*, 'and formerly those of the "Friends" who came to visit the graves used to rest for a while in the little house which he has near here, and partake of tea and *ḳalyáns*. The Musulmáns, however, found this out, made a raid on his house, abused and threatened him, and, before they departed, destroyed his tea-things and pipes. He is very poor,' he added in a whisper, 'give him a *ḳrán* [qirán] for his trouble; it is an action which has merit.'

I accordingly gave a small present to our guide, who departed with expressions of gratitude. After sitting a little while longer we too rose to go, and, taking a last look at the graves, from each of which I carried away a small stone as a memento, we once more turned our faces towards the city. On our way towards the gate of the cemetery we again passed the poor grave-digger with his little boy, and he again greeted me with expressions of thankfulness and good wishes for my journey.

I was much touched by the kindliness of these poor people, and communicated something of my thoughts to my companion.

[As Edward Browne relates, Áqá Javád then told him:] '. . . we are taught to regard all good men as clean and pure, whatever their religion. . . . Has it not struck you how similar were the life and death of our Founder (whom, indeed, we believe to have been Christ Himself returned to earth) to those of the Founder of your faith? Both were wise, even in their childhood, beyond the comprehension of those around them; both were pure and blameless in their lives; and both at last were done to death by a fanatical priesthood and a government alarmed at the love and devotion which they inspired in their disciples.* But besides this the ordinances enjoined upon us are in many respects like those which you follow. We are recommended to take to ourselves only one wife, . . . we believe that women ought to be allowed to mix more freely with men, and should not be compelled to wear the veil.' (ibid. pp. 234–6)

In suchwise the *dallál* of Iṣfahán went on to speak to Browne, on their walk back to Iṣfahán. 'Conversing thus,' Browne writes:

. . . we arrived at the side of the river, just where it is spanned by the bridge called Pul-i-Khájú, a much finer structure than even the bridge of thirty-three arches which I had admired so much on my entry into Julfá. My companion suggested that we should sit here awhile on the lower terrace (for the bridge is built on two levels) and smoke a *ḳalyán*, and to this I readily consented. (ibid. p. 238)

The final paragraph of the chapter on Iṣfahán in Edward Browne's imperishable book has no connection with the story of the Núrayn-i-Nayyirayn or the author's encounter with the followers of Bahá'u'lláh; but it is truly worth quoting in full because it well describes the depredations and the havoc wrought by the unholy hands of Ẓillu's-Sulṭán and his minions in the splendrous city of 'Abbás the Great:

* The Bábís for the most part, unlike the Muḥammadans, believe that Christ was actually crucified by the Jews, and not, as the latter assert, taken up into heaven miraculously, while another, resembling Him in appearance, was crucified in His stead. But few of the Muḥammadans are conversant with the Gospels, while the reverse holds good of the Bábís, many of whom take pleasure in reading the accounts of the life and death of Jesus Christ. (EGB)

After admiring the massive piers and solid masonry of the bridge, and the wide sweep here made by the Záyanda-Rúd, we resumed our way along the southern bank in the direction of Julfá. On our way we visited the deserted palace called *Haft-dast* ('Seven Hands'). Here was visible the same neglected splendour and ruined magnificence which was discernible elsewhere. One building, the *Namak-dán* ('Salt-cellar'), had just been pulled down by one of the ministers of the Ẓillu's-Sulṭán to afford material for a house which he was building for himself. Another, called *Á'íné-kháné* ('the Chamber of Mirrors'), was nearly stripped of the ornaments which gave it its name, the remainder being for the most part broken and cracked. Everywhere it was the same – crumbling walls, heaps of rubbish, and marred works of art, still beautiful in spite of injuries, due as much to wanton mischief as to mere neglect. Would that some portion of that money which is spent in building new palaces in the capital, and constructing *mihmán-khánés* [hotels, guest-houses] neither beautiful nor pleasant, were devoted to the preservation of the glorious relics of a past age! That, however, is as a rule the last thing an Oriental monarch cares about. To construct edifices which may perpetuate his own name is of far more importance in his eyes than to protect from injury those built by his predecessors, which, indeed, he is perhaps not sorry to see crumbling away like the dynasties which reared them. And so it goes on – king succeeding king, dynasty overthrowing dynasty, ruin added to ruin; and through it all the mighty spirit of the people 'dreaming the dream of the soul's disentanglement', while the stony-eyed lions of Persepolis look forth in their endless watch over a nation which slumbers, but is not dead. (ibid. pp. 238–9)

Unfortunately, Consular Reports of Iṣfahán, for the period concerned, do not exist in the Public Record Office in London. They seem to have been destroyed. However, a dispatch dated June 1879 is extant, sent by Sir Ronald Thomson, the British Minister in Ṭihrán, to Lord Salisbury, the Foreign Secretary, informing him of the execution of the two brothers of Iṣfahán and its circumstances. Sir Ronald writes:

Several serious disturbances have lately occurred in Isfahan and unfortunately the governor of that province, being the Zil-i-Sultan a son of the Shah, instead of being censured or withdrawn was supported by the government.

The Imam-i-Joomeh, or Chief Priest, owed sum of Eighteen thousand Tomans (Ts. 18,000) to two respectable and wealthy Seyeds, and to avoid payment of the debt he accused them of being Bábis and Socialists; they were accordingly seized, their property made away with by the authorities, and they themselves put to death. This gave rise to great excitement in Isfahan and news of the occurrence having been telegraphed to me, I immediately made representations through the Minister for Foreign Affairs to the Shah, and orders were sent down to Isfahan which resulted in putting a stop to further atrocities which were in contemplation. (Cited Momen, *The Bábí and Bahá'í Religions*, p. 277)

Let it not be imagined that 'Raqshá' – the She-Serpent – that faithless Imám-Jum'ih of Iṣfahán thus castigated and designated by the Most Exalted Pen, lightly escaped the consequences of his treachery to enjoy his ill-gotten gains. At one time there was a moment when it seemed that wise counsels might prevail. Some people were reluctant to allow the spilling of innocent blood. These two brothers, they averred, were of impeccable record and conduct; they were noble scions of the noble House of Muḥammad, distinguished descendants of Fáṭimih; why should their deaths be envisaged? The unprincipled Imám-Jum'ih, sensing that he might lose his prey, struck his neck and exclaimed: 'Their blood be on my neck [the same as 'be it on my head'], I accept full responsibility.' Thus he envisaged his own destruction, and that dastardly deed, the slaying of those two brothers, came to pass.

Hardly had a year elapsed since the martyrdom of the Núrayn-i-Nayyirayn, when on that very spot of the Imám-Jum'ih's neck which he had struck, in token of his acceptance of full responsibility for the spilling of innocent blood, there appeared a swelling which soon turned into a nasty and troublesome boil and the matter collecting in it was exceedingly unpleasant. That wicked divine had to abandon Iṣfahán and his seat of authority, going from village to village, nowhere finding relief. Finally his whole body became so malodorous that his own family could not bear to be anywhere near him. And when he died after months of extreme misery, porters had to be brought to carry unceremoniously his corpse to an unknown grave.

And there is a strange sequel to the death of that Imám-Jum'ih of Iṣfahán which took place on 21 June 1881. The British Agent S. P. Aganoor, reporting to the Minister in Ṭihrán, wrote on 4 July: '. . . people of Isfahan, in his honer [sic], shut the shops and Bazars, but the Prince Governor sent ferashes [*farráshes*] and ordered to open them.' (Public Record Office, FO 248/384)

Years rolled on, decades passed, the graves of the Núrayn-i-Nayyirayn remained obscure and forlorn – but not forgotten by those who cherished their memory. At the beginning of the second Bahá'í century a beautiful monument was raised over their remains, and although it has in recent years been destroyed by the same fanatical spirit that encompassed their deaths and now rules over Írán, the time will come when the Bahá'ís of the world will honour these great heroes of their Faith in a manner befitting their courage, fidelity and sacrifice.

4

Lamentation of the Most Exalted Pen

MANY AND MOST POIGNANT were the verses which flowed from the Most Exalted Pen in lamentation over the appalling tragedy, the cruel extinction of the Núrayn-i-Nayyirayn – the Twin Shining Lights of the city of 'Abbás the Great.

The heart-rending cry: 'O Land of Sád [Iṣfahán] . . . Where is My Ḥasan! . . . Where is My Ḥusayn! . . .' was wrung from the lips of the Supreme Manifestation of God.

Addressing the Son of the Wolf, Bahá'u'lláh wrote in the evening of His life:

O heedless one! Rely not on thy glory, and thy power. Thou art even as the last trace of sunlight upon the mountain-top. Soon will it fade away as decreed by God, the All-Possessing, the Most High. Thy glory and the glory of such as are like thee have been taken away, and this verily is what hath been ordained by the One with Whom is the Mother Tablet. Where is he to be found who contended with God, and whither is gone he that gainsaid His signs, and turned aside from His sovereignty? Where are they who have slain His chosen ones and spilt the blood of His holy ones? Reflect, that haply thou mayest perceive the breaths of thine acts, O foolish doubter! Because of you the Apostle [Muḥammad] lamented, and the Chaste One [Fáṭimih] cried out, and the countries were laid waste, and darkness fell upon all regions. O concourse of divines! Because of you the people were abased, and the banner of Islám was hauled down, and its mighty throne subverted. Every time a man of discernment hath sought to hold fast unto that which would exalt Islám, you raised a clamor, and thereby was he deterred from achieving his purpose, while the land remained fallen in clear ruin.

O My Supreme Pen! Call Thou to remembrance the She-Serpent [Imám-Jum'ih of Iṣfahán] whose cruelty hath caused all created things to groan, and the limbs of the holy ones to quake. Thus biddeth Thee the Lord of all names, in this glorious station. The Chaste One [Fáṭimih] hath cried out by reason of thine iniquity, and yet thou dost imagine thyself to be of the family of the Apostle of God! Thus hath thy soul prompted thee, O thou who hast withdrawn thyself from God, the Lord of all that hath been and shall be. Judge thou equitably, O She-Serpent! For what crime didst thou sting the children of the Apostle of God [King of Martyrs and Beloved of Martyrs], and pillage their possessions? Hast thou denied Him Who created thee by His command 'be, and it was'? Thou hast dealt with the children of the Apostle of God as neither 'Ád hath dealt with Húd nor Thamúd with Ṣáliḥ, nor the Jews with the Spirit of God [Jesus], the Lord of all being. Gainsayest thou the signs of Thy Lord which no sooner were they sent down from the heaven of His Cause than all the books of the world bowed down before them? Meditate, that thou mayest be made aware of thine act, O heedless outcast! Ere long will the breaths of chastisement seize thee, as they seized others before thee. Wait, O thou who hast joined partners with God, the Lord of the visible and the invisible. This is the day which God hath announced through the tongue of His Apostle. Reflect, that thou mayest apprehend what the All-Merciful hath sent down in the Qur'án and in this inscribed Tablet. This is the day whereon He Who is the Dayspring of Revelation hath come with clear tokens which none can number. This is the day whereon every man endued with perception hath discovered the fragrance of the breeze of the All-Merciful in the world of creation, and every man of insight hastened unto the living waters of the mercy of His Lord, the King of Kings. . . . Didst thou imagine that martyrdom could abase this Cause? Nay, by Him Whom God hath made to be the Repository of His Revelation, if thou be of them that comprehend. Woe betide thee, O thou who hast joined partners with God, and woe betide them that have taken thee as their leader, without a clear token or a perspicuous Book. How numerous the oppressors before thee, who have arisen to quench the light of God, and how many the impious who murdered and pillaged until the hearts and souls of men groaned by reason of their cruelty! The sun of justice hath been obscured, inasmuch as the embodiment of tyranny hath been stablished upon the throne of hatred, and yet the people understand not. O foolish one! Thou hast slain the children of the Apostle and pillaged their possessions. Say: Was it, in thine estimation, their possessions or themselves that denied God? Judge fairly, O ignorant one that hath been shut out as by a veil from God. Thou hast clung to tyranny, and cast away justice; whereupon all created things have lamented, and still thou art among the wayward. Thou hast put to death the aged, and plundered the young. Thinkest thou that thou wilt consume that which thine iniquity hath amassed? Nay, by Myself! Thus informeth thee He Who is cognizant of all. By God! The things thou possessest shall profit thee not, nor what thou hast laid up through thy cruelty. Unto this beareth witness Thy Lord, the All-Knowing. Thou hast arisen to put out the light of this Cause; ere long will thine own fire be quenched, at His behest. He, verily, is the Lord of strength and of might. The changes and chances of the world, and the powers of the nations, cannot frustrate Him. He doeth what He pleaseth, and ordaineth what He willeth through the power of His sovereignty. Consider the she-camel. Though but a beast, yet hath the All-Merciful exalted her to so high a station that the tongues of the earth made mention of her and celebrated her praise. He, verily, overshadoweth all that is in the heavens, and on earth. No God is

*Núrayn-i-Nayyirayn (The Twin Shining Lights). Mírzá Muḥammad-Ḥasan, the King of Martyrs (*left*), and Mírzá Muḥammad-Ḥusayn, the Beloved of Martyrs (*right*)*

there but Him, the Almighty, the Great. Thus have We adorned the heaven of Our Tablet with the suns of Our words. Blessed the man that hath attained thereunto, and been illumined with their light, and woe betide such as have turned aside, and denied Him, and strayed far from Him. Praised be God, the Lord of the worlds! (*Epistle to the Son of the Wolf*, pp. 99–103)

And thus did the Most Exalted Pen* address Shaykh Káẓim of Qazvín, whom Bahá'u'lláh had honoured with the designation of Samandar:

He is the Consoler in this sublime, supreme station. O Samandar! Verily, He, Who is the Supreme Ordainer, consoleth Himself for that which came upon Him from those who took to oppression and turned their backs on justice, following the path of satanic souls who aspire to evil ways. Verily, the people of 'Ád and Thamúd meted unto Ṣáliḥ and Húd that which caused the Sadratu'l-Muntahá to lament and the Concourse on high to wail. Unto that beareth witness this Wronged One, sorrowful and exiled. By God, they crucified the Spirit [Jesus], hamstrung the She-Camel [of Ṣáliḥ] and smashed the Ark of the Covenant. Thy Lord well knoweth and expoundeth this unto

* Bahá'u'lláh

thee. He eulogizeth His chosen ones and consoleth His loved Ones on this affliction which hath caused justice to moan and the Faithful Spirit [Gabriel] to wail. Verily, verily, they have slain My chosen ones and pillaged their property. Thus hath the decree been fulfilled and yet most of the people are of the heedless.

O Samandar! Verily, We have seen the beloved Joseph caught by the fangs of wolves, and Ḥusayn captive in the claws of tyrants. By God, this nation hath done what the Jews did not do to the Spirit [Jesus] nor Abú Jahl to Muḥammad, My Apostle, Whom We adorned with the mantle of the 'Seal', and sent unto the denizens of heaven and earth. They have, verily, committed that which no one in the world had committed, and to that beareth witness the Lord of Eternity from this Scene of transcendent glory. After Ḥasan and Ḥusayn had attained their station, and some days passed, We laid hands on the source of tyranny and oppression, through Our Sovereignty. Verily, thy Lord is the All-Powerful, the Almighty. Great is the blessedness of those who drew nigh unto them and visited their resting-places. They are, verily, the people of God in the kingdom of creation. Thus did the Most Exalted Pen decree in this glorious, incomparable Book. Woe betide them who have cast the Tablet of God behind them and followed everyone who hath been a worker of iniquity and hath gone far astray.

Ponder, O My Samandar, My patience and forbearance notwithstanding My power and might, and My silence in spite of the penetrative influence of My word which standeth supreme over all the worlds. Should We have wished We could have seized those who have wronged Us outwardly with the hand of one of the servants of God, or through the intervention of well-favoured angels. We act according to the dictates of wisdom which We have set to be a guiding light for My people and the denizens of My Kingdom. Verily, thy Lord is the All-Knowing, the Wise. Ere long We shall take hold of those who have acted with tyranny as We seized others before them. Verily, thy Lord commandeth what He willeth. (Quoted in Is͟hráq-i-K͟hávarí, *Kitáb-i-Núrayn-i-Nayyirayn*, pp. 172–4)

And the Tongue of Power and Might* thus spoke to the bereaved family of the Núrayn-i-Nayyirayn:

He is the Consoler

O Scions of that House! Verily, there hath come upon you in the path of God that which came upon the descendants of the Apostle and their women and children in the Land of Ṭaff [Karbilá] and elsewhere. Be ye confident of the grace of God and of His mercy. He is, verily, with you in every world of His worlds, and He is the Ever-Watchful, the Ever-Present, the All-Seeing. Woe unto those who wronged you and slew you and pillaged your possessions. By My life, they are in manifest loss. Ere long the gales of chastisement will beat upon them from every side. Verily, He is the All-Informed, the All-Knowing. Put your trust in God and say: 'Well is it with us, and blessed are we

* Bahá'u'lláh

for that which hath come upon us in His straight Path. Praise be to God, the Lord of all worlds.' (ibid., p. 172)

The Most Exalted Pen was moved, once again, by the tragedy of Iṣfahán thus to inscribe:

In the Name of God, the Almighty, the All-Powerful

Thy letter was received and studied. Verily, that people hath been guilty of such oppression as hath cast gloom over the dominions of earth and heaven; those Twin Shining Lights were so wronged that the hosts of the Supreme Concourse have bewailed their plight. Ponder the fate of the Son of Zechariah [John the Baptist]: his head was stricken from his body at the whim of the adulteress of that age; and ponder what befell the Scion of the Apostle of God [the Imám Ḥusayn]: he was slain by order of the most debased man of his time. Was it those who were martyred who found themselves in great loss, or was it the tyrants? All created things have loudly proclaimed that it was the tyrants who went down into manifest perdition.

How burdensome was this affliction, and how profound the abasement that it caused, yet it was, by God, a supreme exaltation which but appeared in the guise of abasement. Protect this sublime station and regard not that which is seen in this day. Verily, God hath taken hold of these people in the past and will seize them now and will cleanse the earth of the defilement of their presence. And He will raise you to that station towards which all faces shall turn, and in the mention of which all the tongues in the world shall be moved.

Hearken to the call of this Wronged One and cling unto that which He hath mentioned. Verily, He is a trusted Counsellor . . . Comfort and console all the kindred on behalf of this Wronged One. Verily, He is the Consoler, the All-Knowing . . . That which is required of thee is to win the goodpleasure of the family of the Two Martyrs, upon whom be the Glory of God. Shouldst thou ponder for a while thou wouldst come to know for a certainty that that which hath transpired is infinite exaltation now and in the future. To this testifieth He with Whom is the knowledge of the Book. Praise be to God, the Lord of Lords. (ibid. pp. 182–3)

And the Tongue of Might and Power thus addressed the eloquent poet, Mírzá 'Alí-Muḥammad, master of limpid verse, himself a glorious martyr of later years, whom Bahá'u'lláh had honoured and extolled with the designation of 'Varqá' – Nightingale:

He is the Most Holy, the Supreme

O Varqá! The Servant in Attendance* attained My presence and mentioned what thou hadst written and We found thy letter a mirror reflecting thy love for the Beloved of the world and thy turning towards Him. Great is thy blessedness for having drawn nigh, for having drunk thy fill, and for having been

* Mírzá Áqá Ján

caused to attain. Verily, thy Lord is the Resplendent Expounder. Verily, We witness the fire that hath encompassed thee in thy love for thy Lord, We see its flaring up and hear the crackling of its flames. Exalted be He Who hath ignited it, He Who hath made its flames to leap high, He Who hath revealed it to all men. He is that Almighty Lord before the evidence of Whose might the essence of power acknowledgeth its helplessness. Verily, thy Lord is He who heareth and seeth, and is the All-Knowing. Rejoice, for this Wronged One maketh mention of thee as He hath in the past, and even in this instant, as He paceth, He giveth utterance to these words: 'Verily, We have sensed the sweet scent of thy love, and have witnessed thy sincerity and thy humility, as thy heart was occupied with the mention of Me and thy tongue with My wondrous praise.' Thus hath the Sea of life sprinkled its waters upon thee, that thou mayest rejoice in the days of thy glorious, incomparable Lord.

O Varqá! Thy call was heard and thy letter was presented before the Throne. Praise be to God! By it the fire of divine love blazed up . . . Some of the believers are seen to be sorrowful, even fearful at the events in the Land of Ṣád [Iṣfahán]; whilst it was the Hand of Divine Might which graciously singled them out and, from the heaven of His mercy and the clouds of His generosity, caused the overflowing rains of affluence and abundance to shower upon them. The consummate power of God adorned them with honour among the people, so that the tongues of the sincere who enjoyed near access unto Him spoke forth in their praise. They reached such heights that their adversaries bore witness to the elevation of their high rank. Then, at the end of their days, they attained the most exalted station which is that of supreme sacrifice; this is a station which God's chosen ones and His loved ones have at all times desired and everlastingly sought. Notwithstanding, some are sad and sorrowful. It is hoped that this grief hath appeared because of the love entertained for them. I swear by the ocean of divine mysteries that should the station of but one of the servants now engaged in their service be made manifest, the people of the world would be shaken asunder. Great is the blessedness of him who pondereth over that which hath transpired, that he may be informed of the greatness of this Cause and its sovereignty. This station which they attained was that which they themselves implored God – exalted be His glory – to grant them, and which they wished and desired with the utmost eagerness.

Say: O friends! Ye have endured much in the path of your love for the Beloved of the worlds; ye have witnessed that which it was not seemly to behold, and have heard that which ill became your ears, and have endured such burdens in the path of the Friend as were truly heavier than mountains. Great is the blessedness of your backs, your eyes and your ears, for that which they bore and they saw and they heard. Now ye should value this highly exalted station, and not allow it to be squandered. In all cases this ephemeral world and all who are therein will suffer death, and all things therein will be caught in the claws of change. At all times ask ye God – exalted be He – to keep you in His safekeeping, and to cause you to be constant in the path of His Cause. Know ye well that whatever ye have endured or seen or heard for His sake hath been as a token of His special bounty unto you. And among His eternal bestowals is the mention of you in His Tablets. Verily, ye have tasted the cup of calamity in His path; now drink your fill of the purest elixir from the goblets of His remembrance of you and of His tender mercy unto you . . . Be not saddened by what appeareth to be your weakness, your abasement and your distress. I swear by the Sun of the Heaven of Independence that honour, wealth and affluence are revolving around you, are making mention of you and are turning towards you. If, in accordance with the dictates of divine wisdom, their appearance is for some days as yet veiled, days will come when each and all of them will become evident and manifest as the sun. We beseech God that men will partake of the sweetness of His divine Utterance. (ibid. pp. 184–7)

Let it be said unmistakably and unhesitatingly that, despite the fearfulness of a few mentioned in this Tablet, the vast majority of those who had given their allegiance to Bahá'u'lláh remained firm and steadfast as the immovable rock, happy and blissful to have entered His fold, and confident of that ultimate victory which the Báb promised to His Letters of the Living, when He bade farewell to them. History bears ample witness to this.

5

The Vazír of K͟hurásán

IN ADRIANOPLE Bahá'u'lláh revealed one of His most momentous and most significant Tablets, the *Súriy-i-G͟huṣn* (The Súrih of the Branch), and addressed it to Mírzá 'Alí-Riḍá of Mas͟hhad, known as Mustawfí. The recipient, who came originally from the town of Sabzivár in the province of K͟hurásán, was a remarkable man, well-famed as a Bahá'í, and high in the service of the government. It was Mullá Ḥusayn-i-Bus͟hrú'í, the Bábu'l-Báb, who had guided him to range himself under the standard of the new Theophany. He had remained true to that allegiance throughout all the storms and stresses that followed. When the Persians were beaten by the Turkamáns and the renowned city of Marv was lost to them, one of the Persian officers who fell into the hands of the Turkamáns was 'Abdu'l-'Alí K͟hán of Marághih in the province of Ád͟harbáyján, then a colonel in the Persian army. As soon as Mírzá 'Alí-Riḍá was apprised of the plight of his fellow-believer, he sent eight hundred *túmáns* (a substantial sum in those days) through an intermediary to the Turkamáns in Marv, and obtained the release of the colonel. Thus, Mírzá 'Alí-Riḍáy-i-Mustawfí was always ready and well equipped with the riches he had, to serve the Cause which he had embraced so ardently. And he never made it a secret that he had given his allegiance to the Báb and Bahá'u'lláh.

It is well to quote here the following lines from the *Súriy-i-G͟huṣn* with which Mírzá 'Alí-Riḍáy-i-Mustawfí was honoured:

There hath branched from the Sadratu'l-Muntahá this sacred and glorious Being, this Branch of Holiness; well is it with him that hath sought His shelter and abideth beneath His shadow. Verily the Limb of the Law of God hath sprung forth from this Root which God hath firmly implanted in the Ground of His Will, and Whose Branch hath been so uplifted as to encompass the whole of creation. Magnified be He, therefore, for this sublime, this blessed, this mighty, this exalted Handiwork! O People! Draw ye nigh unto Him and savour from Him the fruits of wisdom and knowledge which come from God, the Glorious, the All-Knowing. Whosoever doth not taste thereof shall be deprived of the bounties of God, even if he should partake of all that is on earth, did ye but know. Say: A Word hath, as a token of Our grace, gone forth from the Most Great Tablet – a Word which God hath adorned with the ornament of His own Self, and made it sovereign over the earth and all that is therein, and a sign of His greatness and power among its people that thereby they would extol their Lord, the Lord of might and power and wisdom, praise their Creator, and exalt the sanctity of the Godhead, Who standeth supreme over all things. This is naught but that which hath been revealed by Him, the All-Knowing, the Ancient of Days. Say: Render thanks unto God, O people, for His appearance; for verily He is the most great Favour unto you, the most perfect bounty upon you; and through Him every mouldering bone is quickened. Whoso turneth towards Him hath turned towards God, and whoso turneth away from Him hath turned away from My Beauty, hath repudiated My Proof, and transgressed against Me. He is the Trust of God amongst you, His charge within you, His manifestation unto you and His appearance among His favoured servants . . . We have sent Him down in the form of a human temple. Blest and sanctified be God Who createth whatsoever He willeth through His inviolable, His infallible decree. They who deprive themselves of the shadow of the Branch, are lost in the wilderness of error, are consumed by the heat of worldly desires, and are of those who will assuredly perish. (Quoted in Shoghi Effendi, *The World Order of Bahá'u'lláh*, p. 135, and Ishráq-i-Khavárí, *Ayyám-i-Tis'ih*, p. 362)

One cannot overrate the significance of the *Súriy-Ghuṣn*, for in it, in the very early years of His Ministry, Bahá'u'lláh indicated the powers given to His eldest Son, as well as the developments still in the womb of a distant future.

Mírzá 'Alí-Riḍáy-i-Mustawfí served the Cause of Bahá'u'lláh faithfully and fearlessly until old age overtook him and he became infirm. His brother, younger than he, was there to take his place: Mírzá Muḥammad-Riḍá, the Mustasháru'l-Mulk, later entitled Mu'taminu's-Salṭanih. Rising high in the service of the State, he became the Vazír of Khurásán, a post which he kept to the end of his days until Náṣiri'd-Dín Sháh treacherously encompassed his death. Like his illustrious brother he never concealed the fact that he was a follower of Bahá'u'lláh and totally dedicated to His Cause. Because the State needed him, needed his profound knowledge of affairs, his integrity and unblemished honesty, he stayed firmly at the helm and prospered as the Vazír of Khurásán.

Just once in his remarkable career he ran into trouble with men standing above him, and that was due to the faithlessness and perjury on the part of his niece, a daughter of the late Mustawfí. It was in the

Mírzá Muḥammad-Riḍá, entitled Mu'taminu's-Salṭanih, the Vazír of Khurásán

year 1883 and Náṣiri'd-Dín-Sháh, on pilgrimage to the holy Shrine of Imám Riḍá (the Eighth Imám) in Mashhad, was presented with a petition by that lady, who was the wife of Ḥájí Qavám, commander of the Sabzivár cavalry. No doubt goaded by the adversaries of the Faith of Bahá'u'lláh, she claimed that her stepmother had left 80,000 *ashrafís* (gold coins), which belonged to her father, in the keeping of her uncle, the Vazír of Khurásán. Being a Bahá'í, her uncle was using that money, she alleged, to further the interests of his co-religionists who would soon be powerful enough to destroy the State. Náṣiri'd-Dín Sháh was naturally frightened by the tone and contents of that malicious petition; not only that, he scented a substantial amount of money to add to his own wealth. So affrighted was the Sháh that, on the day following the receipt of that document, he ordered four lines of armed soldiers to guard the route from the *arg* (citadel) to the Shrine of Imám Riḍá, before he would venture out to visit the Shrine. Next, he ordered the confiscation of the estate of Mírzá 'Alí-Riḍáy-i-Mustawfí, and held a board of enquiry to ascertain the facts. There, in

Náṣiri'd-Dín Sháh (reigned 1848–1896)

the presence of Shaykh 'Abdu'l-Karím (a noted divine of Mashhad), Mírzá 'Alí-Aṣghar Khán (the Amínu's-Sulṭán) and the Vazír of Khurásán himself, it was proved conclusively that the claim of the vazír's niece was wholly false and that the vazír was not in possession of any sum of money which had belonged to his late brother.

In the course of this enquiry it came to light that Áqá 'Azízu'lláh Jadhdháb (see chap. 15) had been entrusted with six hundred *ashrafís* by the late Mustawfí. Áqá 'Azízu'lláh himself had declared this trust, although nobody else had any knowledge of it and there was no record in the Mustawfí's own ledgers and papers. This fact greatly impressed Amínu's-Sulṭán, who declared that Áqá 'Azízu'lláh was an angel, because of his transparent honesty. The sum was paid to the progeny of the late Mustawfí, none of whom measured up to their father's calibre. However, Náṣiri'd-Dín Sháh, as was his wont, made good pickings from the riches of Mírzá 'Alí-Riḍá.

The Vazír of Khurásán was utterly fearless. One day during that same visit of Náṣiri'd-Dín Sháh mention was made, in the court, of a poetess of Bus͟hrúyih whose fame had reached the ears of the S͟háh. He told Ḥájí Muḥammad-Báqir K͟hán, the 'Imádu'l-Mulk and governor of Ṭabas, that it seemed that the town of Bus͟hrúyih still harboured some Bábís. 'Imádu'l-Mulk tried to evade the issue, replying that there was a girl there with hallucinations for whom a husband had been found, and she was cured. Of course the S͟háh knew how flimsy was the answer of the Governor of Ṭabas, and, trying to cajole the Vazír, commented: 'Oh! and we slew your Qá'im.' Then the Vazír spoke out: 'O Asylum of the Universe! What did it matter! The One Who is now sitting there in 'Akká is greater than the Qá'im; and do you know, Sire, He claims Divinity.' Náṣiri'd-Dín S͟háh was both abashed and frightened. He determined to rid himself of the courageous Vazír of K͟hurásán. But that was not an easy task. Because of his fairness and his boundless generosity, the vazír had, to the chagrin of the S͟háh, become a well-loved figure in that vast province.

Another incident which occurred during that same visit of Náṣiri'd-

S͟hujá'u'd-Dawliy-i-Qúc͟hání, hereditary chief of the Za'faránlú tribe of K͟hurásán

Dín Sháh served to arouse further the baseless fears of that highly suspicious potentate. From Mashhad he went to the town of Bujnúrd. There it was arranged that he should meet all the kháns and chieftains of Khurásán and watch a march past of the soldiery of that province. Shujá'u'd-Dawlih of Qúchán was one of those chieftains, a very powerful man.* Not only was he well disposed towards the followers of Bahá'u'lláh, but he had a son, Ḥasan-'Alí-Khán, who was devoted to the Bahá'í Faith. The soldiery of Khurásán were not alone in coming to Bujnúrd to present arms to the monarch of Írán; General Kropotkin of Russia had also arrived with troops and a regimental band, to greet the Sháh. Náṣiri'd-Dín Sháh took his position on a hillock, surrounded by spectators. When Shujá'u'd-Dawlih appeared on the scene leading his celebrated and well-equipped cavalry, the Sháh noticed that the Vazír of Khurásán was riding with him; he was not at all pleased by what he saw, although he could not help admiring the equipage of Shujá'u'd-Dawlih. General Kropotkin also expressed his keen admiration. Náṣiri'd-Dín Sháh was thus even more alarmed by the position of the Vazír of Khurásán. Then it fell to the vazír to present the kháns and chieftains to the sovereign. Amongst them was Sulaymán Khán of Darjiz, a brave and courageous Bahá'í who was very ugly in appearance. The Sháh asked him jokingly: 'Sulaymán Khán! Where were you on the day they were giving out *jamál* (beauty)?' Sulaymán Khán replied: 'Sire! I was going about looking for *kamál* (perfection).' It was a perfect answer and even the vazír was taken aback by it.

Náṣiri'd-Dín Sháh felt that a combination of the Vazír of Khurásán and Shujá'u'd-Dawlih would be ruinous for him, a sentiment totally false. He took them both with him to Ṭihrán, intending to destroy them. However, Ḥasan-'Alí Khán, the son of Shujá'u'd-Dawlih, could not and would not sit idly by and see his father eliminated because of the misplaced fears of the Sháh. He kept sending threatening letters to Ṭihrán, until Náṣiri'd-Dín Sháh had to let his father return to Qúchán. But the Sháh detained the Vazír of Khurásán in the capital, on the pretext of wishing to offer him a portfolio in his court. Then he gave him the governorship of Káshán. It seems that Káshán was the place to which the two Qájár monarchs, Náṣiri'd-Dín Sháh and his father, consigned dignitaries who had fallen foul of them. Mírzá Áqá Khán-i-Núrí, a future Ṣadr-i-A'ẓam

* He was the hereditary chief of the Za'faránlú tribe.

(prime minister), was sent there in the days of Muḥammad Sháh, when Ḥájí Mírzá Áqásí, the Antichrist of the Bábí Revelation, held the reins of power. And when Náṣiri'd-Dín Sháh, the ingrate, dismissed Mírzá Taqí Khán, the Amír Kabír, he directed the unseated prime minister to go to Káshán, and there had him put to death. (See Balyuzi, *Bahá'u'lláh, The King of Glory*, chap. 14.)

That one year in Káshán, although he was the governor of the city, came very hard to the Vazír of Khurásán, but he faced his banishment bravely. Then Náṣiri'd-Dín Sháh relented, summoned him to Ṭihrán, gave one of his sisters in marriage to him and conferred on him the

The Governor of Káshán with his attendants (Dieulafoy, La Perse*)*

Mírzá Taqí Khán, the Amír-Nizám, first Prime Minister of Náṣiri'd-Dín Sháh

title: Mu'taminu's-Salṭanih. The Vazír went back to Mashhad to his old post, where he was badly needed. Towards the end of the year 1890, Mu'taminu's-Salṭanih was once again in Ṭihrán, lodging in the house of Ruknu'd-Dawlih, a brother of the Sháh, who was the governor-general of Khurásán. In the last days of that year the Vazír died suddenly, poisoned by order of Náṣiri'd-Dín Sháh. The poison was administered to him in a cup of what has gained notoriety as the 'Qájár coffee'.

The remains of the Vazír were taken to Mashhad and buried in a stone sarcophagus, which he himself had prepared some years before. His eldest son, Mírzá 'Alí-Muḥammad Khán, inherited his title. With the premature death of the second Mu'taminu's-Salṭanih, some fifteen years after his father's, the glory centred in the holy city of Mashhad for seven decades passed into history.

The Vazír of Khurásán resembled Bahá'u'lláh in his build and height. In a Tablet revealed in his honour, Bahá'u'lláh thus addressed him: 'O thou whose temple beareth resemblance to Mine.'

6

The Nightingale

THE EMINENT BRITISH ORIENTALIST, Edward Granville Browne, was in Yazd as a young man in the spring of 1888. He had letters of introduction, addressed to the Afnáns (relatives of the Báb) living in that city, written by the father of the present writer. Ḥájí Siyyid Mírzá – a son of Ḥájí Mírzá Siyyid Ḥasan, a brother-in-law of the Báb known as Afnán-i-Kabír (the Great Afnán) – sent a man to guide Edward Browne to his house on receiving one of these letters. In his immortal book, *A Year Amongst the Persians*, Browne describes the discussion to which he listened:

On arriving at Ḥájí Seyyid M—s' house, I was delighted to find a theological discussion in progress. An attempt was evidently being made to convert an old mullá, of singularly attractive and engaging countenance, to the Bábí faith. [It is strange that Edward Browne kept naming Bahá'ís as Bábís.] Only one of the Bábís was speaking, a man of about thirty-five years of age, whose eloquence filled me with admiration. It was not till later that I learned that he was 'Andalíb (the 'Nightingale'), one of the most distinguished of the poets who have consecrated their talents to the glory of the New Theophany. 'And so in every dispensation,' he resumed, as soon as I had received and returned the greetings of those present, 'the very men who professed to be awaiting the new Manifestation most eagerly were the first to deny it, abandoning the "Most Firm Handhold" of God's Truth to lay hold of the frail thread of their own imaginings. You talk of miracles, but of what evidential value are miracles to me, unless I have seen them? Has not every religion accounts of miracles, which had they ever taken place, must, one would have thought, have compelled all men to believe; for who would dare, however hard of heart he might be, to fight with a Power which he could not ignore or understand? No, it is the Divine Word which is the token and sign of a prophet, the convincing proof to all men and all ages, the everlasting miracle. Do not misunderstand the matter: When the Prophet of God called his verses 'signs' (*áyát*), and declared the Ḳur'án [Qur'án] to be his witness and proof, he did not intend to imply, as some vainly suppose, that the eloquence of the words was a proof. How, for instance, can you or I, who are Persians, judge whether the eloquence of a book written in Arabic be supernatural or not?

Ḥájí Siyyid Mírzá, a son of Ḥájí Mírzá Siyyid Ḥasan (Afnán-i-Kabír)

No: the essential characteristic of the Divine Word is the penetrative power (*nufúdh*): it is not spoken in vain, it compels, it constrains, it creates, it rules, it works in men's hearts, it lives and dies not. The Apostle of God said "in the month of Ramaẓán [Ramaḍán] men shall fast from sunrise* to sunset". See how hard a thing this is; and yet here in Yezd there are thousands who, if you bade them break the fast or die, would prefer death to disobedience. Wherever one arises speaking this Word, know him to be a Manifestation of the Divine Will, believe in him, and take his yoke upon you.'

'But this claim,' said the old Mullá, 'this claim! It is a hard word that He utters. What can we do or say?'

'For the rest, He hath said it,' replied 'Andalíb, 'and it is for us, who have seen that this Divine Word is His, to accept it.' There was silence for a little while, and then the old Mullá arose with a sigh, and repeating, 'It is difficult, very difficult,' departed from our midst. (pp. 401–2)

Áqá 'Alí-As͟hraf of Láhíján (of the Caspian province of Gílán), whose sobriquet, 'Andalíb, was given to him by his tutor, wrote a

* It is actually from the moment dawn appears in the sky, when a white thread can be distinguished from a black thread. (HMB)

booklet addressed to Edward Browne, but it is not certain that it ever reached him. It is a lucid apologia, highly learned and concise.

Mírzá 'Alí-Ashraf lost his father early in life. However, he had as his mother a very remarkable woman named Khánum-Ján, who bravely faced the future and made every effort to give 'Alí-Ashraf and his sisters, Bilqís and Gawhar, a sound upbringing. 'Alí-Ashraf showed soon, in his early teens, that he had remarkable talents. He excelled in calligraphy, and his poetic talent became evident before long. His tutor felt very proud that he had a pupil so well endowed. Not only was his intellectual achievement brilliant; his handiwork was superb, particularly with the production of papier mâché pen-cases (an art in which the Persians excelled) and illuminated pages in manuscripts. He could easily earn his living by practising these arts. But he still craved for more knowledge and set out to learn Arabic. His mastery of that rich language was equally noteworthy.

There lived in Shíráz an excellent calligraphist named Mírzá 'Abdu'r-Raḥmán. 'Abdu'l-Bahá instructed him to make two copies of the Tablets of Bahá'u'lláh, such as *Tajallíyát* (Effulgences), *Ṭarázát* (Ornaments) and *Ishráqát* (Splendours), and ask 'Andalíb to illuminate the margins on every page. These books He intended, He wrote, to donate to the British Museum in London and the Bibliothèque Nationale of Paris.

Áqá 'Alí-Ashraf, apart from his accomplishments which made of him an outstanding person in Láhíján, was also a seeker of truth. To begin with he followed the Shaykhí school. Whatever the Shaykhís became and did under the leadership of Ḥájí Karím Khán of Kirmán, it should always be remembered that all those who set out in search of the promised Qá'im, and found Him in the person of the Báb, were disciples of Siyyid Káẓim.

In the days of the Báb two brothers, merchants of Qazvín who had become Bábís, went to Láhíján to engage there in trade. One was named Ḥájí Shaykh Muḥammad – the father of Mullá Káẓim-i-Samandar, a prominent Apostle of Bahá'u'lláh (see chap. 16) – and the other was Mashhadí Muḥammad-Raḥím. Before long, the former went back to Qazvín, and the second made Láhíján his home. There he married and settled down. Although he exercised great caution in teaching the Faith, soon he became known as a Bábí. Time and again the rabble of the town pillaged his goods and knocked him about. He was nearly beggared. But his faith in the Báb was as firm as ever.

Some time later, a number of Bahá'ís of Qazvín went to Láhíján, one of whom was Ḥájí Naṣír (to be martyred before long). They were followed by still others seeking refuge there from the persecutions in Qazvín. Mullá Ja'far, a very learned man, was one of the second group. In Láhíján he became a tutor. Then another citizen of Qazvín, named Siyyid Javád, arrived in their midst. But he was a confirmed Azalí (follower of Ṣubḥ-i-Azal). There were also many Shaykhís in Láhíján, from the governor and his entourage to smallholders. Naturally, Siyyid Javád did not associate with the Bahá'ís, who were his compatriots. But being surrounded by influential Shaykhís, and he himself being an agent for one of the wealthy landlords, Siyyid Javád had to watch his step.

As it happened, Siyyid Javád became friendly with a resident of Láhíján named Karbilá'í Bábáy-i-Vakíl. This Karbilá'í Bábá was a just man and free of prejudice. In his careless moments, Siyyid Javád had spoken such words as made his friend suspect him of being a Bábí. When Karbilá'í Bábá asked Siyyid Javád whether his guess was correct or not, the latter readily admitted that he was, and once the veil was drawn he spoke openly, until soon Karbilá'í Bábá embraced the Faith of the Báb. And he, in his turn, aided by Siyyid Javád, led Áqá 'Alí-Ashraf to become a Bábí. Siyyid Javád, who was going away for a short while, told the two new Bábís that they should eschew the company of the other men of Qazvín who were in Láhíján. Áqá 'Alí-Ashraf was too intelligent not to try to find out why Siyyid Javád had banned associating with all those Qazvínís in the town.

And so Áqá 'Alí-Ashraf went to the trading-house of Mashhadí Muḥammad-Raḥím, whose reputation as a Bábí was, as the Persian proverb has it, more widespread than the devilry of Satan, and put his question without any hedging: 'I know and everyone knows that you are a Bábí. Siyyid Javád, who is from your own home town, has made me see the truth and I have become a Bábí. But why did he warn me against you? I must know.' Mashhadí Muḥammad-Raḥím was delighted and told him the reason. Áqá 'Alí-Ashraf listened and when the truth dawned upon him, he, without any hesitation, became a Bahá'í, to be followed by Karbilá'í Bábá. When Siyyid Javád returned, these two made it known to him that they had found the truth: they were now followers of Bahá'u'lláh. Then began a period of discussion and debate which ended six months later when Siyyid Javád also embraced the Faith of Bahá'u'lláh.

Now 'Andalíb (whom henceforth we shall name as such, because soon it was his sobriquet that gained fame while his name 'Alí-Ashraf was almost forgotten), afire with the zeal of his newly-found faith, occupied a central position in the teaching field. The former Azalí, Siyyid Javád, was no less active in propagating the Faith of Bahá'u'lláh. These two, newly enrolled, were joined by the veteran Ḥájí Naṣír, and the three of them moved to Rasht – the seat of the governor of Gílán – a provincial capital where greater opportunities existed for making the Cause of Bahá'u'lláh known to the public. As a result of their efforts five brothers, whose surname was Báqiroff, became interested and were to render outstanding services to the Faith of Bahá'u'lláh (as do their descendants today), particularly Siyyid Naṣru'lláh who lived in Ṭihrán and offered the major share of the expenses of 'Abdu'l-Bahá's travels in Europe and America. Siyyid Aḥmad, son of one of these brothers, travelled to Europe, attended 'Abdu'l-Bahá in Paris and travelled with Him in 1913 when He visited Stuttgart, Budapest and Vienna. The descendants of those five brothers have chosen Sádát-i-Khamsí as their surname, bestowed by Bahá'u'lláh. 'Khams' means 'five' in Arabic, and the five siyyid brothers were known as such.

Back in Láhíján, 'Andalíb, who was still dressed in the garb of a student of theology, turned his attention to some of his fellow-students and brought two of them into the Faith. One of these was to become in future years a pillar of the Faith in the capital, and found a family distinguished by outstanding Bahá'í services. He was Mírzá Siyyid Muḥammad, entitled Náẓimu'l-Ḥukamá, the father of the late General Shu'áu'lláh 'Alá'í, elevated by the Guardian of the Cause of God to the rank of Hand of the Cause.

Náẓimu'l-Ḥukamá writes this about the man who introduced him to the Faith of Bahá'u'lláh:

> Gradually he became known as a Bábí . . . I stopped associating with him . . . because keeping his company would cause accusations to be levelled against me . . . Then the month of Ramaḍán arrived and the period of fasting. He came during that month to the Jámi' Mosque and engaged in prayer. At the end of the ritual prayer, he began his devotionals silently, in deep meditation. After an hour he left the mosque. One of the people present commented after he had gone that he was a Bábí. 'This is simulation' said another, adding that he had gone to buy a piece of cloth (*Máhút*) from him and found him finishing his lunch. ['Andalíb had already quitted the circle of the theological college and had set himself up in business as a draper

Siyyid Naṣru'lláh (1857–1921), one of the five Báqiroff brothers

'Abdu'l-Bahá in Stuttgart, 1913. Siyyid Aḥmad, a son of one of the Báqiroff brothers, stands immediately behind 'Abdu'l-Bahá on the right of the photograph

Three of the five Báqiroff brothers (front row)*, whose descendants use the surname of Sádát-i-Khamsí. They are Siyyid Naṣru'lláh* (left)*, Mír 'Alí Naqí* (centre)*, Siyyid Asadu'lláh* (right)*. Two of the second generation stand behind: Siyyid Mihdí* (left) *and Mír Náṣir* (right)*.*

*Siyyid Muḥammad, entitled Náẓimu'l-Ḥukamá, the head of the 'Alá'í family, is seated with his children around him. They are (*front row from left to right*): 'Aṭá'u'lláh, Riḍá, Qudsíyyih, Ni'matu'lláh, Ḍíyá'u'lláh, Shu'á'u'lláh (the late Hand of the Cause of God), and (*back row, left*) Mihdí; the other man is unidentified.*

and cloth merchant.] Still another added: 'Yesterday, when he came out of his house I met him and we walked on together. His hand smelt of fish. He goes home to have his lunch, then comes to the mosque to say his prayers just to deceive the people, and goes to his shop to sell his goods.' All those who spoke were his friends as well as mine. Not far from the place where we were sitting, there sat a number of divines.

Apparently the divines were also talking about 'Andalíb in such vile terms that Náẓimu'l-Ḥukamá, overhearing them, resolved to go and have it out the same night with 'Andalíb. He has written fully about all that passed between him and 'Andalíb during the next months. It is a very stirring and exciting account, and it ended with the conversion of Náẓimu'l-Ḥukamá. As he himself describes his spiritual odyssey:

At last after a whole year of struggle, similar to being in the throes of death, I obtained a new lease of life. I made my way out of the grave and beheld a new world. I had tormented the soul of the Mírzá ['Andalíb]. It was again the month of Ramaḍán. He told me reprovingly: 'What more do you want of me? You have tired me out. With all the proofs that I have given you, what more do you require? Go away. I have given you up.' I answered: 'Will declaring my faith suffice you or myself? And if someone has truly come to believe, but does not speak of it, will you or he come to any harm?' Hearing me say that convinced the Mírzá that I had reached the end of my quest, that it was all up with me now, that after a whole year's experience of the throes of death, I had been born again and had attained life eternal.

'Andalíb had by this time become known all over the town as a 'Bábí'. When his mother became aware of it she was furious. 'Andalíb had already, very quietly, led his sisters to give their allegiance to Bahá'u'lláh, but had left his mother alone. However, the time had come to win her over to the Cause. She resisted, just as Náẓimu'l-Ḥukamá had resisted for a year. But like him, she too found it impossible to resist any longer. The whole family was now united in one common allegiance. Externally, however, pressures were mounting. Men were heard denouncing 'Andalíb from pulpits. And then a dervish, who was also a siyyid, appeared on the scene.

In time past, dervishes were indeed men who deserved respect. Certainly there were still dervishes about who were pious and unworldly. But the vast numbers of them were parasites, greedy and ungodly. They prospered on simple people's credulity. The dervish now haunting the bazars of Láhíján was of the latter category. And he made it a duty to pester 'Andalíb. Although 'Andalíb paid him no attention, encouraged by the example of some of the divines, the dervish waxed bolder and bolder, until the climax was reached on a Friday. Another Javád of Qazvín, who had come to replace the aforementioned Siyyid Javád, had on that Friday invited a number of the Bahá'ís, including 'Andalíb, to lunch. Before going to Mírzá Javád's house, 'Andalíb went to his shop on some errand. Although it was a Friday and shops were shut, that dervish appeared outside 'Andalíb's shop and began to taunt him, first with personal abuse and then with insults to his family. All the while 'Andalíb kept his peace and went on with what he had to do in the shop. But when the dervish insulted the Báb and Bahá'u'lláh, 'Andalíb could bear it no longer; he picked up his metal yardstick and brought it down with all his force on the head of that insolent man. When he saw that the dervish was bleeding, he closed his shop and hurried to Mírzá Javád's house. There he found his companions talking of how to stop the impudence of the dervish. There was no need to talk of him anymore, said 'Andalíb, because he himself had hit him so hard with his metal yardstick that he would soon be dead. 'Andalíb was still beside himself with rage, but his host immediately realized that the consequences of that attack, even were the dervish to live, would be dire. He sent all the guests home at once, but kept 'Andalíb and found him a hiding-place.

Sure enough, the whole town was now in uproar, and the populace demanded 'Andalíb's blood. Some had seen him entering the house of Mírzá Javád, who, because of his position as the agent of one of the wealthiest landlords of the district, connected with the Court of Náṣiri'd-Dín Sháh, was treated with respect. At last the tumult of the mob reached the ears of the Governor of Láhíján. He asked to know the reason. When told that Áqá 'Alí-Ashraf, the Bábí, had grievously injured a dervish, and to compound his felony had failed to observe the respect due to a siyyid, a descendant of the Prophet, the Governor immediately ordered the arrest of the 'aggressive Bábí'. The officials, hearing that Áqá 'Alí-Ashraf had been seen that morning entering the house of Mírzá Javád-i-Qazvíní, hastened to it. Mírzá Javád invited them to search his house. 'Andalíb was there but they could not find him. He was hidden behind a huge cauldron. The mob, however, convinced that 'Andalíb was in Mírzá Javád's house, continued to crowd the street, keeping watch.

As it happened, Mashhadí Ḥusayn, an uncle of 'Andalíb who had gone to Rasht, arrived back the same day. Learning that the mob was seeking 'Andalíb to kill him, he flew into a rage. Then, taking with him a set of clothing, he first visited a bazar in the quarter where he lived, and where most of the shops belonged to 'Andalíb's cousins and other relatives. He denounced them as poltroons for not having gone to the aid of his nephew. 'I don't understand', he said, 'most of the things which 'Alí-Ashraf says, but I do know this, that he has time and again invited the 'ulamá to meet him at their convenience and discuss the matter with which he is concerned; and I know this also, that they have declined to meet him, but are now inciting a vagabond to bring him to harm. Had I not returned today 'Alí-Ashraf would have been in mortal danger.' Having castigated the members of his family for their lack of courage, Mashhadí Ḥusayn went to Mírzá Javád's house, gained admittance, made 'Andalíb change his clothes and led him out of the house. He had also brought two stout clubs with him. Giving one of them to 'Andalíb, he commanded him to use it if attacked. 'If you don't use it, I myself will beat you with this other club I am holding.' Mashhadí Ḥusayn was indeed very angry. His mien and the club in his hand struck terror in the hearts of the would-be assailants. 'Andalíb reached home safely and, in order to let tempers cool down, kept to his house. He had also to consider the perils which beset other Bahá'ís in Láhíján. But the rabble kept on agitating; they were still after 'Andalíb's blood. The Governor of Láhíján wrote to him that although the dervish's wound had healed, people were restive; should he leave the town for a while, that episode would soon be forgotten. 'Andalíb went to Qazvín.

A year later he returned to Láhíján for a short stay. But soon we find him again in the provincial seat of government – Rasht. Now that city became once more a scene of intense Bahá'í activity. The year 1882 (in which the fourteenth century of the Hejira [Hijrah], according to the lunar reckoning, was inaugurated) saw 'Andalíb tirelessly at work. That year also witnessed a reinvigorated persecution of the Bahá'ís, which had its beginning in Ṭihrán. Soon a number of Bahá'ís were detained in Rasht, and the Governor of Láhíján, where 'Andalíb had gone for a short visit, was directed to arrest 'Andalíb and Áqá Muḥammad-Ṣádiq, an uncle of the celebrated Samandar of Qazvín, and send them on to Rasht in the company of a few others.

The governor of the province of Gílán, in the year 1882, was the notorious 'Abdu'lláh Khán-i-Válí, who, as a grandson of Muḥammad-Báqir Khán-i-Biglarbagí,* a maternal uncle of Muḥammad Sháh, was therefore one of the Qájárs. Faḍlu'lláh Khán, the brother of 'Abdu'lláh Khán-i-Válí, was the Governor of Láhíján, and, according to the Válí's decree, had 'Andalíb arrested. He was hauled before Faḍlu'lláh Khán with something like a hundred books, none of them related to the Bahá'í Faith for he had succeeded in effectively concealing those. Once 'Andalíb was arrested, the Governor's men went to find other Bahá'ís in the town. A few were detained, while others fled, making their way to Mázindarán where they found conditions to be even worse. Some eventually managed to reach Mashhad, the holy city of Khurásán.

* In all probability Muḥammad-Báqir Khán was on the same ship which the Báb boarded in Búshihr, on His pilgrimage to Mecca.

A few days after his arrest 'Andalíb sent a message to the Governor, enquiring why he was arrested and what crime he had committed to earn this punishment. If his detention was related to the Faith which he professed, that was a matter of one's conscience, a matter over which no court could exercise jurisdiction. The right way of dealing with the problem would be to summon the divines of the town to debate the matter with him. His wish was granted. The divines of Láhíján were summoned and 'Andalíb was brought out of gaol to meet them, but the confrontation proved to be a complete fiasco. To begin with the divines started shouting all at once. 'Andalíb courteously pointed out that that was not the proper procedure for holding a debate. When the shouting had died down, one by one he was able to vanquish them all. The last one of those distinguished divines was a certain Mírzá Ibráhím, inordinately proud of his knowledge and attainment. He tried very hard to get the better of 'Andalíb, but when he realized it was impossible, he resorted to the usual device and declared that 'Andalíb was a heretic meriting death. By then, all their faces were glowing with anger and 'Andalíb saw that nothing could be achieved by talking with men who were beside themselves with rage. They had already condemned him to death. And so he rose and walked out, first pointing out to the Governor the failure of the divines to conduct a proper investigation.

The Governor's next step was to send 'Andalíb to Rasht. Wherever he was seen by the public during that transfer from Láhíján to the provincial capital, he was jeered, mocked and reviled. People spat on him, pelted him with eggs and threw missiles at him. As he was being led out of Láhíján, his mother and sisters followed him, surrounded by the rabble of the town. Although veiled, they were recognized and insulted. But they continued to walk to the outskirts of the town until, without having had a chance to speak with 'Andalíb, they had to turn back and go home. Throughout that walk to the edge of the town, although tried beyond the limit of human endurance, 'Andalíb never lost his composure, but trod the ground with firm gait, his armour never dented.

In the pestilential gaol of Rasht, 'Andalíb found many of his compatriots. Before long, two of them, Ḥájí Naṣír, a survivor of Shaykh Ṭabarsí, and Áqá Muḥammad-Ṣádiq of Qazvín succumbed to the hardships constantly encountered in the prison of Rasht. Even there, 'Andalíb and his fellow-believers were unceasingly assailed by

A view showing the condition of prisoners in a gaol in Írán during the period of this book. Two Bahá'ís are among them.

the abuse and reviling which not only the gaolers, but the other wretched inmates of that prison, hurled at them.

'Andalíb languished there for more than two years. A number of his compatriots were freed, but he and two others, Siyyid Mihdí of Iṣfahán and Siyyid 'Abdu'lláh of Burújird, were left to suffer. He petitioned 'Abdu'lláh Khán-i-Válí in a fine poem. These were its opening lines:

> O thou of the arched eyebrows, didst thou take me to be
> the renowned Sám,* son of Narímán,
> That thou didst put me in chains, and send me
> to a horrid dungeon?

But his cry went unanswered, save for a poem in rebuttal from the pen of a poet in the service of the válí.

Then release came in an unexpected way. In all probability those who had put him in that gaol, and particularly the válí, became bored with keeping him and ordered him out. The end of this notorious válí a decade later was to be sudden and miserably dramatic. In the year AH 1310 (26 July 1892–14 July 1893) a cholera epidemic hit Írán, starting in Khurásán, and soon reaching Ṭihrán. Mírzá 'Ísá, the Vazír of Ṭihrán, died at the time the epidemic invaded the capital, and 'Abdu'lláh Khán-i-Válí was appointed to his office. He put on his

* Sám was the grandfather of Rustam, the legendary hero of Firdawsí's *Sháhnámih* (The Book of Kings).

robe of honour in a summer resort in S̲h̲imrán (which these days adjoins Ṭihrán), and mounted his horse to ride to the capital. On the way cholera laid him low. His attendants, seeing their master thus afflicted, fled in horror. He was left alone, totally helpless, to die by the roadside, and his corpse was ravaged by beasts.*

After his release 'Andalíb went back to his home town, but soon realized that after all that had happened, it would be impossible for him to live in Láhíján. Samandar writes that he invited 'Andalíb to come and make his home in Qazvín. After a stay there of one year, 'Andalíb went to Ṭihrán and then to Yazd, where we found him with Edward Browne in the year 1888. (See p. 60.) In a letter dated 2 July 1889, the father of the present writer informed Edward Browne that 'Andalíb had come to S̲h̲íráz:

A few nights ago we were together in our own garden. We stayed there for two nights. We talked much about your good self. Indeed, we wished that you were with us. He ['Andalíb] is a very, very fine person, and has some sweet and excellent poems to his credit. It is not decided where he should go from here. I shall let you know where he goes next. All the friends here send you their salaams.

As it happened, 'Andalíb stayed in S̲h̲íráz for the rest of his life and made that city his permanent home. He settled down, found the means of earning a living and married.

Before long, 'Andalíb received all that his soul craved, permission to travel to the Holy Land and attain the presence of Bahá'u'lláh. There he found as a fellow-pilgrim the sixteen-year-old son of Samandar, the future Hand of the Cause of God, Ṭarázu'lláh Samandarí. Both of them were there when the Ascension of Bahá'u'lláh immersed the Bahá'ís in a sea of grief. The soul of the poet responded to this harrowing sorrow which wrung from his heart a dolorous song declaring that his eyes had witnessed the morn of the Day of Resurrection on the plain of 'Akká. 'Andalíb was also there when the contents of the *Kitáb-i-'Ahdí* – Bahá'u'lláh's Will and Testament – became known. Although for many years past, Bahá'ís had come to see that the Most Great Branch was indeed that 'Mystery of God' – Sirru'lláh, a designation which His Father had given Him – they now rejoiced to find that they would march on under His infallible

* Hájí Sayyáh-i-Maḥallátí has given the above account of the death of 'Abdu'lláh K̲h̲án-i-Válí in his memoirs. He had suffered at the hands of 'Abdu'lláh K̲h̲án-i-Válí who was instrumental in bringing about his imprisonment, together with a number of others.

Mírzá 'Alí-Ashraf, an eloquent poet, whose sobriquet was 'Andalíb

guidance. 'Andalíb and Varqá, the two most eloquent of Bahá'í poets, penned such lines in praise of the Most Great Branch as are the finest of their genre, rarely equalled in the whole range of Bahá'í history. 'Abdu'l-Bahá, while graciously and kindly accepting their offerings, administered a gentle rebuke to them for their extreme adulation, pointing out that such praise should only be uttered in homage to Bahá'u'lláh. For Himself, He had chosen the name 'Abdu'l-Bahá – the Servant of Bahá – betokening the essence of His being.

'Andalíb, on his return from the Holy Land, once more engaged in propagating and teaching the Faith. Twenty-three years later, he was again given the bounty of visiting the Holy Land and sitting at the feet of the Master. 'Abdu'l-Bahá had aged considerably in those years. The faithlessness of Mírzá Muḥammad-'Alí and his associates – who included two other sons of Bahá'u'lláh, the descendants of the loyal Mírzá Músá (Áqáy-i-Kalím), and a number of well-known teachers of the Faith – as well as the intrigues of the dwindling followers of Mírzá Yaḥyá, had left their mark on Him. Apart from the obnoxious activities of the violators of the Covenant of Bahá'u'lláh and the misdeeds of the Azalís, 'Abdu'l-Bahá had to meet other darts from enemies of old. Even from Christian quarters voices of opposition and denigration were raised from time to time. Indeed, the Centre of the Covenant had to face the whole concourse of mankind, as did His Father.

Having drunk his fill from the chalice of grace and knowledge proffered by the Master, 'Andalíb returned to Írán by way of the Caucasus. Reaching Rasht, he found many whom he had guided to embrace the Faith thirty years before rejoicing at his return. Of course there were some who had departed from this world. That homecoming must have been both happy and sad for 'Andalíb. In Láhíján, his mother, grieving for years at her separation from him, had passed away; and so had Mashhadí Ghulám-'Alí, the husband of one of his sisters, whose children were all active in the service of their Faith. 'Andalíb stayed for a year in Láhíján, and his nephew, Mírzá Kúchik, always stood ready to serve him. Next, 'Andalíb went to Qazvín, where his other sister lived with her husband, Áqá Muḥammad-Taqí 'Amughlí, staying at their home. In Qazvín, too, there were many who remembered him of old and welcomed him most joyously.

He had been away from his family in Shíráz for more than two years. At last, he bade farewell to his relatives in Qazvín and set his face towards Shíráz, where misfortune awaited him. Shortly after his return his wife died, and in his declining years he was left alone to bring up his young children, with the help of his eldest daughter who was then old enough to share his responsibility. His closing years brought him infirmities, as well, and he passed away in the early part of 1920. He was buried in the vicinity of the tomb of the great poet and songster, Ḥáfiẓ. The passage of time has effaced his grave and the area where it was is now a public park.

'Abdu'l-Bahá wrote a prayer of visitation for 'Andalíb and directed that these words should be inscribed on his tombstone:

> Verily, life in the nest of this world was too confined for 'Andalíb, the beloved. He winged his flight to the Supreme Concourse, to limitless heights, that he might rapturously sing melodious tunes on the branches of the blessed tree. (Unpublished)

7

Varqá, The Silver-Tongued Nightingale

O Thou! whence God's Beauty shineth,
I know Thee.
Would my being, my soul Thy ransom be,
I know Thee.
Shouldst Thou behind a hundred-thousand veils cover seek,
By God, O Thou, the Visage of God,
I know Thee.
Shouldst Thou a King choose, or a Servant appear to be,
Apart – at the crest of each Station – apart,
I know Thee.
Varqá

VARQÁ'S NAME was Mírzá 'Alí-Muḥammad. His father was Ḥájí Mullá Mihdí, a native of Yazd: a simple man, not of the rank of the mujtahids, but yet very learned. Speaking of Varqá's father, 'Abdu'l-Bahá said:

. . . he was an expert in the field of Muslim sacred traditions and an eloquent interpreter of orally transmitted texts . . . He was one of those who penetrate mysteries, and was a confidant of the righteous. As a teacher of the Faith he was never at a loss for words, forgetting, as he taught, all restraint, pouring forth one upon another sacred traditions and texts.

When news of him spread around the town and he was everywhere charged, by prince and pauper alike, with bearing this new name, he freely declared his adherence and on this account was publicly disgraced. Then the evil 'ulamás of Yazd rose up, issuing a decree that he must die. Since the mujtahid, Mullá Báqir of Ardikán, refused to confirm the sentence of those dark divines, Mullá Mihdí lived on, but was forced to leave his native home. ('Abdu'l-Bahá, *Memorials of the Faithful*, pp. 84–5)

Driven to quit Yazd, Ḥájí Mullá Mihdí, accompanied by two sons, Mírzá 'Alí-Muḥammad and Mírzá Ḥusayn, set out for 'Akká. It was a long, long way to go and much hardship awaited him on the road. Let the Centre of the Covenant conclude this story:

. . . He was imprisoned along his way; and as he crossed the deserts and climbed and descended the mountain slopes he endured terrible, uncounted hardships. But the light of faith shone from his brow and in his breast the longing was aflame, and thus he joyously, gladly passed over the frontiers until at last he came to Beirut. In that city, ill, restive, his patience gone, he spent some days. His yearning grew, and his agitation was such that weak and sick as he was, he could wait no more.

He set out on foot for the house of Bahá'u'lláh. Because he lacked proper shoes for the journey, his feet were bruised and torn; his sickness worsened; he could hardly move, but still he went on; somehow he reached the village of Mazra'ih and here, close by the Mansion, he died. His heart found his Well-Beloved One, when he could bear the separation no more. Let lovers be warned by his story; let them know how he gambled away his life in his yearning after the Light of the World. May God give him to drink of a brimming cup in the everlasting gardens; in the Supreme Assemblage, may God shed upon his face rays of light. Upon him be the glory of the Lord. His sanctified tomb is in Mazra'ih, beside 'Akká. (ibid. pp. 85–6)

It is by his sobriquet that Mírzá 'Alí-Muḥammad, the most accomplished son of Ḥájí Mullá Mihdíy-i-Yazdí, eternally lives: Varqá, the silver-tongued nightingale, who in dulcet and exultant tones sang, throughout his life, the praise of Bahá'u'lláh and His eldest Son, 'Abdu'l-Bahá, the Centre of His Covenant. The lines which adorn the opening of this chapter were addressed to the Centre of the Covenant, and they have their own story to which we shall come in a later page.

Varqá was born and brought up in Yazd. He was in his early twenties, when, in the company of his father, he had perforce to turn his back on his native town and seek other climes. Ḥájí Mullá Mihdí and his two sons reached Tabríz, where they tarried for a while. Varqá must have had a good knowledge of the rudiments of medicine, for in Tabríz a well-known Bahá'í of that city, Mírzá 'Abdu'lláh Khán-i-Núrí, who served as attendant to the Crown Prince, Muẓaffari'd-Dín Mírzá, called him in for consultation. The truth of the matter was that he was most eager to invite Ḥájí Mullá Mihdí and his sons to his home and to entertain them, but his wife, a woman of the Sháhsavan tribe, was exceedingly hostile towards the Faith of Bahá'u'lláh, and therefore Mírzá 'Abdu'lláh Khán had to find ways and means to facilitate visits of these new arrivals from Yazd.

Mírzá 'Abdu'lláh Khán-i-Núrí and his wife, the Sháhsavan lady, had only one daughter and they longed to have another child. Various medicaments had so far been of no help. Now Mírzá 'Abdu'lláh Khán suggested to his wife that she let a physician who had recently come to

Tabríz attend her. She gladly accepted. The medicine which Varqá prescribed proved effective, and before long she was with child, to her overwhelming delight. Next, Mírzá 'Abdu'lláh Khán, who had become greatly devoted to Varqá and wholly captivated by his accomplishments, proposed to his wife that they should wed their daughter to him. At first she demurred, because he was an unknown young man from a far-off city while she was a person of consequence with high connections in Tabríz; but finally, overcoming her scruples, she agreed. Mírzá 'Abdu'lláh Khán was truly overjoyed.

The nuptials over, Ḥájí Mullá Mihdí and his two sons continued their journey to the Holy Land. As we have seen, just before reaching the presence of Bahá'u'lláh, Ḥájí Mullá Mihdí succumbed to the rigours he had endured. And Varqá, as soon as he attained and set eyes on His majestic mien and heavenly visage, was certain that he had seen them before – but where and how? Then, as he himself has related, he recalled a dream he had had in childhood. He had dreamt that he had been playing with his dolls, when God had come and, taking his dolls away from him, had thrown them onto the fire. The next day he had spoken of this strange dream to his parents, who had upbraided him, telling him not to speak of it again as no one could possibly see God. Now, because of words spoken to him by Bahá'u'lláh he recalled that childhood dream and realized that it had been the countenance of Bahá'u'lláh which appeared to him in his vision. Here is Varqá's own recollection of the words spoken by Bahá'u'lláh: 'O Varqá! Cast into fire idols of vain imaginings.'

From the Holy Land Varqá returned to Tabríz, and made that city his home. Mírzá 'Abdu'lláh Khán-i-Núrí took his son-in-law to the Court of the Crown Prince, and Muẓaffari'd-Dín Mírzá was equally charmed by Varqá's attainments and qualities. It is related that the Crown Prince oftentimes asked Mírzá 'Abdu'lláh Khán to bring Varqá with him to the Court whenever there was to be an assemblage of learned men, that he might participate in their talks and discussions to everyone's delight. And the young poet would always rise to the occasion. Despite his years Varqá was a man of many parts. He was very eloquent, not only as a composer of lucid verse but as a writer of excellent prose. He had also a good hand at calligraphy and other arts which nimble fingers can perform. Besides these, his knowledge of medicine, scriptures, and the history and literature of his country, made him an exceptional person.

Mírzá 'Alí-Muḥammad-i-Varqá, the Martyr, referred to by 'Abdu'l-Bahá as a Hand of the Cause of God

Varqá had his home in Tabríz and travelled a good deal throughout the expanse of the province of Ádharbáyján, to teach and promote the Faith of Bahá'u'lláh. Here and there he met with bitter hostility and stern opposition; his life was even endangered and he was imprisoned. But he always enjoyed the protection of his influential father-in-law and, in extremity, the helping hand of the Crown Prince of Írán. In contradistinction to his two brothers, Ẓillu's-Sulṭán and Kámrán Mírzá (the Náyibu's-Salṭanih), Muẓaffari'd-Dín Mírzá never showed any ill will towards the followers of Bahá'u'lláh. He had his faults but cruelty and avarice were not among them, whereas the other two powerful princes had major shares of both.

However, in that fateful year of AH 1300 (AD 1882–3), Varqá decided to visit after many years' absence his native town of Yazd, whose people were blindly fanatical and easily swayed by self-seeking divines. Yazd was part of the domain of Mas'úd Mírzá, the Ẓillu's-Sulṭán, which he governed most injudiciously. Very soon, Varqá fell into the hands of his minions, and there in Yazd he languished for a whole year in its foul prison. Then he was carried in chains from Yazd to Iṣfahán, where Mas'úd Mírzá resided. As it happened, another well-known Bahá'í, also an accomplished poet with the sobriquet of Síná, had just been set free. (See chap. 11.) Having heard that a 'Bábí' had been brought from Yazd, Síná was most eager to find out who his Yazdí co-religionist was, but was told that he could neither hear nor speak. Síná was greatly astonished when he saw Varqá there in chains, but greater was the astonishment of the gaolers when their prisoner began to speak fluently. The guards escorting him from Yazd to Iṣfahán had been so insolently abusive that to spare himself the taunts of those brutish men Varqá had pretended to be deaf and dumb. After their joyous encounter, Síná, pained to see that Varqá was placed in a prison where the worst criminals were kept, tried, with the help of the Bahá'ís of Iṣfahán, to have him moved to a more salubrious gaol reserved for men of rank. That end was achieved through the assistance of Ḥájí Muḥammad-'Alí, Sayyáḥ-i-Maḥallátí, and here is how it happened.

This amazing man* was a confidant of Ẓillu's-Sulṭán, the eldest son of Náṣiri'd-Dín Sháh, and made no secret of it. We know now of a particular mission entrusted to him by the scheming and seditious Ẓillu's-Sulṭán, whose ardent but unfulfilled wish it was, throughout his plot-ridden and turbulent life, to supplant his younger brother, Muẓaffari'd-Dín Mírzá, and obtain the throne of Írán. This he could not achieve because his mother was not of the royal House of Qájár. During one of his mysterious journeys to Ádharbáyján, which may have been connected with Ẓillu's-Sulṭán's plots, Sayyáḥ fell into the hands of Muẓaffari'd-Dín Mírzá's men in Tabríz. Having rightly or wrongly found him guilty, it was almost certain that they would have put him to death, had not Mírzá 'Abdu'lláh Khán-i-Núrí intervened to bring about his release. Sayyáḥ, a much chastened man, went back to Iṣfahán and was there at the time Varqá was brought from Yazd. The Bahá'ís of Iṣfahán, knowing how it had fared with him in Tabríz, approached Sayyáḥ and told him that the 'Bábí' prisoner brought from Yazd was the son-in-law of that same Mírzá 'Abdu'lláh Khán-i-Núrí who had saved his own life, suggesting that he should use his influence to ease the circumstances of Varqá's imprisonment. Sayyáḥ persuaded Ẓillu's-Sulṭán to order the transfer of Varqá to the prison where distinguished men were detained.

* His autobiography and Book of Reminiscences has been published in recent years. Therein he conceals much that is now common knowledge.

Sulṭán-Mas'úd Mírzá, Ẓillu's-Sulṭán

About that time, Ẓillu's-Sulṭán had treacherously put to death Ḥusayn-Qulí Khán, the Bakhtíyárí chieftain. Isfandíyár Khán, the son of the murdered chieftain, was still a prisoner of the Prince-Governor of Iṣfahán, and Varqá was sent to join him. It is said that consorting with Varqá led Isfandíyár Khán to embrace the Faith of Bahá'u'lláh. Whatever the case, Varqá's poetic talent charmed the Bakhtíyárí leader. Even the boorish Ẓillu's-Sulṭán could not withhold his admiration, and before long he set Varqá free, thinking it would be to his own advantage, as he was about to send Sayyáḥ on a secret mission to 'Akká.* Varqá returned to Tabríz.

The second time that Varqá attained the presence of Bahá'u'lláh was about a year before His Ascension. Varqá was then accompanied by two of his sons: 'Azízu'lláh and Rúḥu'lláh. The heroic Rúḥu'lláh, who was destined to die a martyr's death together with his father, was then no more than seven years old, but at that tender age his pure soul responded, in all its intensity, to the truth and reality of God as revealed to the world in the human temple of Bahá'u'lláh. He had

* Sayyáḥ's mission was to win the support of Bahá'u'lláh for Ẓillu's-Sulṭán's plots against his father. Of course Sayyáḥ was sent away – a disappointed man.

Mírzá Valíyu'lláh Khán (left) *and Mírzá 'Azízu'lláh Khán* (right)*, the third and the eldest sons of Varqá, in Ṭihrán in 1908. The former was later appointed a Hand of the Cause of God.*

inherited an ample share of his father's poetic talent, and thus he composed, when only two or three years older, his paean of praise and adoration:

> O the joy of that day, when eyes at me stare,
> As on gallows-tree, I the praise of the King of Glory declare.

In the course of this second visit to 'Akká, Varqá was summoned to attend Bahá'u'lláh as a physician, and, after prescribing some medicine which Bahá'u'lláh took, was sent for a second time for the same purpose. Mírzá Valíyu'lláh Khán,* Varqá's third son, recalled decades later:

My father was much with Bahá'u'lláh. One night as He walked back and forth in His room [at the Mansion of Bahjí], Bahá'u'lláh said to my father: 'At stated periods souls are sent to earth by the Mighty God with what we call the Power of the Great Ether. And they who possess this power can do anything; they have all power . . . Jesus Christ had this power. People thought of Him as a poor young man Whom they had crucified; but He possessed the Power of the Great Ether. Therefore He could not remain

* Elevated to the rank of Hand of the Cause of God by the Guardian of the Bahá'í Faith.

Rúḥu'lláh, son of Varqá, who was martyred in 1896 with his father, when about twelve years of age

underground. This ethereal Power arose and quickened the world. And now look to the Master, for this power is His.'

When Varqá heard these words from Bahá'u'lláh, he yearned to lay down his life in the path of the Master. And that wish was granted him.

Varqá, once again, returned to Tabríz. However, the hostility of his mother-in-law, the Sháhsavan lady, allowed him no peace at home. She had never reconciled herself to the fact that both her husband and her son-in-law were dedicated Bahá'ís. Varqá had thought of divorcing his wife, to rid himself of the bane of his mother-in-law's constant opposition. But Mírzá 'Abdu'lláh Khán would not hear of it and advised him not to remain in Tabríz, but to travel throughout Ádharbáyján to teach the Faith. Then his mother-in-law sought an accomplice who would kill Varqá. As it happened, some enemies who could sway the mind of the Crown Prince succeeded in making him suspicious of his faithful attendant, Mírzá 'Abdu'lláh Khán, who had to leave Tabríz in haste because Muẓaffari'd-Dín Mírzá, his mind totally poisoned, was on the point of ordering his arrest. When his wife became certain that her husband could not and would not return to Tabríz, she planned the death of her son-in-law. She told a servant in their house named Khalíl, not knowing that he had been converted to the Faith of Bahá'u'lláh, that should he kill Varqá she would give him a horse and 250 *túmáns*. Instead, Khalíl informed Varqá of the evil designs of his mother-in-law. Then Varqá realized, at last, that the time had come for him to turn his back on Tabríz, the city hallowed by the blood of the Báb, wherein he had found refuge after abandoning his own native city of Yazd. He left Tabríz and Ádhar-báyján with a heavy heart, as a letter which he wrote soon after his arrival at Zanján amply testifies. In it he quoted from the writings of Mírzá Abu'l-Qásim, the Qá'im-Maqám, to draw a parallel between his own feeling and that of the great minister whom Muḥammad Sháh had treacherously put to death.

Varqá had to leave home and depart from Tabríz in such a way as to thwart any interference on the part of his mother-in-law. In the dead of night, he threw his Tablets and all that appertained to his Faith from a window overlooking the street, left the house very quietly, collected all that he had thrown into the street, and then went to the home of a fellow-Bahá'í who was also a native of Yazd. When the inimical Sháhsavan lady learned what had happened, Varqá was well beyond her reach. Enraged, she sought the help of one of the mujtahids of Tabríz, related to herself, to obtain a death warrant from him. 'My son-in-law is a Bábí', she roundly declared, 'and ought to be put to death.' The mujtahid refused to comply with her demand and pleaded ignorance of the case; whereupon she rushed away and brought Rúḥu'lláh to him. 'I will prove to you through this child', she told the mujtahid, 'the apostasy of my son-in-law.' Rúḥu'lláh was then asked whether he could say his daily prayer. The child made his ablutions and said the long Bahá'í prayer, in a mellifluous voice. Now it was the turn of the mujtahid, who was a just man, to expostulate. He told the lady, in no uncertain terms, that what she had been trying to do, in obtaining the condemnation of a man who had reared such a wonderful child, was a deed heinous and unforgivable.

By now the breach between Mírzá 'Abdu'lláh Khán, Varqá and their wives had so widened that no alternative but divorce was left. Varqá took with him the two sons 'Azízu'lláh and Rúḥu'lláh, but

Valíyu'lláh and the youngest Badí'u'lláh had to be left with their mother because of their ages. Badí'u'lláh did not live long. The Sháhsavan lady and her daughter both married again, and their lives thereafter were anything but happy; at the end both had cause to rue their fates, which were of their own making, and to feel bitter remorse.

In Zanján, Varqá married Liqá'íyyih Khánum, a daughter of Ḥájí Ímán, and had both 'Azízu'lláh and Rúḥu'lláh with him.

It was not long after the Ascension of Bahá'u'lláh that the perfidy of those who had resolved to break His Covenant came into the open. Many were those, once shining lights, who became centres of darkness. But Varqá never wavered. He made his third and last pilgrimage to the Holy Land, again taking with him both 'Azízu'lláh and Rúḥu'lláh. He sang the praises of 'Abdu'l-Bahá, the Centre of the Covenant, as fervently as he had sung the praises of Bahá'u'lláh, and addressed a poem to 'Abdu'l-Bahá, some lines of which appear at the head of this chapter. Another line* of the same poem is this:

> O Thou, the Root, Thou the Limb of Revelation,
> In any garb, any garment, with any mantle,
> I know Thee.

'Abdu'l-Bahá gently reproved him because of the poem's extravagance. Responding, Varqá composed another poem which begins thus:

> Cease either, O shining Orb, shedding Thy rays on the world,
> to flare,
> Or strike blind the eyes of those of insight, who witness
> dare.

Having mentioned the excellence of the poetical work of 'Andalíb (see chap. 6) and Varqá, it is meet to mention here too the achievement of a young Bahá'í poet of these days, now in his thirties. He also is a native of Írán. His name is Bahá'u'd-Dín Muḥammad. 'Abdí is both his surname and his sobriquet. The depth of feeling and the mastery of the language which he shows, put him on a par with those veterans of the Faith, even surpassing them in his imagery and tenderness of expression. Indeed, it can be said that he is the precursor of a new school of poetry in the domain of the Bahá'í Faith. Thus ends his eulogy of Varqá:

* One line in the original poem.

My heart, aflame, sends forth from its narrow cage,
Such fire as puts the rays of sun to shame.
From one drop of my tears that on this earth is shed,
Tulips, red tulips grow from the martyred Varqá's grave.

In the same year that Náṣiri'd-Dín Sháh was to meet his death at the hands of a disciple of Siyyid Jamálu'd-Dín-i-Asadábádí, circumstances impelled Varqá to move out of Zanján. He was most anxious to gain Ṭihrán. In the first instance he wanted to carry out the oral instructions of 'Abdu'l-Bahá, Who had advised him to take his Tablets and all his Bahá'í archives away from Zanján. He also desired a reunion with Mírzá 'Abdu'lláh Khán-i-Núrí, the maternal grandfather of his sons, who had established himself in the capital. Varqá asked Ḥájí Ímán, the father of his second wife, to hire a number of horses for travelling to Ṭihrán. It was, however, winter time, there was a good deal of snow on the ground, and steeds were difficult to come by. As days dragged on, Mírzá 'Azízu'lláh Khán, the eldest son of Varqá, became impatient, and without informing anyone of his intention took the road to Ṭihrán on foot. When Varqá learned of his son's departure and took measures to bring him back, it was too late; 'Azízu'lláh had put a good many miles between himself and Zanján.

By the time that Mírzá 'Azízu'lláh Khán had got well away, pack animals had been procured. Varqá put his Tablets and books in two trunks, well locked and secured. The night before leaving Zanján with Rúḥu'lláh and Ḥájí Ímán, Varqá, accompanied by a number of the Bahá'ís of that city, went to the Telegraph Office to say farewell to Mírzá 'Alí-Akbar Khán, the director, and to offer him condolences on the death of his mother which had occurred shortly before. All went well, but on coming out of the Telegraph Office they ran into an ill-intentioned divine of Zanján named Mullá 'Abdu'l-Wási', who immediately reported what he had seen to the master of the curfew, and he, in turn, informed 'Alá'u'd-Dawlih, the newly-appointed governor, that a number of 'Bábís' had been spotted coming out of the Telegraph Office.

Aḥmad Khán, the 'Alá'u'd-Dawlih, was a Qájár, though not of the royal clan. He was imperious, suspicious, unbearably autocratic; and some of his rash deeds, in future years, were highly questionable. But it is not at all clear why the fact of a number of 'Bábís' leaving the Telegraph Office should have irked him to such an extent as to order the arrest of Mírzá Ḥusayn and a few other local Bahá'ís, and direct his men to go outside the city and search for those who were believed to have left Zanján. Varqá, Rúḥu'lláh and Ḥájí Ímán, who were well on their way to the capital with a caravan, were thus intercepted and brought back to join the others in 'Alá'u'd-Dawlih's prison. It may have been that this haughty grandee, suspicious by nature, had thought that the 'Bábís' were hatching a plot against his own person. In those days, and for many years after, a telegraph office was one of the places where people, who either had a grudge or a genuine complaint, rushed to take refuge – a '*bast*', as it was called. Whatever the case, Varqá was back in Zanján and in its gaol, where the governor could interrogate him closely. 'Alá'u'd-Dawlih, though of a generation much younger than the old despotic Qájár princes – like Mu'tamidu'd-Dawlih (Ḥájí Farhád Mírzá) and Ḥisámu's-Salṭanih (Sulṭán-Murád Mírzá), even younger than Ẓillu's-Sulṭán (Sulṭán-Mas'úd Mírzá) and Náyibu's-Salṭanih (Kámrán Mírzá) – proved no exception to them. On his first encounter with Varqá, he began a harangue of abuse, to which Varqá replied that such language was demeaning and not meet for such an assemblage. Whereupon Varqá was sent back to prison.

When Varqá was stopped on the road to Ṭihrán, miraculously the pack animal that carried the two trunks of Tablets and books and other archival material was not halted, and it went all the way safely to Qazvín, where trusted hands received the trunks and preserved their contents. But, alack, the personal property of Varqá fell into the hands of enemies. Amongst all that rich material, rich both in worth and value, was a water-colour painting of the Báb. And here is the place to record the marvellous story of that painting, told to the present writer by Mírzá Valíyu'lláh Khán Varqá, the Hand of the Cause of God.

During his long sojourn in Ádharbáyján, Varqá met an artist, a Naqqásh-Báshí (Chief Painter) whom he guided into the fold of the Faith of Bahá'u'lláh. And this artist, Áqá-Bálá Bag, a native of Shíshván (a village on the banks of Lake Urúmíyyih), had a remarkable tale to tell. He had in his possession a portrait of the Báb, the only one in existence, that he had done himself. It happened when the Báb was on His way to Tabríz for cross-examination by the Court of the Crown Prince. At Urúmíyyih the governor, Malik-Qásim Mírzá, who was a descendant of Fatḥ-'Alí Sháh, received the Báb with tokens of great respect but, at the same time, he worked out a scheme to test Him. He owned a horse notorious for its unruliness, and on a Friday when the Báb was going to the public bath, Malik-Qásim Mírzá ordered that charger to be brought for Him to ride. Those who were in the know watched with trepidation as the Báb came out to mount, but to the astonishment of all the horse proved exceedingly docile. The Báb mounted it with ease and rode to the public bath; the Prince-Governor, crestfallen and ashamed, followed Him all the way on foot. Before reaching the bath, the Báb turned to Malik-Qásim Mírzá, who was then walking beside him, to ask him not to come any further but return to his house. When the Báb came out of the public bath, the horse was still there for Him to ride; and it behaved exactly as before. As the news of this extraordinary incident spread like a bonfire throughout Urúmíyyih, the populace broke into the public bath and carried away every drop of water they could find there.

The people of Urúmíyyih were certain that a miracle had come to pass in their midst and they flocked, day after day, to the governor's residence to see the Báb. One of them was Áqá-Bálá, the Chief Painter. He told Varqá, all those years later, that on his first visit, as soon as the Báb noticed him, He gathered His 'abá round Him, as if sitting for His portrait. The next day He did the same. It was then that Áqá-Bálá Bag understood it to be a signal to him to draw His portrait. On his third visit, he went to the residence of Malik-Qásim Mírzá with the equipment of his art. He made a rough sketch or two at the time, from which he later composed a full-scale portrait in black and white. Varqá wrote and informed Bahá'u'lláh of this tremendous discovery. And Bahá'u'lláh directed him to instruct Áqá-Bálá Bag to make two copies of the portrait in water-colour, one to be dispatched to the Holy Land, and one for Varqá himself to keep. The copy sent to the Holy Land is now preserved in the International Bahá'í Archives on Mount Carmel, but the one which belonged to Varqá was amongst his possessions which were looted when he was arrested outside Zanján. The original portrait, in black and white, was found long after by Siyyid Asadu'lláh-i-Qumí, who took it with him to the Holy Land and presented it to 'Abdu'l-Bahá.

During the weeks that followed his detention, Varqá had, almost daily, to endure verbal assaults by the divines of Zanján, and by the governor himself. 'Alá'u'd-Dawlih was a man of many moods.* It

* In the autumn of the year 1903, Lord Curzon, the Viceroy of India, who had always been an

apparently amused him to sit day after day and listen to the devious arguments of the divines, making his own interjections every now and then. Endless these futile argumentations seemed to be, and as endless were the brilliant retorts of Varqá. 'Alá'u'd-Dawlih, by all accounts, was trying in some tortuous way to entice Varqá to deny his faith in order to gain his release, while Varqá determinedly rejected those inducements.

'Alá'u'd-Dawlih, despairing of having any influence over Varqá, to bend his will told him that he and his son would be sent to Ṭihrán, and Mírzá Ḥusayn, a fellow-Bahá'í, would be blown from a cannon. Varqá cautioned him not to act so impetuously where Mírzá Ḥusayn was concerned. This co-religionist of his, he informed 'Alá'u'd-Dawlih, had come from 'Ishqábád at the behest of Náṣiri'd-Dín Sháh and with the full knowledge of the Russian consul-general. Moreover, his son-in-law was a dragoman in the service of the said consul. It would be more prudent, he advised the haughty governor, to send Mírzá Ḥusayn away from Zanján, and let his fate be decided by others. 'Alá'u'd-Dawlih came to his senses and ordered his *farrásh-báshí* to arrange the transportation of Mírzá Ḥusayn, as well, to Ṭihrán, and collect the cost of the hiring of a horse from his relatives. They were to be escorted to the capital by the cavalry in the service of the family of a local grandee, Jahánsháh Khán. Moreover, the possessions of Varqá were to be sorted by himself, placed in boxes and

advocate of a forward policy anywhere in Asia, sailed with an imposing escort into the Persian Gulf. This official visit of the Viceroy, with the ostentatious showing of the flag, was meant not only to stamp on the minds of the rulers of lands bordering on the Gulf, large and small alike, the fact of the supremacy of Great Britain in those waters, but also to warn off any European Power, notably Russia and Germany, who might have had designs of their own in that inhospitable clime. 'Alá'u'd-Dawlih was then Governor-General of the province of Fárs, and at loggerheads with Sálár Mu'aẓẓam (later Niẓámu's-Salṭanih the Second), the Governor of the Gulf Ports and Isles. He was commissioned by the government of Írán to go to Búshihr and there receive the Viceroy ceremoniously. But as 'Alá'u'd-Dawlih had no knowledge of English, he took with him from Shíráz the father of the present writer, who had received part of his education in Britain, and had served a term of office as the Consul-General of Írán in Bombay, where he had met Lord Curzon in the course of his duties.

My father's role was to assist in receiving the Viceroy, and to hold parleys as well with Sir Arthur Hardinge, the British minister in Ṭihrán who was coming to Búshihr to be there when the Viceroy arrived. 'Alá'u'd-Dawlih came out of Shíráz with a large retinue and escort of soldiery, and spent a vast sum of money. Unfortunately an idiotic misunderstanding – a rigid adherence to meaningless protocol and unbending stances shared by both sides (with Lord Curzon in the lead) – prevented the Viceroy leaving his boat in the harbour of Búshihr, and left 'Alá'u'd-Dawlih fuming on the shore. And to add to his chagrin, his rival, Sálár Mu'aẓẓam, had stolen a march on him and had gone to Bandar 'Abbás to receive the Viceroy there, thus avoiding meeting 'Alá'u'd-Dawlih in Búshihr. The present writer has gained the impression from his father's letters and diaries that 'Alá'u'd-Dawlih was, although capable and efficient, a grandee demanding obeisance, whose hauteur and air of superiority were hard to match and to bear, and who was easily swayed by his conflicting and fleeting emotions.

trunks, and locked up to be taken with him, while the keys and a full list of the contents would be delivered in Ṭihrán to Amínu's-Sulṭán, the Ṣadr-i-A'ẓam.

Mírzá Ḥusayn writes:

Government *farráshes* entered the prison, took away the chain on my neck and carried me to the house of the *farrásh-báshí*. I saw that Varqá's feet were heavily fettered . . . he and Rúḥu'lláh both looked at me smilingly and Varqá said, 'See, what a difference there is.' But immediately a carpenter was brought in who put my feet also in heavy fetters. Then they produced a long chain and attached it to my neck. They wanted to attach the other end to Varqá's neck. However, the guards would not have it, because of the difficulty of managing two men chained together. That chain remained on my own neck, and I carried it all the way to Ṭihrán. Ḥájí Ímán had been taken away one day prior to us by the artillerymen, on a gun-carriage, who had tied his arms to the cannon. He had suffered a great deal by being carried in that fashion to the capital. But we were given pack horses to ride and were fully equipped.

This was the Jubilee year of Náṣiri'd-Dín Sháh . . . Jahánsháh Khán's cavalry were going to Ṭihrán to take part in the celebrations . . . grooms were holding the halters of the horses, pulling us through the bazar. Horsemen were surrounding us. Crowds of the populace swirled around with people getting on each other's shoulders to have a good look. We were taken to the caravanserai of Ḥájí 'Alí-Naqí, and were made to dismount and wait for all the cavalry to foregather, so that all could march out of the city gate as one body. Spectators kept increasing. There was no passage left. It was impossible to move. In the end, they put us in a room and locked it. We were left in peace and sat down to eat. They had sent some *dulmih* (a Persian dish) from my home . . . Rúḥu'lláh said: 'We have been starving since last night. They would not give us anything to eat.' And Varqá added: 'The *farrásh-báshí* displayed such miserliness . . . gave us no supper last night. We were very hungry. Your bread and *dulmih* came to our rescue' . . . He then observed: 'These horsemen, without knowing it, are giving victory to the Cause of God, taking us with such pomp to Ṭihrán. One does not know what is hidden behind the veil of the future. Whatever it may be it will redound to the victory of the Cause. We do not know, but He Who is the Master of Providence knows.' After a while they opened the door of the room and took us out. The horses were all ready and we were made, one by one, to mount. Rúḥu'lláh and I had little else on the saddle and had no difficulty in mounting, but Varqá had saddle-bags on his horse and found mounting it rather difficult. The head horseman told one of the bystanders to help Varqá mount his horse. That man, a Muslim, replied: 'Why should I defile my hands [by touching him]; let him mount by himself.' The sergeant-major was infuriated and dismounted. First he whipped that man, then bent his own knee for Varqá to step on and reach the saddle. While thus engaged, he was saying: 'Now I know.

Aping and imitation cause a people to wither and die,
May a hundred curses on that imitation lie.'*

When we were all mounted the pressure of the crowd and the rush of increasing numbers of people, milling around, blocked all the thoroughfares. The horsemen of the government began beating back the crowds, who were like a billowing ocean. A way was opened for the horses to gallop through, and thus we reached the city gate and went out of Zanján.

It was almost a triumphal exit. Within a few miles of the city, this cortège stopped at a village called Dízij. Villagers were out to view the 'Bábís', as if they were exotic animals taken around for exhibition. The Sartíp of Dízij had asked Jahánsháh Khán's cavalry to be his guests. Shortly after their arrival, one of the Sartíp's servants came to conduct the prisoners to an assemblage of the notables and divines. Soldiers with their rifles were well in evidence. Mírzá Ḥusayn writes, 'I was sure they had brought us from Zanján to this place to kill us. Varqá had thought likewise.' They were made to sit on a dais, all eyes fixed on them. Then they were collectively arraigned. Varqá bravely withstood their assaults. Having failed to shake him, their tormentors turned to Rúḥu'lláh, whose cryptic remarks made them hopeful at first. But when the divines realized that Rúḥu'lláh was ingeniously holding them up to ridicule, their wrath knew no bounds. 'This child is insulting holy divines,' they kept shouting, 'and why is he not fettered? Send for the carpenter to come and put fetters on him.' Mírzá Ḥusayn writes: 'They went in search of the carpenter, and when he came he was so ebullient and elated that he hardly knew how to proceed. It was as if he had been given the treasures of heaven and earth. Blithely he fixed fetters on Áqá Rúḥu'lláh's feet.' However, the cavalrymen paid no attention to the ringing demands for slaughter. From that village of ill renown, the cavalrymen made their way to Sulṭáníyyih, giving a wide berth to Khayrábád which was the district from which Mírzá Ḥusayn hailed. Strangely, the people of Sulṭáníyyih received the 'Bábís' with cordiality. Learning that Varqá was a physician, they came to him asking for remedies.

The son of Jahánsháh Khán treated the prisoners very well, providing them with good meals. The sergeant-major who represented that chieftain was also very kind and considerate. At the end of that journey to Ṭihrán he became a convert to the Faith of the prisoners. But there were two guardsmen who vied with each other in making life

* Famous couplet from the *Mathnaví* of Jalálí'd-Dín-i-Rúmí.

hard and unpleasant for the prisoners. Varqá, in particular, was brutally made to bear much pain, riding as he was atop saddle-bags with his legs fettered. The guardsmen would not relent to allow his impedimenta to be shifted. And mulishly they turned a deaf ear to the sergeant-major's remonstrances. To Atákíshí, one of those two, the sergeant made the observation that indeed by the way he maltreated the prisoners he bore resemblance to Azraq the Syrian. (Azraq-i-Shámí was a man notorious for causing the captive family of Imám Ḥusayn to suffer gravely, after the tragedy of Karbilá.) To that appropriate observation Atákíshí had the temerity to retort: 'Not so, not so. It is these people who are Azraqs of the present day. Now we must take our revenge. They think that they are the Imáms and we are the Syrians (Shimrs), while it is we who are the Imáms and they who are the Syrians.' Varqá was greatly pained when he heard that observation and this retort. He told Atákíshí, 'May God judge between us. You have been very insolent.' Mírzá Ḥusayn writes that Varqá's remark greatly angered Atákíshí, who galloped a long way ahead of the others, only to stop at a spring to have a drink and smoke. There, as he sat relaxing, unbearable pain gripped him. Mírzá Ḥusayn writes:

> Afar we could see someone writhing like a slaughtered cock. He was shouting, 'My belly is on fire, I am dying, help me.' The horsemen came along and took him, somehow, off to the next stage, which was Karaj. Varqá was greatly distressed by his condition and prescribed a remedy for him. But it did not cure him, and on reaching Ṭihrán the man died. His death invigorated the faith of the sergeant-major, but it made Varqá very unhappy. He kept saying, 'I should not have put such an injunction upon him. We should not heap curses on our enemies, who are ignorant, but pray for them.'

Fearing lest the Bahá'ís of Qazvín would make a bid to free the prisoners, the horsemen skirted that city. Then, at long last, Ṭihrán was gained, and the prisoners were taken to the stables of the house of Jahánsháh Khán, the Zanján magnate, where they were lodged for the night. The next day they were visited by Mírzá 'Azízu'lláh Khán, the eldest son of Varqá who had made his way to the capital by himself. He was sorrowful that he had separated himself from his father. But Varqá bade him never to come near them again, because, should he be recognized, he would also be arrested and put in gaol; whereas outside the gaol he could be of help and service to them all. Thus Mírzá 'Azízu'lláh Khán remained free, and in future years rendered outstanding service to the Cause of Bahá'u'lláh.

Mírzá Ḥusayn gives a graphic account of their first days in Ṭihrán. The day after their arrival they were taken to the house of Ḥusayn-'Alí Khán, the Mu'ínu'd-Dawlih, brother of the Governor of Zanján. There they found Ḥájí Ímán, like themselves in chains. It is not at all clear why they were taken to the house of Mu'ínu'd-Dawlih. On the third day another brutish official named Náyib (Deputy or Lieutenant) Naṣru'lláh descended upon them, to convey them to governmental quarters for interrogation. Avenue 'Alá'u'd-Dawlih (later Avenue Firdawsí), Mírzá Ḥusayn writes, was teeming with bystanders, gathered to have a look at the 'Bábís' as if they were a different species of men. They were marched down that avenue, surrounded by *farráshes* and executioners dressed in red, to Maydán-i-Túpkhánih (Artillery Square) – later Maydán-i-Sipah (Army Square) – dragging their chains with them. There, governmental quarters were close by. Proceedings in the Chamber of Justice (which Mírzá Ḥusayn called the 'Quintessence of Tyranny') were futile and inconsequential. And from the first day, in the house of Mu'ínu'd-Dawlih, the captors began their shameless spoliation of Varqá's very precious belongings. High and low alike helped themselves to whatever they could. Ḥájibu'd-Dawlih, the murderer-to-be, laid hands on the portrait of the Báb and took it to Náṣiri'd-Dín Sháh. The brutal Náyib Naṣru'lláh incessantly clamoured to take possession of a white robe which had been a garment belonging to Bahá'u'lláh. Varqá's entreaty not to dispossess him of that robe, so highly prized, did not have the slightest effect on the hard-hearted Náyib, who took it away and appeared dressed in it, to taunt Varqá. At the end, when all had gone, Varqá remarked that everything mulcted from him was of the very best, worthy to lose in the path of God.

Mírzá Ḥusayn writes: 'In short, they heaped injuries upon us. They had fastened heavy chains on our necks to extort money from us. We had no money to give them and those chains remained on our necks.' The gaolers also starved them. Mírzá Ḥusayn mentions a grandee of Qazvín, entitled Ghiyáth Niẓám, who had fallen foul of the government and was pushed into prison. But he was a man of substance, had plenty to spend and a servant to attend to his needs. This servant informed his master of the plight of the Bahá'í prisoners. The grandee had it announced that on a certain night all the prisoners (numbering sixty, apart from the Bahá'ís) would be his guests for *chilaw-kabáb* (a Persian rice dish with kebab and other ingredients).

Varqá and Rúḥu'lláh, with their fellow-Bahá'ís of Zanján, Mírzá Ḥusayn and Ḥájí Ímán (reading from left to right)*, shortly before the first two met their death in the royal palace in Ṭihrán following the assassination of Náṣiri'd-Dín Sháh in 1896*

On that night, Mírzá Ḥusayn writes, every prisoner was given his portion, but it was denied to the Bahá'ís. That had been the decision of the gaolers. On being told by his servant that the Bahá'ís had been deprived of their share, Ghiyáth Niẓám flew into a rage and ordered that a fresh supply of *chilaw-kabáb*, even better garnished, should be sent in immediately to the Bahá'í prisoners. The Náyib had tried to exonerate himself, saying that it was by the order of Ḥájibu'd-Dawlih that the 'Bábís' had not been served with that favourite dish.

Now, Náṣiri'd-Dín Sháh's jubilee was drawing near. Mírzá 'Abdu'-lláh Khán-i-Núrí, the maternal grandfather of Varqá's children, sent him a message to compose an ode for that occasion that it might be presented to Náṣiri'd-Dín Sháh and thus obtain his release. Varqá's response was that a poetic talent that had been moved to render praise unto Bahá'u'lláh and His Son, could not be induced to utter the praise of any other. And Varqá had no doubt that neither he nor his son would ever come out of that dungeon alive.

Then came that fatal Friday preceding the day of jubilee celebrations when Náṣiri'd-Dín Sháh, proud and arrogant as ever, fell dead within the Shrine of Sháh 'Abdu'l-'Azím, with a bullet in his heart. Amínu's-Sulṭán, the Ṣadr-i-A'ẓam, by his presence of mind and sound tactics saved the day and prevented riots and worse. But as soon as it became known that Náṣiri'd-Dín Sh͟áh had been assassinated, the generality of people accepted it as a fact that the deed had been committed by the 'Bábís'. But it was Siyyid Jamálu'd-Dín working for a long time on the disordered mind of Mírzá Riḍáy-i-Kirmání, smarting under injustices, who was responsible for placing that bullet in the chest of Náṣiri'd-Dín Sh͟áh, thus bringing to its end his inglorious and disastrous reign.* In the eyes of the people 'Bábí' and 'Bahá'í' were the same. Varqá had tried in vain to make Ḥájibu'd-Dawlih aware of the difference. However, no matter how much the Bábís – the partisans and followers of Ṣubḥ-i-Azal – might have wished to have a hand in destroying Náṣiri'd-Dín Sh͟áh, they too were not involved in regicide. It was entirely the subtle work of Siyyid Jamálu'd-Dín.

Ḥájibu'd-Dawlih, beside himself with rage, on his own initiative and without informing either Amínu's-Sulṭán, the Ṣadr-i-A'ẓam, or Kámrán Mírzá, the Governor of Ṭihrán (who had cravenly gone into hiding, totally neglecting his urgent duties), rushed into the prison to avenge as he thought the death of his sovereign. Stampeding, roaring and, as Mírzá Ḥusayn expresses it, behaving like a mad dog, he struck terror into the hearts of the inmates of the dismal dungeon of Ṭihrán. It was a hideous scene. Chains were strengthened, locks were fastened and made more secure, everything was done to impede the movement of the startled prisoners; but no one knew what had happened, no one had the slightest notion of what had put Ḥájibu'd-Dawlih into such a rage as to act like a man deranged. And he had not come just by himself to display such antics. He had brought a host of underlings, as if he expected a massive uprising on the part of those helpless and brutally chained men. Mírzá Ḥusayn writes of roof-tops swarming with soldiers, their rifles trained on the prison yard where a row of executioners were standing, ready and alert, as if on the lookout for a signal to commence their gruesome task. So it seemed that all the prisoners, Bahá'í and non-Bahá'í alike, were about to receive a new measure of chastisement. But, on that day, the wrath of the ferocious Ḥájibu'd-Dawlih was focused on Varqá. It was that silver-tongued poet whom he particularly intended to destroy. He had already had his contretemps with the poet, at the time he sequestered the portrait of the Báb. Varqá's respectful reference to the person of

* He was assassinated on 1 May 1896.

the Báb, which he had written to identify that portrait, had angered Ḥájibu'd-Dawlih, and driven that uncouth, brutish courtier to belabour the poet with his walking-stick.

The Bahá'ís were unchained and hauled out of the dungeon. Ḥájibu'd-Dawlih ordered them to be brought, two by two, through a long corridor, which, Mírzá Ḥusayn writes, led from the prison yard to an inner room. Varqá and Rúḥu'lláh were the first to go through that corridor, and as soon as they had gone the intervening door was shut in the faces of Mírzá Ḥusayn and Ḥájí Ímán. Those two, left behind, were, as Mírzá Ḥusayn himself writes, both perplexed and distressed. As they waited, they heard voices raised on the other side of the partition, and soon after, a *farrásh* appeared to fetch the instrument of bastinado, followed in a little while by one of the gaolers carrying a dagger covered with blood, which he washed in the pool within the prison yard. And before long, one of the executioners came through with Varqá's garments. Then, to their mortification, Mírzá Ḥusayn and Ḥájí Ímán knew that the worst had happened. But they had yet to learn of the heroism of Rúḥu'lláh.

Those two now prepared to go through the door to their inevitable fate, but suddenly the door was shut in their faces, and they could hear noises and voices beyond it which, in their state of affliction, they found hard to comprehend. Then, as suddenly as the door had shut, it was flung open, and out rushed that evil courtier, Ḥájibu'd-Dawlih, panic-stricken. All that he could or would say was: 'Take these two back to the gaol, I will deal with them tomorrow.' But that morrow never came. Ḥájí Ímán and Mírzá Ḥusayn were returned to the dungeon and, as the latter writes, they saw that all they had of quilts and bedding, clothing and rugs, had been taken away in their absence. Mírzá Ḥusayn writes that they were too numbed to feel much and they sank down forlorn and dejected on the bare, damp floor of the dungeon. There could be no doubt that the inimitable Varqá had been put to death, but where was Rúḥu'lláh, what had happened to him? And what exactly had occurred behind that closed door? Still more puzzling: what had caused Ḥájibu'd-Dawlih, a man bereft of common humanity, such distress and bewilderment as they had witnessed? Not all the gaolers were as vindictive and hard-hearted as that brutish courtier and his minion, Náyib Naṣru'lláh. Some of them responded to the piteous entreaties of Ḥájí Ímán and Mírzá Ḥusayn and told them the full story of the martyrdom of Varqá and the immolation of

Rúḥu'lláh. This is the story they heard, to their horror and marvel – horror at the hideous cruelty of the deed, marvel at the unshakeable constancy of the fearless poet and his glorious son.

Brought face to face with Varqá in that inner room, Ḥájibu'd-Dawlih had gone immediately into a fierce tirade: 'You did at last what you did', he had shouted at Varqá, to which the poet had quietly answered that he was unaware of having done anything wrong. Varqá's calm reply had added to the fury of Ḥájibu'd-Dawlih. It had indeed maddened him. Dragging his dagger out of its sheath, he had plunged it into the chest of Varqá, saying with great relish: 'How are you?' And Varqá had answered him thus: 'Feeling better than you.' 'Tell me,' said Ḥájibu'd-Dawlih, 'which one shall I slay first, you, or your son?' And quietly Varqá had replied, 'It is the same to me.' Then, having torn open Varqá's chest, Ḥájibu'd-Dawlih had handed him over to his executioners, whereupon four of them had fallen on the poet, tearing him apart, limb from limb. As his blood kept flowing in profusion, Rúḥu'lláh was crying out: 'O dear father, father dear, take me, take me, take me with you.'

Having destroyed Varqá, the unspeakable Ḥájibu'd-Dawlih had turned to Rúḥu'lláh, who had just witnessed the dismemberment and slaughter of his father: 'Do not weep. I shall take you with myself, make you an allowance, obtain for you a post from the Sháh.' And bravely, Rúḥu'lláh had replied: 'I do not want you. I do not want your allowance. I do not want any post that you might obtain for me. I want to join my father.' Then, he had begun weeping afresh. Defied, baulked, repelled, Ḥájibu'd-Dawlih had ordered his minions to bring a rope and strangle that brave boy. No rope was available there, and so they had put Rúḥu'lláh's neck in the loop of the instrument of the bastinado. When he had become still, they had dropped the senseless corpse on the floor. Elated, Ḥájibu'd-Dawlih had told his minions to bring in the other two 'Bábís'. The moment they had opened the door, the corpse of Rúḥu'lláh had sprung up and come down with a thud, a yard away. It was that which had terrified the blood-thirsty Ḥájibu'd-Dawlih, and made him flee away, exclaiming that he would deal with the other two on the morrow, a morrow which never came. That was how Ḥájí Ímán and Mírzá Ḥusayn escaped from the clutches of Ḥájibu'd-Dawlih. That was how Mírzá Ḥusayn lived to see another day, and to recall the story of the martyrdom of that father and his matchless son.

In a dream, Mírzá Ḥusayn writes, he saw Rúḥu'lláh coming towards him, all smiles, saying: 'Mírzá Ḥusayn, did you see how I rode on the neck of the Emperor?' During their last pilgrimage to the Holy Land, 'Abdu'l-Bahá had patted Rúḥu'lláh on his back and had said: 'Should God will it, He can make Rúḥu'lláh ride on the neck of an emperor to proclaim the Cause of God.'

8

The Gourmet Who Was a Saint

Mullá Muḥammad-Riḍáy-i-Muḥammadábádí of Yazd is one of the most distinguished amongst the Bahá'í martyrs.

He was a God-fearing man, whom nothing of this world ever daunted, outspoken, courageous to the extreme. He went to prison and accepted its rigours blissfully, although he was a bon viveur; indeed a gourmet, a connoisseur of good food.

In his historical work, Samandar writes of him:

He himself has been heard to say: 'When Raḍíu'r-Rúḥ,* one of the most eminent divines to believe, came from Baghdád to Yazd, he had certain Writings with him, including *Qaṣídiy-i-'Izz-i-Varqá'íyyih*. [Bahá'u'lláh composed this ode in Sulaymáníyyih.] As soon as I set eyes on it, I exclaimed spontaneously: "Man-Yuẓhiruhu'lláh† of the Bayán has come." He said: "The One Whose words these are has not made such a claim." I replied: "On the throne of these words I see the Promised One of the Bayán seated." Then Raḍíu'r-Rúḥ said: "Henceforth it is difficult to consort with you." Ere long, that same eminent man, subsequent to high endeavour, embraced the blessed Cause of Abhá and served it for years, engaged in promoting the Word of God. The Friends [Bahá'ís] of Manshád and its environs were led to the light of faith by him. For a long time, because of the transgressions of the enemies, he had to spend both summers and winters in caves and on mountain-tops, suffering untold hardships, until the day of his death. Upon him be the peace of God and His glory.' Mullá Muḥammad-Riḍá himself, when detained in Ṭihrán and summoned to the court of Kámrán Mírzá [the Náyibu's-Salṭanih, son of Náṣiri'd-Dín Sháh], where the most eminent of the princes and the high officials of the State had gathered for interrogation, fearlessly gave appropriate replies to any matter raised and any question asked. And when Farhád Mírzá, the Mu'tamidu'd-Dawlih [uncle of Náṣiri'd-Dín Sháh] made an abusive remark, he [Mullá Muḥammad-Riḍá] gave an answer which so accorded with the law of religion that no one had any more to say and the session ended in deep silence. (*Táríkh-i-Samandar*, pp. 220–21)

* Mullá Muḥammad-Riḍáy-i-Manshádí, whom Bahá'u'lláh honoured with the designation: Raḍíu'r-Rúḥ (Contented Spirit). He was poisoned by a certain Ḥájí Rasúl-i-Mihrírí.

† He Whom God shall manifest.

Mullá Muḥammad-Riḍáy-i-Muḥammadábádí of Yazd

We shall presently see what Prince Farhád Mírzá's remarks and Mullá Muḥammad-Riḍá's comments were.

Samandar goes on to say:

After his release from that long detention, he [Mullá Muḥammad-Riḍá] went to 'Akká and attained the presence [of Bahá'u'lláh]. Subsequently, by way of Qazvín, he gained Ṭihrán. Then, when Náṣiri'd-Dín Sháh was assassinated, he was, once again, arrested and thrown into prison. He passed away while in gaol. Upon him be the essence of God's mercy and His light. (ibid. pp. 221–2)

Ḥájí Farhád Mírzá, the Mu'tamidu'd-Dawlih

Mullá Muḥammad-Riḍá was truly fearless. Hearing, at the time of his sojourn in Yazd, that the merchants of that city had come together to devise ways and means of improving trade and bringing more prosperity to their people, Mullá Muḥammad-Riḍá unhesitatingly wrote them a memorandum, telling them that the surest way to gain their end was to accept and follow the polity of Bahá'u'lláh.

That confrontation with Ḥájí Farhád Mírzá, the Mu'tamidu'd-Dawlih, which Samandar has mentioned, occurred in the year AH 1300 (12 November 1882–1 November 1883). In the course of his discussions with Mullá Muḥammad-Riḍá, Prince Farhád Mírzá said: 'O Ákhúnd!* You cannot push aside so lightly all the traditions and the sayings of the past. We have most reliable and trustworthy traditions and references to the cities Jábulqá and Jábulsá. It is not possible to ignore them all and uphold the belief that Siyyid-i-Báb, a young mercer of Shíráz, is the promised Qá'im.' Mullá Muḥammad-Riḍá replied: 'Your Royal Highness! You yourself have written a book on geography. If such a city exists, a city which is claimed to have 70,000

* Ákhúnd is a term applied to the turbaned men of learning, particularly the divines.

gates, and according to others 100,000, please tell me in which part of the world you have placed it in your geography; show me where in your book you have referred to it and described it; then I shall accept all your arguments.' This retort went home and incensed the prince. He kept hitting the ground with his walking-stick and shouted: 'Ákhúnd! Ákhúnd! Stop! This Bahá'u'lláh to whom you have lost your heart, I know well. Many a time he has been my companion in drinking bouts: he is a bibber of wine.' Mullá Muḥammad-Riḍá kept his composure and replied: 'Your Royal Highness is, must be, well aware of the law of Islám: the testimony of a wrongdoer regarding another cannot be entertained. You yourself have here owned to drinking wine; therefore, your testimony regarding Bahá'u'lláh is inadmissible.' Prince Farhád Mírzá could bear it no longer, and angrily stamped out of the room. Mullá Muḥammad-Riḍá's repartee was truly brilliant and accorded with the prescriptions of Islám.

Mullá Muḥammad-Riḍá came out safely from that imprisonment. Some thirteen years later Náṣiri'd-Dín Sháh was assassinated [1 May 1896]. Mullá Muḥammad-Riḍá was then in Qum. He was present in a mosque, when one of the clergy ascended a pulpit and called to the people assembled: 'Look! O men, these detested Bábís have murdered the sovereign. He has fallen a martyr at their hands. They are pestilential. They ought to be crushed!' Amidst the hush of the people and the raging of the divine, Mullá Muḥammad-Riḍá spoke out: 'Ákhúnd! Ákhúnd! You are mistaken: this is not the doing of these people. They cannot have committed this crime.' The people were astounded and turned to Mullá Muḥammad-Riḍá: 'Ákhúnd! How dare you defend these Bábís? Are you one of them?' Mullá Muḥammad-Riḍá calmly replied: 'Of course I am one of them.' He was seized, sent to Ṭihrán and thrown into the Síyáh-Chál. This second time he did not leave the prison alive.

The incomparable Bahá'í scholar and teacher, Mírzá Abu'l-Faḍl of Gulpáygán, writes in his great work *Kitáb-i-Fará'id* (pp. 110–14), a book unparalleled in both its range and depth:

In the year AH 1300, certain events came to pass in Írán. In most of the cities they set upon these people [Bahá'ís]. Everywhere they seized a number of them, who were innocent of any wrongdoing, and put them in prison. In Ṭihrán too by the orders of Náyibu's-Salṭanih, Prince Kámrán Mírzá, who was the Minister of War as well as the Governor of the capital and the province of Mázindarán, a number were detained and gaoled. Amongst

Mírzá Abu'l-Faḍl-i-Gulpáygání

these prisoners, four came from the ranks of the learned and the rest were tradesmen and merchants. Mírzá Muḥammad-Riḍáy-i-Muḥammadábádí of Yazd was one of the four – a man distinguished by his old age and constancy. Although, at the beginning, the aim of the Amír* was only to ease the situation and silence the mischief-makers; yet bit by bit, due to the uprising of the divines, the aiding and abetting of powerful men, the incitement of the high-positioned, and the promptings of self, views were greatly changed and the matter assumed considerable importance. The flare-up of prejudices caused the authorities to overlook that which was for the good of the state and the nation, until most of the leading figures of the country became determined to destroy these greatly-wronged people. To carry out their corrupt and impossible designs they resorted to all kinds of means and intrigues. Briefly, in those days, time and time again, meetings were held for enquiry and argument in the governing circles. All manner of debate and proof-seeking was introduced. Evidently, with them, it is a canon of opposition to begin by resorting to that which they consider to be axioms of faith and belief. And when they receive irrefutable answers and find themselves unable to pose any proof, they turn to miracle-seeking and the supernatural. Having been worsted and brought to their knees in that arena as well, they resort to the last weapon of the transgressor and the evil-intentioned and that is slaying of the innocent and incarcerating the helpless. Thus it was that in those meetings, after repeated argumentation and verbal assaults, lengthy and detailed, the end came with demanding miracles. Those who were

* Mírzá Abu'l-Faḍl refers to Prince Kámrán Mírzá as Amír Kabír.

prominent amongst the friends, one and all, said: 'So be it: the way is clear, the post and the telegraph afford ample facility for presenting your request. While the Sun of Truth is here effulgent, and the Most Sacred Person of the Manifestation of God is here unveiled, how good it would be if the holders of governmental authority and the learned of the land would combine and choose a miracle, a supernatural deed, decide on the day for its fulfilment, inform the inhabitants of Ṭihrán, and then cable their request to His Blessed Person; so that truth might be revealed and differences effaced from the midst of the nation.'

One day, the Amír summoned me to one of those assemblages already mentioned. A number of the grandees and men holding positions of authority were present at that meeting. The Amír, after bidding me sit down, turned to me and said: 'Abu'l-Faḍl! Mírzá Muḥammad-Riḍáy-i-Yazdí says: "You choose whatever miracle you wish and cable your choice to the Most Sacred Presence, and declare it also; undoubtedly, God, great is His glory, will evince and grant that supernatural deed which you have asked for, and will reveal His power to the people. But, were that to happen which I consider to be impossible, and that power should not be revealed, I would rise to assist you and would make public everywhere my repudiation of the Bábís."' I replied: 'Your Royal Highness well knows of the Mírzá's veracity and constancy in the Cause of God. Without the slightest doubt, he must have total assurance to make such a bold, emphatic assertion.' The Amír then said: 'What is your view and what do you think of it?' I replied: 'Why do you

Kámrán Mírzá, Náyibu's-Salṭanih, third son of Náṣiri'd-Dín Sháh

hesitate, why linger? You who, in all of these gatherings, after resorting to every means, cling to miracles and constantly say that if this Advent is that Advent promised to us, why does He not bring forth miracles; now that the leading figures of this Cause show such constancy and promise you the working of miracles, why do you hesitate and who or what prevents making the request? By God! They have completed their proof and have with strength and assurance established their case. Why do you not pay heed, but instead, for the sake of those who if closely looked at and investigated would be found to be the worst enemies of the State, do not follow the dictates of wisdom in such grave matters?'

In these respects, such matters were discussed and presented as must engage the attention of those who are possessed of discernment and cause them wonderment. However, to tabulate and marshal all the arguments here would unnecessarily lengthen this narrative. But to cite a few examples, I said: 'My Lord! Do not assume that slaying and imprisonment will stem the influence of this Cause, and do not think that faith and belief will alter by torment and suppression. Rather, should the matter be viewed with a discerning eye, it could be plainly seen that putting people to death will tend to increase the worth of this Cause, and the harshness of injunction will serve to intensify the desire of the people to enquire and investigate. If you desire your own good and the good of the nation you should resort to provisions of justice, and view this Cause with perception and not hostility, that perchance a good name, an admired name should become your legacy to posterity in books and written accounts; and whatever has been said regarding the deniers of past ages should not be said regarding you.' Much of this manner of advice, devoid of self-interest, was offered. But jealousy prevailed. The enmity of divines and the assault of vain imaginings stood in the way. Advice was discarded. Consequences were not taken into account, until the hands of the All-Powerful rolled up all the outspread circumstances and the hallucinations [of the adversary] did not materialize. That which remained eminent and proven was that neither could the influence of the Cause of God be stemmed by oppression and suppression, nor could one wipe out the story of these events from the pages of history, as if they had never happened.

Mírzá Abu'l-Faḍl has paid glowing tribute to the quality of Mullá Muḥammad-Riḍá's courage and his unswerving faith. 'Abdu'l-Bahá mentions it, when He Himself was lauding Mírzá Abu'l-Faḍl's humility and selflessness. 'Abdu'l-Bahá recounted in a meeting, held in His house in Haifa after the death of Mírzá Abu'l-Faḍl, that despite his own brilliant contribution to the arguments conducted in the presence of Prince Kámrán Mírzá, Mírzá Abu'l-Faḍl always stoutly and meekly maintained that on those occasions the pride of place belonged to Mullá Muḥammad-Riḍá, and he outshone them all by his boldness, firmness and certitude.

One night, it is related, Prince Kámrán Mírzá called Mullá Muḥammad-Riḍá to his own private apartments to have dinner with him. Dinner over, he suddenly turned to the prisoner with this abrupt question: 'Ák͟húnd! Tell me: whom do you consider Bahá'u'lláh to be – an Imám or a Prophet?' Not at a loss for an answer, Mullá Muḥammad-Riḍá replied: 'Your Royal Highness! We recognize in Him the Ancient Beauty, the Manifestation of God, the Dawning-Place of the Sun of Divinity, the Horizon whereupon has appeared the Light of the Unseen Who is beyond all comprehension. Should we do otherwise we would have denied all the Prophets Who came in past ages, and the Glad Tidings imparted by Them would have been made senseless, since They have foretold the Advent of the Lord of Hosts, the Heavenly Father, the day when men will come face to face with the Godhead. We refer to Him by these names, which are not of our own invention. Moreover, it is not names that we look up to, because Bahá'u'lláh is sanctified beyond all names, designations, appellation and description. He is both the Lord of Names and independent of names.' Then Mullá Muḥammad-Riḍá went on to present the Prince with proofs and pointers.

The next day the prisoners were, as usual, brought to the assemblage where the great and mighty of the land had gathered, although that whole pretence of investigation was a mockery of justice, as is seen elsewhere in this volume. 'Well,' said Prince Kámrán Mírzá, turning to Ḥájí Mullá 'Alí-Akbar-i-S͟hahmírzádí, known as Ḥájí Ák͟húnd, 'what is your view of Mullá Muḥammad-Riḍá; do you consider him to be a truthful person, is he an honest man?' To which query Ḥájí Ák͟húnd replied: 'Indeed and indeed, he is a truthful person; he never lies.' Now Kámrán Mírzá found his chance to score a decisive point. 'If that is so,' he said, 'then the rest of you are all liars and deceivers. You have been telling me all along that in Bahá'u'lláh you witness the Return of Ḥusayn [Rij'at-i-Ḥusayní], whereas Mullá Muḥammad-Riḍá tells me that the Light of the Invisible Godhead is shining in the Person of Bahá'u'lláh.' Ḥájí Mullá 'Alí-Akbar was amazed and said mildly, 'Your Royal Highness! Mullá Muḥammad-Riḍá is the Ṣúfí of the Bábís, waxing extravagant.' Then, Mullá Muḥammad-Riḍá himself intervened: 'Your Royal Highness! You listen to me. What I have said is the truth. These are the samovar-centred Bahá'ís: when the samovar is boiling and they are seated somewhere safe and secure, they all say the same

Ḥájí Mullá 'Alí-Akbar-i-Shahmírzádí, known as Ḥájí Ákhúnd, one of the four Hands of the Cause of God appointed by Bahá'u'lláh

as I have told you. That is the belief of all; but now, at the time of testing, they draw a veil over it all and follow the dictates of circumspection.' After that there was only silence.

Mullá Muḥammad-Riḍá's courage and outspokenness contributed in no small measure to the eventual release of all the Bahá'ís.

This erstwhile divine of Yazd was a man of great vision. He had a clear picture in his mind of a vast and magnificent town with a splendorous House of Worship (Mashriqu'l-Adhkár) dedicated to the glory of Bahá'u'lláh. His notion of a Mashriqu'l-Adhkár was one constructed with translucent crystal. In the vicinity of Kirmán he came upon a lake which was fed with melting snow and rainwater, and below the lake there was an extensive area of barren land. All by himself, he set about working on that land. Here he was going to have his dream realized. But it was not to be. He was arrested, taken to the city and put into gaol. When he was taken away, some five hundred digging tools of various kind were left around that wasteland. His labour was necessarily slow because of his advanced age, and when he was arrested and his work was halted he said that there would be another day. Then people from neighbouring villages came and helped themselves to the tools which Mullá Muḥammad-Riḍá had gathered in that desolate spot.

And yet this saintly and selfless man was a bon vivant. The life he lived was a testimony to the fact that detachment and monasticism are poles apart. Detachment is not denying oneself all the good things that this world has to offer; but disallowing anything, abstract or material, to pose a barrier between oneself and the recognition and acceptance of Truth, however hard and exacting it might be to take and tread that shining path. Mullá Muḥammad-Riḍá always stood fearlessly by the side of the Truth which he professed. And he lived well and ate very well, for he was a keen connoisseur, in fact an unashamed gourmet. He chose his lamb while still a suckling, and fed it with delicious sweets, with nuts and spices, such as cardamom and cloves. Frequently he had guests to share with him his repast. The tidiness of his mien and manners was extraordinary. Once, in his native city of Yazd, the divines vented their rage on him and caused the governor to have him bastinadoed in public. That was done in seven thoroughfares. In each spot Mullá Muḥammad-Riḍá would neatly divest himself of his turban, his 'abá and his socks, place them in an orderly fashion on a handkerchief and stretch out his feet, inviting his tormentors to do their caning. And he never flinched, never uttered a cry of pain, to the amazement of the passers-by and the discomfiture of those who wanted to humiliate and torture him.

In the course of his first imprisonment in Ṭihrán, Mullá Muḥammad-Riḍá's frankness so aroused the ire of Ma<u>sh</u>hadí 'Alí, the gaoler, that he took him out into the prison yard, stripped him of his clothes and lashed him so hard on his bare skin that soon his back became a mass of weals and wounds. Siyyid Asadu'lláh-i-Qumí, who shared his chain with him at night, wished to smear that lacerated back with yolks of eggs, to bring the saintly sufferer some relief. Mullá Muḥammad-Riḍá told him: 'Áqá Siyyid Asadu'lláh! Do you think that when they were punishing me, I was aware of what they were doing? O Siyyid! I was in the presence of the Blessed Perfection, speaking with Him!' A certain Ghulám-Riḍá Khán, one of the notables of Ṭihrán, also happened to be incarcerated at this very time. He particularly noticed the heroism and endurance of Mullá Muḥammad-Riḍá. And that led him to give his allegiance to Bahá'u'lláh. Whenever asked what it was that made him a Bahá'í, he always said 'lashing', and would quickly add: 'Nothing but what I saw of the blissful constancy of that man under the impact of those lashes could have ever induced me to turn to the Faith of Bahá'u'lláh.'

Another fellow-prisoner was a poor Jew – sad, forlorn, helpless and shunned. He was not allowed into the bath, and he had no change of clothing. Mullá Muḥammad-Riḍá watched the miserable plight of that solitary figure with increasing concern, until he could stand it no longer. He proposed to Siyyid Asadu'lláh that together they should give that poor Jew a decent wash in the pool of the prison yard and provide him with a clean shirt, which they proceeded to do. The Jew was overwhelmed and wished to know why they were so kind and considerate to him. Mullá Muḥammad-Riḍá told him that it was the command and counsel of his Heavenly Father which made him do what he was doing. He, the Father of them all, had made it a duty to consort with the followers of all religions in perfect harmony.

During his second imprisonment in Ṭihrán two of his fellow-Bahá'ís chained with him were Ḥájí Ímán and Mírzá Ḥusayn, both natives of Zanján. Mírzá Ḥusayn has bequeathed to posterity the story of that time, and particularly of Mullá Muḥammad-Riḍá. He witnessed also and has described the martyrdom in that prison of the noble poet Varqá together with his heroic young son, Rúḥu'lláh, at the hands of the brutal Ḥájibu'd-Dawlih (see chap. 7). And it was to Mírzá Ḥusayn that 'Abdu'l-Bahá addressed these lines, after his release from prison:

> O thou imprisoned for the sake of the Ancient of Days! Don a pilgrim's garb, and then give Me My fill to drink and tell Me: Lo, this is wine. O Cup-bearer! When thou givest Me that wine to drink, tell Me: Lo, this is wine, so that My ears too may take delight. In numerous letters we have read the astounding story of Varqá and Rúḥu'lláh, yet I desire to hear it with Mine Own ears as well. (Quoted in Sulaymání, vol. 1, pp. 210–11)

Áqá Mírzá Ḥusayn relates that one day they brought in a young man named 'Alí, a native of Hamadán, and chained him with them. He had been accused of robbery.

[He] had no shirt. Mullá Muḥammad-Riḍá said to me: 'Mírzá Ḥusayn! This man too is a servant of the Blessed Beauty, although he does not know his Master. He is bare and we have an extra shirt between us; let us give it to him.' I replied: 'I have just washed that shirt; I will give it to you to wear, and you give the shirt that you are wearing now to this young man.' At that, Mullá Muḥammad-Riḍá flared up: 'Do you know what you are saying, Mírzá Ḥusayn? Are you not a Bahá'í? I would be ashamed to offer my dirty shirt to the Blessed Beauty.' I gave the clean shirt to 'Alí, who gratefully wore it. And that was a lesson to me.

Mírzá Ḥusayn writes that he prayed to be granted the same degree of certitude which Mullá Muḥammad-Riḍá had attained; and says that whatever was given to him Mullá Muḥammad-Riḍá considered to be a bounty from Bahá'u'lláh, and whatever he, himself, gave to others, he considered to be an offering to Bahá'u'lláh.

By now the nightmarish reign of Náṣiri'd-Dín Sháh had reached its end and Muẓaffari'd-Dín Sháh was the ruler of Írán. He was not vindictive and erratic, but weak, kind-hearted and vacillating. A number of Bahá'í ladies sent him a cable from Sháh-'Abdu'l-'Aẓím, begging him to set the Bahá'ís free. The capable but devious Amínu's-Sulṭán had fallen from power, and in his place as Prime Minister sat Mírzá 'Alí Khán, the Amínu'd-Dawlih, a disciple and friend of Prince (or Mírzá) Malkam Khán. Muẓaffari'd-Dín Sháh gave him the telegram he had received from the Bahá'í ladies, and asked him to investigate the matter.

It was decided to take the five prisoners to the house of Amínu'd-Dawlih. Áqá Muḥammad-Qulíy-i-'Aṭṭar (the Druggist), Siyyid Faṭṭáh, Ḥájí Ímán and Mírzá Ḥusayn tied by one chain, and Mullá Muḥammad-Riḍá tied by a smaller one, were moved out of the prison and, escorted by soldiers, were paraded in the streets amidst a gaping, jeering populace, all the way to the home of the Prime Minister. Their progress was slow, both because of the press of people, and their own inability to keep a steady pace after sixteen months of little exercise in gaol. The four managed to go ahead, but Mullá Muḥammad-Riḍá, a much older man, collapsed. Porters had to be forced into service to carry him. Mullá Muḥammad-Riḍá jested so much with the sergeant in charge about the quality of his 'steed', to the annoyance of the porters, the amusement of the public and the consternation of the Bahá'í ladies who moved with them mixed with the crowd, that the porter carrying him on his back nearly dropped him in the middle of the road. Then one of the ladies went near him and whispered:

Mírzá 'Alí Khán, the Amínu'd-Dawlih

'Ákhúnd, for God's sake, keep quiet.' Mullá Muḥammad-Riḍá replied: 'I shall obey! I am both deaf and dumb.' Mírzá Ḥusayn says that it took them nearly two hours to reach the house of Amínu'd-Dawlih, who was at the door to meet them. To his query, Mullá Muḥammad-Riḍá made no answer, pretending now that he could neither hear nor speak. The people were now doubled up with laughter.

The crowd was thickening outside the house of Amínu'd-Dawlih as the prisoners were led to the house of his *farrásh-báshí*. There they were relieved of their chains, given a decent meal sent from the kitchen of the Prime Minister, and had a good night's rest, after languishing for all that long time in prison. The *farrásh-báshí* was awaiting the arrival of the royal rescript to let the prisoners go, but Amínu'd-Dawlih himself, without any further ado, ordered their release. However, at this critical juncture, as the prisoners were about to leave, a divine, who was a siyyid as well, accompanied by a number of theological students, came riding by as they returned from the house of the Prime Minister. It was raining and the *farrásh-báshí* invited them to take shelter in his house while the rain lasted. Learning that the Bahá'í prisoners were there and would shortly be going to their homes, the siyyid expressed his desire to meet them. But all refused to see him, saying that they were not well enough, except for Mullá Muḥammad-Riḍá. The other four begged him to desist and not to put his neck into a noose, but he was adamant and would not listen to them: he would not run away, he stoutly asserted. Áqá Muḥammad-Qulí, Mírzá Ḥusayn writes, exclaimed in anguish: 'May God preserve us from the ill-advised actions of this Á<u>kh</u>únd and that Siyyid.' The four sat in trepidation as Mullá Muḥammad-Riḍá went into another room to meet the siyyid. Within fifteen minutes, according to Mírzá Ḥusayn, pandemonium broke loose in the other room: the theological students were beating Mullá Muḥammad-Riḍá and he was shouting at the top of his voice to the siyyid: 'You who could not prove the truth of the Faith of your forefathers, how dare you tell me to curse Ṣubḥ-i-Azal? You who do not know who Ṣubḥ-i-Azal is and why he should be cursed, are trying to make me soil my tongue.' Then Mullá Muḥammad-Riḍá rejoined his fellow-believers, who admonished him, but he was unrepentant and replied: 'I did well to go . . . I put him in his place.' The siyyid must have been terribly confused, taking Mullá Muḥammad-Riḍá to be a follower of Azal. He immediately wrote a letter to the Prime Minister, saying: 'It will be most injudicious to set this old, insolent Bábí free.' On receipt of that letter, Amínu'd-Dawlih ordered the release of the four Zanjánís and further detention of Mullá Muḥammad-Riḍá, whose case he would personally investigate at a later date.

Now it became obvious that Mullá Muḥammad-Riḍá was not reprieved, at least for the time being. Mírzá Ḥusayn, in despair, appealed to the sergeant not to return the old man to the prison, as he had no one there to look after him, and promised the sergeant seven *túmáns*, in consideration of his kind-heartedness. Hearing this, Mullá Muḥammad-Riḍá said laughingly that it reminded him of the story of <u>Sh</u>ay<u>kh</u> Farídi'd-Dín-i-'Aṭṭár and his Mongol captor. He told the sergeant: 'You are offered seven *túmáns*, but I am not worth it. Give me two *túmáns*, and I will walk straight back to the prison.' However, the sergeant promised not to put Mullá Muḥammad-Riḍá once again in the gaol, but he did not keep his word. Ḥájí Ímán visited that noble man in the dreary gaol the next day. Mullá Muḥammad-Riḍá asked for some kind of broth. Ḥájí Ímán took it to him, and left him some money as well.

Being left alone, Mullá Muḥammad-Riḍá soon succumbed to the rigours of prison life. Within ten days he passed out of this world; at peace with himself, with his fellow-men and with his Maker.

9

Nabíl-i-Akbar

'THERE WAS, in the city of Najaf,' 'Abdu'l-Bahá has recounted,

> among the disciples of the widely known mujtahid, Shaykh Murtaḍá,* a man without likeness or peer. His name was Áqá Muḥammad-i-Qá'iní, and later on he would receive, from the Manifestation, the title of Nabíl-i-Akbar. This eminent soul became the leading member of the mujtahid's company of disciples. Singled out from among them all, he alone was given the rank of mujtahid – for the late Shaykh Murtaḍá was never wont to confer this degree.
>
> He excelled not only in theology but in other branches of knowledge, such as the humanities, the philosophy of the Illuminati, the teachings of the mystics and of the Shaykhí School. He was a universal man, in himself alone a convincing proof. When his eyes were opened to the light of Divine guidance, and he breathed in the fragrances of Heaven, he became a flame of God. Then his heart leapt within him, and in an ecstasy of joy and love, he roared out like leviathan in the deep. (*Memorials of the Faithful*, p. 1)

Indeed, Áqá Muḥammad-i-Qá'iní, Nabíl-i-Akbar, also known as Fáḍil-i-Qá'iní (the Learned One of Qá'in), was a man of great knowledge. It has been claimed that no one within the enclave of the Bahá'í Faith has ever surpassed the profundity of his erudition. As far as the accomplishment demanded of a Shí'ih mujtahid is concerned, his attainment was superb, but naturally he had little knowledge of the lore and the scholarship of the West. Mírzá Abu'l-Faḍl of Gulpáygán, on the other hand, was well versed in Islamic studies and had a wide and comprehensive knowledge of Western thought as well. This comment is just a diversion, and certainly is not meant to cast a slur on the intellectual eminence of Nabíl-i-Akbar, the learned sage of Qá'in.

When Áqá Muḥammad of Qá'in had completed his studentship under Shaykh Murtaḍáy-i-Anṣárí, and had obtained his sanction and blessing, he moved from Najaf to Baghdád. Here, in the city of the

* When at the instigation of the cleric, Shaykh 'Abdu'l-Ḥusayn-i-Ṭihrání, Shí'ih divines gathered together to concert plans against Bahá'u'lláh in Baghdád, Shaykh Murtaḍáy-i-Anṣárí refused to associate himself with their aims and objects. (See Balyuzi, *Bahá'u'lláh, The King of Glory*, pp. 142–3.)

'Abbásids, he found himself in the presence of Bahá'u'lláh. As Áqá Muḥammad himself has related, having received him most graciously, Bahá'u'lláh asked him smilingly and in a light vein: 'Do you not know that we are offenders in the eyes of the government and have been cast out? People, too, regard us as outlaws and spurn us. You are a learned man, a mujtahid, and highly respected. Whoever comes to meet us and consorts with us, he too becomes suspect and blameworthy in the eyes of the public. How then did you dare to come to us, not sparing yourself and without concern for your own position and status?'* Then, very kindly, Bahá'u'lláh invited Áqá Muḥammad to stay as His guest, instructing Mírzá Áqá Ján to act as host and see to the comfort of that distinguished pupil of Shaykh Murtaḍá.

* * * * * * * * * *

Nabíl-i-Akbar was born in a village, Naw-Firist, near Bírjand in the district of Qá'in, on 29 March 1829. He came from a family of eminent clerics and received the usual religious education, going first to Mashhad to study under the distinguished divines of that town. While there, he became interested in the study of philosophy and so he travelled to Sabzivár where Ḥájí Mullá Hádí, the most eminent Persian philosopher of the nineteenth century, was delivering classes. After five years of study, Nabíl set out for the Holy Shrines of Najaf and Karbilá in order to complete his education. It was the year 1852 and the persecutions of the Bábís following the attempt on the life of the Sháh were at their height as Nabíl entered Ṭihrán. Through the instrument of certain ill-disposed persons Nabíl found himself arrested as a Bábí. He protested his innocence and obtained his freedom but the incident set him thinking, and later when he had an opportunity he studied the writings of the Báb and became a believer.

In 'Iráq, Nabíl attended the classes of the eminent mujtahids there and, in particular, those of Shaykh Murtaḍáy-i-Anṣárí, obtaining the rank of mujtahid. On his way back to Írán, Nabíl stayed in Baghdád for a time where he met Bahá'u'lláh. Nabíl himself has written how at first he was blind to Bahá'u'lláh's station and would always take the most prominent position at the meetings of the Bábís and deliver an address. Then one day Bahá'u'lláh began to discourse on a point and resolved the matter in such a manner that Nabíl realized his own ignorance in comparison.

* The above are reported words of Bahá'u'lláh, not to be equated with His writings.

Áqá Muḥammad-i-Qá'iní, Nabíl-i-Akbar, referred to by 'Abdu'l-Bahá as a Hand of the Cause of God

Having returned to his home town, Nabíl began to teach the Faith. Although he was received at first with great honour and distinction, opposition began to mount. Eventually he was arrested and after a period of imprisonment in Bírjand he was sent to Mashhad. The governor there, Sulṭán-Murád Mírzá, Ḥisámu's-Salṭanih, released Nabíl, but on his return to Qá'in, he was again arrested and taken to Ṭihrán in 1869. The 'ulamá of Ṭihrán plotted to kill Nabíl and he had to flee. He proceeded to 'Akká where he remained a short time before being instructed by Bahá'u'lláh to return to Írán to teach the Faith. Nabíl travelled through all parts of Írán and was soon being hunted by the authorities as a believer. He was eventually arrested in Sabzivár but so impressed the governor of that town that he enabled Nabíl to slip away to 'Ishqábád. From 'Ishqábád, he proceeded with Mírzá Abu'l-Faḍl to Bukhárá. There Nabíl fell ill and died on 6 July 1892.

'Abdu'l-Bahá designated Nabíl-i-Akbar a Hand of the Cause of God, the Guardian of the Faith included him among the Apostles of Bahá'u'lláh, and it was to him that the *Lawḥ-i-Ḥikmat* (Tablet of Wisdom) was addressed. In the words of 'Abdu'l-Bahá, '. . . because he stood steadfast in this holy Faith, because he guided souls and served this Cause and spread its fame, that star, Nabíl, will shine forever from the horizon of abiding light.'*

* The reader is referred to the inspiring description of Nabíl-i-Akbar's life and achievement in *Memorials of the Faith*, pp. 1–5.

10

The Nobleman of Tunukábun Conqueror of India

ONE OF THE BÁB'S Letters of the Living was an Indian: Shaykh Sa'íd-i-Hindí. Almost nothing is known about him except that he was a disciple of Siyyid Káẓim-i-Rashtí. His end is also shrouded in total obscurity. It is certain that he left almost no imprint in the annals of the Faith.

Then, at the time the Báb was incarcerated in Chihríq, an Indian dervish arrived there. His identity was known to no one, and to this day no one knows who that dervish was. The Báb named him Qahru'lláh (The Wrath of God). And all that Qahru'lláh would say about himself was this:

> In the days when I occupied the exalted position of a navváb in India, the Báb appeared to me in a vision. He gazed at me and won my heart completely. I arose, and had started to follow Him, when He looked at me intently and said: 'Divest yourself of your gorgeous attire, depart from your native land, and hasten on foot to meet Me in Ádhirbáyján. In Chihríq you will attain your heart's desire.' I followed His directions and have now reached my goal. (Nabíl-i-A'ẓam, *The Dawn-Breakers*, p. 305)

The Báb told Qahru'lláh to go back to India, in the same garb and by the same way he had come. Then, this strange dervish passed as swiftly out of the arena of history as he had entered it. Who he was and what happened to him remain mysterious.

The next man from India who comes into view in Bábí-Bahá'í history is a descendant of the Prophet Muḥammad, named Siyyid Baṣír, who was devoid of sight but possessed of a keen mind and remarkable spiritual susceptibilities. Nabíl-i-A'ẓam maintains that it was Shaykh Sa'íd-i-Hindí who, in the town of Mooltan (Multan), met Siyyid Baṣír and gave him the tidings of the Advent of the Báb. But Mírzá Ḥusayn-i-Hamadání records this of him in his *Táríkh-i-Jadíd* (New History):

. . . at the age of twenty-one, he set out with great pomp and state (for he had much wealth in India) to perform the pilgrimage; and, on reaching Persia, began to associate with every sect and party (for he was well acquainted with the doctrines and tenets of all), and to give away large sums of money in charity to the poor, submitting himself the while to the most rigorous religious discipline. And since his ancestors had foretold that in those days a Perfect Man should appear in Persia, he was continually engaged in making enquiries. He visited Mecca, and, after performing the rites of the pilgrimage, proceeded to the holy shrines of Karbilá and Najaf, where he met the late Ḥájí Siyyid Káẓim, for whom he conceived a sincere friendship. He then returned to India; but, on reaching Bombay, he heard that one claiming to be the Báb had appeared in Persia, whereupon he at once turned back thither. (Quoted in Nabíl, pp. 588–9n)

Let the inimitable Nabíl relate the rest of the story of this Indian scion of the Prophet Muḥammad. 'Casting behind him the trappings of leadership, and severing himself from his friends and kinsmen, he arose with a fixed resolve to render his share of service to the Cause he had embraced.' (p. 589)

Siyyid Baṣír first visited Shíráz, but to his great disappointment found that the Báb was not there. So despondently he took the road to Ṭihrán and from Ṭihrán he went to Núr. Nabíl writes that in Núr Siyyid Baṣír 'met Bahá'u'lláh'. He goes on to say:

This meeting relieved his heart from the burden of sorrow caused by his failure to meet his Master. To those he subsequently met, of whatever class or creed, he imparted the joys and blessings he had so abundantly received from the hands of Bahá'u'lláh, and was able to endow them with a measure of the power with which his intercourse with Him had invested his innermost being.

I have heard Shaykh Shahíd-i-Mázkán relate the following: 'I was privileged to meet Siyyid Baṣír . . . during his passage through Qamsar . . . Day and night, I found him engaged in arguing with the leading 'ulamás who had congregated in that village. With ability and insight, he discussed with them the subtleties of their Faith, expounded without fear or reservation the fundamental teachings of the Cause, and absolutely confuted their arguments . . . Such were his insight and his knowledge of the teachings and ordinances of Islám that his adversaries conceived him to be a sorcerer, whose baneful influence they feared would ere long rob them of their position.'

I have similarly heard Mullá Ibráhím, surnamed Mullá Báshí, who was martyred in Sulṭán-Ábád [present-day Arák], thus recount his impression of Siyyid Baṣír: 'Towards the end of his life, Siyyid Baṣír passed through Sulṭán-Ábád, where I was able to meet him. He was continually associated with the leading 'ulamás. No one could surpass his knowledge of the Qur'án and his mastery of the traditions ascribed to Muḥammad. He displayed an understanding which made him the terror of his adversaries . . . He stood unrivalled alike in the fluency of his argument and the facility with which he brought out the most incontrovertible proofs in support of his theme.' (ibid. pp. 589–90)

Next, according to Nabíl-i-A'ẓam, Siyyid Baṣír journeyed to Luristán and visited Íldirím Mírzá, a brother of Muḥammad Sháh, who received him with honours due to him, as a nobleman from India and a descendant of the Prophet. However, one day Siyyid Baṣír spoke of Muḥammad Sháh in a way that aroused the ire of the prince. Nabíl writes: 'He was furious at the tone and vehemence of his remarks, and ordered that his tongue be pulled out through the back of his neck.' This savage treatment, which Siyyid Baṣír patiently endured, led to his death. Nabíl goes on to say:

The same week a letter, in which Íldirím Mírzá had abused his brother, Khánlar Mírzá, was discovered by the latter, who immediately obtained the consent of his sovereign [Náṣiri'd-Dín Sháh] to treat him in whatever way he pleased. Khánlar Mírzá, who entertained an implacable hatred for his brother, ordered that he be stripped of his clothes and conducted, naked and in chains, to Ardibíl, where he was imprisoned and where eventually he died. (ibid. p. 590)

Nabíl-i-A'ẓam had some time before, at the request of Mírzá Aḥmad-i-Kátib, taken a copy of the *Dalá'il-i-Sab'ih*, one of the well-known works of the Báb, to Íldirím Mírzá. Apparently the Qájár prince had been glad to receive it and had told Nabíl that he was devoted to the Báb. He had also written a letter to Mírzá Aḥmad and given it to Nabíl to deliver to that amanuensis of the Báb. When Nabíl returned from the prince's camp, he heard from Mírzá Aḥmad at Kirmansháh that Bahá'u'lláh was in that town, on His way to Karbilá. Going into His presence in the company of Mírzá Aḥmad, Nabíl spoke of the mission he had fulfilled on behalf of his companion and of Íldirím Mírzá's response. Bahá'u'lláh had observed: 'The faith which a member of the Qájár dynasty professes cannot be depended upon. His declarations are insincere. Expecting that the Bábís will one day assassinate the sovereign, he harbours in his heart the hope of being acclaimed by them the successor. The love he professes for the Báb is actuated by that motive.' (ibid. p. 588)

And to bring to its end the story of that wonderful and courageous nobleman from India, it ought to be noted that Siyyid Baṣír was one of

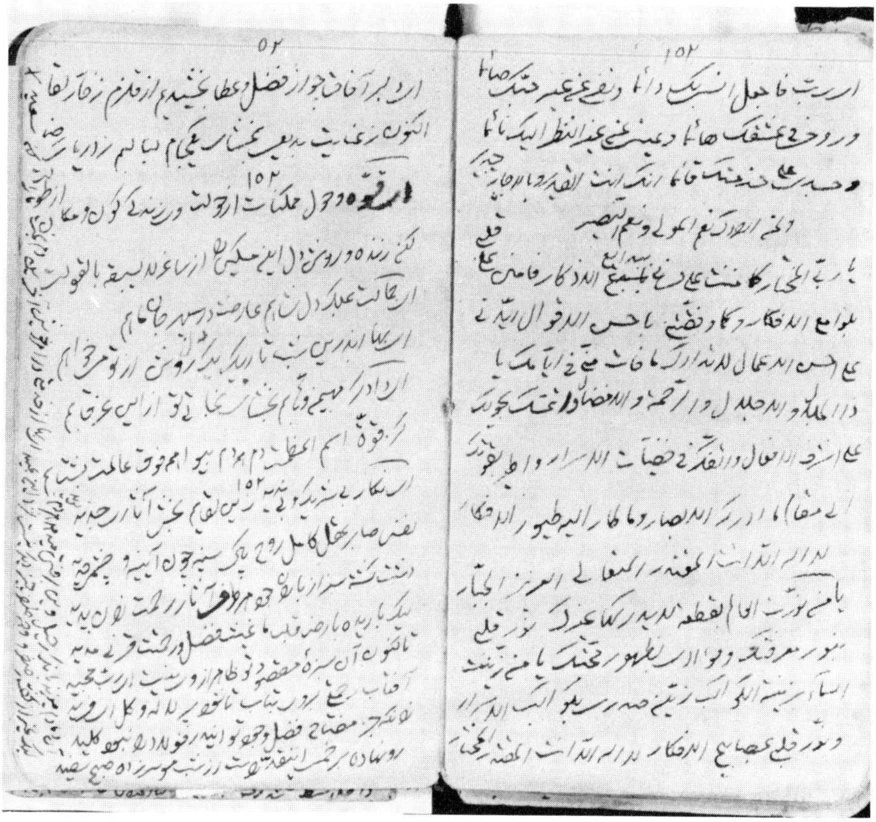

A specimen of the writing of Muḥammad-i-Zarandí, Nabíl-i-A'ẓam; the pages contain prayers of Bahá'u'lláh

the first to see the hollowness of the contentions of Ṣubḥ-i-Azal.

Neither Shaykh Sa'íd, nor Qahru'lláh, nor Siyyid Baṣír left a permanent trace of their work in the land of their birth. The man whom Providence had destined to become the spiritual father of the subcontinent and of Burma was a nobleman of the same province of Írán which had been the home of the ancestors of Bahá'u'lláh. His name was Sulaymán Khán and he was a native of Tunukábun. But when he set out in the world to serve the Cause of Bahá'u'lláh, he left behind the garb of a nobleman and attired in the garment of a humble man of the cloister travelled far and wide. 'Abdu'l-Bahá says that he 'was given the title of Jamáli'd-Dín'. He became known as Jamál Effendi.

Jamál Effendi

Sulaymán Khán was the son of 'Isá Khán-i-Tunukábuní. 'Isá Khán was a man of substance and influence in his area of Mázindarán. But his son decided to try his luck in Ṭihrán. It was in the capital city of Írán, the city in which Bahá'u'lláh was born, that Sulaymán Khán had his tryst with fate. There he met his destiny, which was not to rise to high position in the temporal realm, but to scale spiritual heights. He gave his allegiance to Bahá'u'lláh, donned the garb of a dervish and took to the road. Forsaking his wealth, his earthly attachments, his position and station in life, and possessing an Ottoman passport, he roamed for a long time over the Ottoman domains, making his way to the Holy Land. 'Abdu'l-Bahá says:

Here for a time he rested, under the protection of the Ancient Beauty; here he gained the honor of entering the presence of Bahá'u'lláh, and listened to momentous teachings from His holy lips. When he had breathed the scented air, when his eyes were illumined and his ears attuned to the words of the Lord, he was permitted to make a journey to India, and bidden to teach the true seekers after truth.

Resting his heart on God, in love with the sweet savors of God, on fire with the love of God, he left for India. There he wandered, and whenever he came to a city he raised the call of the Great Kingdom and delivered the good news that the Speaker of the Mount had come. He became one of God's farmers,

Sulaymán Khán-i-Tunukábuní, known as Jamál Effendi

scattering the holy seed of the Teachings. The sowing was fruitful. Through him a considerable number found their way into the Ark of Salvation . . . To this day, in India, the results of his auspicious presence are clear to see, and those whom he taught are now, in their turn, guiding others to the Faith. (*Memorials of the Faithful*, pp. 135–6)

The Afnáns in Bombay

In the course of the nineteenth century Bombay had developed into a thriving commercial centre. The Afnáns, relatives of the Báb, had gradually built up what amounted to a trading empire, stretching from Hong Kong to Báků. They had a branch in Bombay, where a number of them resided. Mírzá Ibráhím, a son of Ḥájí Mírzá Abu'l-Qásim, one of the two brothers of the wife of the Báb, established a printing-press and publishing house in Bombay. Ḥájí Mírzá Abu'l-Qásim lived in S̲h̲íráz, but the other brother, Ḥájí Mírzá Siyyid Ḥasan, known as Afnán-i-Kabír – the Great Afnán – lived in Beirut, until he retired to 'Akká, where Edward Granville Browne met him with obvious delight in the year 1890. A son of the Great Afnán, Ḥájí Siyyid Mírzá, had a long sojourn in Bombay, later to be replaced by one of his brothers named Ḥájí Siyyid Muḥammad. Another of the Afnáns, Áqá Mírzá Áqá Núri'd-Dín, also resided in Bombay for a while, but he soon moved to Port Sa'íd. Ḥájí Mírzá Maḥmúd, a grandson of Ḥájí Mírzá Siyyid Muḥammad (the maternal uncle of the Báb, in answer to whose questions Bahá'u'lláh revealed the *Kitáb-i-Íqán* – The Book of Certitude), also took part for a while in the affairs of the Bombay branch.

It was in the printing-press and by the publishing house, named Náṣirí, which the Afnáns owned in Bombay, that the Writings of Bahá'u'lláh were printed for the first time. The eminent calligraphist, Mis̲h̲kín-Qalam, went to Bombay for the purpose of writing copies to be lithographed. And so too did Mírzá Muḥammad-'Alí, the second son of Bahá'u'lláh who was also a distinguished calligraphist, as well as Muḥammad-Ḥusayn K̲h̲artúmí.

The Afnáns in Bombay had a few other Persian Bahá'ís with them, similarly engaged. With them also was Ḥájí Mírzá Muḥammad-i-Afs̲h̲ár of Yazd, a learned man who wrote the book entitled: *Dalá'ilu'l-'Irfán* (Proofs of Knowledge), a polemical work setting forth proofs gleaned from Scriptures and Traditions sustaining the truth of the Bahá'í Faith. That book was printed in Bombay, three to

Áqá Ḥusayn-i-Iṣfahání, Mishkín-Qalam, holding an example of his calligraphy

four years after the Ascension of Bahá'u'lláh. Despite this gathering of a number of Persian Bahá'ís in Bombay, no effort had been made to bring the Faith of Bahá'u'lláh to the notice of the Indian people. The Afnáns and others became acutely aware of the fact that they needed a teacher and sent a petition to Bahá'u'lláh, stating their case. They undertook to meet all the expenses. Thus it was that Bahá'u'lláh directed Sulaymán Khán, now generally spoken of as Jamál Effendi, to India. And thus it was that the nobleman of Tunukábun became the spiritual father of the subcontinent.

Jamál Effendi in India and Beyond

In the year 1878, Jamál Effendi, accompanied by Mírzá Ḥusayn, a relative, reached Bombay. There he began his sojourn and travelling in the subcontinent, which lasted for eleven years. Dressed as a dervish he lived the simple, dedicated life of a true *darvísh*. He met people from all walks of life, fearing nothing, asking no favour. He became known as Darvísh Jamálu'd-Dín, the Bábí. He had some of the Writings of Bahá'u'lláh printed and widely circulated. Thus he guided a considerable number, here and there in the subcontinent, to embrace the Faith of Bahá'u'lláh. He visited Ceylon (Sri Lanka of today), which was known to the Persians as the island of Sarandíb. In Colombo, Sulaymán Khán met strong opposition from some of the leaders of the Buddhists and suffered much hardship. Mírzá Ḥusayn was taken ill in Ceylon and died there: the first Bahá'í to be buried in that delectable island, where, as legend had it, Adam, the first man, came down upon the Earth. Jamál Effendi visited Burma as well, but did not prolong his sojourn there.

After more than a decade of constant travelling and teaching, Jamál Effendi asked two of the newly-converted Bahá'ís of the subcontinent – one an engraver and the other a hatter – to accompany him, and also he took with him a lad named Bashír whom he had chosen for service in the household of Bahá'u'lláh. The four of them sailed for Egypt, whence they went to the Holy Land. But soon after reaching the presence of Bahá'u'lláh, Jamál Effendi was directed by Him to return to India and continue the excellent pioneering work he had begun. Thus we find him once again in the subcontinent, in the year 1888, accompanied by Ḥájí Faraju'lláh-i-Tafrishí, one of the 'Akká exiles.

Jamál Effendi with an unidentified boy of the Indian subcontinent

Now, he spent a period of time in Burma and went beyond the subcontinent east to Java, Siam (Thailand) and Singapore; and in the north from Kashmír to Tibet, from Tibet to Yárqand and Khuqand (in Chinese Turkistán), then to Badakhshán and Balkh (in Afghánistán).

Amír 'Abdu'r-Raḥmán Khán of Afghánistán, ruthless and harsh, refused to allow Jamál Effendi to visit Kábul. In reply to his letter, written from Yárqánd, in which he had mentioned wounds afflicting his feet, the Amír threatened him that should he come to Kábul, his hands would go the way of his feet. At Badakhshán and Balkh the semi-barbaric people of those regions acted so abominably that he was forced to fall back on Ladakh (Laddákh) where there was a British commissioner. Aḥmadu'd-Dín, employed as chief secretary by the British official, had been converted to the Faith of Bahá'u'lláh by Jamál Effendi himself. There, supported by Aḥmadu'd-Dín, he found a safe place to rest awhile and recuperate, before going on to the eastern areas of Transoxania.

He was still travelling when the news reached him of the Ascension of Bahá'u'lláh. 'Abdu'l-Bahá instructed him to stay in the field, which he did for another five years. Now, old age was creeping on him. For almost twenty years he had been traversing, back and forth, vast tracts of the Asian mainland, and visiting islands of the Indian Ocean and the Pacific. He had suffered grave hardships at the hands of opponents and adversaries, apart from the toils of the road. Now, he took with him two of the outstanding Bahá'ís of Rangoon, Ḥájí Siyyid Mihdíy-i-Shírází and Dr Khabíru'd-Dín, and set out once more for the Holy Land. His companions had been brought into the orbit of the Bahá'í Faith by himself. Shortly after his arrival in 'Akká, 'Abdu'l-Bahá chose Jamál Effendi to carry out a delicate mission, which Bahá'u'lláh had desired to be undertaken by one of His followers. And that was to deliver a message to Mírzá 'Alí-Aṣghar Khán, the Amínu's-Sulṭán. The message which Bahá'u'lláh had wished to be given to the Grand Vizier of Náṣiri'd-Dín Sháh was this:

> You took steps to help the prisoners; you freely rendered them a befitting service; this service will not be forgotten. Rest assured that it will bring you honor and call down a blessing upon all your affairs. O Amínu's-Sulṭán! Every house that is raised up will one day fall to ruin, except the house of God; that will grow more massive and be better guarded day by day. Then serve the Court of God with all your might, that you may discover the way to a home in Heaven, and found an edifice that will endure forever. (Quoted in 'Abdu'l-Bahá, *Memorials of the Faithful*, p. 136)

*Mírzá 'Alí-Aṣg̲h̲ar K̲h̲án, the
Amínu's-Sulṭán*

'Abdu'l-Bahá explains the nature of the service rendered by Amínu's-Sulṭán:

In Ád̲h̲irbáyján the Turkish clerics had brought down Áqá Siyyid Asadu'lláh, hunted him down in Ardabíl and plotted to shed his blood; but the Governor, by a ruse, managed to save him from being physically beaten and then murdered: he sent the victim to Tabríz in chains, and from there had him conducted to Ṭihrán. Amínu's-Sulṭán came to the prisoner's assistance and, in his own office, provided Asadu'lláh with a sanctuary. One day when the Prime Minister was ill, Náṣiri'd-Dín S̲h̲áh arrived to visit him. The Minister then explained the situation, and lavished praise upon his captive; so much so that the S̲h̲áh, as he left, showed great kindness to Asadu'lláh, and spoke words of consolation. This, when at an earlier time, the captive would have been strung up at once to adorn some gallows-tree, and shot down with a gun. (ibid. pp. 136–7)

The day Náṣiri'd-Dín S̲h̲áh was assassinated, Amínu's-Sulṭán displayed a high measure of sagacity and competence, and saved Írán from potential disturbances. The next S̲h̲áh, Muẓaffari'd-Dín, confirmed Amínu's-Sulṭán in his post, but intrigues by the S̲h̲áh's favourites, and the conflicting policies of Russia and Britain, forced him out. He was replaced by Mírzá 'Alí K̲h̲án, the Amínu'd-Dawlih, who was a friend and collaborator of Prince (or Mírzá) Malkam K̲h̲án.

Amínu's-Sulṭán was sent in disgrace to reside in Qum. And as 'Abdu'l-Bahá further relates:

Thereupon this servant dispatched Sulaymán Khán to Persia, carrying a prayer and a missive written by me. The prayer besought God's aid and bounty and succor for the fallen Minister, so that he might, from that corner of oblivion, be recalled to favor. In the letter we clearly stated: 'Prepare to return to Ṭihrán. Soon will God's help arrive; the light of grace will shine on you again; with full authority again, you will find yourself free, and Prime Minister. This is your reward for the efforts you exerted on behalf of a man who was oppressed.' That letter and that prayer are today in the possession of the family of Amínu's-Sulṭán.

From Ṭihrán, Sulaymán Khán journeyed to Qum, and according to his instructions went to live in a cell in the shrine of the Immaculate [Fáṭimih, the sister of the eighth Imám: Imám Riḍá]. (ibid. p. 137)

Sulaymán Khán, then, met Amínu's-Sulṭán and delivered to him 'Abdu'l-Bahá's letter. He received it with great respect and told Sulaymán Khán: 'I had given up hope. If this longing is fulfilled, I will arise to serve; I will preserve and uphold the friends of God . . . Praise be to God, I hope again; I feel that by His aid, my dream will come true.' 'Abdu'l-Bahá says that Amínu's-Sulṭán was joyous and grateful.

The rest is well known to history. Amínu'd-Dawlih's premiership did not last long. His fall was swift. And Muẓaffari'd-Dín Sháh summoned Amínu's-Sulṭán from Qum and installed him once again in the office of Ṣadr-i-A'ẓam. In the words again of 'Abdu'l-Bahá: 'He assumed the position and functioned with full authority; and at first he did indeed support the believers, but toward the end, in the case of the Yazd martyrdoms, he was neglectful. He neither helped nor protected the sufferers in any way, nor would he listen to their repeated pleas . . . Accordingly he too was dismissed, a ruined man; that flag which had flown so proudly was reversed . . .' (ibid. p. 138) Amínu's-Sulṭán had a third period of office in the first year of the Constitutional period, but it was only for a brief space of time. He was assassinated in August 1907, sharing the fate of his monarch: Náṣiri'd-Dín Sháh.

Many are the stories related about the twenty-year odyssey of Jamál Effendi, Sulaymán Khán, the nobleman of Tunukábun, who was destined to be the spiritual conqueror of the Indian subcontinent and Burma. His first companion, Mírzá Ḥusayn, laid down his bones in

Siyyid Muṣṭafá Rúmí, builder of the Burmese Bahá'í community, appointed posthumously by Shoghi Effendi as a Hand of the Cause of God

The tomb of Siyyid Muṣṭafá Rúmí in Daidanaw, Burma

the island of Sarandíb (Sri Lanka) and the second, Ḥájí Farajulláh-i-Tafris͟hí, passed away in Bombay, in April 1894. Another eminent associate of Jamál Effendi was Siyyid Muṣṭafá Rúmí, whom he converted in Madras and took with him to Burma. Siyyid Muṣṭafá stayed on to build the Burmese Bahá'í community and on his death in 1945 was named a Hand of the Cause of God by the Guardian of the Bahá'í Faith. He is buried in Burma.

As for Jamál Effendi himself, he passed away on 20 August 1898 in 'Akká.

11

Na'ím of Sidih, a Poet Superb

MÍRZÁ MUḤAMMAD, who adopted Na'ím (Blissful) as his sobriquet, was a poet of the first rank. His poems mainly touch themes pertaining to the Bahá'í Faith. Yet their fame has reached circles well beyond the Community of Bahá'u'lláh. Their lambent, persuasive quality always enchants.

He was born in the village of Furú<u>sh</u>án, in the spring of 1856. Furú<u>sh</u>án, one of the three villages that constituted a larger unit, Sidih of Iṣfahán, had never known the burgeoning of such remarkable talent as Na'ím's within its confines.

Ḥájí 'Abdu'l-Karím, his father, had no other son. That made him particularly devoted to Mírzá Muḥammad, giving priority to his education. But Muḥammad had not gone very far with his studies when his father decided that it was time for him to get married and settle down to earn a living. Na'ím (as we shall henceforth call him) was then only sixteen years old. His father was a farmer and that was the only occupation which was open to Na'ím. So he put aside his studies and became a worker on the land. However, he had a cousin, named Ḥájí Mullá Ḥasan, who was a prosperous merchant in Iṣfahán. As Na'ím was a sturdy, hard-working, trustworthy young man, this cousin took him on to manage his substantial farming and commercial interests in the district of Sidih and its environs. In a poem which is autobiographical, Na'ím describes how it was that he had to abandon his studies and adopt a business career. Compelled by his talent he sought the company of poets and cultivated the friendship of two brothers, both poets of note whose sobriquets were Nayyir and Síná. These three found that they had much in common; they would spend hours reciting their poems, and proposing and selecting new themes as subjects. And as Muḥsin-i-Na'ímí, the Dabír-Mu'ayyid and husband of the daughter of the poet, comments, these three founded a literary circle in that lowly village.

Nayyir and Síná were, a good deal of the time, travelling about in search of their livelihood. In October 1880, Síná was in Tabríz and there he met a stranger. That very remarkable man, famed for his humour and jest, whose name was Mírzá 'Ináyatu'lláh 'Alíyábádí, is today very little known, even in his native land and in the memory of his co-religionists. But there was a time when his pranks and wise-cracks were often told and retold with glee.

Síná has thus related the story of his encounter with 'Alíyábádí:

> We were seated in our chamber in the caravanserai of Tabríz, when Mírzá 'Ináyat came riding in. He stopped in front of our chamber, dismounted, and having exchanged greetings, entered and sat down. Then he asked one of those present to go and fetch him a *nargileh*. To another he gave the task of tending his horse. When he had cleared the room of the two who lacked capacity and understanding, he paused awhile to rest, and then addressed us: 'O descendants of the Rasúl! [Messenger, i.e. the Prophet Muḥummad] I bring you tidings of the rise of two great Luminaries in the world of humanity. The first was the Orb of the Qá'im, rising in the year 1260. Then after nine years came the effulgence of "Ḥusayn Returned" and the world was illumined.'

Síná went on to recount how 'Alíyábádí proceeded to adduce proof after proof in substantiating his theme. Later, he brought out of his pocket the *Tablet of Náqús* (The Clarion Bell), chanted it with great fervour, and followed it by reciting a verse from the Qur'án (from the 36th súrih: 'Yá Sín'). 'Afterwards he kissed the Tablet,' Síná related, 'put it on his head, made a present of it to us and departed.' All that narrative Na'ím has put into a gripping and translucent poem.

This entry, declaration and exit of Mírzá 'Ináyatu'lláh 'Alíyábádí caused consternation as well as disputation. There and then, Siyyid Mírzá, a companion of Síná, left to go to 'Akká and investigate the truth of what they had heard.

Síná, telling Na'ím of that strange experience in Tabríz, could not add much more to it, and soon after he went on another journey, this time to Ras<u>h</u>t. Na'ím's interest had been greatly aroused. He craved to know more, and fate threw him into the company of an Azalí, Ismá'íl-i-Ṣabbágh (Dyer), who was also a native of Sidih. This Ismá'íl in later years changed his name to Mírzá Muṣṭafá, migrated to Ṭihrán and became a scribe. He provided Edward Granville Browne with many Bábí and Azalí manuscripts. Na'ím met others as well who were confirmed Bahá'ís. They met surreptitiously; the books lent to Na'ím

*A group of Bahá'ís including Síná (*middle row, 4th from left*) and Na'ím (*back row, 3rd from right*), both poets of note*

had to be taken away with great caution and kept well hidden. In the dead of night Na'ím would take out the books he had borrowed and, at a time when all others were fast asleep, would concentrate on reading and studying, and sometimes he copied them. Thus he became well versed in his study of the *Bayán*. One day the dyer spoke to him of Azal and his successorship to the Báb. Na'ím had learnt from the *Bayán* that there could be no successor to the Báb. However, he took with him one of Azal's works: *Jadhbíyyih* (Attraction). That night he had to wait impatiently for a long while, sitting through dinner until everyone had retired. At last all was quiet. Na'ím gathered together his writing material, brought out the book hidden in his pocket, and sat down to read it, prepared to copy it by candlelight. But soon he was bitterly disappointed. Azal's composition was a mockery of authorship. Na'ím had wasted his time, denied himself sleep and was deeply disappointed. Soon he fell into meditation. Three points stood out before him in prominent relief.

Firstly, he saw and admitted that the *Bayán* was divine script, come from God. And the *Bayán* was only the prelude to an Advent greater than the Advent of the Báb. This he came to believe truly without a shadow of doubt.

Secondly, he saw that the Báb had divided the *Bayán* into nineteen unities (wáhids). But what He had revealed consisted only of nine unities and ten chapters (Bábs). This fact was indicative of the nearness of the Advent of 'Him Whom God shall make manifest', because God never leaves His Revelation incomplete. The Manifestation promised by the *Bayán*, he realized, must come very soon to complete the unfinished task.

The third point of truth which confronted Na'ím was the fact that the laws and ordinances prescribed in the *Bayán* were so onerous and difficult to observe that a very rapid renewal of the Law was imperative.

In other words, Na'ím came to believe in Bahá'u'lláh before he had seen any of His Writings. He had already rejected Azal's pretensions as he had recognized his words to be fatuous and ignorant. That was how Na'ím found his spiritual home in the Community of Bahá'u'lláh.

By then the circle of poets in Sidih had three more members, namely Mírzá Manẓar, Muḥammad-Taqí and Siyyid Muḥammad. Gradually people became aware that a group of Bahá'í poets was meeting regularly in their midst. Tongues wagged and the rabble decided to make life impossible for those six men, who had been brought together by literary concerns. They became almost housebound, except that Síná and Nayyir were most of the time on the road, and therefore spared a good deal of the hatred. They also managed to obtain from Prince Ẓillu's-Sulṭán a decree forbidding the people to molest them. Na'ím's father, in order to rescue his son from persecution, advised Na'ím to take himself away to the holy cities of 'Iráq. But when he returned, after an absence of several months, he found that the situation had not altered.

Na'ím, by then, was so afire with his love for the Cause of Bahá'u'lláh that he could not refrain from preaching and teaching it, although he did not abandon all discretion. Ḥájí Mullá Káẓim, a local divine, brought together a number of his leading colleagues to investigate this Faith, including Ḥájí Shaykh Muḥammad-Taqí of Iṣfahán, well known as Áqá Najafí, whom Bahá'u'lláh has stigmatized as Ibn-i-Dhi'b (the Son of the Wolf). Naturally, Na'ím came too, and wisely and discreetly carried on a dialogue with the host and the other notables present. This debate became very prolonged, and it is said that Ḥájí Mullá Káẓim found himself so cornered by Na'ím's eloquent dissertation that thrice he retired to his private chamber to change his shirt which was drenched with perspiration. And he surrounded

Mírzá Muḥammad, whose sobriquet was Na'ím, a poet of the first rank

himself with such an enormous pile of books (for reference in search of proofs and arguments to buttress his contentions) that in the end only his huge turban and the upper part of his face could be seen. Meanwhile Na'ím calmly and quietly used the same material, which that divine was digging out of his books, to substantiate his own case. The most crushing testimony to Na'ím's amazing knowledge and debating skill came from no less a person than Áqá Najafí, never a friend of the Faith of Bahá'u'lláh, who told the divines of Sidih: 'This young man today scored a triumph over you and divested you of your honours as men of learning'. Ḥájí Mullá Káẓim, himself, remained silent and later avowed his own conversion, but alleged that he could not come into the open and declare himself a Bahá'í due to old age and the lack of any other means of support.

After that gathering in the home of Ḥájí Mullá Káẓim, the fame of Na'ím, in the villages of Sidih, became more pronounced and more widespread. And the malice of adversaries was correspondingly intensified. Let us learn his story from his own words:

I embraced the Faith in the year 1298 (4 December 1880–22 November 1881). Previously I used to visit Mullá Ismá'íl [the Azalí dyer of Sidih] and some people became suspicious. Síná had described to Mírzá Ja'far [a crony of the dyer] the experience he had had in Tabríz (see p. 130). Mírzá Ja'far and I resolved not to visit Síná again. But I knew that he kept visiting Síná. One night 'Alí Abu'l and myself were at Síná's, and he related the story of the martyrdom of the Báb. 'Alí said: 'Whoever rides a donkey, and thus comes to Iṣfahán, cannot be the Qá'im.' I said: 'The Prophet also rode a donkey' . . . Then I became known in Sidih as a Bábí, the butt of insults. Gradually it became impossible to leave the house, because of the abuse hurled by the people and their insolence. Mosques and gatherings buzzed with talk, hearts brimmed with hate, they wished to kill or eject us. Thus, we lived a whole year in utmost deprivation and abasement and had to bear countless afflictions, until the siyyids [the two brothers: Síná and Nayyir] returned from their travels. Taqí Abu'l went to visit them. In the mosque, Baḥru'l-'Ulúm asked him: 'Why do you go to the home of these siyyids and cause mischief?' Taqí answered back rudely: 'Ẓillu's-Sulṭán has given them a letter, forbidding the people to trouble them, and I am seeking an opponent like you.' At that, Baḥru'l-'Ulúm, enraged, rushed up the minaret, screaming: 'The Faith is in mortal peril! The Faith is in mortal peril.' His shouts brought the people out, who seized Taqí and trounced him. They were about to kill him when Ḥájí Amín Khán-i-Yávar [the Major] threw himself upon him and prevented his murder. The [two] divines of Furúshán – Mír Siyyid 'Alí, the Imám-i-Jum'ih, and Baḥru'l-'Ulúm – complained to Shaykh Muḥammad-Báqir, the Dhi'b [the Wolf], who told Ruknu'l-Mulk, the deputy-governor, to put matters right. He sent two *farráshes* to Sidih to take Taqí to Iṣfahán. When the news came that *farráshes* were on their way, I was sent for before their arrival and taken to the house of Baḥru'l-'Ulúm. Taqí was there, bound up. I was told that Taqí had said: 'Na'ím has made me wayward.' I commented: 'He has said that under duress.' They replied that they had found a letter in his pocket, written by Mírzá Asadu'lláh-i-Iṣfahání, addressed to me. 'If the letter was written to me,' I asked, 'what was it doing in his pocket?' We were thus engaged in conversation when the *farráshes* arrived. They said that this man [Na'ím] and Taqí and some others ought to be sent to the city [Iṣfahán]. A *farrásh* tied up my arms and, together with Taqí, I was marched off to my own house, which was some distance away, and a number of spectators surrounded us. Next, they sought out Nayyir, Síná and Siyyid Muḥammad. They were also tied up and brought to our house. My late father was detained too. He was dragged by his beard to a butcher's shop where they purchased a quantity of meat, and then brought to join us. In the meantime, a man sent by Ḥájí Mírzá Asadu'lláh, the Kadkhudá [the Magistrate] came and ordered us to have ready a suitable tip for the *farráshes*, and to start right away for the city. Baḥru'l-'Ulúm also sent his man to have us moved. They had made everything ready for our departure. About a hundred men, each holding a cane in his hand and shouting, preceded our procession. They had tied the five of us together in such a way that we were forced to walk, step by step, in line.

That day was Friday when crowds of people were free to gather, and spectators had swarmed in from all the neighbouring villages. We were led on, in that strange way, bare-headed and barefooted. Streets and roof-tops were so crowded with people that one could not see where a street opened and where it ended. They took us round the village, and in the midst of a spacious carrefour we were ushered into the upper room of a building overlooking the square. There they tied us to the door-frames, and the *farráshes* fell upon us with their canes. We were beaten for two hours. Next, around sunset, they took us, half alive, to the house of Áqá Muḥammad-Taqí where the *farráshes* kept beating us throughout the night. During the fourteen hours of that night, only while the other four were undergoing beating could one of us have a chance for some rest. As morning came, with snow lying on the ground, they took us barefooted to the gate of the mosque, to be beaten there too. Later they pushed us into our house, took up their rifles and shot five hens that were running about in the courtyard. While they were roasting the birds they kept bastinadoing me, leaving the others alone because they knew that no tips could be forthcoming from them. In the afternoon, word came from Ruknu'l-Mulk that the guilty men should be taken to Iṣfahán.

[Elsewhere, Na'ím reverts to these same events:] During those days, when the five of us were tied together, more than six thousand spectators were around us, pelting us with stones, throwing ashes and refuse over us from roof-tops, abusing and cursing us. Yet we were laughing as we walked through that crowd. One of my companions commented: 'God has tied our hands and brought us amongst these people to complete His proofs.' A few

*Bahá'ís of Iṣfahán, including the poet Síná – Siyyid Ismá'íl – (*last on right in first row*) and Áqá Mírzá Asadu'lláh Khán-i-Vazír (*2nd from left in first row*), who became the secretary of Ẓillu's-Sulṭán, the Governor of Iṣfahán*

steps further, he said, 'We have become the evidence of "Believers are together one personality"', and still further on, he said, 'This pomp and magnificence He has ordained for us' and again, 'this being cursed and spat upon – this affliction God sends only to His loved ones' . . . and we laughed all the way. Hours on end we suffered from the lashes of the footmen until, chained, we were thrown into a prison and sat there awaiting the descent of the sword.

Mírzá Asadu'lláh Khán-i-Vazír, a distinguished Bahá'í of Iṣfahán and its Vazír for some three decades. Following Bahá'u'lláh's instruction, he assisted in the protection and transport of the remains of the Báb from Ṭihrán to 'Akká in 1899.

Na'ím has related orally that when he was under those lashes his sister, although not a believer, was so overcome by the piteous sight which her brother presented that she pulled off her ear-ring so forcefully as to tear open the ear itself, throwing it to the *farráshes* in the hope that it would make them relent. His aged father, holding his beard, was imploring that heartless crew to show mercy to his only son, but with no effect. To compound their villainy they took off the clothes of those five innocent men, exposed them to the bitter cold of winter and painted their bodies with different colours to amuse the gaping, swearing crowd. Of course there were some here and there who took pity, who questioned it all, but they were a small minority. The majority were purblind and motivated only by animal instincts. Such is the mob. Such will always be the mob. Na'ím also spoke of his body being very swollen because of the blows he had received and of his shirt being soaked with blood and sticking to his body. Later, it was impossible to pull off his shirt and scissors had to be used to cut it open.

With bare heads and bare feet, in the heart of winter, the five Bahá'ís were marched off to Iṣfahán and gaoled. After a time Ẓillu's-Sulṭán ordered the release of Nayyir. Then Ruknu'l-Mulk sent for the other four to tell them that he had summoned their opponents to come and sit with them, to resolve the issue. He meant to set them free. When the others arrived, Ruknu'l-Mulk informed them that the prisoners had said 'We are not Bábís'. 'In that case, they should curse the Báb,' they replied. 'How can they?' Ruknu'l-Mulk retorted. 'They do not know Him.' The Law does not permit a Muslim to curse someone not known to him, but the adversaries were persistent. 'In their homes', they declared, 'the writings of the Báb have been discovered.' Ruknu'l-Mulk called in his attendant, gave him his keys and told him to fetch a certain box, from which he extracted diverse books about a variety of Faiths. Showing the books, Ruknu'l-Mulk told them: 'These books are mine; the follower of which of these religions do you consider me to be?' Thus silenced they went away, and Ruknu'l-Mulk had the prisoners freed and instructed them to leave Iṣfahán that very night.

In Furúshán, the cleric, Baḥru'l-'Ulúm, declared that Na'ím being an apostate, his wife should consider herself divorced from him. That pitiless woman took possession of all that Na'ím had, and would not give him even a small sum of money to take him to Ṭihrán. Penniless, Na'ím, Síná, Muḥammad-Taqí and Mírzá Manẓar took the road into the wilderness, their destination Ṭihrán. They depended on the charity and hospitality of Bahá'ís on the long road to the capital. Day by day they trudged on, occasionally stopping to rest wherever a Bahá'í home offered them shelter. When, after weeks of trekking, they reached 'Alíyábád (a stage between Qum and Ṭihrán), they had nothing left and they were hungry. There they came upon a dervish who lent them one *qirán*. On that paltry sum, the four travel-weary men subsisted until they reached Ṭihrán. When, after a long search in the capital, they found the whereabouts of that dervish, to return the money he had lent them, they also gave him the tidings of the Advent of Bahá'u'lláh, and he became a Bahá'í.

But there is more to relate about that walk to Ṭihrán. One day, on the road to Qum, the travellers found themselves without water, having drained their vessel. Seized by thirst with no source of water in sight, and hardly able to walk on, they joyously noticed a traveller (riding, of course) coming towards them. When he reached them, they implored his help. Could he point out to them any source of water in that expanse of barren ground? He could and did. Na'ím, stronger than the rest, took their water vessel and set out in the direction given by the stranger. He found the place, filled the vessel and started back to his companions. But, although his thirst had been allayed, his strength was sapped. As he drew near to his companions, he found that he could not take one further step. And they were begging him to hurry, as they too had collapsed and were unable to move. In his own parlous state, Na'ím finally managed by almost crawling to get close to them.

With life at a low ebb the four men entered Ṭihrán, and by following directions given to them, they found the orchard in the street, in a poor quarter of the city, where Bahá'ís had their gatherings. It is still called the street of the Bábís. That orchard had to be their home for they had nowhere else to go. Shorn of all material possessions, they had, first of all, to find means of livelihood. Na'ím chose the only occupation he was capable of following: to do the work of a scribe and make copies of Tablets for the Bahá'ís of Ṭihrán. That brought him a little money. Later he was paid fifteen *qiráns* a month to teach Bahá'í children. (In those days there were no schools as we know them in Ṭihrán.) It was hardly a living wage. Na'ím and his companions had to burn dead branches of trees at night, both for warmth and light. They could not afford candles.

When Na'ím found a room of his own, it had no rug to cover the floor. For fuel, he had to go out early in the morning and collect the dung he could find in the streets. His small tin samovar was heated with dung. It all took a long time before he could have a sip of tea in the morning. When winter came again, it was only that dung-fuelled tin samovar which could give him some heat. Yet living out this life of penury never made him complain. And he served the Cause of Bahá'u'lláh to the utmost of his ability. Whenever he could afford to buy charcoal and a few pieces of white wood, he would invite the Bahá'ís in his neighbourhood to come to tea on a Friday, and join him in reading and reciting Tablets and verses.

Years and years later, when Na'ím prospered, one day a Bahá'í came to his home and found him supervising masons and builders. Seeing workmen busy at one side making mud bricks, and at the other end of the compound a mason raising a wall, he reminded Na'ím jestingly of a couplet from one of his poems: 'The mud and brick of

Bahá'ís of Ṭihrán, among whom are (first row, seated, from left)*: (1) Mírzá Muḥammad Na'ím, (2) Mírzá 'Alí-Akbar-i-Muḥibbu's-Sulṭán;* (seated behind, from left) *(3) Dr Yúnis Khán-i-Afrúkhtih, (4) Mírzá Maḥmúd-i-Furúghí, (5) the Hand of the Cause Ibn-i-Abhar, (6) Siyyid Mihdíy-i-Gulpáygání, (7) the Hand of the Cause Ḥájí Ákhúnd, (8) Mírzá Maḥmúd-i-Nayyir, (9) Siyyid Ismá'íl Síná*

this abode so fleeting,/We used to raise our home everlasting'. 'How can you square all this building activity with the sentiment you expressed in those lines?' asked Siyyid Muṣṭafáy-i-Simnání. Na'ím's answer was: 'The construction of this house itself is preparation for that "home everlasting", because here believers will come together and remember their Lord.'

Na'ím, an undoubted master of verse, of a poetic ability rarely matched in his days, was a very unassuming man. The renowned Ḥájí Amín describes a meeting addressed by Mírzá 'Alí-Akbar-i-Rafsanjání* which was attended by a knowledgeable man newly introduced to the Faith. Na'ím was also present, listening attentively

Mírzá 'Alí-Akbar-i-Rafsanjání, London
11 January 1914

and not saying a word. The newcomer was greatly impressed by all he heard, and was particularly delighted by some lines of Na'ím's poem which closed the talk. Eagerly he asked the name and identity of the poet and, if he were living, where he could be found. When hearing that the poet was there in that very room, and Na'ím was pointed out to him, that discerning man was truly astonished that one who could write such poetry was so modest!

Na'ím, despite all he had suffered and despite the grinding poverty of his early years in Ṭihrán, always presented a cheerful face, and his humour never deserted him. One day in Ṭihrán, one of the minions of the Court ran into him in the street. The man was haughty and insolent; using an insulting epithet, and a very common mode of

* Mírzá 'Alí-Akbar-i-Rafsanjání was an eminent teacher of the Bahá'í Faith. He and Ṭarázu'lláh Samandarí (in later years a Hand of the Cause of God) travelled together a good deal. Rafsanjání visited London at the bidding of 'Abdu'l-Bahá in 1914.

threat, he said to Na'ím: 'Do you want me to burn your father?' Na'ím smilingly replied: 'No sir, by God, oh no sir.' The self-satisfied official was very pleased, and thought that he had nonplussed Na'ím.

There lived in Ṭihrán a physician of note, Dr Sa'íd Khán-i-Kurdistání. He had, justly, a high reputation for honesty and integrity, and was a good and competent physician, a man of profound learning. However, he had abandoned Islám in favour of Christianity, for which he was an ardent proselytizer. On one occasion Na'ím and Dr Sa'íd Khán chanced to meet in a street of Ṭihrán. They were not total strangers. Na'ím, very solemnly, asked the doctor whether he thought it possible that Christ could have come once again. Immediately and emphatically, Dr Sa'íd Khán said: 'Never'. To which Na'ím retorted: 'Then know for certain that Christ said: "I come at a time when you know not". He did come a while ago.' Dr Sa'íd Khán, it is reported by Na'ím himself, was dumbfounded, but he said nothing except goodbye and departed.

Hard times were at last over for Na'ím. Bahá'u'lláh had assured him in a Tablet that, before long, far more than had been harshly taken from him would be granted to him. He found employment teaching Persian in the British Legation, and he prospered. But poverty and wealth were alike to Na'ím. His one goal, whatever his material condition, his heart's desire at all times, was service to the Faith of Bahá'u'lláh. Not only was his poetic talent put brilliantly into the service of the Faith, but his eloquent tongue made many a soul realize that the Day of God had indeed dawned.

Na'ím married again in the same year that witnessed the Ascension of Bahá'u'lláh. His wife, Ruqayyih Sulṭán, a native of Iṣfahán, proved a true helpmate to her husband, always supporting him loyally through thick and thin. They had one son and one daughter. The son, 'Abdu'l-Ḥusayn Na'ímí, whose great service besides many others was to publish the invaluable poetical work of his father, lies buried in the New Southgate Cemetery, close to the grave of the Guardian of the Faith. The daughter was married to Muḥsin-i-Na'ímí, the Dabír-Mu'ayyid, biographer of his father-in-law, and a devout teacher of the Bahá'í Faith.

Indeed, Na'ím the lucid poet, Na'ím the eloquent teacher, Na'ím the servant of Bahá'u'lláh, has left a heritage of praise, fidelity and selflessness whose fame will only brighten more and more as the years roll by. And one day the whole world will bow to it.

12

An Eminent Grandson of Fatḥ-'Alí Sháh

SHAYKHU'R-RA'ÍS had been the designation of the great Avicenna. It was also the designation of Prince Abu'l-Ḥasan Mírzá, a grandson of Fatḥ-'Alí Sháh; his father Muḥammad-Taqí Mírzá, the Ḥisámu's-Salṭanih, was the seventh son of that uxorious monarch.

Prince Abu'l-Ḥasan Mírzá was born in Tabríz in the year 1847. His father, who had been the governor of Luristán, was one of the several princes who had either rebelled and risen up to resist the accession of Muḥammad Sháh to the throne or had shown overt displeasure. Eleven of these princes were sent to Ádharbáyján to be detained in the citadel of Ardibíl. Muḥammad-Taqí Mírzá was one of them. Four of the princes, one of whom was 'Alí Sháh, the Ẓillu's-Sulṭán, dug a tunnel and escaped. They gained safety outside Írán. Then it was that the other seven were moved to Tabríz and kept there, but not in gaol. Throughout the rest of Muḥammad Sháh's reign, Tabríz was the home of Muḥammad-Taqí Mírzá and his family. Later, Náṣiri'd-Dín Sháh restored his freedom. One report has it that he died soon after, because his title Ḥisámu's-Salṭanih was given to Sulṭán-Murád Mírzá, uncle of Náṣiri'd-Dín Sháh and conqueror of Hirát. But there are other instances of two men receiving the same title; it is confidently related that Muḥammad-Taqí Mírzá was still living well beyond the date when Sulṭán-Murád Mírzá came to be known as Ḥisámu's-Salṭanih.

According to Prince Abu'l-Ḥasan Mírzá's own evidence, his devotion to the Bábí-Bahá'í Faith was a precious gift, in his childhood, from his mother, which was later reinforced by the wise guidance of the great Ḥujjatu'l-Islám, Ḥájí Mírzá Muḥammad-Ḥasan, generally known as Mírzáy-i-Shírází. (See chap. 19.) His mother was Khurshíd Bagum, daughter of Suhráb Khán, a Georgian and grandee of Caucasia, who was taken prisoner when Ághá Muḥammad Khán, the eunuch king, stormed the city of Tiflís

Fatḥ-'Alí Sháh (reigned 1797–1834)

(Tbilisi). Abu'l-Ḥasan Mírzá was a sickly child. Very early in life, he lost the sight of one eye through smallpox but it was miraculously restored before long. When a cholera epidemic reached Tabríz, his parents, despairing of the child's life, left him with a wet nurse and hurried to the safety of the countryside. But Abu'l-Ḥasán Mírzá was destined to live on and become distinguished as the Bahá'í grandson of Fatḥ-'Alí Sháh. Cholera did not touch him.

At the age of six, Prince Abu'l-Ḥasan Mírzá was sent for tuition by Mullá 'Abdu'l-'Alí, who had as pupils many of the scions of the nobility of Tabríz. When he was eleven, it is stated, he accompanied his father to Ṭihrán, and there attended the classes of Mullá 'Alíy-i-Núrí, a divine who taught in the Madrisiy-i-Mullá Áqá Riḍá. Under him Abu'l-Haṣan Mírzá studied logic and syntax, and made rapid progress in mastering the intricacies of Arabic, arousing the jealousy of his brothers. Three years later we find him again with his father in Mashhad, where Muḥammad-Taqí Mírzá was taken ill and died. His last word to Abu'l-Ḥasan Mírzá was to go on with such studies as would entitle him to become a cleric.

After the death of his father, Prince Abu'l-Ḥasan Mírzá returned to

Ṭihrán, where, against the wishes of both his mother and himself, his brothers sent him to the military academy. Yet he managed to attend daily the classes of Shaykh Ja'far-i-Turk, where again he made rapid progress in his study of literary subjects. Two years later he was able to leave the military academy and was freed from that oppressive environment. Now, he and his mother moved to Mashhad and made that holy city their home. This happened at the time when Ḥájí Mírzá 'Alí-Akbar, the first Qavámu'l-Mulk of Shíráz (son of Ḥájí Ibráhím Khán, the king-maker) had been directed by Náṣiri'd-Dín Sháh to Mashhad and appointed custodian of the sacred Shrine of the Eighth Imám. Ḥájí Qavámu'l-Mulk was well disposed towards Khurshíd Bagum and her sons. He organized a great fête to celebrate the entry of Prince Abu'l-Haṣan Mírzá, who must have been about seventeen years of age, into the ranks of the clerics. His cap was changed to a turban, the garb of a prince was shed, and he put on the long robe of learned men. Even at that early age Prince Abu'l-Ḥasan Mírzá had shown poetic talent of a high order and the mastery of a fluent pen. And at that fête, encouraged by Ḥájí Qavámu'l-Mulk, he adopted the sobriquet of Ḥayrat. Now he was qualified to follow the advice of his late father, and became a theological student.

His studies, to which he applied himself assiduously, were varied and fundamental. With Mullá Muḥammad-Taqíy-i-Mazniyání, an accomplished teacher, he continued with literary subjects. He followed courses in mathematics with Mírzá Naṣru'lláh-i-Shírází.

Prince Abu'l-Ḥasan Mírzá

Philosophy and scholastic theology were pursued with Mullá Ibráhím-i-Sabzivárí, considered to be one of the most learned men of his age. Three of the leading divines of Mashhad – Mullá Muhammad-Riḍáy-i-Sabzivárí, the mujtahid, Mírzá Naṣru'lláh, and Ḥájí Mullá 'Abdu'lláh, the mujtahid of Káshán – gave him lessons and directed his studies of jurisprudence and theology. As soon as opportune, he was resolved to go to the holy cities of 'Iráq to sit at the feet of the great divines there and obtain from them the writ which would entitle him to *Ijtihád*.* He stayed six months in Karbilá and four months in Najaf, adding all the time to his knowledge. Thus, at last, he reached at Sámarrá the circle of the greatest Shí'ih divine of his age, Ḥájí Mírzá Muḥammad-Ḥasan, Mírzáy-i-Shírází, who was a second cousin of the glorious Báb. For two years Prince Abu'l-Ḥasan Mírzá attended eagerly upon him, until at the end of that time Mírzáy-i-Shírází gave him the certificate of *Ijtihád*. Even more, from that unmatched divine he received further incentive to strengthen his faith in the Revelation of Bahá'u'lláh. We cannot be certain that Prince Abu'l-Ḥasan Mírzá then knew that Mírzáy-i-Shírází was related to the Báb. One day he asked the Mírzá: 'What do these Bahá'ís say?' and was answered: 'Go and investigate'.

Having received his writ from Mírzáy-i-Shírází, Prince Abu'l-Ḥasan Mírzá went on pilgrimage to Mecca and Medina. From Ḥijáz he returned to 'Iráq, and stayed another year in Sámarrá. Then he turned homewards, a mujtahid given his authority to practise by no less a person than the great Ḥujjatu'l-Islám, and a man of profound learning, possessed of a remarkable poetic talent, a fiery and eloquent speech, and an able pen. He had also the advantage of royal descent, and enough of this world's riches to dress resplendently. He had already been noted with great reverence by Muḥammad Ibn ar-Rashíd, the Emir of Jabal, while a pilgrim to Mecca, and had composed a poem in Arabic praising the emir.

Now, in Mashhad, Prince Abu'l-Ḥasan Mírzá soon made his mark in the pulpit. People flocked to hear him preach. The governors of Khurásán held him in high respect and he had the support of Mu'taminu's-Salṭanih, the Vazír of Khurásán. All went well, until Mírzá 'Abdu'l-Vahháb Khán, the Áṣafu'd-Dawlih of Shíráz, was appointed the Válí of the province. Gradually, relations between Prince Abu'l-Ḥasan Mírzá and the haughty grandee of Shíráz became

* The power of the Shí'ih divine to issue *ex cathedra* decrees and judgments.

strained, until it became impossible for the prince to stay any longer in Mashhad. He fled to Qúchán, where he found a haven with Ḥusayn-Qulí Khán, the Shujá'u'd-Dawlih, hereditary chief of Qúchán, who had also lately given his allegiance to Bahá'u'lláh, and his protection saved Prince Abu'l-Ḥasan Mírzá from the evil designs of Áṣafu'd-Dawlih. Shujá'u'd-Dawlih was not only powerful; he was, as well, a man of iron will and action, who would not suffer fools gladly.

His character is portrayed in an incident involving the celebrated Ḥájí Mírzá Ḥaydar-'Alí (the 'Angel of Mount Carmel') and two companions, who were once set upon by a mob of some two thousand, incited by a divine named Mullá Káẓim whom Ḥájí Mírzá Ḥaydar-'Alí had worsted in debate in the presence of Shujá'u'd-Dawlih. Mírzá Ḥaydar-'Alí suffered grave injuries. With his clothes tattered and blood-stained, bare-headed, shoeless, bleeding from wounds, he just managed to stagger into a village. The people there took pity on him and made him comfortable. (Ḥájí Mírzá Ḥaydar-'Alí writes that Bahá'u'lláh had foretold what would befall him.) When Shujá'u'd-Dawlih learned of this event in his own territory he flew into a terrible rage and ordered condign punishment for all the culprits amongst whom were theological students. He had their school closed. Even Mullá Káẓim, who was an influential man in his own sphere, was not spared the lashing of his tongue. Ḥájí Mírzá Ḥaydar-'Alí was brought into Qúchán, where, he writes, he was besieged by some three to four hundred weeping women and children begging him to intercede for their menfolk whom Shujá'u'd-Dawlih had punished and detained.

Prince Abu'l-Ḥasan Mírzá stayed for one year in Qúchán. But a man of his talents and accomplishment, if he was to reach the public, required a much wider field than was afforded by a small township in a corner of Khurásán. He first wrote to Mírzá 'Alí-Aṣghar Khán, the Amínu's Sulṭán and grand vizier of Náṣiri'd-Dín Sháh, and put his case before him. He also sent to Kámrán Mírzá, the Náyibu's-Salṭanih, son of Náṣiri'd-Dín, a couplet which has gained fame, and took the road to 'Ishqábád. And this is that well-famed couplet,* the last line of which is borrowed from a *ghazal* of Ḥáfiẓ:

> O Náyibu's-Salṭanih, tell the sovereign, good and true, to note
> That a man of Khurásán to him this letter wrote:

* The original poetic line is longer than a line in translation. (Ed.)

Áṣaf and the land of Khurásán be thine to boot,
We took the road to Love, mosque or temple is of little
note.

Náṣiri'd-Dín Sháh also used a couplet to reply, taking his last line too from the same *ghazal* of Ḥáfiẓ:

Náyibu's-Salṭanih! Tell the Khurásání, a man of spite,
Thus did the Sháhansháh to thee this letter indite,
Áṣaf, good or bad, thine own steps thou watch,
For no one will, in thy account, the sins of others write.

It should be noted that the name of 'Ishqábád, the city to which Prince Abu'l-Ḥasan Mírzá went from Qúchán, means the 'City of Love'. The Prince's arrival at that city, the home of a considerable number of Bahá'ís, caused a sensation. However, he did not stop there for long, and was soon on his way to Istanbul, whence he embarked on a second pilgrimage to Mecca and Medina. On his return, he stayed for two years in the Ottoman capital – the metropolis which Bahá'u'lláh had designated as 'Madíniy-i-Kabírih' (the Great City) – commanding the respect of high and low alike. His profundity of knowledge, mastery of language and lucidity of both tongue and pen, made him an outstanding, highly respected figure in the leading circles of the Turkish capital. Even Mírzá Áqá Khán-i-Kirmání, who could not have been unaware of his allegiance to the Cause of Bahá'u'lláh, could not but praise him.

The Persian ambassador, Shaykh Muḥsin Khán, the Mu'ínu'l-Mulk, whom Bahá'u'lláh commends in the *Epistle to the Son of the Wolf* for his sense of justice, encouraged the prince to return to Persia, saying the authorities would make amends for the past. Abu'l-Ḥasan Mírzá was almost certain that these promises would remain unfulfilled. Yet he went back. Amínu's-Sulṭán received him with due consideration, presented him with a diamond ring, and wrote to Ruknu'd-Dawlih, a brother of Náṣiri'd-Dín Sháh, who was, by then, the governor-general of Khurásán, to treat him with respect. It was rumoured that the Ṣadr-i-A'ẓam had promised the prince the custodianship of the sacred Shrine at Mashhad. This rumour made Ruknu'd-Dawlih so jealous that he joined hands with the old enemies of Abu'l-Ḥasan Mírzá, and had him detained and banished to Kalát-i-Nádirí. There Prince Abu'l-Ḥasan Mírzá suffered hardships. As soon as he was freed, he went back to Mashhad, collected his family, and once again took the road to 'Ishqábád in the spring of 1892. Then he began a tour of the renowned cities of Transoxania, such as Samarqand and Bukhára. From Transoxania he passed on to Caucasia, and in that area, too, the Persian residents gathered round him with expressions of reverence and goodwill.

Next, we find him again in Istanbul and once again embarking on a pilgrimage to Ḥijáz, after which he returned to Istanbul and stayed for nearly a year. He was received by Sulṭán 'Abdu'l-Ḥamíd, which aroused suspicion at the Persian Embassy that, because of his shabby treatment at home, he might plot with 'Abdu'l-Ḥamíd against Írán. Finding it best to leave the Ottoman metropolis, he went to take his leave from the Sulṭán, who presented him with a bejewelled snuff-box. Now, at long last, Prince Abu'l-Ḥasan Mírzá set his face towards the Holy Land. He reached Beirut, Jerusalem, and then the city of 'Akká.

Abu'l-Ḥasan Mírzá was a confirmed Bahá'í and, by his own admission, while at Qúchán he had been honoured by a Tablet from Bahá'u'lláh which had set him afire, evoking from his superb poetic talent one of his finest odes. He arrived at 'Akká as a guest of the Mutaṣarrif. The notables of the city, hearing that a distinguished member of the Royal House of Írán was staying in the residence of their governor, called on him to pay their respects. 'Abdu'l-Bahá also visited him in the house of the Mutaṣarrif. It was a brief visit. Abu'l-Ḥasan Mírzá, although a Bahá'í, had not fully comprehended the station of the Centre of the Covenant. He spoke boldly in the presence of 'Abdu'l-Bahá and continued smoking a water-pipe. A few days later he returned 'Abdu'l-Bahá's visit. A number of Bahá'ís were present when he arrived and they witnessed 'Abdu'l-Bahá walking with him slowly and speaking to him – words which they did not hear. Then all of a sudden the whole mien of the prince changed. He had been walking shoulder to shoulder with 'Abdu'l-Bahá; now he drew back to follow Him. He became far more attentive. When he left, it was seen that tears had reddened his eyes.

When Abu'l-Ḥasan Mírzá (whom we shall henceforth call Shaykhu'r-Ra'ís) came to depart, 'Abdu'l-Bahá told him to teach the Faith, but with great circumspection. The Master knew that should the prince become too well known as a Bahá'í, both his enemies and the adversaries of the Faith would be so infuriated that their show of hostility and acts of hostility would be redoubled. In a Tablet

Prince Abu'l-Ḥasan Mírzá, Shaykhu'r-Ra'ís

Ḥájí Mírzá Muḥammad-Taqí, known as Ibn-i-Abhar, one of the four Hands of the Cause of God appointed by Bahá'u'lláh

addressed to the Hand of the Cause Ibn-i-Abhar, 'Abdu'l-Bahá laid particular stress on this fact: the imperativeness of not allowing the true allegiance of such eminent men to become common knowledge. He did not even mention Shaykhu'r-Ra'ís by name in that Tablet, and referred to him as 'the illustrious man of Khurásán'.

We do not know how and when it was that Prince Abu'l-Ḥasan Mírzá received his designation of Shaykhu'r-Ra'ís. But gradually, he came to be called by that renowned title, and hardly ever Abu'l-Ḥasan Mírzá. From the Holy Land he went to India. Bombay was his first port of call, which he reached early in 1894. In Poona, Sulṭán Muḥammad Sháh, Aga Khan III (then seventeen years old) offered him hospitality in his palace at Yevorda with signal honours. They were related. The mother of the Aga Khan, Lady 'Alí Sháh (Shams'ul-Mulúk) was a granddaughter of Fatḥ-'Alí Sháh. Even more, the mother of 'Alí Sháh, Aga Khan II, was Sarv-Jahán Khánum, the twenty-third daughter of the same Qájár monarch, a paternal aunt of Shaykhu'r-Ra'ís.

Then Shaykhu'r-Ra'ís made a tour of the subcontinent, and about a year before the assassination of Náṣiri'd-Dín Sháh, he returned to Írán and resided for a long time in Shíráz. The fact that he was a dedicated follower of Bahá'u'lláh had become well known. It is related that at one time, when he came face to face with Náṣiri'd-Dín Sháh, that capricious monarch remarked that Shaykhu'r-Ra'ís had brought shame both to his status as mujtahid, and to his position as a Qájár prince. In Shíráz, Shaykhu'r-Ra'ís continued to make use of the pulpit. His powers of speech and his eloquence were such that, despite the overt displeasure of some of the divines, people flocked to hear him. However, Ḥájí Shaykh Yaḥyá, the illustrious Imám-Jum'ih of Shíráz, was very friendly. Finally, opposition to him mounted high and he took the road to Iṣfahán, where he met open hostility from Shaykh Muḥammad-Taqí, known as Áqá Najafí.

One reason apparently for the departure of Shaykhu'r-Ra'ís from Shíráz was the altercation between Muḥammad-Riḍá Khán, Qavámu'l-Mulk III, and Malik Manṣúr Mírzá, the Shu'á'u's-Salṭanih, Governor-General of the province of Fárs, who was a son of the reigning monarch, Muẓaffari'd-Dín Sháh. Shaykhu'r-Ra'ís took the side of the Prince-Governor. Added to the ill-will of powerful divines, Shaykhu'r-Ra'ís had also to contend with the opposition of the

Malik Manṣúr Mírzá, the Shu'á'u's-Salṭanih, Governor-General of the province of Fárs

imperious and powerful Qavámu'l-Mulk. So he was forced to quit Shíráz. Shu'á'u's-Salṭanih was also forced to leave his post. According to a remarkable book by Majdu'l-Islám of Kirmán, which bears the title *Táríkh-i-Inḥilál-i-Majlis* – The History of the Dissolution of the Majlis (Parliament) – both Ẓillu's-Sulṭán (Mas'úd Mírzá) and Áqá Najafí were displeased by Shaykhu'r-Ra'ís's intention to visit Iṣfahán. Ẓillu's-Sulṭán took himself away for the time being; thus he evaded offering hospitality to the visitor. Shaykhu'r-Ra'ís cabled Mu'ayyidu's-Salṭanih, the head of the Telegraph Office in Iṣfahán, to rent a house for him. Mu'ayyidu's-Salṭanih was also a prince of the Qájárs, as well as a Bahá'í. Observing the attitude of the Governor of Iṣfahán and Áqá Najafí (whom Bahá'u'lláh referred to as the 'Son of the Wolf'), Shaykhu'r-Ra'ís decided to prolong his visit. Anything else would have been an admission of defeat. Within the spacious ḥouse rented for him, he made arrangements to make use of the pulpit. Here too his eloquence attracted large crowds which further infuriated the jealous Áqá Najafí. Prominent Bahá'ís of Iṣfahán, such

Bahá'ís of Iṣfahán, with Prince Abu'l-Ḥasan Mírzá, Shaykhu'r-Ra'ís (first row, centre), *and including Áqá Muḥammad-Javád-i-Ṣarráf* (back row, 3rd from right)

as Mírzá 'Alí Khán-i-Ṣarráf (Money-changer) and Áqá Muḥammad-Javád-i-Ṣarráf, were to be seen oftentimes serving and supporting Shaykhu'r-Ra'ís. All these happenings were noted by Áqá Najafí and his men, who were biding their time to strike, and strike hard, at the Bahá'ís of the city of 'Abbás the Great. They could not touch Shaykhu'r-Ra'ís: for one thing, he was a very distinguished member of the Royal House; for another, the public was enchanted by him.

At last Shaykhu'r-Ra'ís, having successfully defied both Ẓillu's-Sulṭán and Áqá Najafí, left for Ṭihrán. Soon after, Írán was plunged into the revolution which led to the establishment of constitutional government. Shaykhu'r-Ra'ís chose to play a leading and conspicuous part in that revolution. His intervention was contrary to the clear advice given by 'Abdu'l-Bahá that Bahá'ís should keep out of that struggle, although it ought to be said that Shaykhu'r-Ra'ís had involved himself at an early date. 'Abdu'l-Bahá, learning of the involvement of Shaykhu'r-Ra'ís, wrote that Bahá'ís should keep silent in regard to him. Then came the *coup d-état* of Muḥammad-'Alí Sháh in June 1908 and the bombardment of Baháristán, the seat of the Majlis (Parliament), together with the arrest of a sizeable number of the leaders of the Constitutional Movement and the execution of

Muḥammad-'Alí Sháh, (reigned 1907–1909)

some of them. Shaykhu'r-Ra'ís was amongst those detained and chained.

> Take away this chain from my neck, O Sháh!
> And make a chain of people to thee indebted, O Sháh.

Thus did Shaykhu'r-Ra'ís now petition the stubborn monarch who had thrown his country into chaos and confusion, breaking his oath into the bargain. Shaykhu'r-Ra'ís was pardoned and set free. He admitted that he had reaped the harvest of disobedience. 'I failed to obey my Master', he said, 'and I had to pay the penalty.' Whatever penalty he paid was through action by forces of despotism. 'Abdu'l-Bahá never reproached him.

Now, Shaykhu'r-Ra'ís gradually retired from public life. He once again visited 'Ishqábád. In Mashhad, he had to meet the challenge of the newly-formed Democratic party, led by Mírzá Muḥammad, known as Áqá-Zádih, son of Mullá Muḥammad-Káẓim-i-Khurásání, the celebrated pro-Constitutionalists divine who was resident in 'Iráq. A famous ode composed by Shaykhu'r-Ra'ís was printed, and thousands of copies were widely distributed to prove to the public that the veteran prince was a Bahá'í. One day a number of theological students stopped Shaykhu'r-Ra'ís, as he was about to enter the Shrine of Imám Riḍá, telling him that as he was a 'Bábí', he could not be allowed to enter the sacred precincts. Their action was instigated by the Áqá-Zádih, supported by the Governor – Nayyiru'd-Dawlih, himself a Qájár prince – who sided with him. And Shaykhu'r-Ra'ís had to take once more the road to 'Ishqábád.

At last old age was telling on Shaykhu'r-Ra'ís and he became a recluse. He died in the year AH 1336 (17 October 1917–6 October 1918) and was buried in a room next to that which harbours the grave of Náṣiri'd-Dín Sháh, within the precincts of the Shrine of Sháh 'Abdu'l-'Aẓím. The Áqá-Zádih, in Mashhad, carried his vendetta beyond the grave; he declared openly that should the remains of Shaykhu'r-Ra'ís be brought for interment in the holy city, he would consign them to flames.

Prince Abu'l-Ḥasan Mírzá, the Shaykhu'r-Ra'ís, bore proudly a title which had belonged to one of the greatest savants of all time. By his indirect method and his most effective use of the pulpit he guided many a soul to the truth of the Revelation of Bahá'u'lláh. His poetic talent produced a long and wondrous ode on the Advent of

Bahá'u'lláh, with its refrain, '*tamashshí kun, tamáshá kun*' – 'walk on and witness'. Here are two of its lines:

The One, by all beloved, stepped out of the Realm Unseen,
On His visage, indeed, the Light of Truth can be seen.
Captivated is the world by His beauty rare!
Walk on and witness.
Lo, by bounty and grace is the Earth replete,
Lo, the Effulgent Light of the Godhead
From a Human Temple shines!
Walk on and witness.

Similarly striking is the *ghazal* which Shaykhu'r-Ra'ís composed in praise of 'Abdu'l-Bahá:

The King whose crown 'Him Whom God hath purposed'
doth proclaim withal,
After the Ancient Beauty is Sovereign unto all.*

His poem in Arabic, commemorating the construction of the Shrine of the Báb, remains unmatched. His rejection of Mírzá Muḥammad-'Alí's pretensions is emphatically, powerfully and eloquently worded.

To him 'Abdu'l-Bahá addressed the following Tablet:

The Lamp of the Assemblage of the high-minded, the Prince of the enlightened, Shaykhu'r-Ra'ís: May he be a ray of God, and a dazzling moon!

O kind Friend! What thy musk-laden pen hath inscribed bestowed joy and brought delight. It was not a dew-drop, but an ocean; not a lamp, but a beam of sunlight. Praise and glory be to God, Who hath endowed Creation with such beatitude and conferred such tranquillity upon the hearts, and by imparting heavenly knowledge made the friends stars of the East, brilliant moons, so that they would enkindle the Light of Understanding, and with the showers of the rain of their utterance make human hearts the envy of meadows and rose-gardens. O kind Friend! The All-Bountiful God guided thee and led thee to traverse mountains and deserts, to reach the City of thine ancestors. That Land stood in great need of one mighty soul like that loving friend to enter therein, engage in discussion, show the Way of God, embellish the assemblage of men with mysteries unveiled, and watch over their spiritual lives so that they might abide under the shade of the tree of hope. Thou shouldst speak forth, wax eloquent, divulge the hidden secrets, share the Word of God, inaugurate a school of the Kingdom and give instruction in heavenly Books, ignite a shining lamp and burn down the veils of the imaginings of the ignorant. May thy soul be joined to the Beloved. (Unpublished)

* Bahá'u'lláh refers to 'Abdu'l-Bahá in the *Kitáb-i-Aqdas* as 'Him Whom God hath purposed'.

13

A Stalwart Teacher of the Faith

AS FAR AS THE RECORDS of history show, Mírzá Maḥmúd-i-Furúghí is the only Iranian Bahá'í teacher who was given the chance to meet face to face a Sháh of the Qájárs, for the purpose of making him comprehend the nature and the aim of the Bahá'í Faith, and to set his mind at rest by assuring him that Bahá'ís are not anarchists, that they do not wish to jeopardize the tranquillity of the realm and foment rebellion and contention. That monarch was Muẓaffari'd-Dín Sháh, the ruler whose edict terminated autocracy in Írán.

The meeting of Mírzá Maḥmúd with Muẓaffari'd-Dín Sháh lasted

Muẓaffari'd-Dín Sháh, (reigned 1896–1907)

more than two hours and the details of that historic encounter are given by Mírzá Maḥmúd in a short autobiography which he, at last, consented to write. It is a very precious document. Later, we shall note the circumstances in which he wrote it, after having resisted for long the demand for a comprehensive autobiography.

'Abdu'l-Bahá, commenting on the meeting between Muẓaffari'd-Dín Sháh and Mírzá Maḥmúd, wrote: 'Consider how a servant of the Abhá Beauty, all alone, outwardly bereft of all aid and assistance, converseth in the way he did with such a person, proveth equal to the task, and causeth wonder.' (Quoted in Sulaymání, vol. 3, p. 456)

Mírzá Maḥmúd came from a remote village in Khurásán named Dúghábád, which was situated in the environs of Turbat-i-Ḥaydaríyyih. Bahá'u'lláh honoured that village with the designation of Furúgh (Splendour, Light). That is why Mírzá Maḥmúd is known as Furúghí. Fáḍil-i-Furúghí – the Savant of Furúgh – is also an appellation by which he is remembered.

Mírzá Maḥmúd had as his father a distinguished survivor of Shaykh Ṭabarsí: Mullá Mírzá Muḥammad, who, prior to his conversion to the Faith of the Báb, was a highly-respected and influential Shí'ih divine. Mullá Mírzá Muḥammad's grandfather was a man of Iṣfahán, but it was in Khurásán that his grandson, the great cleric who was destined to become a devoted follower of the Báb, had his fulcrum of power. Whenever people had a grievance or had actually been wronged by a government official, they appealed to Mullá Mírzá Muḥammad. He always thoroughly investigated any case brought before him, and if his findings showed that an official had been guilty of a misdeed he would personally take action to redress the wrong. No matter how highly placed the malefactor was, he could not escape the sentence decreed by the cleric of Dúghábád, who would even send a deputy-governor to gaol.

Then came the Call of the Báb. There were genuine seekers in the area of Turbat-i-Ḥaydaríyyih, but there were also quite a number seeking only their own gain and concerned only with lining their pockets. These hypocrites simulated great interest and told Mullá Mírzá Muḥammad that they wished him, in whom they placed their trust, to investigate the claim of the Báb for them. That was the way to get rid of the 'meddlesome' cleric, they thought. And so they provided him with a horse and offered him the expenses of his journey. A few men volunteered to accompany him. Mullá Mírzá Muḥammad set out on his quest and hearing that Mullá Ḥusayn had gone towards Mázindarán, he took the same direction. Of those who had accompanied him, some, finding it toilsome to cover vast distances, and also being unsure of their motives, turned back. But five brave and sincere men stayed with him and went with him into the fortress of Shaykh Ṭabarsí. Their names ought not to be forgotten. They were Shaykh 'Alí of the village of Fayḍábád, Mullá Muḥammad of Mahnih, Áqá Aḥmad and Mírzá Ḥasan Khán of 'Abdu'lláhábád, and Mullá 'Abdu'lláh of Dúghábád. Meeting Quddús and Mullá Ḥusayn left them in no doubt that the Call of the Báb was not of human invention, that it was indeed divine.

Thus the renowned and just cleric of Dúghábád became one of the heroic defenders of Shaykh Ṭabarsí. As he had no desire for martyrdom, Quddús assured him that he would leave Shaykh Ṭabarsí with his life spared. Now we see a man who had never had to wield a sword or a dagger, who would have been mightily astonished, a year before, if someone had put a sword in his hand and totally at a loss as to how to use the unfamiliar weapon, one who knew only the law, its intricacies and its applications, for whom fortifications and battlements and trenches were phantasmagoria removed from the world of reality, going out of Shaykh Ṭabarsí, sword in hand, to drive away the relentless enemy. He was wounded five times by bullets or sword; but as promised by Quddús he came through. Triumphantly he returned to Dúghábád to inform those ringleaders, who had sent him to Mázindarán in search of truth, that he had indeed found it. A few accepted his testimony and embraced the Faith of the Báb. But the hard of heart, desirous only of material gain, with little concern for justice and truth, leagued together to rid themselves, once for all, of this troublesome cleric who had dared much and come home with laurels of faith and certitude. Mullá Mírzá Muḥammad was ordered by the authorities to go to Ṭihrán. He obeyed, but once again returned to Dúghábád. Further incensed, his adversaries planned afresh to have him cast out of Dúghábád.

Their intrigues bore fruit. Mullá Mírzá Muḥammad was arrested and put in chains. Mírzá Aḥmad-i-Azghandí and twenty-two others from Azghand were also chained and taken to Mashhad in the company of the undaunted survivor of Shaykh Ṭabarsí. Their internment in the citadel of Mashhad lasted a long while, but when release came Mullá Mírzá Muḥammad, now a devoted follower of

Mírzá Maḥmúd-i-Furúghí

Bahá'u'lláh, went back for the third time to his village. He was old and frail and infirm, but he had testified to truth to his last breath, and he had a son of the stature of Mírzá Maḥmúd to don his mantle. 'Azízu'lláh Sulaymání, the biographer of many of the prominent teachers of the Faith, recalls the person and the personality of Furúghí, a memory of the days of his childhood in 'Ishqábád.

Of middle height, he was a dignified figure possessed of an attractive and handsome face, a thick beard which was dyed and a commanding voice. Dressed in the garb of the divines, his speech and his demeanour reflected his inner strength. One particular distinction of this man was the fact that he never, never engaged in backbiting, and no one in his presence ever committed backbiting, so much was he held in high respect. And if anyone wanted to break the code, he was denied the chance to proceed; for in whatever meeting Furúghí was present, from start to finish, he kept people entranced by the recital of scriptures, the narration of the services and sufferings of early believers, and by relating something of his own life. (Sulaymání, *Maṣábiḥ-i-Hidáyat*, vol. 3, pp. 420–21)

Such a man was the son of Mullá Mírzá Muḥammad.

A Bahá'í of 'Ishqábád has recalled a particular occasion, a Friday evening, when believers had gathered in that part of the Mashriqu'l-Adhkár specified for meetings and a booklet had reached them from the Bahá'ís of the United States, conveying the news of fresh victories. One of the young men asked Mírzá Maḥmúd whether he might read from that booklet for all to hear. As the young man began reading, it was 'Alláhu-Abhá' that came first. Immediately Furúghí stopped him and, turning to the audience, said: 'Your brethren in America have greeted you. Let us make our response.' They all stood up, as Furúghí had done, and their voices rang out: 'Alláhu-Abhá'. They could be heard several streets away. Thus did the Bahá'ís of 'Ishqábád reciprocate, at Furúghí's bidding, the greetings sent them by American Bahá'ís.

Furúghí always paid particular attention to the welfare of the youth: not only their upbringing in the spirit of the Faith, but also their civilized behaviour. But he was never impatient, never autocratic. Kind and considerate, he led the youth gently to better manners, better understanding, better conduct. And he was exceedingly modest. Time and again he had been asked to write his autobiography. He would have had a rich tale to tell. What he considered important, however, was not the record of his own person, but the record of the victories of the Faith. It was only when he was assured that the Greatest Holy Leaf, with the approval of the Guardian of the Faith, was eager that he should write the story of his life, and he was given a note-book in Haifa to fill, that he took up his pen and wrote, regrettably not at length, but long enough to make the reader see the mettle and the true greatness of this dedicated Bahá'í. When, in his early youth, he went with a fellow-believer on his first teaching trip, visiting a number of localities in his native province of Khurásán, he presented an account of his journey to Bahá'u'lláh. In response a Tablet was revealed in his honour:

> Verily, We were with thee when thou didst journey away from home, and didst travel in the land to propagate the Cause of thy Lord, the Ruler of this world and the Kingdom. We heard thy call giving the Most Great Announcement, and thy words regarding this wronged Exile. (Quoted in ibid. p. 431)

Before long Furúghí's zeal and eloquence roused the fury of the divines of Dúghábád. Their clamour caused the Governor of the district, who was a grandson of Fatḥ-'Ali Sháh, to send Furúghí to Mashhad. From his prison-cell there, he managed secretly to send out a petition to Náṣiri'd-Dín Sháh. His appeal was so worded that it touched the heart of that cruel monarch who issued orders for the release of Furúghí. As it became known that Furúghí would be set free, the clerics of Mashhad began agitating. The Governor-General of Khurásán yielded to their demands and banished Furúghí to Kalát, a corner of Khurásán which has seen scores of exiles. Such were the qualities of Furúghí that the Governor of Kalát fell under his spell. And one day that benevolent man gave him the shattering news of the Ascension of Bahá'u'lláh. Furúghí was so grief-stricken that it seemed his senses would part from him. He began a three-day fast, breaking it each sunset with only a drink of water, and prayed throughout the night. On the fourth night, Bahá'u'lláh appeared in his dreams. The consolation which that dream imparted to Furúghí gave him new life.

Now, the Governor of Kalát asked him to occupy the pulpit every day, recite the sufferings of the House of Muḥammad, and give the people good advice in the ways of faith. Furúghí did as he was bidden. The power of his speech, once again, caused the clerics to league themselves in opposition to him. They took their case to the Governor-General of Khurásán, alleging that Mírzá Maḥmúd had robbed half of the inhabitants of Kalát of their true faith, had led them astray. The Governor-General, a weak man, was frightened, and ordered the good Governor of Kalát to send Furúghí away to Bájgírán, which was a frontier post. The Governor was naturally very annoyed, but Furúghí remained calm and composed and left the safety of Kalát with confidence. Bájgírán was close to 'Ishqábád, and the Bahá'ís of that renowned city came and took Furúghí away. He was a free man at last. That was his first journey outside his country.

After a short sojourn in 'Ishqábád, Furúghí went on to the Holy Land: his first pilgrimage. 'Abdu'l-Bahá took him to Bahjí, to the Shrine of Bahá'u'lláh. Furúghí, after many a month of tests and hardship, had found his paradise on earth. A few yards away from the Shrine stands the stately Mansion where Bahá'u'lláh lived and where He ascended to His Kingdom. And at this point of time, when Furúghí experienced the supreme thrill of lowering his brow on the threshold of the Shrine, in the presence of the beloved Master, there lived in the Mansion that infamous band of men and women who had the temerity to violate the Covenant of Bahá'u'lláh.* They had been conspiring for long to undermine the position of 'Abdu'l-Bahá. He,

* See Balyuzi, *'Abdu'l-Bahá*, chap. 5.

Mírzá Maḥmúd-i-Furúg͟hí (seated, left) *and S͟hayk͟h Muḥammad-'Alí* (right)*, both designated Apostles of Bahá'u'lláh*

the forgiving Master, had tried to protect them from the consequences of their devilish designs. The more assiduously He endeavoured to save them and protect them, the more blatant became their impertinence; until a time came when 'Abdu'l-Bahá, compelled by the demands of the trust reposed in Him, had to take measures to cleanse the Community of the Most Great Name of the poison which the violators of the Covenant were instilling into it. During this first pilgrimage of Furúghí still only a few of the Bahá'ís had come to know of the treachery of Mírzá Muḥammad-'Alí, the arch-breaker of the Covenant of Bahá'u'lláh. Furúghí, amazingly perspicacious, was one of them. The warning imparted by a tradition of Islám had found its verification in the spiritual susceptibilities of this very gifted man of Khurásán: 'Beware of the perspicacity of the believer, because he observes with the light of God.'

One day, a son of Mírzá Muḥammad-'Alí came in with a dish of tangerines and laid it before Furúghí. 'Sarkár-i-Áqá' (His Excellency the Master), he said, 'asks you to distribute this dish of fruit amongst the friends.' 'And who is Sarkár-i-Áqá?' Furúghí asked. 'Why, of course,' replied the son of Mírzá Muḥammad-'Alí, 'it is Áqáy-i-Ghuṣnu'lláhi'l-Akbar' (the Greater Branch, Mírzá Muḥammad-'Alí). Furúghí shook his head. 'No!' he exclaimed. 'The only Sarkár-i-Áqá is Haḍrat-i-Ghuṣnu'lláhi'l-A'ẓam' (the Most Great Branch).

Many years before, Mírzá Ḍíyá'u'lláh, a full brother of Mírzá Muḥammad-'Alí, had presented a request to Bahá'u'lláh on behalf of 'Áqá'. He was asked, 'Who is Áqá?' Mírzá Ḍíyá'u'lláh replied, 'Áqáy-i-Ghuṣn-i-Akbar'. And Bahá'u'lláh very sternly reminded him that there is only one 'Áqá' (one Master); others have names – but He who is totally 'Áqá' is 'Ghuṣn-i-A'zam' ('Abdu'l-Bahá).

Furúghí did not stop at telling the son of Mírzá Muḥammad-'Alí that there was only one 'Master'. He made it clear that anyone who broke the Covenant of Bahá'u'lláh and waxed proud before the Most Great Branch would forfeit any title or station he had. A branch which is dried only serves as fuel: no more, no less. And then he instructed the son of Mírzá Muḥammad-'Alí to take the dish of fruit away. But, it is related, because the Covenant-breakers had not, as yet, come into the open, Furúghí was apprehensive. Had he overstepped the mark and talked out of turn? It was not his, he pondered, to make public the defection of the members of the family of Bahá'u'lláh. But when he was once again in the presence of 'Abdu'l-Bahá, the smile of the beloved Master reassured him that all was well. On a table he saw a dish piled up with tangerines. 'Abdu'l-Bahá picked up one, peeled it Himself and offered it to Furúghí. He knew then that indeed he had acted rightly, that the beloved Master had approved what he had done.

Next, we find Furúghí in Cairo, where the matchless Mírzá Abu'l-Faḍl was, at that time, resident. At a large gathering of the Bahá'ís, Furúghí took up the theme of the Covenant and the necessity of

A gathering of Bahá'ís with Mírzá Abu'l-Faḍl in Cairo, April 1907 (seated, 3rd from right), *on the occasion of the pilgrimage to 'Akká of Thornton Chase, the first American Bahá'í* (seated next to him) *and Mr and Mrs Arthur S. Agnew* (seated across the table). *Also identified are Ḥájí Mírzá Níyáz, one of the early believers of Persia, loved by all, who lived many years in Cairo until his death in 1919* (seated at front, with white turban); *Ḥusayn Rúḥí, who owned and directed two schools in Cairo* (at table, centre foreground); *and Shaykh Muḥyiddín Sabrí Sanandají al-Kurdí* (standing, hatless, below the tree at left), *a disciple of Mírzá Abu'l-Faḍl and a well-known scholar and Bahá'í teacher invited by 'Abdu'l-Bahá to go to Tunisia and North Africa*

obedience, unreserved and unqualified, to Him Who was the Centre, the Pivot of the Covenant: the Most Great Branch. Once again Furúghí was very outspoken. Mírzá Abu'l-Faḍl intervened to ask Furúghí to exercise a measure of restraint. Furúghí retorted at once that in the field of oratory he had not become so unsaddled as to have to call out, 'O Abu'l-Faḍl! Rescue me.* Besides,' he continued, 'do you not know that the Master, in a Tablet with which He has honoured me, has said: "be a leader of this legion"?' As soon as Mírzá Abu'l-Faḍl heard this reference to the Tablet of 'Abdu'l-Bahá, he stood up, went close to Furúghí and said, 'I am the very first person to kiss the knee of this commander!' Furúghí, too, was immediately on his feet. Those two men, both truly great, embraced each other and kissed each other's cheeks. The union of the fidelity and constancy of these spiritual giants galvanized the faith of all who witnessed it. The shafts of hate and malice flung by the faithless could never pierce the armour thus forged.

The Egyptian journey over, Furúghí set out for home. His arrival at Ṭihrán caused a great stir. Bahá'ís gathered in their hundreds to hear him speak of the beloved Master, of His all-encompassing love, of the treachery of the Covenant-breakers, of the triumphs of the Covenant. The news of these gatherings reached the ears of Náyibu's-Salṭanih (Kámrán Mírzá, governor of Ṭihrán). And he was alarmed. Are the Bábís hatching a plot to seize power, was his immediate reaction, fantastic as it sounds! He set spies to find out who the newcomer was, and how many these 'Bábís' were. At one gathering, his minions counted nine hundred pairs of shoes shed outside the room. Then Náyibu's-Salṭanih ordered the detention of Mírzá Maḥmud. Officials went in search of him, discovered his house, and not finding him at home laid hold of his servant, a Bahá'í named Siyyid 'Alí, who readily confessed his faith and marshalled arguments to prove the truth of his beliefs. Náyibu's-Salṭanih listened to Siyyid 'Alí and then told him to go home and inform his master that Náyibu's-Salṭanih desired to meet him.

As soon as Furúghí received that message, he wrote a letter to the prince, intimating that he would keep a tryst the next day. He had no fear, although his fellow-believers thought that he would be walking into the lion's mouth. However, Furúghí could not be persuaded to

* Abu'l-Faḍl was the patronymic of 'Abbás, a brother of Ḥusayn, the third Imám, who suffered martyrdom with him at Karbilá. He is always invoked by the Shí'ites for help.

change his mind. Moreover, he had made a solemn promise which he could not, would not revoke. A man notorious for his wild ways had only recently embraced the Faith of Bahá'u'lláh, bidding farewell to his indulgences. His name was Abu'l-Qásim, his nickname Khammár (Vintner). Furúghí asked Khammár whether he would be prepared to hold the reins and lead his horse to the gates of the palace. Khammár was delighted and felt proud to serve Furúghí in that manner. But arriving at the prince's residence, Furúghí was informed that Náyibu's-Salṭanih was too busy to receive him that day; would he come on the morrow? The following day, once again, Náyibu's-Salṭanih was said to be much occupied.

It was on the third day that Furúghí was admitted to see the prince. Náyibu's-Salṭanih expressed astonishment at Furúghí's fearlessness. He had had full opportunity to take himself to a place of safety; instead he had kept his tryst. In a corner, away from others, a rug was spread for the two of them to sit and talk. Some lettuce and a bowl of syrup was brought to them for refreshment. A knife was there too for cutting the lettuce. At that moment the Prince referred to Bahá'u'lláh as Mírzá Ḥusayn-'Alí. Furúghí was greatly angered. Upbraiding the Prince for his display of irreverence, he asked for the knife. 'What do you want it for?' Náyibu's-Salṭanih remarked. 'To cut my throat, that you may drink my blood' was Furúghí's answer. 'It seems that your thirst has not been slaked; perchance, drinking my blood may give you satisfaction.' Seeing Furúghí thus enraged, Náyibu's-Salṭanih made an attempt to pacify him and asked, 'Tell me, what is your view of Him?' Furúghí replied: 'He [Bahá'u'lláh] lives on two planes; one is the human plane which is common to all; that is the plane alluded to in the Qur'án: "I am a human being like you, to whom Revelation comes."* Then there is the Divine plane, the plane of Lordship, which lies beyond human understanding. The Prophet [Muḥammad] has thus spoken of it: "For me, in relation to God, there are various stages: once He is I and I am He."'†

Next Náyibu's-Salṭanih put this question to Furúghí, 'I am told that you are convening many meetings; do you intend to cause mischief?' Furúghí knew that Náyibu's-Salṭanih would ask him something on those lines and was prepared. 'Your Royal Highness,' he said, 'our

* 18: 110.
† Paraphrase of an Islamic tradition on the authority of the Prophet, quoted in *Gleanings from the Writings of Bahá'u'lláh*, XXVII.

books are in your possession; you can easily verify what they teach. Moreover, our community is composed of all sorts of people. Within every community you find both good men and bad men. We hold our meetings to warn the wayward, to still uncontrolled passions, to help the people distinguish clearly that which is right from that which is wrong. These are our reasons for holding meetings, for bringing men together, and not to foment discontent and disorder. Holding these meetings is also to your advantage. In the early years of this Faith, some of its followers, because of their ignorance of the true purport of the teachings of the Báb, made an attempt on the life of the sovereign which led to great upheavals and suffering. That event was never repeated, because at our meetings we help the people to be on their guard and not to slip into negligence and waywardness.' Náyibu's-Salṭanih was greatly pleased to hear all this and replied to Furúghí: 'Now I am assured. I am satisfied and know that Bahá'ís mean no harm. Go, and hold your meetings. No one will try to stop you.'

As Furúghí came out of the orchard, he noticed Abu'l-Qásim, the vintner, disengaging himself from the shelter of a tree. Very astonished, he asked Abu'l-Qásim what he was doing there in the prince's orchard. Khammár replied that, knowing the precarious situation in which Furúghí had been placed, he had stealthily come into the orchard with a revolver, intending to use it were the prince found to have devilish designs. He definitely meant to shoot the prince. Now, he asked, in such a case would he have been forgiven, or would he only have added one more transgression to all the rest? Furúghí told him that it was a question not at all easy to answer, but at the earliest opportunity he would present it to 'Abdu'l-Bahá.

Time passed. One day, Áqá Jamál-i-Burújirdí, still ensconced within the ramparts of the Faith, made a remark which was obviously impertinent. He faulted 'Abdu'l-Bahá regarding an opinion which He had expressed. It so incensed Furúghí that he immediately jumped up and pulled the cushion on which Áqá Jamál was sitting away from him, saying, 'You have waxed so insolent as to match the perspicuous text with your puny understanding.'

Before long Furúghí returned to 'Ishqábád. In that city, now teeming with Bahá'ís, a young man had been guilty of an offence, and the believers asked Furúghí to teach him a lesson. So when this young man approached Furúghí he slapped him hard in the face. The offender realized immediately what that slapping was meant to convey. 'I am sincerely sorry' he said, 'and I regret what I have done.' The next day he brought a bag of silver and gave it to Furúghí, to give a Feast on his behalf when in the Holy Land.

When Furúghí found himself in the presence of 'Abdu'l-Bahá, he was moved to offer his life as a ransom, so grievous were the Master's sufferings at the hands of the Covenant-breakers. 'You wish to be relieved of this world and repair at the earliest to the presence of Bahá'u'lláh,' observed 'Abdu'l-Bahá. 'But, no, you must live. And the Covenant-breakers will soon receive their desserts.'

One day 'Abdu'l-Bahá pointed out to him a ship which was about to depart and worked out his itinerary for him. Then Furúghí, remembering all that he had missed or forgotten, the questions that he had not asked, felt at a loss, wondering what he could do. As he was pondering the matter, 'Abdu'l-Bahá got up to walk away and told Furúghí to follow Him. When He had gone a little way ahead, He turned to Furúghí and said, 'There is little time left. Tell me, what did you say to Abu'l-Qásim-i-Khammár, outside the Amíríyyih garden?' Furúghí was taken aback and tried to explain it implicitly, but 'Abdu'l-Bahá said, 'Tell me in your own words'. Furúghí replied, 'I made it all dependent on the bounty of the Master.' Then 'Abdu'l-Bahá replied: 'Do you not know your Qur'án? Is it not written there that "Good deeds blot out misdeeds?"* Give him my greetings and tell him that his transgressions committed previously are forgiven, but leave those ways alone in future.'

Next, 'Abdu'l-Bahá asked him what he had done to Jamál-i-Burújirdí. Furúghí said that because he matched the text with his own verdict, 'I pulled away the cushion on which he was sitting'. 'The Blessed Perfection inspired you to do what you did,' 'Abdu'l-Bahá said. 'He has joined the Covenant-breakers. Tell the friends to beware of him and not to be beguiled by him.'

Then 'Abdu'l-Bahá asked him, 'What did you do to that young man in 'Ishqábád?' Furúghí replied: 'I punished him in front of the people.' 'What you did was wrong,' said 'Abdu'l-Bahá.

* * * * * * * * * *

'This type of person should be chastised in private. But God has forgiven both your wrong and his.'

Furúghí returned to Írán by the route that 'Abdu'l-Bahá had

* An Arabic proverb.

indicated, visiting a number of towns and encouraging the believers. In Ṭihrán, he delivered 'Abdu'l-Bahá's reply to the overjoyed Abu'l-Qásim-i-Khammár. Then a few years later he returned to the Holy Land. Here 'Abdu'l-Bahá indicated to him that he would be beaten and persecuted for the sake of the Faith; He also foretold the assassination of Náṣiri'd-Dín Sháh, instructing Furúghí to warn the believers in Írán to be on their guard. And so it occurred.

On the way back, Furúghí visited the Bahá'ís of Ábádih. While there he was set upon by an angry mob and severely beaten. He only just escaped death in that town. Later in Ṭihrán, Náṣiri'd-Dín Sháh died at the hand of one of the disciples of Siyyid Jamálu'd-Dín-i-Afghání, and although there was an attempt to lay the blame at the door of the Bahá'ís this was thwarted. It was shortly after this that Furúghí was given an opportunity of meeting the new Sháh, Muẓaffari'd-Dín, and of apprising him of the tenets of the Faith of Bahá'u'lláh in such a manner that the Sháh was induced to look favourably upon it.

At this time Furúghí fell ill and a physician pronounced his case to be beyond hope. But undaunted, Furúghí asked permission to go to the Holy Land. Although very ill by the time he arrived there, he was brought back to complete health by 'Abdu'l-Bahá's ministrations. He returned to Ṭihrán and went from there to Yazd in order to answer a challenge by the mujtahid Siyyid 'Alíy-i-Háyirí to an open debate. But on Furúghí's arrival, Háyirí pleaded ill-health and would not come forward.*

From Yazd, Furúghí proceeded to Khurásán and his home village of Dúghábád. He had been there but a short while when he was set upon by a mob, beaten and forced to leave the village. He retired to 'Ishqábád for a time before returning to Mashhad. It was in Mashhad in October 1910 that two men attempted to assassinate Furúghí. But although they discharged their pistols at his chest at close range, Furúghí survived this attack. He returned to Dúghábád for a short time before setting out once more for 'Ishqábád and Egypt where 'Abdu'l-Bahá was at that time resident, following His strenuous travels in Europe and America. Furúghí was sent to Haifa to announce 'Abdu'l-Bahá's return in December 1913 after an absence of more than three years from the Holy Land.

* It should be noted that although there were frequent persecutions of the Bahá'ís in Yazd at this time, Háyirí never participated in these.

On his return to Írán, Furúghí again survived an attempted assassination in Mashhad and retired to Dúghábád where he was frequently under attack from the enemies of the Faith. His last pilgrimage to Haifa was in the time of Shoghi Effendi, and it was shortly after his return to Dúghábád that he was invited to a feast by one who pretended to be his friend, but who administered poison to him during the meal. The poison caused a severe illness that Furúghí's advanced age could not withstand. Within a short while he passed away, in AH 1346 (AD 1 July 1927–19 June 1928).

14

Ibn-i-Aṣdaq

MÍRZÁ ʿALÍ-MUḤAMMAD, known as Ibn-i-Aṣdaq, whom the Exalted
Pen (Baháʾuʾlláh) addressed as <u>Sh</u>ahíd Ibn-i-<u>Sh</u>ahíd (Martyr, son of
the Martyr), was the distinguished son of that great veteran of the
Bábí Faith, Mullá Ṣádiq-i-Muqaddas-i-<u>Kh</u>urásání, who, haltered and
in the company of the incomparable Quddús was paraded in the
streets of <u>Sh</u>íráz; fought on the battlements of <u>Sh</u>ay<u>kh</u> Ṭabarsí under
the banner of Quddús, and came safely through the holocaust;
attained the Day of 'Him Whom God shall make manifest', gave Him
his whole-hearted allegiance, served Him with exemplary devotion,
and was honoured by Him with the designation of Ismuʾlláhuʾl-
Aṣdaq. (See p. 7.)

Ibn-i-Aṣdaq was the son of such a father. He was a boy of tender
years when, together with his saintly father, he was consigned to the
dungeon of Ṭihrán. And he was still in his teens when, in the company
of his father, he travelled to Ba<u>gh</u>dád, and into the presence of
Baháʾuʾlláh. Not only did he have that supreme bounty, but the Most
Exalted Pen moved to reveal a prayer for him, in which we read these
very significant words: 'I ask Thee, O my God! to give him to drink of
the milk of Thy bounty so that he may raise the standards of victory
through Me, – a victory which is Thine – and arise to serve Thy Cause,
when he groweth up, just as, when a youth, he hath arisen at Thy
Command.' (Unpublished)

Indeed, Baháʾuʾlláh chose the son of Ismuʾlláhuʾl-Aṣdaq to be a
promoter of His Cause, a faithful servant at His threshold, when that
future Hand of the Cause of God was still a child. And he was still a
child when the hands of the ungodly brought lashes to bear on his
flesh.

Ibn-i-Aṣdaq craved martyrdom in the path of his Lord. In the Most
Great Prison ('Akká) he attained once again the presence of
Baháʾuʾlláh. 'We testify that thou didst enter the prison, that thou

didst present thyself and didst stand at the door, and thou didst hear the words of this Wronged One by Whom all lamps are ignited.' (Unpublished) Thus again the Most Exalted Pen moved to address him. Then he supplicated Bahá'u'lláh to grant him the station of martyrdom. In January 1880 his supplication was answered.

Thou didst beg the Supreme Lord . . . to bestow upon thee a station whereat in the path of His love thou wouldst give up everything: thy life, thy spirit, thy reputation, thine existence, all in all. All of these behests were submitted in the most sanctified, most exalted Presence of the Abhá Beauty. Thus did the Tongue of the Merciful speak in the Kingdom of Utterance: 'God willing, he shall be seen in utmost purity and saintliness, as befitteth the Day of God, and attain the station of the most great martyrdom. Today, the greatest of all deeds is service to the Cause. Souls that are well assured should with utmost discretion teach the Faith, so that the sweet fragrances of the Divine Garment will waft from all directions. This martyrdom is not confined to the destruction of life and the shedding of blood. A person enjoying the bounty of life may yet be recorded a martyr in the Book of the Sovereign Lord. Well is it with thee that thou hast wished to offer whatsoever is thine, and all that is of thee and with thee in My path.' (Bahá'u'lláh, through His amanuensis, Mírzá Áqá Ján; unpublished)

Mírzá 'Alí-Muḥammad, known as Ibn-i-Aṣdaq, one of the four Hands of the Cause of God appointed by Bahá'u'lláh

Later, we find Mírzá Áqá Ján writing again on the same theme, bringing to Ibn-i-Aṣdaq the life-imparting words of Bahá'u'lláh:

What thou hadst written regarding martyrdom in the path of God, was presented and He spoke thus, supreme is His Power: 'We, verily, have ordained for him this exalted station, this high designation. Well it is with him that he attained this station prior to its appearance, and We accepted from him that which he intended in the path of God, the One, the Single, the All-Knowing, the All-Informed.' (Unpublished)

In such manner was Ibn-i-Aṣdaq honoured with the designation Shahíd Ibn-i-Shahíd in the year 1882.

It was then that Ibn-i-Aṣdaq took to the road, moving from town to town, city to city, visiting large centres of population as well as rural areas, teaching with all his ardour the Faith of his Lord, in the path of which he had begged for martyrdom. 'The movement itself from place to place,' the Most Exalted Pen instructed him, 'when undertaken for the sake of God, hath always exerted, and can now exert, its influence in the world. In the Books of old the station of them that have voyaged far and near in order to guide the servants of God hath been set forth and written down.' (Quoted in Shoghi Effendi, *The Advent of Divine Justice*, pp. 70–71)

The first time in the Writings of Bahá'u'lláh that we encounter the mention and concept of Hand of the Cause of God is within a Tablet which He revealed through His amanuensis in honour of Ibn-i-Aṣdaq, dated April 1887. 'This evanescent Khádim [Mírzá Áqá Ján was called Khádimu'lláh: Servant of God] beseecheth the All-Abiding Lord to confirm the chosen ones, that is those souls who are Hands of the Cause, who are adorned with the robe of teaching, and have arisen to serve the Cause, to be enabled to exalt the Word of God.' (Unpublished)

Ibn-i-Aṣdaq's marriage brought him close to men of high rank, associated with royalty. His wife, 'Udhrá Khánum, entitled Ḍíyáu'l-Ḥájíyyih, was a great-granddaughter of Muḥammad Sháh. A sister of the wife of Ibn-i-Aṣdaq was married to Intiẓámu's-Salṭanih, who had entrée in the circles of the nobility, and had already become a stalwart Bahá'í. Ibn-i-Aṣdaq's marriage took place in Khurásán, the ancestral home of his father, Ismu'lláhu'l-Aṣdaq; and when the newly-married couple moved to Ṭihrán, they found a home made ready for them by Intiẓámu's-Salṭanih and his wife, in one of the best residential quarters of the capital.

Ibn-i-Aṣdaq

Ibn-i-Aṣdaq was thus well placed, well prepared and well equipped to meet and talk with people who had a hand in guiding the destinies of the nation: royalty, nobility, priesthood, men of letters, devotees of learning. It is related that Ibn-i-Aṣdaq himself referred time and again to 'hunting the lion rather than the fox'. 'Abdu'l-Bahá, in later years, directed him, in particular, to stay with the course he had taken: give the message of Bahá'u'lláh to those who were at the helm. Whilst holding converse with the prominent men in the capital, Ibn-i-Aṣdaq was also undertaking journeys far and wide to teach the Faith. His travels were not confined to Persia. He visited India and Russian Turkistán wherein 'Ishqábád was situated. In the historical city of Marv, Ibn-i-Aṣdaq began preliminary work for the construction of a Mashriqu'l-Adhkár; the land for the temple was donated by the government, and an architectural plan was drawn up which was sent to the Holy Land. Moreover, he founded a hospice and a junior school in Marv.

In India, Ibn-i-Aṣdaq visited Bombay, Lahore and Delhi. In Burma, he visited Rangoon and Mandalay, and everywhere he met and talked with men occupying positions of responsibility. At home Ibn-i-Aṣdaq pioneered the establishment of teaching classes for the Bahá'í women of Ṭihrán.

* * * * * * * * * *

The years immediately following the passing of Bahá'u'lláh were difficult years for the Bahá'í community. The breakers of Bahá'u'lláh's Covenant were active in Írán, spreading their claims and causing agitation and bewilderment. Ibn-i-Aṣdaq, in conjunction with the other Hands of the Cause, countered the activities of the enemies of the Faith, travelling throughout Persia to explain to the believers the Covenant of Bahá'u'lláh and confirm them in it. 'Abdu'l-Bahá instructed the Hands of the Cause to establish in Ṭihrán a Spiritual Assembly to administer the affairs of the Faith. The Hands of the Cause were appointed permanent members of this body that

*The Consulting Assembly of Ṭihrán, 1899, established at the behest of 'Abdu'l-Bahá, which eventually became the National Spiritual Assembly of the Bahá'ís of Írán. Members shown are (*front row, left to right*) Ḥájí Mírzá 'Abdu'lláh-i-Ṣaḥíḥ-Furú<u>sh</u>, Mírzá 'Azízu'lláh <u>Kh</u>án Varqá, Mírzá Zakaríyyá; (*second row, from left*) Dr Ásifu'l-Ḥukamá', the Hand of the Cause Mírzá Muḥammad-Ḥasan, known as Adíb, the Hand of the Cause Mírzá 'Alí-Muḥammad, known as Ibn-i-Aṣdaq, the Hand of the Cause Ḥájí Mullá 'Alí-Akbar-i-<u>Sh</u>ahmírzádí, known as Ḥájí Á<u>kh</u>únd, Ḥájí Mírzá Muḥammad-i-Afnán, Mírzá Síyáva<u>sh</u>; (*back row, from left*) *Mírzá Muḥammad <u>Kh</u>án Ja<u>dh</u>bih and Áqá Muḥammad-Ḥusayn-i-Ká<u>sh</u>í*

eventually evolved to become the National Spiritual Assembly of the Bahá'ís of Írán.

Ibn-i-Aṣdaq was the instrument whereby 'Abdu'l-Bahá's Treatise on Politics (*Risáliy-i-Siyásíyyih*) was presented to the Sháh and distributed among the notables of Írán. 'Abdu'l-Bahá also made him responsible, with Aḥmad Yazdání, for delivering in person the Tablet addressed to the Central Organization for a Durable Peace at the Hague, in 1919.

Ibn-i-Aṣdaq was fortunate to be in the presence of 'Abdu'l-Bahá on several occasions as a pilgrim. On the last of his pilgrimages, he was in Haifa for some thirty months and left shortly before 'Abdu'l-Bahá's ascension.

Back in Írán, Ibn-i-Aṣdaq continued to travel and serve the Faith until his death in 1928 in Ṭihrán.

15

The Honest Merchant of Mashhad

ÁQÁ 'AZÍZU'LLÁH-I-JADHDHÁB, the merchant, whose honesty so surprised Mírzá 'Alí-Aṣghar Khán, the Amínu's-Sulṭán, as to declare him to be an angel, came from the Jewish fold. (See p. 55.)

Mashhad is a holy city and it had had a sizeable Jewish population. They suffered considerably at the hands of unruly fanatics. As happened in Europe in medieval times, when Jews were forced to renounce their faith although many of them whilst ostensibly professing Christianity kept to their old allegiance, so it happened in Mashhad in recent times. Let Lord Curzon tell us what occurred in Mashhad, during the reign of Muḥammad Sháh:

There still exists a considerable number of Jewish families in Meshed, although the practice of their own worship is strictly forbidden, and is only pursued in secret. The story of their enforced conversion to Moḥammedanism* in the year 1838 is well known, and has been repeated by more than one traveller. Dr. Wolff,† who was twice at Meshed, both before and after the incident, described it in these terms:

The occasion was as follows: A poor woman had a sore hand. A Mussulman [Muslim] physician advised her to kill a dog and put her hand in the blood of it. She did so; when suddenly the whole population rose and said that they had done it in derision of their prophet. Thirty-five Jews were killed in a few minutes; the rest, struck with terror, became Mohammedans. They are now more zealous Jews in secret than ever, but call themselves *Anusim*, the Compelled Ones. [*Narrative of Mission to Bokhara* in 1843–1845, vol. i p. 239, and vol. ii p. 72]

Wolff does not add – what is necessary to explain the sudden outburst – that the incidents of the Jewess and the slaughtered dog unfortunately occurred on the very day when the Mohammedans were celebrating the annual Feast of Sacrifice.‡ Superstition and malice very easily aggravated an innocent act into a deliberate insult to the national faith; and hence the

* It is both incorrect and insulting to speak of Islám as Mohammedanism. Fortunately the use of that designation has been largely abandoned. (HMB)

† Dr Joseph Wolff (father of the British diplomat, Sir Henry Drummond-Wolff) himself came from the Jewish fold but had converted to Christianity. He was highly polemical. (HMB)

‡ The tenth day of Dhu'l-Ḥijjah: 'Íd al-Aḍḥá or 'Íd-i-Qurbán. (HMB)

> outbreak that ensued. There is much less fanaticism now than in those days; but it still behoves a Yehudi [Yahúdí], or Jew, to conduct himself circumspectly and to walk with a modest air in Meshed. (*Persia and the Persian Question*, vol. 1, pp. 165–6)

It must also be added that the poor Jewess could not bring herself to slaughter the stray dog they had cornered. A Muslim was asked to do it for her, and it was this man, perhaps out of fear, who dashed about shouting that the Jews were guilty of insolence and deliberate affront, offering for sacrifice a dog on the day when sheep or camels are sacrificed in memory of the act of Abraham. Whatever the case, the Jews of Mashhad, dwelling in the quarter of the city called the 'Ídgáh, paid heavily in human lives on that tenth day of Dhu'l-Ḥijjah. Some fifty of them suffered death, their synagogue was demolished, their Torahs consigned to the fire. It is reported that only one Torah remained; it had been secreted in a safe place. Then, as that forcible conversion took shape, the holy city came to have a *Jadíd-Khánih* (New House): the quarter of the *Jadídu'l-Islám* (newly converted to Islám).

Of course it is impossible to say how many of those repressed Jews genuinely became Muslims and how many remained attached to their old faith. But there was one Jew in Mashhad of whose true allegiance we have ample evidence; he was Mullá Ḥizqíl (Ezekiel), known as Námdár, the father of Áqá 'Azízu'lláh. Mullá Ḥizqíl was a merchant, but he was also very learned, and held classes to teach his pupils the Torah, the Talmud and other religious works. Even more, he had a copy of the *Mathnaví* of Jaláli'd-Dín-i-Rúmí, written in Hebrew characters, from which he taught his favourite pupils. Some twelve years prior to that episode of forcible conversion, Mullá Ḥizqíl invited Mírzá 'Askarí, an eminent Muslim divine of Mashhad whom he knew personally, to give him the word of testifying to utter. He told Mírzá 'Askarí that studying Torah and other holy scriptures had convinced him of the truth of Islám. So, years before the tumult of 1838, Mullá Ḥizqíl had, of his own accord, become a Muslim, but no one in his family other than his wife, and certainly none of his pupils, knew of it. Then one day, when engaged in reading from Rúmí's *Mathnaví*, he turned to his eldest son and said: 'Shamúyíl [Samuel]! Holy scriptures indicate that today is the day of the Advent of that greatest Manifestation of Yahweh [Jehovah], Who is the Redeemer of all. I shall be leaving this world, but beware lest you all remain heedless.'

Áqá 'Azízu'lláh was two years old when his father died, and under his mother's care he grew up mindful of his religious duties. However, when he was eight years of age, and attending a Muslim school in their quarter, one day a boy tried to cheat him, not giving back to him some of his writing materials which he had purloined. Another boy intervened and ordered the cheat: 'Give it back to him; these people are still Jewish.' Áqá 'Azízu'lláh, not being cognizant of his own origins, was terribly hurt; he told his mother, 'I will never go again to that place for my lessons; today, a boy insulted me and called me "Yahúdí" [Jewish].' His mother explained their situation to him, of which the boy had been totally ignorant, and it revolted him. At that early age, he decided to revert to the Faith of his forefathers. His mother had said to him: 'Being Yahúdí meant that we are descendants of Yahúdá, the son of Jacob. We have been forcibly converted to Islám; but your own father had, years before that forced conversion, by his own free will come into the Islamic fold. During that awful night of massacre and murder, at the instance of Mírzá 'Askarí, who himself had given your father the word of *Shahádat* [testifying] to utter, we were all taken to the house of Áqá Rajab, who was called Rajab Bahádur. We ourselves remained safe, but all that we possessed was pillaged.' Horrified, Áqá 'Azízu'lláh ceased going to that Muslim school for his lessons, and at a tender age started trading. And he became a master in his work.

Now, the divines of Mashhad had appointed one among themselves to keep a close watch over the Jadíd-Khánih. All the Jadíds, even old ones over seventy, were expected to attend congregational prayers, and no kosher meat was allowed. Despite all these pressures Áqá 'Azízu'lláh was determined to take up the Jewish Faith. He asked a cousin to teach him the Torah in secrecy, and he never left his home on a Saturday to avoid setting his eyes on the face of a Muslim on the Sabbath.

Thus the matter stood with Áqá 'Azízu'lláh until the martyrdom of Badí', who was a youth of Khurásán. Áqá 'Azízu'lláh had a half-brother named Áqá Sháhvirdí, who had already, unbeknown to all, embraced the Faith of Bahá'u'lláh. One day Áqá Sháhvirdí came to speak of the courage of that youth and of his glorious martyrdom. It was the first time that Áqá 'Azízu'lláh had heard the name 'Bahá'í' and wanted to know more, but his brother, well aware of fanaticism all around him, was very circumspect and kept silent. Two other brothers of Áqá 'Azízu'lláh, named Áqá Asadu'lláh and Áqá Raḥmatu'lláh, resided and traded in the town of Turbat-i-Ḥaydarí, whilst he and Áqá Sháhvirdí lived in Mashhad. Áqá 'Azízu'lláh's merchandise consisted mainly of goods in silk and most of his customers were Turkamáns who frequented Mashhad in search of trade.

One day in the year AH 1291 (18 February 1874–6 February 1875), when Áqá 'Azízulláh was newly married, Áqá Sháhvirdí came to him with a proposal: 'I have a very large quantity of damask, the price has fallen by two-thirds in Mashhad, and more than that there is no ready cash; if I sell it will have to be against future payment. But I am told that the market for this fabric is very good at Bádkúbih. Should I go there alone and die on the way all will be lost. Would you accompany me for a month to put this deal through?' Ties of kinship were too strong and Áqá 'Azízu'lláh could not refuse his brother's request. He gave the charge of his own trading-house to Áqá Yúsuf, one of the Jadíds of Mashhad, and the two brothers set out for the Caucasus. When they reached Níshápúr, Bahá'ís, such as Shaykh Muḥammad-i-Ma'múrí (uncle of the martyr, Shaykh Aḥmad-i-Khurásání) and Shaykh Muṣṭafá, came to visit Áqá Sháhvirdí. By then, Áqá 'Azízu'lláh was certain that his brother had become a follower of the new Faith, but, although much disturbed, he kept his peace. In every town and city they passed through, there were Bahá'ís whom Áqá Sháhvirdí wished to meet and so he did: in Sabzivár there was Ḥájí Muḥammad-Riḍá (martyred some years later in 'Ishqábád); in Kúshkbágh lived Mullá Muḥammad-i-Kúshkbághí; in Sháhrúd, Mullá Ghulám-Riḍáy-i-Hirátí; in Bádkúbih itself (their destination), Mírzá 'Abdu'l-Mu'min and Mullá Abú-Ṭálib; in Shirván, Karbilá'í Ismá'íl and the family of Samadov. But everywhere Áqá Sháhvirdí would ask the Bahá'ís not to speak to his brother of their Faith. 'He is a zealot for our old Faith,' Áqá Sháhvirdí would tell them, 'and he will not listen to you.' For his part Áqá 'Azízu'lláh kept silent, and in the homes of his brother's co-religionists would not touch their cooked food, taking only cups of tea and boiled eggs offered to him. Thus the two brothers went about in Caucasia. Bádkúbih did not provide, after all, a good and profitable market for damask, and Áqá Sháhvirdí thought that he should try their luck in Tiflís (Tbilisi). He went there by himself, leaving Áqá 'Azízu'lláh behind in the town of Shakí, with most of their merchandise. The peregrinations of the two brothers in the Caucasus had taken several months and nowhere had they been able to dispose of their goods profitably.

Áqá 'Azízu'lláh then decided to go on alone to the renowned and historic city of Gandzha (now Kirovabad) where there were better prospects. Taking his seat in a four-horse carriage (with his goods) at Shakí, Áqá 'Azízu'lláh was put on the alert by the looks of his fellow-passengers. Had it not been for his sagacity, he would not have lived to see another day. Although he had learned some Turkish, he pretended to have no knowledge at all of that language, and thus, listening to the cartman and the other passengers talking in Turkish, he realized that they were plotting to murder him and steal his goods. Reaching Gandzha, he sought out Mashhadí Muḥammad-Ja'far, the rentier of a well-known caravanserai of that city, to whom he had a letter of introduction from Ḥájí 'Alí-Akbar, a Persian merchant of Shakí. Through his host he was rescued from the clutches of the villainous cartman and his passengers. But being on his own in Gandzha, he apparently did not take full advantage of the favourable market. Later, it was seen that a temporary situation created by a Christian festival had limited his sales.

From Caucasia, the two brothers made their way to Istanbul. It took them fourteen months in the Ottoman capital to sell all their silken goods. Áqá 'Azízu'lláh, who had abandoned his schooling at an early age, was most anxious to improve his knowledge. During those months of travelling he brought his mind to it, and being well endowed with a high intellect, he made rapid progress. His brother, Áqá Sháhvirdí, had a case with him which contained books and papers. These he would take out, from time to time, and peruse. This had not

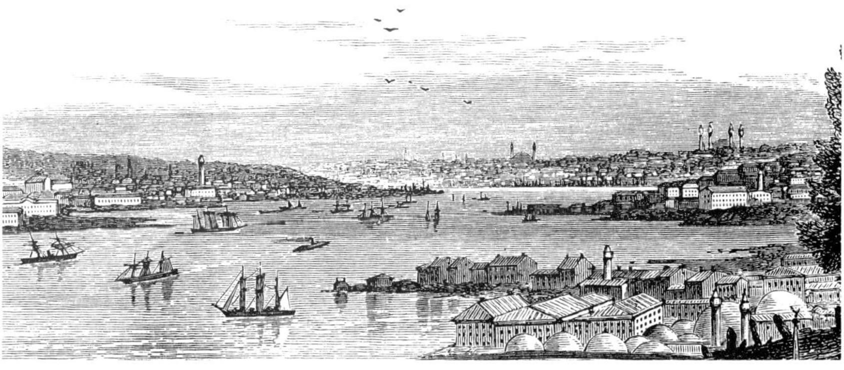

A view of Istanbul, the Golden Horn, in the late nineteenth century

escaped Áqá 'Azízu'lláh's notice. One day, when Áqá S͟háhvirdí had gone to the bazar, Áqá 'Azízu'lláh opened that case and came upon writings which he realized appertained to the Bahá'í Faith, and they appealed to him, although he could not fully understand them. Then he had a dream. Let him recount it in his own words:

In my dream I saw it announced that it was the day of the Advent of Yahveh of the Torah, the Promise of all the Scriptures: God watching the march past of all the Prophets and their adherents, examining their deeds and achievements. I went immediately to the direction indicated, and I saw a vast plain. As far as the eye could see people were ranged, rank upon rank. Every Prophet with His followers was seated facing the Qiblih. I marvelled how my eyes were empowered to see them all. Facing all these ranks and ranges of people, a Blessed Being was seated on a two-tiered chair, speaking. I was standing at the end of these ranks and ranges. That Blessed Being was more than fifty years of age, and had a long, black beard and a green *táj* on His head, made of green silk. He beckoned to me with His hand to go to His presence. With both hands I pointed to the people, meaning to say, how could I get through? He beckoned with His blessed hands to all those ranks of people, and they, one and all, prostrated themselves. Then, once again, He beckoned to me to come. I was hesitant, lest He was summoning someone else. Then, when He beckoned a third time, I started to move, walking over the people who were prostrated, one foot on a back, another on a head, until I reached Him, threw myself at His feet and kissed them. He raised me with His blessed hand and said: 'Praise be to God, the best of all creators'.

This dream had a profound effect on Áqá 'Azízu'lláh, but he still remained rooted in his previous beliefs, until he and his brother reached Istanbul and lodged in K͟hán-i-Yúsufíyán. Whilst there Ḥájí 'Abdu'l-Majíd-i-Nís͟hápúrí, the father of the glorious Badí', and a sister of Áqá Ḥusayn-i-Ás͟hchí also arrived at the Turkish metropolis and took lodgings in the same inn. One day, when his brother was absent, Áqá 'Azízu'lláh sat down with Abá-Badí' (the Father of Badí') to talk of the Bahá'í Faith and he opened his heart to him. And soon whatever doubts he had were dispelled. There and then he gave his total, unhedged allegiance to Bahá'u'lláh, Whose Cause he served with distinction to the end of his days. Áqá 'Azízu'lláh said that he thanked God for the long delay in selling their merchandise. That delay had kept them in Istanbul and had made possible the encounter leading him to Truth.

Ḥájí 'Abdu'l-Majíd was on his way to the Holy Land. Áqá 'Azízu'lláh requested him not to inform Áqá S͟háhvirdí, but to mention him in the presence of Bahá'u'lláh and beg for His bounties.

On his return, Ḥájí 'Abdu'l-Majíd brought a Tablet addressed to Áqá 'Azízu'lláh and permission for the two brothers to go to 'Akká. When later the hand of the implacable enemy seized Abá-Badí' and he too drank his fill of the same cup which his son had so heroically quaffed, it was the destiny of Áqá 'Azízu'lláh to give the remains of that stalwart veteran of the Faith a suitable burial.

Before the two brothers departed from Istanbul they heard the commotion which preceded the deposition of Sulṭán 'Abdu'l-'Azíz, saw the tumult in the Ottoman metropolis, and heard the news of the overthrow of 'Abdu'l-'Azíz and of his death a few days later. Ḥájí 'Abdu'l-Majíd had told them that these events would come to pass, as Bahá'u'lláh had presaged them. Áqá 'Azízu'lláh, young as he was and elated as he was by his newly-found faith and the news of the permission to go to the presence of Bahá'u'lláh, did not at first notice that he had badly injured his hand while using a knife. The night when Istanbul was thrown into disarray, the injured hand was so troubling him that he could not sleep. Awake and tossing in his bed, he noticed that the military were on the move, and the warships in the straits had all their lights on. And as dawn came cannons roared: 'Abdu'l-'Azíz, the Sulṭán who had decreed the banishment of Bahá'u'lláh, had fallen. That was the first intimation which Áqá 'Azízu'lláh had of the might of the Revelation of Bahá'u'lláh. And when he attained the presence of Bahá'u'lláh, he went down on his knees to kiss His feet. Bahá'u'lláh raised him up and said: 'Praise be to God, the best of all creators' – the very words which Áqá 'Azízu'lláh had heard in his dream. As he looked up, he saw that Bahá'u'lláh was wearing a green *táj*. That too he had seen in his dream.

Áqá 'Azízu'lláh had unreservedly embraced the Bahá'í Faith, but still certain likes and dislikes of the past persisted. He could not help preferring kosher meat. On the first day of his arrival at 'Akká, Ḥájí 'Alíy-i-Málmírí took him to the market-place and pointed out a butcher's shop to him. Bahá'u'lláh had instructed Ḥájí 'Alí to show Áqá 'Azízu'lláh the shop where he could obtain the kind of meat he still preferred. Áqá 'Azízu'lláh bowed his head in wonderment. While in 'Akká he came to realize, even more than before, his disadvantage because of his neglect of his education in childhood. Appealing to a fellow-believer to teach him some Arabic every day, he found that a start was made with instruction in rudiments of Arabic grammar, which further dismayed him. And he longed for that knowledge of

Arabic which would enable him to understand what flowed from the Most Exalted Pen. He prayed for that knowledge, particularly on those evenings when, admitted to the presence of Bahá'u'lláh, he would have the superb honour of hearing Him dictate His verses to Mírzá Áqá Ján. Later on, in Cairo, he discovered to his own astonishment that he had gained that knowledge.

At last, back in Mashhad after a long absence, Áqá 'Azízu'lláh, because of his fervour and his total dedication to his newly-found Faith, became a cynosure and widely known as a 'Bábí'. He was most generous and hospitable. Bahá'ís from far and wide frequented his home. Then, through a mishap, a Tablet revealed by Bahá'u'lláh in honour of a Bahá'í of Mashhad fell into the hands of this Bahá'í's namesake. The incident led to unrest. Áqá 'Azízu'lláh's relatives, particularly some of his nephews, fearing an assault on their homes, took precipitate action to forestall any untoward event. They seized him, tied his hands and urged him to recant, which he refused to do despite the persistence of their urging and pleading. At this juncture, Mírzá Áqá Ján Mihdízádih, one of the favourite pupils of Áqá 'Azízu'lláh's father, recalled what that sage had said regarding the Advent of that Supreme Manifestation of God Who is the Redeemer of all. Thus reminded, the relatives of Áqá 'Azízu'lláh released him, set about investigating and finally did as he had done: they ranged themselves under the standard of the Faith of Bahá'u'lláh.

However, a number of the Jadíds, moved by fear and jealousy, drew up a statement to the effect that Áqá 'Azízu'lláh was now similar to gangrene at the heart of the Jadíd-Khánih and his baneful influence would, ere long, totally destroy its life. That malicious statement was presented to the elders, who, together with Karbilá'í Muḥammad-Ṣafí, the man placed at the head of Jadíd-Khánih by the government, went up to the trading-house of Áqá 'Azízu'lláh in the caravanserai of Náṣiríyyih. They ordered him to accompany them to the house of a divine and publicly recant. Should he not do so, he was told, they would hand him over to the authorities to deal with and punish as it pleased them. Áqá 'Azízu'lláh retorted that he would gladly accompany them to the presence of the divines, but then he would tell the clergy that these Jadíds, who more than forty years before were forced to profess Islám, had remained Jewish, both in their beliefs and in their practices, whereas he, by embracing the Faith of Bahá'u'lláh, had truly recognized the station of the Prophet, and had come to accept the Qur'án as a holy Book descended from God. Those hypocrites saw that should they persist in persecuting Áqá 'Azízu'lláh, they themselves would be the losers, and crestfallen they departed and took with them the Head of the Jadíd-Khánih. Henceforth, Áqá 'Azízu'lláh began to teach openly and soon the number of Bahá'ís in the Jadíd-Khánih rapidly increased. Some sixty men enlisted in the community of the Most Great Name, as did the wives and children of most of them. 'The Most Exalted Pen addressed them as the children of Khalíl [The Friend, Abraham] and the heirs of Kalím [The Interlocutor, Moses].' (Unpublished Tablet by Bahá'u'lláh)

Áqá 'Azízu'lláh, (whom we shall henceforth sometimes call Jadhdháb, as this was the surname which he adopted in later years), now went travelling about in pursuit of his trading activities. 'Ishqábád (which had a large Bahá'í community) he visited many a time, he traded in Bukhárá long enough for the Amír of that once noble city of Transoxania to give him a passport, he went as far as Táshkand (Tashkent) and stayed there for a while. Marv was another historic city where he lived and traded. Wherever he was, he served the Cause of Bahá'u'lláh and the interests of his fellow-believers assiduously and meritoriously. On his third visit to the Holy Land, in the year AH 1308 (17 August 1890–6 August 1891), Bahá'u'lláh entrusted to him a particular task to carry out in Istanbul. (See *Bahá'u'lláh, The King of Glory*, pp. 399–401.) It was a delicate task, requiring firmness and sagacity. Jadhdháb performed it superbly, to the total discomfiture of the Azalís of Istanbul. He corresponded with Edward Granville Browne and even more significantly with Tolstoy. In his *Materials for the Study of the Bábí Religion* (p. 237), Professor Browne lists three letters which he had received 'From 'Azízu'lláh, a Bahá'í Jew of Bukhárá. (1) May 24, 1892. (2) May 25, 1892. (3) June 24, 1892.' It was from Jadhdháb that Edward Browne learned of the authorship of *A Traveller's Narrative*. In a letter dated 21 May 1892, written from Shíráz, the father of the present writer told Edward Browne: 'The other day a man called Agha Azizullah of Bukhara called on me and asked for your address saying he wanted to communicate with you about some important matter – I hope I haven't done wrong in complying with his request.'

It was at the bidding of 'Abdu'l-Bahá that Áqá 'Azízu'lláh-i-Jadhdháb set out to visit Count Leo Tolstoy. Here is his own account of that unforgettable visit to the great Russian humanist and writer:

Áqá 'Azízu'lláh-i-Ja<u>dh</u>dháb

After hearing the instructions of 'Abdul-Bahá, and returning from the Holy Land, left Odessa, on Sunday [*sic*], 1st Ramaḍán 1320, AD 14th September 1902, in order to visit Graf Tolstoy: ticket to Tula, 11 *manat* and 60 *kopek*, hiring a phaeton: 7 *manat* and 60 *kopek*, driver's tip. [He goes on thus recording his expenses, until the morning of Thursday:] I started for Yasnaya Polyana, where Graf Lif [Leo] Ivan Nikolaeyvich Tolstoy lives (expenses 1 *manat*). On the way, the conductors said: 'They will not let you enter Yasnaya Polyana, because the government has expressly forbidden the entry of any visitors; even his disciples are forbidden. At the railway station, only a one-minute stop is allowed, and no one is permitted to leave the train.' I said: 'I am a Persian Bahá'í. I have come specially from 'Akká to visit him, and it is necessary to see him for some spiritual enquiry.' The two conductors, both of whom were his friends and pupils, consulted together and decided thus after some thought: 'There is no alternative', they told me, 'but for us to let you alight at the signal box, and after passing through the station tell one or two people to seek you and take you away.' I accepted their offer and thanked them. It was a very cold night, very dark and it was snowing. At the signal box where I was let out, it was so dark that had anyone taken my bedding and valise, by my side, I would not have noticed and it was so cold that despite wearing a sable overcoat I was shivering. After the lapse of half-an-hour or more, two men appeared and very kindly took up my bedding and my valise. We walked to the station at Nikharnik, where we came upon the friends of the Graf. They had sent these two men to look for me. The stove was lighted which well heated the room, and by its heat we dried our clothes. In the morning, after partaking of tea, trusting in God, I left my chattels behind and in a droshky drove to Yasnaya Polyana, where the Graf Lif lived. On the road, I met a number of his disciples coming away, some riding in carriages and some on foot. They advised me: 'Do not go any further. The gendarmes will not permit you to proceed.' But I went ahead, and stepping out of the droshky at the entrance to the house I met a gendarme, whom I saluted in Russian. He asked me: 'Why have you come here?' I said in reply: 'I am a Persian, a Bahá'í. There are some spiritual, mystic matters which I would like to discuss with the Count.' He said: 'It is forbidden. I am not permitted to allow anyone to visit him.' I said: 'May I request to ask someone to come to take a message from me?' To this they agreed. A few minutes later someone came. After preliminaries I was informed that he was Chertkov, a philosopher, who had been banished for two years, and had recently returned to Russia to visit Graf Tolstoy. Subsequent to our *pourparlers*, when he realized that I had come from 'Akká, bearing messages from 'Abdu'l-Bahá, he went back to the house to put the situation to the Graf; and when he returned he told the gendarme, on behalf of the Graf: 'This man has come from 'Akká, a long way. He has not met me before. He is not one of my disciples and he is not a Christian. He is a Bahá'í, wishing to discuss some spiritual matters. Let him in to visit me. He will return.' The gendarme agreed. Chertkov became my guide and led me into a room specified for visitors.

The Graf had instructed him to let me rest in that room till lunch-time, since I would be tired, having travelled a distance. Then we were to meet at lunch-time, to have our talk. I said: 'Although I have not studied Russian, I have been for years trading in Transcaspian areas, and have become acquainted with Russian works and press; so I wish to request the perusal of the book which he [Tolstoy] has recently written, and against which the Christian clergy of Russia have risen in protest, leading to the present restrictions.' He [Chertkov] went and fetched me a copy of the book. After having a wash, I was offered tea. 'I have already had my tea,' I said. Then I rested for a while. It was Friday [*sic*], 17 September 1902. From 9 a.m. till noon, I busied myself with the perusal of the book. Despite my poor knowledge, I understood the Count's intention. He wanted to say: What harm is there in this should we, like the Mosaic people and the people of Islám, own that Christ, similar to other Prophets, was chosen and sent down by God, yet refrain from injecting the story of the dove and other imaginings into the

Count Leo Tolstoy

minds of the common people, thus making ourselves the laughing-stock of others. It was just this point which had caused the clergy to denounce him and had led to his house arrest.

At 1 p.m. I was called to meet him. As it happened, that very day they had taken away his secretary and put him in the gaol at Tula, so as to stop his correspondence, because the Graf himself did not write letters; and his younger daughter had gone to Tula to obtain the release of the secretary. To meet him, we directed our steps to a building which stood about three *árshíns** above the ground level. He was seated on a chair – it was a special chair on which he could stretch his legs because of pain. After the encounter and mutual greetings a special table was made ready for Chertkov and myself to serve us our lunch. On my side, glasses for beverages and plates had been arranged according to the present usage. Before the food was brought in, I stated that I did not take alcoholic beverages, and it was now more than three years that I had ceased eating meat. He smiled and said, 'I too do not eat meat, but your avoidance of meat seems to be connected with new teachings.' I replied: 'Nothing is forbidden, but in a Tablet 'Abdu'l-Bahá has written that meat is not the natural food for man, and God has not given man the fangs and the claws for eating meat. How very many are the Buddhists and the Brahmins who do not eat meat and their olfactory sense excels others.' . . . He [Tolstoy] then instructed that an egg dish be brought for me like his own . . .

* Cubits; a cubit is approximately the length of a forearm.

He then said: 'I do not trust newspapers. Some give praise, some become abusive. Three times I wanted to find out facts about the Bábís and Bahá'ís and write truthfully about them in my books, after proper investigation. The last time, twelve days ago, I was talking with Chertkov over this very matter.' I replied: 'Three times I set out according to the instructions given to me. The first time I had messages regarding world peace to deliver to the High Minister and Commander, Kropotkin. Meeting you and him were both forbidden. The second time, I had a letter to deliver to General Kamarov, after which I had to return. And now, this third time, today is exactly twelve days since I left the presence of 'Abdu'l-Bahá in 'Akká.'

Then he began to ask me questions. 'Whom do you consider the Báb to have been,' he asked first; 'when did He appear and what was His claim?' I replied that the Báb was a young Man and His name was Siyyid 'Alí-Muḥammad . . . Then he asked what the state of the Cause was after the ascension of Bahá'u'lláh, and I replied that it was ever progressing. Next, his query was about the claim of the Blessed Perfection, and I answered that He was 'the Speaker on Sinai', 'the Everlasting Father', 'the Spirit of Truth', 'the Heavenly Father' Whom the Sons of Israel and the Christians expect; the Return or Advent of Ḥusayn, according to the beliefs of Shí'ih Islám; and according to the views of the Sunnís the Advent of the Báb was the Advent of the Mahdí (Mihdí), the Advent of Bahá'u'lláh was the Second Coming of the Christ; and according to the beliefs of the Zoroastrians, it was the Advent of Sháh Bahrám. Briefly, His Advent accords with the prophecy of Isaiah and Daniel . . . He has come to rescue all the peoples of the world from vain imaginings.

To summarize the other queries of Tolstoy and Áqá 'Azízu'lláh's replies. He told Tolstoy of the *Kitáb-i-Aqdas*, its laws and ordinances and the legislative powers given to the Universal House of Justice, some of the underlying principles of the Faith, such as equality of men and women, abandonment of all prejudices, the oneness of religion. Tolstoy also wished to know whether people of Faiths other than Islám had embraced the Bahá'í Faith in noticeable numbers. Jadhdháb gave him a satisfactory answer, adding that he himself had come from the Jewish fold. He also told Tolstoy of the Bahá'í School in 'Ishqábád and how it worked. Tolstoy's next query was concerned with the station of 'Abdu'l-Bahá, to which Jadhdháb replied that 'Abdu'l-Bahá was the Expounder of the Book, and His station was that of total 'Servitude'. He also spoke of the rebellion of 'Abdu'l-Bahá's half-brothers, to which Tolstoy commented: 'It should have been so, that opposition should have come from the members of the family of Bahá'u'lláh Himself. This is what has happened to me. I rose up to educate a limited number of people, and my own son is constantly active in Petersburg, day and night, in and out of the Court, to bring about my death.'

With these remarks Tolstoy's queries seem to have ended, and the time had come to give him the message from 'Abdu'l-Bahá, of which Áqá 'Azízu'lláh was the bearer. 'Abdu'l-Bahá wished Tolstoy to leave an indelible mark in the annals of religion. There have been many philosophers who have raised their banners high; Tolstoy could raise his, as a philosopher, even higher, but as a unifier in the sphere of religion, he could leave a greater mark. Then, it seems, Áqá 'Azízu'lláh asked Tolstoy what he thought of Bahá'u'lláh, after all he had heard. Áqá 'Azízu'lláh writes: 'He raised both his hands and said, "How can I deny the One who calls out to the whole of mankind? I tried to educate a limited number of people in Russia, and you have seen how I have been prevented by the gendarmerie."'

Tolstoy seems to have promised Áqá 'Azízu'lláh to write about the Bahá'í Faith, and had presented him with a number of his books and photographs. The rest of the day Áqá 'Azízu'lláh spent in the company of Tolstoy's daughter, his secretary (who had been released), his physician, and Chertkov Zhukovsky. Towards sunset, he writes, he bade them all farewell and left for Bádkúbih.

Jadhdháb had lived also in Bombay for a while. He was always at the service of the Bahá'ís, and travelled a good deal to teach and make the Faith widespread. His home was always open to all. Whenever travelling teachers came to his home, he not only provided hospitality and afforded them every facility, but would always, unbeknown to them, put some cash in their saddle-bag, that they should not find themselves wanting anywhere. His brothers Áqá Sháhvirdí, Áqá Raḥmatu'lláh and Áqá Asadu'lláh were equally active in the service of the Faith, but he excelled them all. Áqá Asadu'lláh met the death of a martyr in Marv.

Áqá 'Azízu'lláh was living and trading in Báyrám 'Alí, in the vicinity of Marv, when the Bolshevik Revolution overtook him. His factory was seized and so was his trading-house. Then he retired to Mashhad, his home town. He was now an old man, well-tried and well-tested. He lived on until the summer of 1935 and passed away in Mashhad, at the age of ninety-four.

16

Samandar
He Who Lived in Fire and Was Not Consumed by It

SHAYKH KÁẒIM-I-SAMANDAR, designated by the Guardian of the Bahá'í Faith an 'Apostle of Bahá'u'lláh', was born in the month of Muḥarram AH 1260 – that same auspicious year which witnessed the dawn of the Day of God. He was the eldest son of Ḥájí Shaykh Muḥammad, entitled Nabíl-i-Akbar, a well-known and highly-respected merchant of Qazvín, and one of the stalwart men of that city – the city of Ṭáhirih the Pure – who, from earliest times, recognized the Manifestation of God and paid homage to him. But let Samandar himself relate his story:

The late Nabíl was the son of Ḥájí Rasúl, and a grandson of Ḥájí Riḍá, famed as Juvayní. Of the public buildings raised by Ḥájí Riḍá, only a caravanserai and a wall remain . . . Ḥájí Rasúl was a merchant. Towards the end of his life he chose to be a resident of Karbilá, where he spent his last twenty-two years, engaged in visitation and devotions. My late father joyfully sent him, all those years, all the money he required for his sustenance. Twice he came home for a short visit. The second time he came, I was a child and I remember him. He was a pious man, and one of the Shaykhís. Although he was a contemporary of Ḥájí Siyyid Káẓim, he did not associate with him. But as it happened, when the Exalted One [the Báb] went to Karbilá he met Him oftentimes in the Shrine of Imám Ḥusayn and was greatly attracted by His mien and devotion. Such a spark was lighted in the heart of Ḥájí Rasúl that it blazed in His remembrance. Although he had no knowledge of that which had come to pass, he came to love His blessed Being and felt submissive towards Him, confessing His superiority.

The best proof of this is the fact that when he came on his last visit to Írán, my father had become enrolled, a servant in the Court of the Exalted One. His brother [Samandar's uncle] complained to their father, saying, 'My brother has joined these people.' The father was alarmed. 'Why should it be so?' he asked. Then they talked about the One Who had put forth a claim, and the identity of the Founder of the Bábí Faith. When all was explained to him, he said: 'The One Whom you name and describe is a merchant, a turbaned Siyyid of Shíráz, Whom I met many a time when he came on pilgrimage to Karbilá. In all these years that I have resided in that holy city, I have come across pilgrims of all sorts and of many a land: siyyids, learned men, mystics, *murshids*, noblemen, grandees, commonalty, merchants – all sorts of men. And I have never met any blessed Being possessed of such humility and such nobility. Firstly, I do not believe that He has come forth with such a claim. And secondly, if it were proved to me that that heavenly Siyyid had indeed made that claim, I cannot consider Him a man of falsehood. That visage and that brow would never, never reflect anything but conspicuous truth . . .' (*Táríkh-i-Samandar*, pp. 15–17)*

Samandar states that because his father was a man deeply devoted to the practices of his Faith, his compatriots had come to call him Shaykh Muḥammad, although he was a merchant. And Shaykh Muḥammad gave his allegiance to Shaykh Aḥmad-i-Ahsá'í, then to Siyyid Káẓim-i-Rashtí (after the passing of the former). Because his male issue did not live long, Shaykh Muḥammad appealed to Siyyid Káẓim and begged his prayers that he might have a son to survive him. His wish was granted, and the son who was born next was given the same name as the Teacher in Karbilá; he grew up to be an Apostle of Bahá'u'lláh. Samandar did not know where and how his father received the tidings of the Advent of the Báb. But he remembered hearing of such great personages as the Bábu'l-Báb, Vaḥíd of Dáráb, Mullá Jalíl-i-Urúmí and Mírzá Muḥammad-'Alíy-i-Qazvíní (both Letters of the Living), whom he did not meet. But those whom he did meet in his father's house make a very impressive list: Mullá Yúsuf-'Alíy-i-Ardibílí (another Letter of the Living), Shaykh 'Alíy-i-'Aẓím, Ḥájí Mírzá Siyyid 'Alí (uncle of the Báb), Mírzá Asadu'lláh-i-Dayyán, Mírzá 'Alíy-i-Sayyáḥ, and the heroic Ḥájí Sulaymán Khán.

Samandar writes:

Because the year of my birth was the same as the year of the Advent [of the Báb], I being born on the 17th day of Muḥarram [7 February 1844], . . . the sires I have named used to hold me, a little boy, in their arms and show great kindness . . . After attaining the honour of belief, my father repeatedly gained the further honour of attaining the presence of the Exalted One: in Tabríz, in Mákú, in Chihríq. During his visit to Mákú, he received a Tablet from the Exalted One, in the handwriting of Áqá Siyyid Ḥusayn, the amanuensis [also a Letter of the Living], which was revealed in answer to a question presented by him . . .

* All quotations from Samandar are from this book unless otherwise attributed.

The Masjid-i-Sháh in Qazvín, in which it is probable that Ḥájí Mullá Taqí, the Ḥujjatu'l-Islám of Qazvín and the father-in-law of Ṭáhirih, was fatally stabbed (Dieulafoy, La Perse*)*

Of the various episodes and happenings [writes Samandar] which touched my late father and about which I heard him speak (others also having knowledge of them), the event of the assassination of Ḥájí Mullá Taqí* is particularly noteworthy. When Ḥájí Mullá Taqí was murdered in Qazvín, my father was in Tabríz. Soon, however, he left to return to Qazvín. It was in Míyánaj that he heard the news of the assassination of a divine of his native town. In Zanján, he found out who the murdered divine was. It occurred to him that men who were makers of mischief might point the finger of accusation at him and cause great trouble. Upon thinking further, he reached the conclusion that the date of his departure from Tabríz was known to a number of men in high position, obtaining their witness by correspondence would be feasible and easy, and people would have the perception to distinguish between fact and fiction. On reaching Qazvín and riding through several quarters, he came upon an acquaintance who showed great surprise and astonishment at seeing him at such a time. Out of kindness, he made my father dismount and walk by paths less frequented to his home. He said, 'I myself will bring your goods and effects. Part of the wall of your house is in ruins; reach your home by that way.' My father did as he was told, and through bypaths and the fallen wall he gained his home. And his acquaintance brought the luggage and took the goods to the owner named by my father.

* The uncle and father-in-law of Ṭáhirih. (HMB)

I myself was a young boy at the time, but was aware of what was happening. I was not allowed to see my father, but I did notice the disposal of the chattels of travel. Witnessing the state my mother was in, I realized that my father had come home. But instead of joy, sorrow and lamentation prevailed. My mother was bemoaning the return of my father. My late aunt kept striking her head and breast, telling my father: 'Why did you return at such a time?' My father retorted: 'If you wish, I shall go in these travel-stained clothes to the governor's house and ask him to write to Tabríz and make enquiries from a number of well-known merchants who were my neighbours there in the same caravanserai.' My mother and aunt replied: 'Alas! it is too late; the time for making such distinctions has passed. They have put your name at the top of the list of wanted men and are all looking for you. So demanding are they that even your brother, who does not share your beliefs and for that reason is hostile towards you, has found living so constricted that, terror-stricken, he has gone into hiding in a subterranean place. Make haste; there is no time to tarry.'

He consented, and was taken to the home of Mashhadí Báqir-i-Ṣabbágh (the dyer), who was the husband of the daughter of my aunt. Only one house separated his house from ours. In it they had a subterranean room . . . which could be reached only in the centre of an upper room. A plank was placed over the entrance. My uncle, Áqá Muḥammad-Riḍá, had also been lodged there.

Within two hours a number of *farráshes*, accompanied by an executioner and a certain Siyyid Muḥsin, appeared outside our house, knocking furiously at the gate which was not opened to them. Then they brought a ladder, stormed the house, poured over the wall and the roof, searched everywhere, and found no one. When they came over the wall and the roof, I, a little boy, was in the courtyard, trembling from head to foot. (ibid. pp. 19–24)

Samandar goes on to say that a woman, a neighbour of theirs, told the murderous crew that a short while before she had seen the man whom they were seeking, being taken to the other house. That house too was stormed, but despite a thorough search no one was found there either. The entrance to the secret subterranean room was well concealed by the carpet covering the floor. Moreover, the cradle of a child had been placed over the spot where the entrance might have been discovered.

At last the tension was eased. Ṭáhirih was taken to Ṭihrán, a move planned and directed by Bahá'u'lláh. And innocent blood was shed because of the vindictiveness of the clerics. Shaykh Muḥammad could leave his hiding-place and ride once again to Tabríz, where he set up his trading-post, as before. Of course the merchants and traders, with whom he had dealings, wished to know the truth of what had

happened in Qazvín. He related the whole story of the murder of
Ḥájí Mullá Taqí and the confession of the assassin, who was a native
of S͟híráz in no way connected with anyone in Qazvín. A few days
later, some men came to the mart seeking him. He was told that Áqá
Mírzá Aḥmad, the mujtahid, wished to see him. Never having met
that divine, S͟hayk͟h Muḥammad was rather perturbed by this
summons. Then those emissaries of the mujtahid got hold of his shawl
and dragged him out. A number of muleteers, who hailed from a
district close to Qazvín and knew S͟hayk͟h Muḥammad personally,
came to his rescue, and in the mêlée that ensued the S͟hayk͟h was
severely beaten.

But that was nothing compared with what came next. On arriving at
the abode of the mujtahid, S͟hayk͟h Muḥammad uttered the words of
attestation: 'I bear witness that there is no God save God; I bear
witness that Muḥammad is the Messenger of God.' The overbearing
divine had a few words with him, and then ordered his minions to
bastinado him, a man totally innocent and without any guile or decep-
tion. It was a cold day in the heart of winter. The minions of the
mujtahid threw him on the ground and began beating him. Spectators
crowded round, spitting on his face. Some of them carried stones and
bricks to hurl at him. Still others, adept at uttering coarse words,
began abusing him. Appealing to men with hearts of stone was
useless. His thoughts and his words were directed to the Primal Point,
the glorious Báb. But his eyes could see the strokes descending upon
him, and he noticed a nail getting looser and looser, about to fall off.
That brought a smile to his lips. At that moment the superintendent or
chief constable (*dárúg͟hih*) arrived and immediately noticed that
smile. Astonished, he said to the S͟hayk͟h: 'They are killing you and
you are smiling!' It was the *dárúg͟hih*'s intervention which saved
S͟hayk͟h Muḥammad. He himself estimated later that he had suffered
two thousand strokes.

Now, the mujtahid ordered the chief constable to expel S͟hayk͟h
Muḥammad from Tabríz. That official managed to move the S͟hayk͟h
to his own home, got him a hat to wear, and brought a physician to see
to his lacerated feet. And S͟hayk͟h Muḥammad answered his
questions, told him who he was and what had brought him to Tabríz.
S͟hayk͟h Muḥammad knew for certain that if he were publicly expelled
from Tabríz, it would make it impossible for him to carry on trading
even in his own native city. Some of his compatriots, whenever they

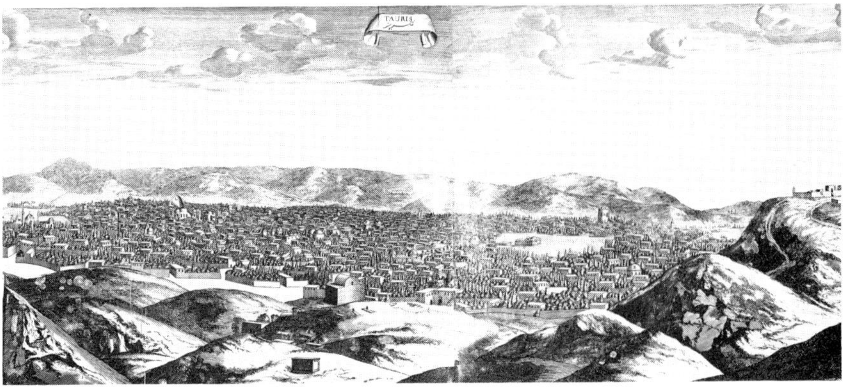

An early panorama view of Tabríz

came to visit him (which was not often), urged him to take himself away; one of them in particular was very insistent, because he had his greedy eyes on the bales of silk which <u>Sh</u>aykh Muḥammad possessed.

Then a certain Ḥájí Siyyid Mihdí, also a native of Qazvín, who, having gone bankrupt, was then engaged in brokerage, found a way to rescue the <u>Sh</u>aykh from his dilemma. He took the case to Ḥájí Mír Muḥammad-Ḥusayn-i-Iṣfahání, a well-known merchant who was famed for his benevolence and good deeds. Having heard the story of <u>Sh</u>aykh Muḥammad, this merchant sent for the chief constable and instructed him to have all the merchandise belonging to <u>Sh</u>aykh Muḥammad moved to the caravanserai known as Ṭabáṭabá'í, which he owned. Although all the rooms there were occupied, they managed to have an upper room prepared for <u>Sh</u>aykh Muḥammad. Under the protection of the Iṣfahání merchant, the <u>Sh</u>aykh found calmness and was freed of interference by ill-wishers. Next, that same kind and God-fearing Iṣfahání merchant interceded with the despotic divine, and obtained permission for <u>Sh</u>aykh Muḥammad of Qazvín to stay in Tabríz. For years, the <u>Sh</u>aykh had his trading-house in that caravanserai, enjoying the sincere friendship of the Iṣfahání merchant. And Ḥájí Mír Muḥammad-Ḥusayn often visited <u>Sh</u>aykh Muḥammad, sometimes twice a week.

When <u>Sh</u>aykh Muḥammad attained the presence of the glorious Báb, it is said, he was told by Him: 'They scourged you and you suffered for My sake; in truth, it was I Who was scourged.' (ibid. p. 30) Not long after, the Báb and His faithful disciple were shot in the public square of Tabríz. And within two years of that dire deed, Írán touched the nadir of inhumanity. In the blood-bath of August 1852, two more of the Báb's Letters of the Living were made to drink the cup of martyrdom: Siyyid Ḥusayn-i-Yazdí, His amanuensis, and the incomparable Ṭáhirih, while in Tabríz they were about to snatch away Shaykh Muḥammad, but the Iṣfahání merchant once again delivered him from the fury of the foe.

Shaykh Muḥammad was further honoured by attaining the presence of Bahá'u'lláh in Baghdád at the time when Mírzá Yaḥyá was also in that city. The Shaykh had received a piece of writing from Mírzá Yaḥyá in which he had clearly shown what a poltroon he was. Trying to hide from all in order to save his life, he had written: 'Whosoever claims to have seen me is an infidel, and whosoever states that he has heard my voice is one who joins partners with God.'

Samandar writes:

My father intended to retire to Baghdád. He ended his trading connections in Tabríz, came to Qazvín, and tried to settle his accounts with his partner by

The fortress, or citadel, of Tabríz where the Báb was confined for about forty days before being sent to the castle of Mákú. His martyrdom occurred in the public square in Tabríz, 9 July 1850, following almost three-years' imprisonment in Mákú and Chihríq (Dieulafoy, La Perse*)*

correspondence and close down the partnership. He told me: 'I have written several times to my partner to send his account, but he has not done so, and time is getting short for travelling.' I said in answer to him: 'You see that the soreness of my eyes has greatly increased; otherwise I would have gone with your permission and settled the whole affair. Now I fear that because of his procrastination the time for travelling will lapse and winter will set in. Therefore I feel that you yourself should go to Láhíján for a few days, settle your accounts with your partner and, God willing, return soon.' He replied: 'Yes, I myself would like to go to Láhíján to see my brother, Mas͟hhadí Muḥammad-Raḥím, and my partner, having shared so many years of our lives together, now that I have reached the end of my journeys and the end of my days.' Divination was also favourable, and the day after that very night he made his preparations, bought a horse, and left for Láhíján. A few days after his arrival there he was taken ill, and departed from this world soon after. That was in the year AH 1278 [9 July 1861–28 June 1862]. (ibid. pp. 32–3)

Samandar thus continues his narrative:

It is a known fact that in Írán, the children of those who bear this name [Bahá'í] are oftentimes not immune [from opposition] in bazars and streets. Youngsters and the ignorant often make verbal attacks on them, particularly at times of perturbation . . . I myself have from the days of my childhood suffered hearing such ridicule, and even to this day such words reach my ears. I wish to record the account of one of these incidents which has a tale to tell, a memory for generations to come.

I well remember a time when I was very young, not yet adolescent, and my father was away. I went to make some purchases from a grocer's shop at the end of our lane. A few men were idling their time around that shop. They saw me approaching from afar, and decided amongst themselves to do me some harm. As I neared the shop, one of them who was a well-built man, to do a good deed approached me and, without saying a word, slapped me hard on the face. I remember that the grocer, knowing that I had come to make purchases at his shop, stopped them and told them to leave me alone. Since I had gone to buy some provisions from him, I went forward and gave him the money. Whilst he was weighing the things, I could hear those men talking about me. I heard one of them say, 'Is he a bastard or not?' Another said in reply: 'If he was conceived prior to his father's ratting and becoming a Bábí, then he is not a bastard; but he is one if his conception took place when his father had already become a Bábí.' (ibid. pp. 34–5)

Samandar goes on to say:

Most of the people, high and low, who caused harm to this sacred Cause had no profit from it, and before long went down in ignominy. Should I put on paper the full story of all, everything we have heard and seen, these pages would not suffice. In brief, some of them were seen fallen on evil days, dying in utmost misery. My father told me this: 'A good while after the episode of

Shaykh Káẓim-i-Samandar, Apostle of Bahá'u'lláh

Tabríz and the beating I received there, I found myself in an assemblage, seated in a place of honour, and noticed a man sitting in a lowly place whose whole mien and bearing spoke of misery. That man turned to me and said: "I beseech your forgiveness." "What for?" I asked. "At one time", he said, "I brought upon you great suffering." I answered: "If you did what you say you have done, in the path of God, do not ask for forgiveness; and if you did it out of selfish desire, turn to God and beseech His forgiveness." Then he replied: "I and two or three others were the men who caused your afflictions. We went to the mujtahid and incited him to have you beaten. They and I were seized by miseries in diverse ways. Forgive us."' (ibid. pp. 35–6)

The son of such a father as Shaykh Muḥammad could not but become in his turn a pillar of the Faith of Bahá'u'lláh in his native city of Qazvín. Throughout his life he followed in the footsteps of his father, engaged in trade. The glorious Báb had been the son of a merchant, and had uncles similarly earning their livings. He Himself began trading at the tender age of fifteen. The Prophet of Arabia traded as the agent of a rich widow of Mecca whom He eventually married, leading caravans with merchandise along the barren wastes of Arabia to the fertile lands of the north. Shaykh Káẓim-i-Samandar excelled both in trade and in learning. One of his teachers was Mullá Zaynu'l-'Ábidín, an uncle of Bahá'u'lláh. This notable of Núr accompanied his nephew, Mírzá Yaḥyá, when the latter hurriedly fled from Írán in a desperate attempt to save his own life, after having endangered the lives of the members of his family and the people close to them, in the province of Mázindarán. On his return from Baghdád, Samandar writes, 'my father kept him [Mullá Zaynu'l-'Ábidín] in our house, ostensibly to teach me'. Another tutor of Samandar was Mullá 'Alí-Akbar-i-Ardistání. He was the one who in very early days suffered indignities in Shíráz, together with Quddús and Mullá Ṣádiq-i-Muqaddas-i-Khurásání. They were flogged, a noose was fastened through their nostrils, and thus they were paraded in the streets of Shíráz. Samandar writes:

In the days of my father, in Tabríz, I studied under him [Mullá 'Alí-Akbar] for two years. Then with my father's permission I accompanied him to Qazvín, whence he went to Ardistán. After the declaration of the Abhá Beauty, he became hesitant for a while, sunk in his own thoughts. Even in a Tablet, He [Bahá'u'lláh] commanded me to bear a message to him, this great teacher of mine. But before long the Will of God prevailed, and that sagacious, acute and subtle man, subsequent to deep investigation, came through the test and attained the highest degree of certitude and knowledge, and engaged in glorifying his Lord and teaching His Faith until he passed away. (ibid. p. 172)

Following his trade, Samandar was oftentimes travelling to Tabríz, to Rasht and Láhíján, to Ṭihrán. And as soon as Bahá'u'lláh made known His Mission, Samandar gave Him his fealty. He was already familiar with the follies of Mírzá Yaḥyá, but as he puts it himself:

I did not know the extent of his folly. A certain Mullá 'Abdu'r-Raḥím, a believer of early days, had written a letter to Mírzá Yaḥyá, and he had answered him in his own handwriting, with which I was familiar. One of the questions which he [Mullá 'Abdu'r-Raḥím] had asked was this: some physicians prepare pills with the flesh of serpents, and sometimes they mix it with other ingredients and make an electuary. At other times they prescribe the cooked meat of a serpent to cure certain ailments. Is it lawful to partake of such flesh? That man, Azal, had written an answer in Arabic. These were his words: 'Is there a dearth of things to eat, that you wish to eat serpents and scorpions?' Yes, that answer made me see that that man was more stupid than I had ever thought him. His answer showed that he had not understood the question. (ibid. pp. 138–9)

Samandar was always engaged in search of knowledge. At the same time as he diligently attended to his business transactions, he was continuously delving into his books, making a thorough study of all the Scriptures of the past, learning all the time. Samandar has left his own testimony indicating his unceasing effort to find truth and investigate it with an open mind. He writes of his studies of the Old and New Testaments, of the text of the holy Qur'án, of traditions of Islám. He takes his stand on the exhortation of Bahá'u'lláh to consort with all peoples, with men of all Faiths, in peace and in harmony. According to his own admission, he even tried to apply the test of independent investigation to the writings of Azal, Mírzá Yaḥyá, whom he calls 'Mir'át' (Mirror). (He had been designated thus by the Báb.) Samandar writes: 'I did whatever was in my power to investigate, to discover, to evaluate. Not a whiff of truth did I ever find coming from the direction of the Mir'át. On the contrary, malodorous is all that is wafted from his bourne . . .' (ibid. p. 144)

In the year AH 1291 (AD 18 February 1874–6 February 1875) Samandar, in the company of Ḥájí Naṣír (one of the survivors of Shaykh Ṭabarsí), attained the presence of Bahá'u'lláh. That pilgrimage inspired Samandar to start on the road to his destiny: to become a pillar of the Faith, an Apostle of Bahá'u'lláh.

Nine years later, that year when the rage of Náṣiri'd-Dín Sháh and his two unprincipled, avaricious sons – Mas'úd Mírzá, the Ẓillu's-Sulṭán, and Kámrán Mírzá, the Náyibu's-Salṭanih – exploded into wholesale arrests and imprisonment of the followers of Bahá'u'lláh, Samandar had to clear the hurdle of mischievous misrepresentation by a man who, in later years, came to see the enormity of his deed. There was in Qazvín a Mullá 'Alí, a man of many talents. The present writer remembers the praises spoken of him by the Hand of the Cause of God, Ṭarázu'lláh Samandarí, who had received tuition from him. Samandar (Ṭarázu'lláh's father), having found Mullá 'Alí to be receptive and willing to listen, had led him to full recognition of the Cause of Bahá'u'lláh, and afterwards had provided him with a home in his own house where he became a tutor to his son. He was called Mu'allim (Teacher) par excellence.

*Bahá'ís of Qazvín, including Shaykh Káẓim-i-Samandar (*seated, centre*), Mírzá Músá Khán, Ḥakím-Báshí (*on his left*), Ṭaráẓu'lláh Samandarí, later appointed a Hand of the Cause of God (* standing 2nd from right*) and (*on his left*) Muḥammad Labíb, author of* The Seven Martyrs of Hurmuzak

Mullá 'Alí had a nephew who was hostile towards the Cause of Bahá'u'lláh. In the first instance, he showed his displeasure at the arrangement which resulted in his uncle's change of residence. He did not wish him to live in the house of a Bábí! Having failed to prevent it, he went about telling tales and bringing grave accusations against Samandar. As Samandar himself writes:

He carried on his vendetta to such an extent that the government became really suspicious. 'My uncle', he said, 'has been kept a prisoner by this Bábí. He does not allow him to leave the house.' Therefore the governor sent his *farrásh-báshí* and a number of *farráshes*, together with the plaintiff himself, to put the matter right. As it happened, the Mu'allim had gone on a journey with Áqá Muḥammad-i-Qá'iní, known as Fáḍil, to accompany him part of the way, leave him at a certain spot, and return [to Qazvín]. (ibid. pp. 44–5)

Then Samandar refers to the events in the capital, the arrests made there and the possibility of the unrest spreading to other places. He goes on to say:

I had come home from the market-place. My son came with a letter from

Tabríz bearing the news at the end of it that 'This very minute a telegram arrived from Yazd to the effect that Varqá has been accused and detained'. My son went back to the bazar, and I was sitting sunk in my thoughts when a hard knock was heard on the gate. It was the second gate. And soon the *farrás͟hes* poured in, saying that they had come to release Mullá 'Alí. I thought they had come to get me. (ibid. p. 45)

Samandar tried then to rescue his papers, but they espied him and held fast to him. He was carried out of his house and subjected to close questioning. All that while the nephew of Mullá 'Alí was lashing him with his waspish tongue. But Samandar kept calm and told his tormentors that they could search everywhere in the house for Mullá 'Alí, but they would be wasting their time because the Mu'allim was not there; he had been there, but had gone away. He was returned to his home, while the search went on, which was in vain. Samandar's household was naturally alarmed, the women and children distressed, but he asked for a hubble-bubble to be brought for him and the *farrás͟h-bás͟hí*. They sat down quietly by the flower-bed and had a smoke together, while the intense search continued for Mullá 'Alí. Once the *farrás͟hes* were satisfied that the man whom they sought was indeed not in that house, they prepared to leave, taking Samandar with them. They realized they had made a great mistake, but no one was prepared to admit it. In the meantime the rabble was growing in number, and the ill-intentioned nephew of Mullá 'Alí was becoming louder with his denunciations. Samandar was threatened with death, but as dignified as ever he kept calm and unruffled. While the mob was thickening and chaos increased, the deputy-governor made his appearance. He and the *farrás͟h-bás͟hí* took counsel together and came to the conclusion that Samandar was telling the truth and others were prevaricating. He was allowed to return home accompanied by *farrás͟hes* who were suitably compensated.

Now, back at home, Samandar was given letters that had come from Ṭihrán. They all conveyed the news that Bahá'ís were being arrested, and more of them would certainly soon be seized. For the time being, however, there was a pause, because Sulṭán-Murád Mírzá, the Ḥisámu's-Salṭanih, had died. This despotic and self-willed uncle of Náṣiri'd-Dín S͟háh had in his time caused misery and hardship in the realm. Bahá'ís too had suffered at his hands. Samandar and his compatriots in Qazvín had been warned to take precautionary measures before they were engulfed. Samandar writes:

This matter caused fresh alarm. It was decided that I should leave that night and go to a place not well known, and see what the unknown morrow would bring. I told my cousin, who, in those days, was with me in the trading-house, to send a number of sugar-cones as a gift to the *farrá*<u>*sh*</u>*-bá*<u>*sh*</u>*í* . . . In the darkness of the night, I gained the residence which was in an obscure quarter. Within two days, a telegram came from Ra<u>sh</u>t announcing that my cheque had not been met. The owner of the goods concerned had rushed to my house and to my place of trading, demanding his money. But I had no ready money available. (ibid. pp. 48–50)

Then Samandar proceeds to explain that it was obvious that adversaries were at work; otherwise there was no reason for dishonouring his cheque. Next he moved to another house, more distant than the previous one. The owner of this second house, in Samandar's own words, was of the 'people of the Evangel' (the New Testament: i.e. Christian). 'He showed the utmost kindness,' Samandar writes. 'He even told me that whatever money I required to go away he would put at my disposal.' But Samandar had sixty *túmáns* brought from his own trading-house, which he left in the care of his host. Samandar had decided to leave because all the news coming from Ra<u>sh</u>t was bad. The Bahá'ís in charge of his trading-house – Ḥájí Naṣír and his son – had been detained. He was on the point of leaving his home town when he received a message from a relative, advising him to consult with a few others before taking an irrevocable step. So, Samandar tells us, he rode the following night to the home of that relative, where two other Bahá'ís had been called to meet him. The man who was owed one hundred *túmáns* had called several times demanding his money. Samandar, as he states himself, had intended to pay him in kind from the goods in his warehouse. One of those present offered to lend Samandar five hundred *túmáns* right away, which he was reluctant to accept. But the host, a very wise man, intervened to persuade Samandar to accept the loan. Thus the creditor was paid the next day. Samandar states that when he came to pay back the loan, the lender refused to charge him any interest.

Samandar had to stay nearly three weeks in the house of this relative, and then a well-known siyyid, also a merchant, who was highly esteemed in Qazvín and was not a Bahá'í, escorted him to his own home; and no one dared to lift a finger against him.

Samandar's own deliverance from grave dangers was dramatic, but he had soon to mourn the cruel loss of a dear and close friend: no less a person than Ḥájí Naṣír, the survivor of the holocaust of Shaykh Ṭabarsí, in whose company he had attained the presence of Bahá'u'lláh. Ḥájí Naṣír was thrown into prison, as was his eldest son, Áqá 'Alí. As a result, Samandar's business activities in Rasht were totally halted. Considerable effort was required to prove to the authorities that the prisoners were agents for Samandar and did not own the trading-house in Rasht. In the meantime, Ḥájí Naṣír, now advanced in years, could not withstand the rigours of incarceration and passed away, a martyr in the path of Bahá'u'lláh. When his corpse was brought out of the prison the rabble of the town assaulted it, tore his eyes out of their sockets, cut off his nose, and subjected the lifeless body to divers insults. A decent burial was denied to it. It was dragged to a ruined spot and there pelted with stones until well covered.

The Mu'allim, Mullá 'Alí, when he returned to Qazvín sought out a friend in the service of the government, and presented his case proving the falsehood of the accusations brought against Samandar. The governor intended to arrest Mullá 'Alí's nephew, who had been the cause of all the mischief. But the young man fled the town, only to come back, years later, apologetic and remorseful. And Mullá 'Alí returned to his post, tutoring the sons of Samandar. In appreciation of the services of Mullá 'Alí, Bahá'u'lláh instructed Ḥájí Amín* to present to him an 'abá on behalf of Himself. The Mu'allim, as Samandar himself has written, lived for nearly thirty-six years in the home of that incomparable promoter of the Faith. Such are the words of Bahá'u'lláh, immortalizing the life-long service of Mullá 'Alí:

> We have accepted that which he hath achieved in the path of God, the Lord of all the worlds. Say: O Mu'allim! Thou art the first teacher who hast attained the good-pleasure of God and hast been mentioned by Him in His conspicuous Book. We bear witness that thou hast attained that which was sent down from My holy Kingdom and recorded in My Most Holy Book, and thou didst observe that which thou wert commanded by thy Lord, the Supreme, the All-Powerful. Verily We have ordained these verses to be thy recompense for that which thou didst accomplish in the path of God, and have sent them unto thee that thou mayest render thanks unto thy Lord, the All-Commanding, the All-Knowing. Thereby have We immortalized thy name and made it to be remembered in all of the centres of learning in the world. Verily, thy Lord is the Omnipotent, the Almighty. Rejoice by reason of what hath flowed from My Most Exalted Pen in the prison of 'Akká, as a token of Our grace unto thee and unto all who have held firmly to the Cord

* Ḥájí Abu'l-Ḥasan-i-Amín-i-Ardikání, the Trustee of the Ḥuqúqu'lláh.

*Ḥájí Amín, Trustee of the Ḥuqúqu'lláh (*seated, right*), with Ḥakím-Bás͟hí and (*standing*) Muḥammad Labíb*

that no man can sever. Glory be unto thee and unto all learned men who have come to recognize this mighty Cause. O Samandar! Convey to him that which hath been revealed for him. God willing yet another revelation of loving kindness will reach him. A garment of honour will also be bestowed on him, though it be only a robe. But that robe is, in the sight of God, more valued than that which the kings and rulers possess. O Samandar! The Mu'allim hath attained unto that which most of the people are unable to comprehend. Verily thy Lord is the All-Knowing, the All-Informed. (Quoted in Is͟hráq-i-K͟hávarí, *Má'idiy-i-Ásmání*, vol. 8, p. 193)

Samandar attained the presence of Bahá'u'lláh in 'Akká twice, and went for a third time on pilgrimage to the Holy Land during the early years of the Ministry of 'Abdu'l-Bahá. Of his first pilgrimage to 'Akká he writes:

In the month of S͟ha'bán AH 1290 [October 1873] this servant, with bales of merchandise consisting of silk and coarse silken material, left Qazvín for Ras͟ht, accompanied by Ḥájí Muḥammad-Ḥasan, the goldsmith, my own maternal uncle (who had his wife and mother-in-law with him), Ḥájí Mullá

Bábá, Kallih-Darri'í, and Áqá 'Abdu'lláh, the son of the late Mullá Malik-Muḥammad-i-Qazvíní. There we attended to our business concerns, and took with us Ḥájí Muḥammad-Naṣír [the martyr]* who was in charge of the trading-house in Rasht, and went on our way. In those days there was as yet no railway between Bádkúbih and Tiflís. We travelled by commercial cart. The late Ḥájí Naṣír and I stayed in Istanbul for trading purposes. Others in our company went on pilgrimage to the Holy Land, while we two asked once again for permission. When it came, we left Istanbul with Manṣúr-i-Uskú'í. We reached 'Akká on 11 Muḥarram 1291, coinciding with the period of fasting [March 1874]. We were in His sacred presence throughout Naw-Rúz and Riḍván. Another pilgrim at the time was Ismu'lláhu'l-Aṣdaq [Mullá Ṣádiq-i-Muqaddas-i-Khurásání]. He spoke to us about what they had experienced in Mázindarán. Ḥájí Naṣír [another survivor of Shaykh Ṭabarsí] was there too. (Quoted in Sulaymání, vol. 7, pp. 32–3)

The encounter of those two veterans of the Faith, who had known Mullá Ḥusayn and Quddús, had campaigned together under their command and had then come into each other's company, once again, under the shadow of the Supreme Manifestation of God, must have been for those who witnessed their reunion an occasion hard to match. Samandar goes on to say:

One day the Blessed Perfection, Who was staying in the house of Áqáy-i-Kalím at the Khán-i-Jurayní,† addressed Ḥájí Naṣír in words such as these, as far as I can remember: 'Jináb-i-Ḥájí! You have toiled much and suffered much in the path of God. If you yourself have forgotten what you have done and endured, God has not. But the worlds of God are not confined to this world. Were it so the Exalted Prophets would not have consented to bear such adversities wrought by men; the Manifestation who preceded Me would not have consented to be suspended and martyred with volleys of malice and malignity; and I would not have consented to be dragged, bare-headed and barefooted, in utmost degradation, from Níyávarán to Ṭihrán to bear untold blows.' In brief, He expounded this theme in most excellent words. He was telling the Ḥájí that he will be recompensed in the worlds to come. (ibid. pp. 33–4)

Then Samandar takes care to explain that he is not reporting the exact words of Bahá'u'lláh, but the purport of His utterance.

Samandar has also recorded what he heard about Napoleon III. It was while Samandar was in Istanbul that the fallen French Emperor died. He says that he intended, when in the presence of Bahá'u'lláh, to ask Him why it was that those who had persecuted the Faith, its

* This pilgrimage occurred a year or so before the death of Ḥájí Naṣír, described a few paragraphs earlier.
† Better known as Khán-i-'Avámíd.

Napoleon III, the French Emperor who first ignored and later spurned the two Tablets which Bahá'u'lláh addressed to him

Founders and followers were still enjoying power while Napoleon III had gone the way predicted in the Tablet addressed to him. But when he went into the presence of Bahá'u'lláh, such were the bounties of that attainment that he gave no more thought to Napoleon; until one day, unrequested, Bahá'u'lláh Himself spoke about the French Emperor, and the enormities committed by the rulers of Persia and Turkey. Napoleon, Bahá'u'lláh said, was godless. Intellect was his god, and he believed that he himself was the wisest of all men. As soon as he was challenged and found wanting, the hand of God seized him and struck him down. Then He spoke of developments in Persia and Turkey and told Samandar that the oppressors of these lands would also, in due time, receive their deserts. Two years later, 'Abdu'l-'Azíz of Turkey met his doom, and in 1896, Náṣiri'd-Dín of Írán, on the very eve of his Jubilee celebrations, fell before the bullet of an assassin.

Samandar attained the presence of Bahá'u'lláh once again, a year before His ascension. He writes: 'In the year 1308 [17 August 1890–6 August 1891], in his company [Mu'allim's] I travelled to 'Akká by way of Istanbul and Alexandria, and together we attained the presence of Bahá'u'lláh' (*Tárí<u>kh</u>-i-Samandar*, pp. 204–5). One day when Samandar had just left Bahá'u'lláh's room at Bahjí and was still standing by the curtained doorway, his ears caught these words of Bahá'u'lláh, Who was pacing within; they were uttered most firmly, most emphatically Samandar relates: 'You are going to 'Akká'; go into the presence of Sarkár-i-Áqá.' And who could Áqá – Sarkár-i-Áqá – be but the Most Great Branch, 'Abdu'l-Bahá? Samandar, who always sought the presence of the Most Great Branch in 'Akká, was greatly surprised, he writes, by Bahá'u'lláh's emphatic command. It was only in after years, when the Covenant-breakers rose in rebellion, that the full purport of those words of Bahá'u'lláh dawned upon him. And Samandar had reason to remember particularly, to the end of his days, the malice of those who had known Light and had called upon Darkness to guide them, those who had sinned against the Holy Ghost, in the judgement of Jesus Christ.

Samandar's account of his return from this pilgrimage with the Mu'allim continues:

> After two months we were permitted to leave. On the way home, Varqá [the martyr] and two of his sons, also Ḥájí Mullá Mírzá Muḥammad-i-<u>Kh</u>unsárí (who was one of the mujtahids, a divine) were our fellow-travellers as far as Ra<u>sh</u>t and Qazvín. Thereafter, he [the Mu'allim] was always in attendance upon the Friends, in their meetings and gatherings, reciting verses and prayers, until his passing from this temporary phase to the world eternal. (ibid. p. 205)

Mulla 'Alí died towards the end of November 1913.

In the year AH 1317 (AD 12 May 1899–30 April 1900), accompanied by his wife, his son Áqá <u>Gh</u>ulám-'Alí, the widow of his brother Ḥájí <u>Sh</u>ay<u>kh</u> Muḥammad-'Alí (he who committed suicide in Istanbul because of the base intrigues of the partisans of Mírzá Yaḥyá),* and Áqá 'Alíy-i-Arbáb (the son of the martyred Ḥájí Naṣír), Samandar again went on pilgrimage to 'Akká. His daughter <u>Th</u>urayyá had been married to Mírzá Ḍíyá'u'lláh, the third surviving son of Bahá'u'lláh and a breaker of His Covenant. By this time Mírzá Ḍíyá'u'lláh was dead and his widow had her home in the Mansion of Bahjí with other Covenant-breakers. Samandar sought a meeting with her and they met within the Shrine of Bahá'u'lláh. Samandar himself has written the full account of all that happened on this occasion, which was

* See *Bahá'u'lláh, The King of Glory*, pp. 387–8, for Bahá'u'lláh's account of his suicide. (Ed.)

published in Egypt shortly afterwards. It is a sorry tale and reveals the lowest depths of human degradation. The infamous crew, entrenched in the Mansion of Bahjí, made this meeting after long years between a distraught, uncertain, grief-stricken woman and her caring, sorrowing parents, a scene of sordid revenge and conflict. Thurayyá, her tears flowing, complained bitterly that they had unjustly neglected her. Samandar tried gently to reason with her and asked her to come away with them, but Thurayyá refused: she would never depart from the vicinity of her husband's grave. Ḍíyá'u'lláh was buried in a room next to the inner Shrine of Bahá'u'lláh.* An old hag had been sent to watch the meeting between Thurayyá and her parents. As soon as Mírzá Ghulám-'Alí caught hold of his sister's hand to lead her to the Pilgrim House nearby, the old woman shouted horribly at Thurayyá, who screamed in return. At that, a number of Mírzá Muḥammad-'Alí's partisans rushed in and dragged Samandar and those who were with him into the Mansion, cursing and beating him all the while. There they were detained, howled at and jeered by a mob. Mírzá Áqá Ján, the faithless amanuensis of Bahá'u'lláh, and Javád-i-Qazvíní were foremost amongst them. And in the meantime, the fickle Mírzá Badí'u'lláh, the youngest son of Bahá'u'lláh, and Mírzá Ḥusayn-i-Khartúmí, who had had the honour of being Ḥájí Mírzá Ḥaydar-'Alí's companion in captivity but had gravitated towards the arch-breaker of the Covenant, hastened to the Seraye [Government House] in 'Akká, shamelessly reporting to the authorities that a group of people had come ostensibly to visit the Shrine of Bahá'u'lláh and had stayed on till nightfall, in order to kidnap a woman. The Mutaṣarrif sent an interrogator with a number of horsemen to Bahjí. They put Samandar, his wife, son and two others who were with them in a carriage and took them to 'Akká. There they were driven straight to the Master's house and left. When informed of the base behaviour of the Covenant-breakers, 'Abdu'l-Bahá Himself went to see the Mutaṣarrif and informed that official of the truth of the matter. The Mutaṣarrif said that Thurayyá should be brought out of the Mansion and united with her parents, but 'Abdu'l-Bahá forbade it. Upon Samandar, who intended to take his case to the courts, He laid the same injunction. He, the very manifestation of mercy, told Samandar that any action to retrieve Thurayyá would

* In recent years, the heirs of the Covenant-breakers moved the remains of Mírzá Ḍíyá'u'lláh to a building they had erected over the grave of Mírzá Muḥammad-'Alí, the arch-breaker of the Covenant of Bahá'u'lláh, in the vicinity of Bahjí.

greatly sadden Mírzá Ḍíyá'u'lláh's mother, who was still grieving over his death. The interrogator who had gone out to Bahjí, when apprised of the facts of the case advised strongly that Samandar should take action, but again 'Abdu'l-Bahá would not allow it. They had been vindictive and foolish, He said, but we should be forgiving.

An incalculable service rendered by Samandar to future generations is his meticulous recording of events and conversations pertaining to the Faith of Bahá'u'lláh. 'Abdu'l-Bahá's pronouncement on the waywardness of Lisánu'l-Mulk-i-Sipihr, the author of *Násikhu't-Taváríkh* (a massive several-volumed world history), which Samandar has put down on paper, is particularly important. Sipihr has commented, in common with many others, that if the Báb had stood where He was when the first volley only severed the ropes suspending Him, and had told the spectators to behold that rifle shots could not harm Him, He would have scored an immediate triumph and people, there and then, would have given Him their allegiance. Sipihr expresses, furthermore, his glee and gratitude that the Báb took refuge in a chamber nearby. Samandar asked 'Abdu'l-Bahá to explain to him the reason for the Báb's action. The Master, he records, felt very strongly the presentation of this reference to the martyrdom of the Báb; His visage changed colour, and He said most emphatically that it was decreed by God as an incontrovertible sign to arouse the people out of their negligence. Had the Báb not retired to that chamber, the adversaries would not have allowed Him to live a minute longer, and thus would have prevented people from realizing what had happened.

Samandar was indeed both a keen observer and a keen recorder. Mírzá Abu'l-Faḍl of Gulpáygán apart, there is no one else amongst the learned men within the Bahá'í fold to match him in those respects. In one of his works, he tabulates and describes his journeys, thirty-one in number, which he undertook from the year AH 1271, at the age of eleven, to the year 1334, when he had reached the seventy-fourth year of his life. These journeys were made either for trading purposes, or for the promotion of the interests of the Faith. Sometimes the two were combined. Here are some of his journeys, presented and described by himself:

Seventh journey, to Ṭihrán: Because the Tablets and communications

> showed evidences of a fresh outpouring of Light causing surprise, I set out for Ṭihrán, accompanied by my brother, the late Ḥájí Shaykh Muḥammad-'Alí. We stayed at Saráy-i-Amír [a well-known caravanserai]. We met the late Ḥájí Mírzá Riḍá-Qulí [brother of Bahá'u'lláh]. As it happened, Áqá Mírzá Hádí, the son of Azal, was also in Ṭihrán. We met him as well . . .
>
> Sixteenth journey, to Ṭihrán: I believe it was towards the end of the year 1312. The rebellion of the Covenant-breakers was being intensified, and coming more into the open. In this journey, Ḥájí Muḥammad Ismá'íl, the son of the late Ḥájí Khalíl, accompanied me. We stayed with Mashhadí 'Ibád Bag-i-Shírvání, the Qavámu't-Tujjár (because at that time we had trading ties). We met all of the prominent Friends. In Ṭihrán, I answered Khartúmí's* letter. Áqá Jamál† wanted to meet me. I refused to go to his house, and said that he should come where I was. He did not. After some twenty days or more and meeting the Friends, we returned to Qazvín . . .
>
> Twentieth journey, to Tabríz: 'Abdu'l-Bahá had sanctioned a journey to Zanján and Ádharbáyján. Developments had delayed this journey. In the year 1321 I embarked upon it. [Here Samandar details the marriages of two of his daughters, taking place at this time.] We [Samandar had taken his nephew, Shaykh Aḥmad, with him] stayed nine days in Zanján, at the house of Ustád Ḥasan, the son-in-law of Ḥájí Ímán. Thence we went to Tabríz, staying for nearly seventy days at the home of Ḥájí Muḥammad-'Alí Áqá, meeting the Friends. (Quoted in Sulaymání, vol. 7, pp. 43–4. The following details of journeys are also from this source.)

Together with his host, Samandar visited Mílán, attending the marriage festivities of Áqá Asadu'lláh, the nephew of the host. Then on his way back to Qazvín, he once again visited Zanján to meet the Bahá'ís there.

His twenty-fifth journey was to Rasht. 'This journey was undertaken at the request of the Friends of that city, to teach the Faith.' He stayed at the homes of Áqá 'Alíy-i-Arbáb and his own son, Mírzá Ghulám-'Alí. He was in Rasht for three months, and held a special class to teach the *Bayán*.

Samandar's twenty-sixth journey, sanctioned by 'Abdu'l-Bahá, was to Ṭihrán. He writes that one of the sons of Siyyid Naṣru'lláh Báqiroff, together with a son of the martyred Varqá, took him from Qazvín to Ṭihrán, again to teach the Faith and particularly the contents of the *Bayán*. This stay in Ṭihrán lasted for two-and-a-half months.

The twenty-seventh journey was to Rasht. 'The members of the Spiritual Assembly of Rasht, once again, asked me, through Mírzá

* See p. 210.
† Áqá Jamál-i-Burújirdí, one of the foremost Covenant-breakers.

Músá Khán, Ḥakím Báshí, to visit Rasht. Although I had just returned from Ṭihrán, I complied.' Accompanied by his wife, the mother of Áqá Mírzá Ṭarázu'lláh (the future Hand of the Cause of God), he left for Rasht. At the request of Ḥájí Yúsuf-i-'Aṭṭár, he also took Mírzá 'Abdu'l-Ghaní, the son of that Bahá'í friend, with him. They travelled by carriage to Rasht. But, before long, a Tablet of 'Abdu'l-Bahá, sent from Ṭihrán by the Hand of the Cause of God, Ibn-i-Abhar, directed him to co-operate with Áqá Mírzá Na'ím (the celebrated Bahá'í poet) and Ibn-i-Abhar, in the writing of a book in refutation of *Kitáb-i-Nuqṭatu'l-Káf.** This book had just been published by Edward Granville Browne, under his own name as editor, in the Gibb Memorial Series. It carried two misleading introductions, one in Persian and the other in English. Decades later, the Persian savant, Mírzá Muḥammad Khán-i-Qazvíní, confessed in writing that he personally had composed the Persian Introduction to the *Nuqṭatu'l-Káf*. The English Introduction, of course, must have been written by Edward Browne.

To go back to Samandar's account, he states that after a stay of only three weeks in Rasht he returned to Qazvín, and then within a week in the company of Ḥájí Abu'l-Ḥasan-i-Ardikání (Ḥájí Amín: the Trustee of Ḥuqúqu'lláh) he and his wife left for Ṭihrán. There he stayed in the house of Áqá Siyyid Háshim, his brother-in-law and son of one of the five Báqiroff brothers. It took them, Samandar writes, about two months and a half to complete the book. Whilst busy with writing, Samandar says, he was meeting the Bahá'ís of Ṭihrán. The task finished, Samandar went back to Qazvín in the company of Ibn-i-Aṣdaq, a Hand of the Cause of God and the son of Mullá Ṣádiq-i-Muqaddas-i-Khurásání, entitled Ismulláhu'l-Aṣdaq.

Samandar's twenty-ninth journey was to Ṭihrán. On the 13th day of Dhu'l-Ḥijjah 1332 (2 November 1914), he received a visit from Mírzá Músá Khán, the Ḥakím-Báshí, another stalwart Bahá'í of Qazvín. The evening of this Friday was closing in, Samandar writes, as the lamps were being lighted. Ḥakím-Báshí came in with an envelope in his hand, addressed to the two of them. It was from the Master,

* See H. M. Balyuzi, *Edward Granville Browne and the Bahá'í Faith*. The present writer has no knowledge of what happened to the book written by Na'ím, Samandar and Ibn-i-Abhar. It certainly was not published. Shortly after, the great scholar, Mírzá Abu'l-Faḍl, began writing such a refutation. But he had not gone far when his death put an end to it. His nephew, Siyyid Mihdí, finished the book. It was published in 'Ishqábád under the title of *Kashfu'l-Ghiṭa'* (Rending the Veil of Error). But, because of its intemperate language and certain inaccuracies, 'Abdu'l-Bahá stopped its circulation.

instructing them to go to Ṭihrán and help in reconciling the members of that Spiritual Assembly, who apparently had been at loggerheads. The next day they were on the road, and a carriage took them quickly to Ṭihrán where they lodged with Ḥájí Ghulám-Riḍáy-i-Iṣfahání. Their host, whom the Guardian of the Bahá'í Faith appointed the Trustee of Ḥuqúqu'lláh after the death of Ḥájí Abu'l-Ḥasan-i-Amín, eventually adopted the surname of Amín-i-Amín. Samandar and Ḥakím-Báshí (who defrayed all the expenses of the journey, returning the money which Samandar had paid) stayed for fifteen days in Ṭihrán. Their mission, carried out with tact and understanding, was successful.

The thirtieth journey of Samandar was again to Ṭihrán, to assist Siyyid Mihdí of Gulpáygán, in co-operation with a number of other distinguished Bahá'ís, with the task of bringing to completion the work begun by Mírzá Abu'l-Faḍl. The way Samandar refers to the course of this task makes it abundantly clear that, at the time he was writing, the work was far from finished.

Ḥájí Abu'l-Ḥasan-i-Amín (centre)*, assisted by Ḥájí Ghulám Riḍáy-i-Iṣfahání, later Amín-i-Amín* (on his left) *and Mírzá Taqíy-i-Qájár* (on his right)

Samandar's last journey, his thirty-first, took place in September 1915. It was to Rasht. His companion in the carriage which set out from Qazvín was Ibtiháju'l-Mulk, whose home was in Rasht. And there lived Samandar's son, Áqá Ghulám-'Alí, who by then had a grown-up family. Samandar's wish was to meet all the Bahá'ís of Rasht, but particularly Áqá 'Alíy-i-Arbáb and Áqá 'Alí's brother. His distinguished companion on that journey was to meet a martyr's death within a few short years of those very happy days which these two devoted servants of Bahá'u'lláh spent together in that waning summer of 1915. In Rasht, Samandar spent most of his time meeting enquirers in the home of a physician, Mírzá Mihdí Khán. This zealous Bahá'í, a native of Hamadán of Jewish background, has written an absorbing autobiography, which unfortunately has not seen the light of day. Those were indeed joyous days for Samandar. More members of his family came over from Qazvín. He stayed in Rasht till 20 March 1916.

Old age had brought infirmities, but despite his failing sight and increasing weakness, Samandar was tireless in serving the Cause of his Lord. Right to the end he was active in the teaching field. Early in 1918, in the midst of winter, Samandar winged his flight to realms beyond. He was truly an 'Apostle of Bahá'u'lláh'. He was both a man of the world, very successful as a merchant, and a saint, the soul of rectitude and integrity. Tablets revealed in his honour by Bahá'u'lláh were legion. Bahá'u'lláh Himself has borne witness to this bounty bestowed on Samandar: 'Were one to collect together all that hath been sent down unto thee of the verses of thy Lord, he would witness a mighty book, greater than other Tablets. This is of the grace of thy Lord. He is sufficient unto thee, by virtue of His truth. No God is there but Him, the Glorious, the Bestower.' (Quoted in Sulaymání, vol. 7, pp. 50–51)

Many, also, are the Tablets which 'Abdu'l-Bahá addressed to Samandar. All of them, Tablets of Bahá'u'lláh and Tablets of 'Abdu'l-Bahá, are mirrors of the station attained by Shaykh Káẓim-i-Samandar.

17

Núri'd-Dín

THE MOST EXALTED PEN addressed Mírzá Siyyid Muḥammad, the son of Mírzá Zaynu'l-'Ábidín, a close relative of the glorious Báb, as Núri'd-Dín: the Light of Faith. He was born in S͟híráz, in the year 1842, and from his infancy was called Mírzá Áqá, as a letter of the Báb to His wife indicates.

At the age of four the child was stricken by smallpox and was so ill that no recovery seemed at all possible. He had a brother, three years his senior, named Mírzá 'Alí-Riḍá, who also contracted smallpox, but his malady seemed not so severe. At this time, in September 1846, the Báb was quietly preparing to leave S͟híráz to turn to other climes, away from the domain of the Ájúdán-Bás͟hí, the governor-general of Fárs. Mírzá Zaynu'l-'Ábidín was a paternal cousin of the father of the Báb, and his wife, Zahrá Bigum, was a sister of the wife of the Báb. Shortly before His departure the Báb went to bid farewell to them. The two children, both very ill, were asleep on a couch in the courtyard. The Báb lifted the sheet on the bed of Mírzá Áqá and prayed over him, but He paid no attention to the elder brother. That child, seven years old, died the same night but Mírzá Áqá recovered. He was the only surviving child of Mírzá Zaynu'l-'Ábidín and Zahrá Bigum.

K͟hadíjih Bigum, the wife of the Báb, was particularly attached to this nephew and that tender feeling was much enhanced by the content of a letter which reached her from her glorious Husband, then cruelly incarcerated in the mountain-fortress of Mákú:

Do not expect any assistance from thy brothers. They will not help, it is enough that they refrain from insults. Overlook their faults.

Even Our enemies have not caused the like of what resulted from the acts of Siyyid 118* in Iṣfahán. God grant that when the light of thine eyes Mírzá

---

* 118 is the numerical equivalent of Hasan, Siyyid Hasan was one of the two brothers of K͟hadíjih Bigum. He is the Afnán-i-Kabír (the Great Afnán) of future years.

Áqá reacheth maturity, he will be thy help and support. O God! Preserve him from all the evil of the envious and the contumacious.

What the Báb had said of Mírzá Áqá made Khadíjih Bigum give special attention to the education and upbringing of the young boy. And Mírzá Áqá was destined to have the distinction of being the third member of the family of the Báb to believe in him.

Then came in rapid succession the triple tragedy of the martyrdom of Ḥájí Mírzá Siyyid 'Alí (the uncle of the Báb), followed by the martyrdom of the glorious Báb Himself, and soon the death of the nineteen-year-old Ḥájí Mírzá Javád, the son of Ḥájí Mírzá Siyyid 'Alí, far away from home at Jiddah.

The relatives of the Báb: two other maternal uncles and in particular the two brothers-in-law, were naturally grief-stricken and, although not believers as yet, were known to a hostile public as men related to the Báb and therefore suspect. No matter how hard they tried to dissociate themselves from the newly-proclaimed Faith and to show themselves as staunch Muslims, currying favour with the Shí'ih priesthood, they were regarded with suspicion. Two brothers of the wife of Ḥájí Mírzá Siyyid Muḥammad, one of the maternal uncles of the Báb – Ḥájí 'Abdu'l-Ḥusayn and Ḥájí Muḥammad-Khalíl – were viciously inimical, shouting abuse and defamation in public and making the life of their sister unbearable. Many a time it was mooted to declare these relatives of the Báb apostate, but they managed to ride the storm although suffering in the process, both mentally and materially. Two of the well-known divines of the day, both related to the Báb and secretly believers in Him, would, as far as it was feasible for them, provide protection for any believer under the scrutiny of public gaze. And yet tongues wagged. Immunity from the effects of the poison constantly instilled into the body politic was not possible. Those mujtahids were Ḥájí Mírzá Muḥammad-Ḥasan, the Ḥujjatu'l-Islám, soon to be famed as Mírzáy-i-Shírází, and Ḥájí Mírzá Javád, the Imám-Jum'ih of Kirmán.

The sorrows of the wife of the Báb, very evident and hard to conceal; the presence of the widow and daughters of Ḥujjat of Zanján in the house where Khadíjih Bigum lived; the occasional visits of the destitute and pitiable captives brought from Nayríz and the reluctance of the elders of the family to become involved, all gave the young Mírzá Áqá cause to think and investigate. But these were matters that his mind could not unravel, and he found himself asking his aunt to throw light upon them. Although he was no more than thirteen years old, his questing mind convinced <u>Kh</u>adíjih Bigum that the time had come to acquaint him with the story of the glorious Báb. And the young soul of Mírzá Áqá responded with its full ardour to the tidings given him by his aunt. The Qá'im of the House of Muḥammad had come in the Person of his own kinsman, Siyyid 'Alí-Muḥammad, the Báb, Whom a wayward generation had rejected and put to death. Love for Him – the glorious Báb, the martyred Qá'im – invaded and conquered completely the heart of the young boy. He desired intensely to quaff of the same cup, to give his life that the Cause of the Báb might live and flourish. <u>Kh</u>adíjih Bigum saw unmistakably the fulfilment of the promise which years ago her Husband had imparted to her from the fortress wherein He was incarcerated. And now <u>Kh</u>adíjih Bigum realized that her lion-hearted nephew was truly destined to be a distinguished and faithful servitor of the Cause of God.

Every day Mírzá Áqá would present himself before his bereaved aunts, <u>Kh</u>adíjih Bigum and the widow of Ḥájí Mírzá Siyyid 'Alí, to carry out their wishes, and would from time to time take them to visit orchards and sanctuaries outside the city, amongst them the mausoleums of the two great poets, Sa'dí and Ḥáfiẓ, and a famous orchard named Pudunak.*

Before long the father of Mírzá Áqá retired from his trading pursuits and confined himself to farming. Mírzá Áqá, now adolescent, formed a partnership with Ḥájí Mírzá Buzurg, the youngest son of Ḥájí Mírzá Siyyid Muḥammad (an uncle of the Báb), who was of the same age as himself. They entered the world of commerce under the supervision of Ḥájí Mírzá Abu'l-Qásim (the brother of <u>Kh</u>adíjih Bigum) and Ḥájí Mírzá Siyyid Muḥammad. Each of them had a capital of seven-hundred-and-fifty *túmáns* to start with.

Mírzá Áqá, whilst embarking on a business career, was also quietly nurturing relationships with a few other Bábís who lived in <u>Sh</u>íráz. Then it was that he determinedly turned his attention to his own parents to help them embrace the Faith revealed by their Kinsman. In this he succeeded and they gave their allegiance unreservedly to the Báb. His next spiritual undertaking was not at all easy to achieve. He

---

* The Báb Himself oftentimes visited these mausoleums, known as Haft-Tanán (Seven Men) and <u>Ch</u>ihil-Tanán (Forty Men), which are resting-places of a number of saintly figures.

Afnán relatives of the Báb and other Bahá'ís of Shíráz in the company of Ḥájí Mírzá Abu'l-Qásim (seated above at right)*, a brother-in-law of the Báb and the great-grandfather of Shoghi Effendi, the Guardian of the Bahá'í Faith. Others identified are:* (front row, from left) *Shaykh 'Alí Mírzá, a nephew of the Imám-Jum'ih; Mírzá Abu'l-Ḥasan, the maternal grandfather of H.M. Balyuzi; Mírzá Mihdí, a poet of note whose sobriquet was Ṣábir; Mírzá Buzurg, a cousin of the Báb; Siyyid Muḥammad-Ḥusayn, the paternal grandfather of Shoghi Effendi; Áqá Mírzá Áqá, Núri'd-Dín;* (second row, from left) *unknown; Mírzá 'Alí-Akbar, the son of Ṣábir; Mírzá Maḥmúd, son of Ḥájí Mírzá Abu'l-Qásim, above; Ḥájí Ghulám-Ḥusayn Khán, the host and an outstanding Bahá'í of Shíráz; Mírzá Hádí, the father of Shoghi Effendi; Mírzá Siyyid 'Alí; Mírzá Muḥammad-Báqir Khán (Dihqán); Mírzá Raḥím, brother of Mírzá Hádí. (The three at the back are unidentified.)*

challenged boldly no less a person than Ḥájí Mírzá Siyyid Muḥammad, the uncle of the Báb. This highly revered merchant, whose brothers-in-law were in the forefront of the bitter adversaries of the Báb, had, as far as discretion allowed, tried to shield those who were associated with his Nephew. He would have gone to any length to save his Nephew from the malevolence of His foes, but to give Him his allegiance he decidedly would not. From the very beginning Ḥájí Mírzá Siyyid Muḥammad had refused to take the path which his martyred younger brother had taken. Now, faced with a determined young man, only seventeen years old, he hedged himself with traditions, both genuine and of doubtful authenticity. To fend off the persistent appeals of his enthusiastic young relative, Ḥájí Mírzá Siyyid Muḥammad used every armour of the orthodox.

Ḥájí Mírzá Ḥabíbu'lláh Afnán, the distinguished son of Áqá Mírzá Áqá, has put on paper his father's reminiscences of that spiritual struggle between himself, a boy of seventeen, and the venerable uncle of the Báb:

At the beginning when I broached the subject the uncle expressed total refusal. I went on presenting proofs supporting my argument. We went through several meetings until one day, when I was strenuously following my line, he said with great amazement: 'Mírzá Áqá! Do you mean to say that the son of my sister is the Qá'im of the House of Muḥammad?' I replied: 'Why not?' Then he showed still more amazement and said: 'It is strange, very strange.' I replied: 'There is nothing strange about it!' Then he became very pensive. That made me smile. He asked me: 'Why do you smile?' I answered: 'It will not be polite if I say why.' He said: 'Do not be shy, tell me.' I replied: 'Now that you allow me I will say it. What you said just now is exactly what Abú-Lahab* exclaimed: "Is it possible for my nephew to be a Prophet!" Indeed it was possible, and the Nephew of Abú-Lahab was the Messenger of God. Now, would you investigate and find out for yourself? This Sun has arisen from your house, this Light has shone from your abode; you must feel proud. Don't be amazed, don't seek avoidance. God the Almighty has the power to have made the Son of your sister the Qá'im of the House of Muḥammad. The hand of God is not tied. As the Qur'án declares: His hand is free!' Then he [the uncle of the Báb] said: 'Núr-i-Chashm, you gave me an answer which is unanswerable! What can I say and what should I do now?' I replied: 'Firstly, it is necessary that you go on pilgrimage to 'Iráq and meet your sister who is there [the mother of the Báb]. Secondly, Íshán [the Blessed Beauty] is in Baghdád. Stop there for a few days. Present your difficulties to Him. Try, endeavour, put your trust in God. Let us hope that you shall attain and reach faith. Man has to strive [a reference to a Qur'ánic verse].' Having

* An uncle of Muḥammad who rejected and opposed His Mission. (Ed.)

listened to me, he commented: 'It is good what you say. It touched my heart.' (pp. 157–60 of unpublished memoirs)

Ḥájí Mírzá Siyyid Muḥammad, we know, went to the holy cities of 'Iráq having his younger brother, Ḥájí Mírzá Ḥasan-'Alí, with him; went into the presence of Bahá'u'lláh without his brother; and presented his questions – questions which evoked from the pen of Bahá'u'lláh the Book of Certitude (*Kitáb-i-Íqán*).*

Ḥájí Mírzá Ḥabíbu'lláh has further written:

Having received and read the *Kitáb-i-Íqán*, which contained answers to his questions, and having attained faith and assurance, he [Ḥájí Mírzá Siyyid Muḥammad] visited the holy cities, and after meeting his sister, the mother of the Báb, returned to Shíráz. Believers came to visit him and received spiritual sustenance from him. He [Áqá Mírzá Áqá] used to say: 'After attaining his presence he thanked me most profoundly and told me: "Although considering age you are as my own son, but in the realm of the Spirit you are as my father, because if it were not for your insistence I would never have attained the measure of faith which is the utmost desideratum of those who seek nearness to God." He then prayed for me with his whole heart.' (ibid. pp. 165–6)

Bahá'u'lláh, in those days, had not as yet declared His Mission, but from Baghdád He was addressing Tablets to the wife of the Báb, and to a number of devout Bábís such as Mírzá 'Abdu'l-Karím, Shaykh-'Alí Mírzá and Ḥájí Abu'l-Ḥasan. His signature read as 152, equivalent to Bahá. The wife of the Báb always turned to Bahá'u'lláh.

Subsequent to the return of Ḥájí Mírzá Siyyid Muḥammad from 'Iráq, Mírzá Áqá and his father, Mírzá Zaynu'l-'Ábidín, wrote and asked permission to travel to Baghdád and visit Bahá'u'lláh. Khadíjih Bigum, in order to introduce her nephew, sent to Bahá'u'lláh the Letter of the Báb, the Letter already mentioned in these pages. Both father and son were honoured with an answer, and the letters were in the handwriting of 'Abdu'l-Bahá.

In the Tablet addressed to Áqá Mírzá Áqá, the receipt of the Letter of the Báb to Khadíjih Bigum is acknowledged in these words:

Then, know thou that the Letter that was of God hath reached Us, and this is loved by Me more than anything else in heaven and on earth, and more than aught that was or shall be. We ask of God to bestow on thee the best of all rewards and to raise thee to an exalted and glorious station. (Unpublished)

* The gist of the questions presented to Bahá'u'lláh by Ḥájí Mírzá Siyyid Muḥammad, found amongst his papers in his own handwriting, is given in *Bahá'u'lláh, The King of Glory*, pp. 163–5. (Ed.)

Time passed, Bahá'u'lláh was called to Istanbul, and on the twelfth day of Riḍván, as He was about to leave the Garden of Najíbíyyah and take the road to the capital of the Ottoman Empire, He revealed a Tablet which exists in His own handwriting addressed to Áqá Mírzá Áqá, reading thus:

Áqá in <u>Sh</u>ín*

He is the Glorious!

Hearken to what the departing Dove revealeth unto thee, as He prepareth to leave the realm of 'Iráq – such are the methods of God decreed for His Messengers. Let this not cause thee sorrow. Put thy trust in thy Lord and the Lord of thy forefathers . . . Those who are endowed with the insight of the spirit are independent of all that was and shall be created, and are able to behold the mysteries of the Cause behind the thickest veils. Say, O beloved of God! Fear none and let nothing grieve thee; be steadfast in the Cause. By God, those who have drunk of the love of God, the Glorious, the Effulgent, have no fear of anyone, and show patience in calamity, like unto the patience of the lover toward the good-pleasure of the beloved. With them affliction ranketh greater than that which the lovers perceive in the countenance of the beloved. Say, O concourse of evil-doers! Ere long the Cause of God will, in truth, be exalted, and the standards of those who join partners with God will perish, and the people shall enter the Faith of God, the Sovereign, the Supreme, the Ancient of Days. Well is it with those who have now hastened forth in the love of God and received the tidings of the breath of the Holy Spirit. Glory be unto you, O concourse of believers in the unity of God.

Know then that thy letter hath reached Us, and We have given this reply to create in thy heart the warmth of yearning, to cause thee to turn to the paradise of this resplendent Name, to make thee detached from all, and to enable thee to soar to such heights as have not been attained by the wings of the worldly-wise who are not under the shadow of God's countenance and who are indeed of the perplexed. (Unpublished)

The news of the departure of Bahá'u'lláh from Ba<u>gh</u>dád, and of the hostile behaviour of the governments and the high officials of the two empires, Persian and Ottoman, trickled through to Persia and caused consternation amongst the Bábís. But when the Tablet addressed to Áqá Mírzá Áqá reached <u>Sh</u>íráz, it brought not only relief from anxiety, but great happiness. The promise of the Báb had been fulfilled: 'Him Whom God shall make manifest' had come forth. Now, at least for the time being, joy and exhilaration prevailed. Although sorrow, much sorrow, was to come; the Manifestation of God was to suffer and suffer grievously; yet the very fact of His

---

* <u>Sh</u>, the 15th letter of the Persian alphabet, is pronounced <u>Sh</u>ín. Here the city of <u>Sh</u>íráz is indicated.

The pulpit of the Masjid-i-Vakíl in Shíráz, where the Báb addressed the Friday congregation on the invitation of the Imám-Jum'ih, Shaykh Abú-Turáb

Advent reanimated the community of the Báb and gave the Bábís, hereafter to be known as Bahá'ís, vigour renewed.

In Shíráz Áqá Mírzá Áqá, the recipient of such a powerful Tablet in the handwriting of Bahá'u'lláh Himself, stepped into the arena of teaching, more than ever determined to serve his Lord, to make his fellow-citizens aware of the precious hour in which they lived. There were still many people alive in Shíráz who remembered vividly the day when the glorious Báb stood on the pulpit of Masjid-i-Vakíl and spoke to the multitude, who remembered the cruelties inflicted on Him and His faithful followers, who remembered the parading of Quddús and Ismu'lláhu'l-Aṣdaq in the streets of their city. Áqá Mírzá Áqá made friends with a number of those men who were well known for their integrity and succeeded in clearing away their doubts.

About fifty of them, members of a family known as Khayyáṭ (Tailor) thus embraced the Faith. Mullá 'Abbás-'Alíy-i-Shamsábádí, who hailed from the district of Marvdasht,* was one who came into the Bábí fold subsequent to the incident in the Mosque of Vakíl. Áqá Mírzá Áqá sought his aid in establishing friendly relations with the prominent men of Marvdasht. His efforts led to the conversion of Ḥájí Muḥammad-Káẓim-i-Naṣrábádí, a mystic of his time and very powerful in the area of Rámjird. Mírzá Mihdí Khán-i-Fatḥábádí, a noted poet, was another convert. Karbilá'í Ḥasan Khán and Karbilá'í Ṣádiq, both of Sarvistán, who had just learned of the Cause of Bahá'u'lláh, and Muḥammad-Háshim Khán of Band-i-Amír† found in Áqá Mírzá Áqá a highly trustworthy and efficient agent to attend to their affairs in Shíráz, which were indeed considerable.

Áqá Mírzá Áqá was regularly corresponding with Sulṭánu'sh-Shuhadá' (King of the Martyrs) and Maḥbúbu'sh-Shuhadá' (Beloved of the Martyrs), the two brothers, Mírzá Ḥasan and Mírzá Ḥusayn, whom the treachery and bad faith of the Imám-Jum'ih of Iṣfahán and Prince Mas'úd Mírzá, the Ẓillu's-Sulṭán, later sent to their deaths. (See chap. 3.) He also had business dealings with them. Unfortunately most of their correspondence has been lost with the passage of time, but what remains speaks eloquently of their intimate friendship and of the conditions under which the Cause of Bahá'u'lláh had to fare in those early days.

It was from Adrianople that Bahá'u'lláh sent Nabíl-i-A'ẓam to 'Iráq and Írán, bearing the tidings of the Advent of Him Whose Name adorns all of the Scriptures of mankind. Furthermore, Nabíl had been appointed by Bahá'u'lláh to perform the rites of pilgrimage on His behalf in the House of the Báb. Nabíl reached Shíráz by the way of Búshihr and stayed at the house of Áqá Mírzá Áqá. Prior to anything else he proceeded to perform the rites of pilgrimage. He knew by heart the *Tablet of Ḥajj* (Pilgrimage). When night fell he left the city, and as dawn broke from the heights overlooking Shíráz, Nabíl could discern the outlines of the city. Then he began to recite the Tablet of pilgrimage and walked on to descend into the plain. Having gone through Darvázih Qur'án – the Gate of Qur'án,‡ within a distance of

* Persepolis is situated in the area of Marvdasht.
† Bendemir of Thomas Moore's 'Lalla Rookh' (Lálih-Rukh).
‡ In an upper room over this gateway there is laid a voluminous copy of the Qur'án, said to be in the handwriting of Imám Ḥasan, the Second Imám.

a thousand paces from the gate to the city he stopped at a building* reared by Karím Khán-i-Zand, and made his ablutions in the waters of Rukní (Áb-i-Rukní). The waters of Rukní or Ruknábád have been eulogized by the great poet Ḥáfiẓ. Then, having completed his ablutions, Nabíl perfumed himself, put on a decorous and costly robe, and walked on towards the city. The sun had not yet risen when he reached the city-gates. There, lost to the world, he prostrated himself and put his forehead on the ground, on the sacred soil of Shíráz. The muleteers and the attendants of caravans, who were leaving the city at that early hour, were puzzled by the sight of Nabíl, and thinking that he had swooned sprinkled rose-water on his face. But at that moment Nabíl was in a world apart. He circumambulated the House of the Báb and completed all the rites of pilgrimage.

Before telling anyone else of the message which Bahá'u'lláh had entrusted to him Nabíl gave it to Khadíjih Bigum, the wife of the Báb. Upon hearing it, she immediately responded without the slightest hesitation, and acknowledged with joy the station of Bahá'u'lláh: He in Whose path her glorious Husband had given His life. It was Khadíjih Bigum, who, weeks before the encounter between her Husband and Mullá Ḥusayn-i-Bushrú'í, had witnessed the effulgent light of God shining from His Person, and had recognized Him as the Qá'im of the House of Muḥammad. And now, at once, she gave her allegiance to Bahá'u'lláh. To this immediate, unqualified response which was evoked from the heart and the soul of Khadíjih Bigum, the Most Exalted Pen has testified abundantly:

O My Leaf! . . . Thou art with the Supreme Companion, and this Wronged One is making mention of thee in the Prison of 'Akká. Thou art she, who, before the creation of the world of being, found the fragrance of the garment of the Merciful . . . Thou art the one who, as soon as the call uttered by the Lord of the Kingdom of Names reached thy hearing, turned to Him, and was so attracted as to lose all restraint! (See Fayḍí, *Khánadán-i-Afnán*, pp. 1 and 3 of a 4-page Tablet attached to p. 185.)

Having delivered the message of Bahá'u'lláh to Khadíjih Bigum, Nabíl turned his attention to others of his co-religionists in Shíráz, meeting them individually or in groups. The Bahá'ís, for their part, became greatly attached to Nabíl, ready to do his bidding. Feeling the great eagerness and total devotion of the Bahá'ís of Shíráz, Nabíl then

* Called Tanúrih-Ásíyábí, it was situated approximately where the headquarters of the Gendarmerie of Shíráz stand today, in the Qur'án Avenue.

took another step. He called all of them together to a large gathering and asked them to bring along every Tablet, every book related to the Cause which they had. Let us hear of what happened in the words of Áqá Mírzá Áqá, as recorded by his son, Ḥájí Mírzá Ḥabíbu'lláh:

As requested by Nabíl I invited the friends to come to a meeting, and I chose the house of Mírzá 'Abdu'l-Karím as the place for holding this meeting because his house was well-appointed. The uncle [Ḥájí Mírzá Siyyid Muḥammad] was particularly invited to come and grace this meeting. When all had arrived Nabíl spoke. He declared the Advent of 'Him Whom God shall make manifest', He Whose Revelation had been promised in the *Bayán*. That Supreme Manifestation of Godhead, he stated, was Bahá'u'lláh and none other. Next he divided the writings which the Bahá'ís had brought with them into three sections. Taking up the first section, he said: 'These are from the pen of the Primal Point [the Báb], sacred, precious, very dear to us.' Then he pointed to the second portion and said: 'These are revealed by "Him Whom God shall make manifest". The Báb promised His Advent, made the acceptance or rejection of all He had revealed in His own Book, the *Bayán*, dependent on the good-pleasure and all-pervading will of that Supreme Manifestation, and warned us not to tarry for a moment but to give Him when He comes instant recognition and allegiance. We have been barred by the Báb from taking the wayward path followed by the people preceding us, thus straying into the wilderness. He [Bahá'u'lláh] is that Supreme Manifestation of Godhead in Whose path the Báb sacrificed Himself, with His own blood pledging His brave and devout followers to remain constant and faithful, not to deprive themselves of the bounty of responding to the call of the Speaker of the Mount. Now all that was promised in the *Bayán* and in the *Qayyúmu'l-Asmá'* has come to pass. Note the Qá'im [the Báb] and the Qayyúm [Bahá'u'lláh]. Note the pronouncement of the Báb regarding the year nine when all good would be realized. Indeed that prophecy is fulfilled. It is Bahá'u'lláh Who is leading us to the understanding of the Cause of God. Whoever ranges himself under His shadow is of the people of the Light, and whoever takes himself away is of the people of the nether world and totally cut off from the reality of the Cause of the Báb.' He [Nabíl] spoke in that vein for nearly an hour.

Then he [Nabíl] took up the third portion of the writings and said: 'These belong to doubters and people of wrong thought and their place is in the fire.' Saying that, he threw them into the fire-place where a fire was burning. This action of Nabíl caused an uproar and protest; particularly Ḥájí Mírzá Siyyid Muḥammad, who did not expect such action on the part of Nabíl in his presence, was very angry and vociferously protested, saying time and again: 'Do you take faith to be like weed; you cut it in daytime and it grows again during the night?'

Then it was that this servant intervened and spoke. Áqá Mírzá 'Abdu'l-Karím, Ḥájí Abu'l-Ḥasan and Shaykh-'Alí Mírzá came to my aid. Courteously and humbly it was put to him: 'Firstly, investigate for yourself to find

> the truth of Nabíl's words. Secondly, you should know for a certainty that, according to the text of the *Bayán*, no one save "Him Whom God shall make manifest" has the temerity to put forth a claim so great. Regard the Báb: despite His virtues, the truth which He bore, the guidance which was His to give, He was made the target of malice and hate. He *was* the Truth, He spoke the truth; and you yourself came to realize it when you attained the presence of Íshán [Bahá'u'lláh] in Baghdád, when He resolved your difficulties and within the span of two nights revealed for you the *Kitáb-i-Íqán*, thus dispelling all your doubts. Even if revealing that book should not provide the proof needed for anyone else, it should be the entire and complete proof for your person, leaving not the slightest doubt and giving you the assurance that He is the Truth, that turning away from Him is the very essence of waywardness. (Unpublished memoirs, pp. 169–73)

Ḥájí Mírzá Siyyid Muḥammad said no more. But Nabíl did not cease following up his course until the uncle of the Báb openly declared his belief and recognized the station of Bahá'u'lláh. In subsequent meetings, in the presence of all, Ḥájí Mírzá Siyyid Muḥammad prostrated himself to render thanks for having been guided to the straight path, and praised the Blessed Perfection for that bounty of recognition. Tears of joy coursed down his cheeks. His acknowledgement of the station of Bahá'u'lláh led everyone else in Shíráz to do the same, everyone that is who had accepted the Báb. And thus not a soul remained in the city of the Báb among His followers who did not turn to Bahá'u'lláh and recognize in Him the Redeemer of Mankind. Shíráz, the city where the Dawn had broken, became free of blemish. It was the grace of the Báb which kept His native town cleansed and purified.

A certain Shaykh Muḥammad of Yazd lived in Shíráz. Prior to the Declaration of Bahá'u'lláh he would state that He was a Manifestation of God, but when the call of Bahá'u'lláh was raised Shaykh Muḥammad rose up in opposition. The Bahá'ís of Shíráz cut him off. Subsequently he left and made his way to Istanbul. Thus Shíráz remained immune from his sedition, but he caused a good deal of mischief in Istanbul, leagued with leading Azalís.

Nabíl, having brought his mission to a successful conclusion in Shíráz, left for Iṣfahán. Soon after, Ḥájí Muḥammad-Ibráhím, whom Bahá'u'lláh had honoured with the designation 'Muballigh' (Teacher, Missioner), moved to Shíráz, his father's native town. Ḥájí 'Abdu'r-Rasúl, the father of Muballigh, was a convert from Judaism to Islám. And the sister of Muballigh, Ḥájíyyih Bíbí Gawhar, was married to

Ḥájí Muḥammad-Ibráhím, whom Bahá'u'lláh designated 'Muballigh' (Teacher)

Ḥájí Mírzá Ḥasan-'Alí, known as Khál-i-Aṣghar, the youngest of the three maternal uncles of the Báb. Ḥájí Muḥammad-Ibráhím was a merchant and his arrival at Shíráz did not at first cause any stir. However, the purpose of his visit was not trading but teaching the Faith, particularly to the remaining members of the Family of the Báb. He directed his attention to Ḥájí Mírzá Buzurg, son of Ḥájí Mírzá Siyyid Muḥammad (uncle of the Báb), to Siyyid Muḥammad-Ḥusayn (paternal grandfather of Shoghi Effendi, the Guardian of the Bahá'í Faith), and to Mírzá Abu'l-Ḥasan and Mírzá Maḥmúd, sons of Ḥájí Mírzá Abu'l-Qásim (the brother-in-law of the Báb). All became Bahá'ís.

Áqá Mírzá Áqá also tried to bring his paternal relatives, who were *mustawfís* (auditors and controllers of governmental accounts), and the Lashkar-Nivís (Paymaster-General) into the circle of the Faith, but there he did not succeed. These men showed such hostility that all family ties were snapped, and two generations later the descendants of Áqá Mírzá Áqá and the descendants of these relatives, although all of them lived in Shíráz, became total strangers. It is a well-told tale in the family that Áqá Mírzá Áqá together with Ḥájí Muḥammad-Ibráhím were one day locked in argument with Mírzá 'Abbás, who was a son of Ḥájí Mírzá Ibráhím-i-Lashkar-Nivís and a cousin of Mírzá Áqá (the son of a paternal aunt). Mírzá 'Abbás remained adamantly opposed. At last he said: 'If there be truth in this claim of the Báb, let me fall down when mounting my horse outside this house, and let the bone in my right thigh crack.' Áqá Mírzá Áqá replied: 'Ask God to illumine your heart with the light of faith, not maim you.' But he refused to change his plea and sure enough, he met with the accident he had mentioned, exactly at the place he had named. The rest of his life he had to hobble with a stick, but to faith he obstinately remained alien.

After a long stay in Shíráz, Ḥájí Muḥammad-Ibráhím went to Yazd and promised to do his utmost to bring Ḥájí Mírzá Ḥasan-'Alí and Ḥájí Mírzá Siyyid Ḥasan, the Afnán-i-Kabír, into the Bahá'í Faith. As it happened, Mullá Muḥammad – Nabíl-i-Akbar – reached Yazd at the same time. The combined efforts of the Muballigh and Nabíl-i-Akbar convinced the uncle of the Báb and His brother-in-law that the Faith of the Báb and Bahá'u'lláh was true. That victory achieved, the only one left to be won over was Ḥájí Mírzá Abul-Qásim, the brother of Afnán-i-Kabír. Nabíl-i-Akbar, after a sojourn of about a year in Yazd, made for Shíráz where he stayed for thirteen months. During that time Ḥájí Mírzá Abul-Qásim yielded to the urgent pleas of his son, Siyyid Muḥammad-Ḥusayn, and his nephew, Áqá Mírzá Áqá, and turned to Bahá'u'lláh. Then he was honoured with a Tablet, and thus the circle was closed. All of the Afnáns were now safe and secure in the enclave of the Faith of Bahá'u'lláh.

There were two grandees in Shíráz, Mushíru'l-Mulk and Qavámu'l-Mulk, who were most of the time at daggers drawn, bitterly fighting over offices and posts of which the Governor disposed. Mushíru'l-Mulk, in particular, striving to create difficulties for his rival and to make the Governor suspicious, made the Bahá'ís the butt of his intrigues. When Sulṭán-Murád Mírzá, the Ḥisámu's-Salṭanih, an uncle of Náṣiri'd-Dín Sháh, arrived as the Governor-General of Fárs, Mushíru'l-Mulk, who enjoyed the post of the Vazír of the province, drew up a list of prominent Bahá'ís of Shíráz which included the names of Ḥájí Mírzá Siyyid Muḥammad and Ḥájí Mírzá Abu'l-Qásim, and gave the list to Ḥisámu's-Salṭanih to persecute them. Qavámu'l-Mulk, on this occasion, intervened and prevented mischief. But Mushíru'l-Mulk would not sit still. He found a way to raise an uproar. Mírzá Áqáy-i-Rikáb-Sáz was one of the early Bábís of Shíráz, having given his allegiance to the Báb after the incident of the Mosque of Vakíl. Strangely, he had close connections with Shaykh Ḥusayn-i-Ẓalim, the Náẓimu'sh-Sharí'ih, a bitter enemy of the Báb. On the very day that the Báb was brought to the Masjid-i-Vakíl (the Mosque of Vakíl) and asked to speak from the pulpit, this Shaykh Ḥusayn insulted Him and tried to hit Him with his walking-stick. Mírzá Áqá's wife was very hostile towards the Faith and, induced by Mushíru'l-Mulk, she sold her husband to the infamous Shaykh Ḥusayn. That treachery led to the arrest of Mírzá Áqá. Not only this excellent calligraphist,* but several Bahá'ís besides him were detained as well and thrown into prison, where they endured several hardships. These were Mashhadí Nabí, Mashhadí Muḥammad-Ja'far-i-Khayyáṭ, Ḥájí Abu'l-Ḥasan-i-Bazzáz (the mercer), Karbilá'í Muḥammad-Háshim, Karbilá'í Ḥasan Khán-i-Sarvistání, Mashhadí Abu'l-Qásim-i-Kharráz (the haberdasher), Mírzá Báqir, Mullá 'Abdu'lláh-i-Fáḍil-i-Zarqání, and Mullá 'Abdu'lláh-i-Buká'.

Áqá Mírzá Áqá (Núri'd-Dín) made every endeavour to bring about their release. At last Mushíru'l-Mulk himself stood bail for Mullá 'Abdu'lláh-i-Fáḍil and Mullá 'Abdu'lláh-i-Buká'. Qavámu'l-Mulk, on the other hand, brought about the release of Karbilá'í Ḥasan Khán, and the Imám-Jum'ih managed to get Ḥájí Abu'l-Ḥasan out of the gaol. Mírzá Báqir was heavily bastinadoed and expelled from Shíráz; he went to Kirmán, where he was martyred. Mírzá Áqáy-i-Rikáb-Sáz, Mashhadí Nabí and Mashhadí Muḥammad-Ja'far-i-Khayyáṭ met their martyrdom in Ḥisámu's-Salṭanih's prison.† The mercer, Ḥájí Abu'l-Ḥasan, after his release, found it impossible to live in Shíráz. He fled to the villages in the districts of Sarvistán and Kurbál, taking with him his two sons, children of tender age (the future Mírzá Muḥammad-Báqir Khán Dihqán [Dehkan] and Mírzá Muḥammad-'Alí Khán). Oftentimes, he had to seek refuge in caves and on the mountain-side to escape the venom of the foe. After a while he returned to Shíráz and took his abode in the House of the Báb. Every now and then he attended the Imám-Jum'ih, so that the

* The frontispiece of *Bahá'u'lláh, The King of Glory* is the first page of the *Kitáb-i-Íqán* from the copy belonging to the author, in the handwriting of Mírzá Áqáy-i-Rikáb-Sáz, who had a good hand at Naskh script.

† When they were martyred, the rabble in Shíráz committed abominations, shameful to describe.

Shaykh Salmán (seated, right)*, the courier between Bahá'u'lláh and the Bahá'ís of Írán, in Shíráz in the year* AH *1288 (1871–72), with Ḥájí Abu'l-Ḥasan-i-Bazzáz* (seated, left)*, the father of Mírzá Muḥammad-Báqir Khán (Dihqán), and* (standing) *'Abbás-Qulí Khán*

public should perceive his attachment to that influential divine. Actually his wife was related to the Imám-Jum'ih. Finally he opened a shop in the bazar known as Bázár-i-Ḥájí.

Shaykh Salmán was the courier who took supplications of the Bahá'ís of Persia to the Holy Land and brought Tablets revealed by Bahá'u'lláh. When in the year AH 1288 (23 March 1871–10 March 1872) he passed through Shíráz, he told Áqá Mírzá Áqá that on his return he would be bringing a pilgrim to the Holy Land to stay with the wife of the Báb whilst in Shíráz. However, caution led him not to mention the identity of this pilgrim and guest. Before long, Áqá Mírzá Áqá received a letter from Maḥbúbu'sh-Shuhadá' (Beloved of the Martyrs), stating that Áqá Siyyid Yaḥyá and his sister would be leaving soon for the Holy Land, and whilst in Shíráz they should be guests of Khadíjih Bigum. Munírih Khánum (soon to be wedded to 'Abdu'l-Bahá) reached Shíráz in Shavvál 1288 (December 1871–January 1872), and stayed for two weeks with the wife of the Báb. Khadíjih Bigum asked Munírih Khánum to present to Bahá'u'lláh a request from her: that the House of the Báb be repaired once again, and that she be permitted to reside in it. (She had been living in the house of the uncle of the Báb.)

Bahá'u'lláh granted Khadíjih Bigum's request, and the task of the restoration of the house was given to Áqá Mírzá Áqá and Ḥájí Siyyid 'Alí, a son of Afnán-i-Kabír. A mason of Shíráz, Ustád 'Abdu'r-Razzáq, a devoted Bahá'í, was chosen for the work, but the house was not restored exactly as it had been in the days of the Báb. The work done, Khadíjih Bigum took her residence there. Fiḍḍih, the faithful negress, attended her, and for a while very few knew that Khadíjih Bigum had moved into that house, but before long Bahá'ís became aware of it and started frequenting it more and more. The fanatical residents of the houses of that street sat up and took notice, began to whimper, and went complaining to the mullás. Very soon it all came to the ears of Prince Farhád Mírzá, the Mu'tamidu'd-Dawlih, an uncle of Náṣiri'd-Dín Sháh, who was at this time the Governor-General of Fárs. And so Mu'tamidu'd-Dawlih decided to damage the House of the Báb. Two of his private secretaries who were Bahá'ís immediately informed Áqá Mírzá Áqá of what the crafty prince intended to do. Mírzá Áqá at once moved his aunt and the negress attendant, at night-time, to his own house which was close to the Jámi' Mosque of Shíráz. Khadíjih Bigum stayed in her nephew's house for nearly six months.

Around this time the Bahá'í community of Shíráz was prospering. There were some two hundred men and women, amongst them a number of very brave and devout believers, raised by the hand of the Almighty to serve His Cause and give it victory. Foremost amongst them stood Mírzá 'Abdu'l-Karím, Mírzá 'Alí-Akbar (son of the poet known as Ṣábir), Mudhahibb-Báshí (the Chief Illuminator), Shaykh-'Alí Mírzá, Ḥájí Mírzá Buzurg-i-Afnán (a son of Ḥájí Mírzá Siyyid Muḥammad), Mírzá Siyyid 'Alí, Ḥájí Ghulám-Ḥusayn Khán and Mírzá Muḥammad-Báqir Khán (Dihqán – Dehkan – of later years). Mu'tamidu'd-Dawlih was still the Governor when, due to the avarice of the Imám-Ju'mih of Iṣfahán and the cunning of Ẓillu's-Sulṭán, the two illustrious brothers, Sulṭánu'sh-Shuhadá' (King of the Martyrs) and Mahbúbu'sh-Shuhadá' (Beloved of the Martyrs), were

Some of the Bahá'í community of Shíráz in AH *1297* (AD *1879*), *identified as follows* (from left to right): (1st row, seated) *Áqá Mírzá 'Alí, son of Ḥájí Mírzá Abu'l-Qáṣim-i-Afnán; Áqá Mírzá Ibráhím, son of Ḥájí Mírzá Abu'l-Qáṣim-i-Afnán; Mírzá 'Alí-Akbar, son of the poet known as Ṣábir;* (2nd row, seated) *Áqá Mírzá Maḥmúd, son of Ḥájí Mírzá Abu'l-Qáṣim-i-Afnán; Áqá Mírzá Abu'l-Ḥasan, son of Ḥájí Mírzá Abu'l-Qáṣim-i-Afnán and grandfather of H.M. Balyuzi; Ḥájí Mírzá Buzurg, son of Ḥájí Mírzá Siyyid Muḥammad, uncle of the Báb; Áqá Siyyid Ḥusayn-i-Afnán, father of Áqá Mírzá Hádí (father of Shoghi Effendi);* (3rd row) *Mírzá Muḥammad-Báqir Khán (Dihqán); Ḥájí Ghulám-Ḥusayn Khán; Mírzá Siyyid 'Alí;* (back row) *Áqá Mírzá Raḥím, brother of Áqá Mírzá Hádí; next two unknown; Áqá Mírzá 'Abdu'lláh-i-Iṣfahání, father of Dr Ḥabíbu'lláh Salmánpúr*

beheaded. They had had commercial dealings with Áqá Mírzá Áqá. As the news of that foul treachery and the martyrdom of such distinguished and well-famed men reached Shíráz, commotion came upon the city, particularly in mercantile quarters. Since amongst the Bahá'í merchants Áqá Mírzá Áqá was the most prominent, the Afnáns felt that he ought to leave Shíráz, at least for a short while, lest Mu'tamidu'd-Dawlih should follow the pattern of Ẓillu's-Sulṭán, his great-nephew, and attempt to extort money and, in the process of lining his pockets, jeopardize the life of this Afnán who was known to everyone as an outspoken member of the Bahá'í Faith. Within twenty-four hours, Áqá Mírzá Áqá was hurried out of Shíráz by his relatives and was on his way to Búshihr, where without lingering he took a boat to Bombay.

The martyrdom of the two illustrious brothers in Iṣfahán was indeed very hard for Áqá Mírzá Áqá to bear. They had been life-long friends and business associates. Bahá'u'lláh honoured him, in this period of engulfing sorrow, with this Tablet:

He is the Comforter, the All-Knowing

O My Afnán! That which thou hadst repeatedly sent to our Name Mihdí was read in Our presence, and from it We sensed the fragrance of sorrow caused by this calamity which hath robed the Temple of Grandeur with the garment of grief. Thy Lord is, in truth, the Source of praise, the All-Knowing. Verily, over this supreme affliction My Most Exalted Pen hath lamented. To this beareth witness what the Maker of the heavens hath sent down in His manifest Book. Well is it with him who recalleth those who met a martyr's death in the path of God, whether in former or in recent times, or in these days, and readeth what was sent down for them from God, the Lord of the worlds. O My Afnán! Verily the divine Lote-Tree hath moaned and the Rock hath cried out, but the evil-doers are deep in slumber. Ere long the scourge of the wrath of thy Lord shall make them aware. Verily, He is the All-Knowing, the All-Informed. O My Afnán! It is incumbent on everyone who hath drunk of the wine of the love of God to share, with the denizens of the Supreme Concourse, in this supreme affliction and great calamity, for they mourn as they see the utmost sorrow of this Wronged One – the evidence of His grace, His fidelity and His bounty. Verily, He is the Gracious, the Ancient of Days. Nevertheless thou and all the other beloved ones of God should evince the utmost resignation, acquiescence, patience and submissiveness to the will of God . . . (Unpublished)

And there were other Tablets revealed by Bahá'u'lláh concerning the martyrdom of the twin luminaries of Iṣfahán, addressed to Áqá Mírzá Áqá and others of the Afnáns in Shíráz and Yazd.

Áqá Mírzá Áqá arose, as was his wont, to propagate the Faith of Bahá'u'lláh in Bombay, where he resided at 5 Appolo Street. Ḥájí Mírzá Muḥammad-i-Afshár and Ḥájí Muḥammad-Ibráhím-i-Muballigh were both in Bombay and aided his efforts. He gave the message of Bahá'u'lláh to anyone who was willing to listen. One of these was named Músá, of Jewish background. This merchant and his family came into the circle of the Faith and went on pilgrimage to the Holy Land.

Although away from Shíráz, Áqá Mírzá Áqá was constantly

attending to the welfare of the wife of the Báb, writing to her and sending on her letters to Bahá'u'lláh. And this brave, dedicated, indefatigable man's services in every field of Bahá'í activity evoked from the Most Exalted Pen a Tablet which conferred upon him the designation of Núri'd-Dín – the Light of Faith.

O My Afnán, upon thee rest My Glory, My Bounty and My Mercy. Verily, the Servant-in-Attendance [Mírzá Áqá Ján] came and made mention of thee in Our presence. We therefore extolled thee in such wise as to cause the cities of remembrance and utterance to be set ablaze. Verily thy Lord is the Supreme Ruler over all things. We have named thee, at this moment, Núri'd-Dín. We beseech God that He may ordain for thee that which will draw thee near unto Him and be of profit to thee. He verily is the All-Gracious, the All-Knowing, the All-Wise. (Quoted in Fayḍí, *Kh̲ánadán-i-Afnán*, p. 201)

* * * * * * * * * *

Then in 1882, the wife of the Báb passed away and Zahrá Bigum – her sister and Áqá Mírzá Áqá's mother – took up residence in the House of the Báb on the instructions of Bahá'u'lláh. Later, Bahá'u'lláh made

Áqá Mírzá Áqá, Núri'd-Dín, in Egypt, circa *1885*

custodianship of the House of the Báb a hereditary office among her descendants. Zahrá Bigum passed away in 1889 and the custodianship became the responsibility of Áqá Mírzá Áqá, although he was at that time resident in Egypt, where he had established his trading-house in Port Sa'íd. In July 1891, less than a year before the Ascension of Bahá'u'lláh, Áqá Mírzá Áqá arrived for pilgrimage in Haifa with members of his family. The story of this pilgrimage, which lasted for nine months and encompassed many episodes of great interest and significance, is the subject of chapter 41 of *Bahá'u'lláh, The King of Glory*, as described by Ḥájí Mírzá Ḥabíbu'lláh, the son of Áqá Mírzá Áqá, in his autobiography.

In 1903, 'Abdu'l-Bahá issued instructions for the restoration of the House of the Báb exactly as it was in the time of the Báb. Áqá Mírzá Áqá (who was the only living person who remembered the details of the house as it had been) came to Shíráz and, with the assistance of the believers there, undertook the task even though these were difficult times for the Bahá'ís and persecutions had erupted in many parts of the land. The restoration was almost complete when Áqá Mírzá Áqá took ill and passed away on 15 November 1903.

18

The Angel of Mount Carmel

> A shining, world-illuminating day is the night
> of godly men,
> Verily, the enlightened know not the gloom
> of a darksome night.
>
> *Sa'dí*

WESTERN BAHÁ'ÍS who came on pilgrimage to the Holy Land in the latter years of the Ministry of 'Abdu'l-Bahá met, at times, on Mount Carmel a very old man, bent with age. His dignity, serenity and vivacity so profoundly impressed and moved them that they spoke of him as the Angel of Mount Carmel. That aged man was Ḥájí Mírzá Ḥaydar-'Alí of Iṣfahán, a well-tested veteran of the Bahá'í Faith. His

Ḥájí Mírzá Ḥaydar-'Alí, the Angel of Mount Carmel, with Sulaymán Khán, known as Jamál Effendi, the Conqueror of India

long life had been a mighty adventure of the spirit – a remarkable and rich story to tell. In the evening of his life, in the shadow of the Mountain of God, he wrote it down at the request of Áqá Khusraw Bimán,* a Persian Bahá'í of Zoroastrian background residing in Poona, India; and gave his book the title: *Bihjatu'ṣ-Ṣudúr* – The Delight of Hearts. Áqá Khusraw had it published in India, in the year 1913. The odyssey of Ḥájí Mírzá Ḥaydar-'Alí does not merely delight the heart; it stirs the soul.

In the Public Record Office in London documents are deposited that touch upon a wondrous episode in the life of Ḥájí Mírzá Ḥaydar-'Alí: his arrest in Cairo in the company of a number of his fellow-believers and their banishment to the Súdán. The archives of Yale University in the United States likewise contain documents that further expose the malignancy of those who were responsible for the banishment of those Bahá'ís.

Some time towards the end of Bahá'u'lláh's sojourn in Adrianople, when the insubordination of Ṣubḥ-i-Azal and his coterie of mischief-makers had already moved to a climax, Ḥájí Mírzá Ḥaydar-'Alí attained the presence of Bahá'u'lláh. He stayed for seven months in that uneasy city. Then, he was directed to Istanbul to take charge of communications. However, before long circumstances made him desirous of a change of residence, and Bahá'u'lláh instructed him to go to Egypt, and to be very circumspect. In a Tablet revealed soon after, addressed to him, Bahá'u'lláh clearly presaged the perils that awaited him. On the same boat which took Ḥájí Mírzá Ḥaydar-'Alí and his companion, Mírzá Ḥusayn, to Egypt there was also another Bahá'í, Ḥájí Ja'far-i-Tabrízí, travelling in commercial pursuits. He was the same dedicated man, who, later in Adrianople, cut his throat when he learned that the Ottoman authorities had decided to exclude him from the group of the Bahá'ís who were to be banished with Bahá'u'lláh. However, on this boat Ḥájí Ja'far and Ḥájí Mírzá Ḥaydar-'Alí were not to show any sign that they had known each other in the past, and their transactions and treatment of one another were to be entirely on the basis of commercial clients: sellers and

* Áqá Khusraw kept a hotel in Poona close to the railway station. It was called the National Hotel and was the best in the town. Many Bahá'í functions of early days took place in that hotel. The present writer has vivid recollections of the dignified, kindly gentleman to whom the National Hotel belonged. (See illustration, p. 260.)

buyers of goods. But, when Ḥájí Mírzá Ḥaydar-'Alí reached Egypt, he found his compatriots there very hostile and suspicious, for Persians of Istanbul had done their worst. The accusations which they had levelled against Ḥájí Mírzá Ḥaydar-'Alí were both ludicrous and enormous; of course they were accusations which stemmed from the fact that he was a Bahá'í. He had been told by Bahá'u'lláh to be very discreet, but now he realized that he must seek a middle course between any attempt at concealment of his faith, which was pointless, impossible and derogatory, and a bold assertion of it in the face of solid, fanatical and blind opposition. And he found that middle course and won the hearts of his prejudiced, hostile compatriots. He told them that they had been sadly misinformed: it was totally untrue that he and his co-religionists had denied the Holy Prophet of Islám and His illustrious Book; he and his co-religionists believed in Muḥammad and the Qur'án with the whole intensity of their souls. It was equally untrue, Ḥájí Mírzá Ḥaydar-'Alí assured those Persians of Egypt, that he and his co-religionists had assumed the appellations that fell exclusively within the domain of the Imáms of the House of Muḥammad. They believed in the Holy Imáms and would never brook any disrespect towards them. He and his co-religionists, Ḥájí Mírzá Ḥaydar-'Alí asserted, were forbidden to engage in futile verbal disputes. They presented what they had to present with love, with compassion, with understanding.

Let us recall what Ḥájí Mírzá Ḥaydar-'Alí told Edward Granville Browne, at Iṣfahán in 1888, two years before Browne visited 'Akká and witnessed the power and the majesty that emanated from the person of Bahá'u'lláh. Browne wrote:

> . . . I learned . . . that he . . . was one of the chief missionaries of the new faith, for which he had suffered stripes, imprisonment, and exile more than once. I begged him to tell me what it was that had made him ready to suffer these things so readily. 'You must go to Acre,' he replied, 'to understand that.'
>
> 'Have you been to Acre?' I said, 'and if so, what did you see there?'
>
> 'I have been there often,' he answered, 'and what I saw was a man perfect in humanity.'
>
> More than this he would not say . . . (*A Year Amongst the Persians*, pp. 229–30)

Having disarmed the adversaries, Ḥájí Mírzá Ḥaydar-'Alí could, then, consort with his compatriots in amity and mutual respect. He says in his autobiography that he and his companion, Mírzá Ḥusayn, were oftentimes invited to the homes of the notables of the Persian community. He gained not only good friends for the Faith which he professed, but eventually he led some of them to give their own allegiance to that Faith. Ḥájí Muḥammad-Ḥasan-i-Kázirúní became a Bahá'í but did not avow it publicly. Ḥájí Mírzá Javád-i-Shírází, who had known the Báb as a young boy and had met Him when He was engaged in trading, opened his heart to Ḥájí Mírzá Ḥaydar-'Alí and spoke admiringly of the martyred Prophet, Whom he had encountered in His early youth. Ḥájí Mírzá Muḥammad-Rafí' was another prominent member of the Persian community in Egypt, who became 'truthfully attracted and strivingly friendly'.

But the case which was indeed miraculous was that of Ḥájí Abu'l-Qásim-i-Shírází. He was a merchant in Manṣúríyyih, very wealthy but miserly, seventy years old. Siyyid Ḥusayn-i-Káshání had told him of the Bahá'í Faith, but Ḥájí Abu'l-Qásim had paid scant attention to what he had heard. Now, meeting Ḥájí Mírzá Ḥaydar-'Alí he became a changed man. For twenty-odd years he had lived away from his family who were in Shíráz, leading a solitary, miserly existence in a caravanserai. When he fearlessly and openly espoused the Cause of Bahá'u'lláh, he sent Siyyid Ḥusayn to Shíráz to bring his family out to Egypt and wedded his daughter to him. As we shall presently see, this marital union caused a stir and a good deal of acrimonious correspondence between the Persian and the British authorities. Next, Ḥájí Abu'l-Qásim applied to Ḥájí Mírzá Ḥusayn Khán, the Mushíru'd-Dawlih, Persian ambassador in Istanbul, specifically for a passport which should take him without hindrance to Adrianople, to the presence of Bahá'u'lláh. Ḥájí Abu'l-Qásim-i-Shírází had, indeed, attained second birth.

As it happened, Ḥájí Mírzá Ḥaydar-'Alí's sojourn in Egypt coincided with Ḥájí Mírzá Ṣafá's periodic visits. Bahá'u'lláh had warned Ḥájí Mírzá Ḥaydar-'Alí that he would meet that self-styled *murshid* and to be on his guard.* Ḥájí Mírzá Ṣafá was a chameleon and changing colour came easily to him. It was known that he had the ear of the Persian ambassador in Istanbul. Although his share of mischief in plotting against Bahá'u'lláh was undeniable, Ḥájí Mírzá Ṣafá now began associating with Ḥájí Mírzá Ḥaydar-'Alí in good rapport, even going to the length of praising Bahá'u'lláh in tones of

* See Balyuzi, *Bahá'u'lláh, The King of Glory*, pp. 198–201 and 481–2. (Ed.)

awe and wonderment. But it soon became evident that the man was indeed false, and that he had his hand in the oppression which soon overtook Ḥájí Mírzá Ḥaydar-'Alí. Nevertheless, only a few short months later when Nabíl-i-A'ẓam was detained in Cairo and thrown into prison, it was the anger and the intervention of Ḥájí Mírzá Ṣafá which brought about his release from the clutches of the Persian consul-general and his transference to a more salubrious place in Alexandria.

In all these cases, the real villain was Ḥájí Mírzá Ḥasan Khán, the consul-general of Írán. His was the false heart, pulsating with greed, replete with envy. All that he cared for was how to fleece his fellow-countrymen, how to break those who were defenceless. To begin with he showed every manner of friendliness to Ḥájí Mírzá Ḥaydar-'Alí.

There was a certain Ḥájí Mírzá Ḥusayn, an engraver of Shíráz [writes this veteran of the Bahá'í Faith], whose faith, affiliation, avocation and path consisted of worldly pleasures and pursuits, of good food and good bedding; and to attain these ends he would sacrifice everything else. The Consul made use of this man covertly to frighten away the Persians so that they should cease consorting with me, while he himself would be associating with me in a friendly manner, simulating sincerity and truthfulness, to learn who were meeting me in secret. One month passed, and the Persians stopped associating with me openly. But at nightfall some came, either singly, or two by two; many of them avowed their belief [in this Faith] and did not speak falsely. Then the Consul and the engraver thought of provoking mischief and arresting me, together with the other believers. But in Egypt there was freedom of conscience and religion, and they could not lay their hands on anyone in the name of faith and belief. Satanic motives and self-ridden thoughts made the Consul and the engraver concoct a plan . . . (*Bihjatu'ṣ-Ṣudúr*, p. 91)

The plan was to inveigle Ḥájí Mírzá Ḥaydar-'Alí into believing that Ḥájí Mírzá Ḥasan Khán really wished to investigate and know the truth. The engraver, an ingenious hypocrite, set about encouraging and persuading him to believe that, and to this end meetings were arranged in the house of the engraver himself. Then, Ḥájí Mírzá Ḥasan Khán twice visited Ḥájí Mírzá Ḥaydar-'Alí in the latter's house, accompanied by the engraver. He was all friendliness, expressing his disgust in regard to the attitude and behaviour of the people. And apparently Ḥájí Mírzá Ḥaydar-'Alí believed that his protestations were genuine.

Next, the Ḥájí writes about another hypocrite, a dervish from

Káshán, named Darvísh Ḥasan. And he, too, succeeded in deceiving Ḥájí Mírzá Ḥaydar-'Alí, for he had played his game well and gained the Ḥájí's confidence. As the Ḥájí writes, Darvísh Ḥasan had made himself an intermediary between the Consul, the engraver and their intended victim. Every day he would come to the Ḥájí with accounts (of his own fabrication) of what the Consul and the engraver had said or done, and would do the same with the others in regard to Ḥájí Mírzá Ḥaydar-'Alí. Whereas when consorting with the Bahá'ís he would avow ardently his belief in their Faith, when meeting the Consul and the engraver he would never pretend that he was a Bahá'í, and they took it that the dervish was just attempting to be discreet.

Ḥájí Mírzá Ḥaydar-'Alí then writes of Ḥájí Mírzá Ṣafá's dissimulation. That self-styled *murshid* claimed that he had known the Báb during the days of His sojourn in Búshihr, and had been greatly impressed by Him. And when he had heard, he said, that a young Siyyid of Shíráz had raised a call, he was certain that this Siyyid could be none other than the young merchant whom he had met in Búshihr. He told Ḥájí Mírzá Ḥaydar-'Alí that before long he had come across the *Aḥsanu'l-Qiṣaṣ* (or *Qayyúmu'l-Asmá'*, the Báb's commentary on the Súrih of Joseph) and also the commentary on the Súrih of Kawthar; and knowing that the Báb had received no formal education, he could not but believe that whatever flowed from the pen of that young Siyyid was divinely inspired. He had been to Tabríz, he averred, to attain the presence of the Báb, but many difficulties and hindrances arose, barring him from his object. Ḥájí Mírzá Ṣafá even went to the length of avowing that the Advent of the Báb was the precursor to the Advent of Bahá'u'lláh. And he visited Ḥájí Mírzá Ḥaydar-'Alí several times. But the Ḥájí had been forewarned.

The man, amongst many of the learned and the erudite, whom Ḥájí Mírzá Ḥaydar-'Alí found to be truly outstanding was Mírzá Ja'far Áqá: a philosopher of immense learning and knowledge, possessed of such eloquence and power of speech as Ḥájí Mírzá Ṣafá could never hope to match. He had attained the presence of Bahá'u'lláh in Adrianople and given Him his allegiance. Mírzá Ja'far Áqá was particularly enchanted by the Most Great Branch, the eldest Son of Bahá'u'lláh, and considered himself to be truly the servant of that 'Mystery of God' (*Sirru'lláh*). Of others in Egypt there was Shafí' Effendi, a Ṣúfí *murshid*, who had his own hermitage and conclave of dervishes, and was led to embrace the Cause of Bahá'u'lláh. Ḥájí

Mírzá Ḥaydar-'Alí states that after what happened to him personally, Shafí' Effendi could no longer live in Egypt and had to leave everything and go away. Still, there was another Ṣúfí *murshid* of the Mawlavís, who had come very close to the Faith of Bahá'u'lláh, a man of great influence. Ḥájí Mírzá Ḥaydar-'Alí had high hopes, he writes, to establish firm contacts with the Egyptians through his good offices. But then the axe fell and the treacherous Ḥájí Mírzá Ḥasan Khán, the consul-general of Írán, wielded that axe whereby all ties were sundered. After the remove of more than a century, that which endures is the shining example of the 'Angel of Mount Carmel', and all that remains of Ḥájí Mírzá Ḥasan Khán is a name coupled with infamy.

It was the night of the 21st day of Ramaḍán, the eve of the anniversary of the martyrdom of 'Alí Ibn Abí-Ṭálib, the first Imám, a night held holy by the Shí'ihs – and not revered by them alone. Ḥájí Mírzá Ḥaydar-'Alí writes:

The Consul invited me to visit him that night in his house. All the Persians, he said, are engaged this night with prayer and meditation until dawn, even the servants of the Consulate go away. There would be no one about, he stated, to cause us concern, and we would have the whole night to consort and to talk.

There was a man, irreligious, inclined to mysticism, eloquent, of good conversation, knowledgeable, who repudiated all faiths. He had known me in Írán and felt kindly towards me. He came to Egypt and heard of the Cause of God and claimed: 'I will answer them, I will prove their falsity.' Some people, to satisfy their own understanding and to test him and me, brought him to my home. When he saw me, he told the intermediary: 'I am neither a believer in this Cause, nor in the previous Causes, but I have seen this man and know that I cannot stand up to him in any respect. To say I do not give way and to behave unjustly, should it confound those who are present, would firstly neither confound him, nor secondly, confound the one who disputes with him. And to act in this manner is far removed from equity, courtesy, wisdom, generosity and humanity.' When the Consul offered me that invitation, this man [whose name Ḥájí Mírzá Ḥaydar-'Alí does not divulge] said: 'Going to the house of the Consul is a rash act and inadvisable, because should the Consul wish to harm thee and detain thee and inflict an injury on thee, he cannot possibly act against thee, Egypt enjoying freedom as she does, unless under the pretence of friendly invitation he gets thee into his own home and under his roof and beneath the flag of his government. Then, whatever the accusation that he levels against thee, whatever the harm that he causes thee, neither the Egyptian government, nor any other government can question him and take him to task. Moreover, you have no one to complain to other governments and stand up to the Consul.' I put down his warning to irresolution, wild imaginings and lack of assurance. (ibid. pp. 95–96)

But this unnamed man, truly discerning, knew his Consul better than did Ḥájí Mírzá Ḥaydar-'Alí, who fell into the trap set for him by Ḥájí Mírzá Ḥasan Khán. A few lines later, Ḥájí Mírzá Ḥaydar-'Alí adds: 'That irreligious man, whose name was Áqá Karím, now I have remembered it . . .' Such are the freshness and spontaneity in the autobiographical writing of the Ḥájí which add immensely to its charm and interest.

Then Ḥájí Mírzá Ḥaydar-'Alí records the contents and some verses of a Tablet of Bahá'u'lláh, addressed to him from Adrianople, in which he is told of perils awaiting him. Thus had Bahá'u'lláh addressed him:

We hear thy cry and supplication at thy remoteness from the Dawning-Place of Lights. Be patient and do not bewail thy plight. Be content with that which God hath ordained for thee. He, verily, payeth the due recompense of those who are patient. Hast thou not seen My incarceration, My affliction, My injury, My suffering? Follow, then, the ways of thy Lord, and among His methods is the suffering of His well-favoured servants. Let nothing grieve thee. Put thy trust in thy Lord. He shall verily confirm thee, draw thee nigh unto Him and grant thee victory. Should affliction overtake thee in My path and abasement in My name, rejoice and be of the thankful. Thus have We imparted unto thee the word of truth so that when calamities descend upon thee, thy feet may not slip and thou shalt be as firm and steadfast as a mountain in the Cause of thy Lord . . . (ibid. pp. 96–7)

Ḥájí Mírzá Ḥaydar-'Alí had shown this Tablet to many, including Áqá Karím. Trying to dissuade him from accepting the invitation of the Consul, Áqá Karím reminded him of that Tablet and the unmistakable warning which it conveyed. But Ḥájí Mírzá Ḥaydar-'Alí was not to be dissuaded. On the appointed night (the eve of the anniversary of the martyrdom of 'Alí Ibn Abí-Ṭálib), he, accompanied by Mírzá Ḥusayn and Darvísh Ḥasan, went to the house of the Persian consul-general. The hypocritical Ḥájí Mírzá Ḥasan Khán received his guests with apparent joy and open arms. They sat down to talk and enjoy refreshments. Then, nearing the dawn, the Consul got up and retired to his private quarters, without uttering a word of farewell. And shortly after, his guests were told that they could go home and a lantern was ready for them. But they soon found themselves surrounded and led away to imprisonment. They had indeed walked into a trap. Thus did nine years of captivity begin for the 'Angel of Mount Carmel'. Describing their capture, he writes:

Such behaviour caused astonishment. What did this mean, subsequent to all that kindliness and expression of kindness? In any case we rose up to depart. Only one lantern was needed, but every few steps that we took, more lanterns and more men appeared, until some thirty to forty men, like wolves, encircled me and the other two, and all of a sudden each one of us was seized by eight or nine men, as if we were Rustams* and men of war. We were carried in such a way to the prison they had prepared that nowhere were our feet touching the ground. In that prison they put chains round our necks and our feet were fettered. Then they disrobed us and took away our clothes, and left nothing undone or unsaid in the way of beatings and abuse. But, praise to God, I was very happy. Day had dawned when they left us and bolted and locked the door of our prison. There we were all alone: Mírzá Ḥusayn, Darvísh Ḥasan and myself. When I spoke with joy and gratitude of our plight, I found that Mírzá Ḥusayn was somewhat unhappy and discontented, while Darvísh Ḥasan was utterly distressed and unresponsive. I managed to comfort Mírzá Ḥusayn to a degree. (ibid. p. 98)

However, Ḥájí Mírzá Ḥaydar-'Alí writes, Darvísh Ḥasan began to show the nature of his duplicity. When the time came for breaking the fast, in the evening the Consul's servants brought the prisoners tea and some food. Ḥájí Mírzá Ḥaydar-'Alí remarks on the abusive language and the impertinence of the Consul's minions. So insulting and so insolent they were, he writes, that the food which they served tasted venomous to the palates of the three men, held unjustifiably and illegally in custody. He goes on to say:

They went to our house and brought everything we had to the Consul. Of Writings, Tablets, best products and specimens of calligraphy, and fine valuables, the Consul, Mírzá Ḥasan Khán of Khuy, took possession himself. What was left the others grabbed. Then they brought some old clothes and bedding most of which were not ours, insisting that they were. We made no enquiry regarding other things, because it was obvious that they had helped themselves to everything. We only said that those old clothes and bedding did not belong to us. Whereupon they so maltreated us, so mocked and reproved us, that we regretted having said anything to them. Next they forced me to write a receipt and put my seal to it, declaring that all the goods and chattels in my house had been given to me except Books and Writings. They wrote that document in the way they wanted, told me to copy it and seal it, and insisted that the other two should sign it as well. Then it was found that Darvísh Ḥasan was illiterate. They intended that this document should serve

* The legendary hero of ancient Írán, immortalized by the *Sháhnámih* of Firdawsí.

as a positive proof to my ownership of those Books and Writings. Having procured what they wanted, they proceeded to put those Books and Writings before the Egyptian authorities, indicating that He [Bahá'u'lláh] was claiming Lordship and Divinity and that He had instituted a new religion. Coupled with these statements were the same sorts of calumnies and insinuations that people have always levelled against the Manifestation of the Light, whenever He has appeared. They told the authorities that these were the men who had intended to assassinate His Majesty the Sháh of Írán, and, having failed to carry out their purpose, were now intent on murdering His Highness the Khedive and taking possession of Egypt. And it is certain that they have accomplices, people who are like-minded: Egyptians, Persians and Turks in other countries . . . With these accusations they beguiled the Khedive, who became apprehensive and frightened. Thus it was that the Consul was empowered to seize anyone whom he knew to be of this Faith. From the third day onward they laid hands on anyone who had been consorting with me and put him in gaol. In Manṣúrah, they arrested Ḥájí Abu'l-Qásim. When they were about to fasten him with chains, this pure-hearted, aged man took the chain with both hands and kissed it. And on his lips were the words: '*Bismi'lláhi'l-Bahíyyi'l-Abhá*' [In the Name of the God of Glory, the Most Glorious]. They had prepared a place near my prison to receive these later detainees. The Consul had some three hundred men arrested, Persians and others, even Christians and Persian Jews. It came to my ears that he had covertly sent for a number of Egyptians, asking them for what reason they had visited my house. These men would have to bribe him to shut his mouth and stop his reporting them to the Egyptian authorities. We could hear the conversation of the people brought in. In any case we were very happy because our captivity and imprisonment had come to us in the path of God. (ibid. pp. 99–100)

However, it is apparent that the behaviour and the talk of Darvísh Ḥasan caused Ḥájí Mírzá Ḥaydar-'Alí great distress at times. And so did the abusive and insulting language which the ruffians and rascals in the service of the Consul used, whenever they came to attend to the needs of the prisoners.

Ḥájí Mírzá Ḥaydar-'Alí goes on to say:

One night, he [the Consul] invited a number of prominent Persians and grandees of Egypt to a sumptuous festivity, and sent for me to be brought to that assemblage, in chains, with hands tied. As soon as I entered there, God is my witness, I saw in my mind's eye a renewal of the court of Ibn-Ziyád* in Kúfih and the hauling in of the prisoners of Karbilá. They wanted to keep me standing while firing questions at me. I salaamed and sat down. (ibid. p. 101)

* 'Ubaydu'lláh Ibn Ziyád, the governor of Kúfih under Yazíd, the second Umayyad caliph, who was greatly instrumental in encompassing the martyrdom of Imám Ḥusayn, the third Imám.

And Ḥájí Mírzá Ḥaydar-'Alí nonplussed the deceitful Consul further still. He himself began addressing the Consul and his guests, declaring first that it had always been the destiny of those who had followed the Light of God to suffer darts and torment, affliction and captivity, hardship and imprisonment in the path of their Faith. Then turning to the guests of the Consul, he told them: 'Ask this man', indicating Ḥájí Mírzá Ḥasan Khán, the Consul, 'what wrong-doing, what wickedness he discovered in me, what plotting, what transgression he uncovered, to subject me to this treatment.' Ḥájí Mírzá Ḥasan Khán of Khuy knew that he was beaten and signalled to his minions to take Ḥájí Mírzá Ḥaydar-'Alí away.

Another day, the Consul, still smarting under the defeat which he had suffered, but still as vindictive as ever, took a number of the people of Ádharbáyján, pilgrims on their way to Mecca, into the prison, and 'in order to show them', as Ḥájí Mírzá Ḥaydar-'Alí puts it, 'his power and authority', as soon as he came in, gave the prisoner a blow with his walking-stick and told him: 'Speak the truth. What is your name?' to which query he received the answer: 'Ḥaydar-'Alí.'

'But', said the Consul, 'you have been called by other names, such as Gabriel, Kátib-i-Vaḥy (the Scribe of Revelation), Amíra'l-Mu'minín (Commander of the Faithful).' I said that I had never applied these designations to myself; someone else must have done that. The Consul affirmed that. Then I said that whoever had related that had not mentioned his name. 'But I know his name: it is Satan, because Satan leads you to evil deeds and enormities, and to speak against people about matters that you do not comprehend.' [See Qur'án 2: 164.] Now, I was hit by a man who said: 'Are you insulting the ambassador?'

Next, they brought a man to the prison who demanded from me his brother's clothes. He said that his brother had given me his clothes to keep for him. Then he mentioned his brother's name. I said that I did not know that man, and knew nothing about his clothes. He became rude and aggressive, but as soon as the Consul's men went away, he kissed me and said: 'I am 'Abdu'lláh-i-Najafábádí; I have attained the Presence [of Bahá'u'lláh]. Now I have come here to go on pilgrimage to Mecca and Medina. I heard of your detention, and knew that you had been robbed of everything. I had two Ottoman pounds and wanted to give them to you.' (ibid. pp. 101–2)

Ḥájí Mírzá Ḥaydar-'Alí then relates the story of that intrepid Bahá'í of Najafábád. Áqá 'Abdu'lláh had found that the only way to meet the prisoners was to make up the fictitious account of his brother's clothes. He stayed with Ḥájí Mírzá Ḥaydar-'Alí for nearly six hours. Then the Consul's men came and took him away. At Jiddah, Áqá 'Abdu'lláh met Ḥájí Mírzá Ṣafá, the Ṣúfí *murshid* whom Bahá'u'lláh had mentioned to Ḥájí Mírzá Ḥaydar-'Alí, and entered his service. Other Persians there told the *murshid* that the man whom he had taken into his service was a 'Bábí' and had been to Adrianople. When questioned, Áqá 'Abdu'lláh readily admitted that everything said about him was correct, and stated bravely that he had never failed the *murshid* in serving him. Ḥájí Mírzá Ṣafá had no complaint on that account, and asked Áqá 'Abdu'lláh what he had seen in Adrianople. He replied: 'Whatever I had heard about the Prophets in the past, I found there.' Then Ḥájí Mírzá Ṣafá said: 'Why is it that so many of the learned, the divines, the philosophers have not seen it and you have?' Áqá 'Abdu'lláh was ready with his answer. The same had happened when Muḥammad came; men of rank and learning failed to recognize Him, but Bilál, an Ethiopian slave, then a shepherd, a seller of dates, and Salmán-i-Fársí (the Persian) did, and came to believe in Him. The *murshid* was nonplussed, increased his wages and told him to go away and not to visit Medina. Áqá 'Abdu'lláh left quietly but he went to Medina, notwithstanding. When he was reproached by Ḥájí Mírzá Ṣafá, Áqá 'Abdu'lláh very politely pointed out that visiting the Shrine of the Prophet took preference. Then the *murshid* took him back into his service, and tried to win him away from his Faith. But, as Ḥájí Mírzá Ḥaydar-'Alí has it:

> . . . he [Áqá 'Abdu'lláh] said: 'The likes of us have to bear the burden and toil, so that you and those like you should live in safety and comfort.' [The *murshid*] asked then: 'What is it that makes you and those like you so brave and so ready with your answers?' He [Áqá 'Abdu'lláh] replied: 'If ye be of the truthful then crave for death [Qur'án 2: 88]. Stating the truth requires no deliberation, no premeditation, no precaution.' May my life be a sacrifice to his power of constancy. (ibid. p. 103)

Then Ḥájí Mírzá Ḥaydar-'Alí relates what he heard a man accused of theft say about the 'Bábís'. The room where he was kept was next door to the main room where all others were housed, and he could hear the conversation of the people there. This man had spoken at length of the 'Bábís', recalled all their past history and had concluded that nothing at all can utterly destroy them. Ḥájí Mírzá Ḥaydar-'Alí says that that poor man was severely beaten and tortured for having sided with the 'Bábís'.

The Ḥájí records that before long the treatment to which they [the

Bahá'í prisoners] were subjected was completely changed. Their food was restricted to half a loaf of bread and the water they were given to drink was so little that they suffered greatly from thirst. 'We were so enfeebled', he writes, 'that we could hardly move ourselves.' At this juncture the two Ottoman pounds, which Áqá 'Abdu'lláh had given to the Ḥájí, came to their aid. Darvísh Ḥasan was all the while whining and reviling the Ḥájí so as to win favours from the Consul's lackeys. All this time, Ḥájí Mírzá Ḥaydar-'Alí relates, the Consul was busy arresting people and fining them – sums varying from a few pounds to five hundred; before releasing them he would send them to spit on the Ḥájí. Some of these wretched men felt so ashamed that they could not raise their heads to look at him, but they were forced to do so and to spit and curse.

Thus days passed. Then one night, as the Ḥájí relates:

. . . six o'clock after sunset, they came and took Darvísh Ḥasan away. Next, they came for Mírzá Ḥusayn; and finally they took me away. In the Consulate there was an array of chairs, occupied by the Consul and members of the Egyptian police. A number of hell's lackeys were also in evidence, as well as a number of men chained whose hands were tied together. The Consul pointed me out and said, 'This man is the source of all mischief, he is their Gabriel and their Prophet.' Then I was handed over to the Egyptian police. My hands were tied very tightly behind my back. Praise be to God, that in the path of His love and for the sake of His name, they put heavy chains on my neck. They wrote down the names of each one of us, and they also recorded our nativity and the names of our fathers, and these were given to the police. We were seven Persians and an Egyptian teacher of English. Because I was teaching him Persian, this Egyptian was accused of being friendly towards me. Amongst those detained were 'Abdu'l-Vahháb-i-Zanjání and Háshim-i-Káshání, outwardly my servants. They were my friends and spiritual brothers. Another one of those detained was Ḥájí Abu'l-Qásim-i-Iṣfahání. They had taken Mírzá Ja'far Áqá to task for being friendly towards me and having been seen in my company, but had been properly told off. Shafí' Effendi, who was a *murshid* and had a hermitage, found it no longer possible to live in Cairo. Ḥájí Abu'l-Qásim-i-Shírází had also been detained. They made him pay a thousand pounds to gain his freedom. He paid it and did not recant faith. He also gave ten pounds to a Christian to give to me. That man came to Súdán and gave me the money. The Ḥájí passed away soon after. His son-in-law, Áqá Siyyid Ḥusayn-i-Káshí, was a British subject, and everywhere he spoke of the Consul's misdeeds. He met a martyr's death at the instigation of the Consul. There was no one to take up the prosecution and the culprit went free. (ibid. pp. 105–6)

The case of Áqá Siyyid Ḥusayn-i-Káshí became a *cause célèbre*, when his nationality was being hotly debated. Dispatches kept in the Public Record Office in London, as well as a number of documents belonging to the Persian Embassy which are now preserved in the archives of Yale University, provide details of the controversies aroused by the chicanery and greed of Ḥájí Mírzá Ḥasan Khán, the Persian consul-general in Cairo. (See Momen, chap. 15.)

* * * * * * * * * *

As for Ḥájí Mírzá Ḥaydar-'Alí, he and his six fellow-Bahá'ís were exiled to Kharṭúm in the Súdán in conditions of the greatest hardship. When they first arrived there, the minds of the Government officials and of the people had been so poisoned against them that they were harshly treated. Later, however, as their true characters became known, they won the respect and admiration of everyone in Kharṭúm from the Governor down. After their exile had lasted nine years, Bahá'u'lláh succeeded in sending one of the Arab believers, Ḥájí Jásim-i-Baghdádí, to Kharṭúm with messages and greetings for them. A short while later, in 1877, General Gordon was made Governor of the city, and by petitioning him the Bahá'í exiles were able to obtain permission to leave.

From Kharṭúm they made their way to Mecca and from there to 'Akká. Here Ḥájí Mírzá Ḥaydar-'Alí spent several months, being frequently in the presence of Bahá'u'lláh. Then he was instructed to leave for Írán. For almost thirty years he travelled around Írán, visiting Bahá'í communities and teaching the Faith. On several occasions, both during the lifetime of Bahá'u'lláh and during 'Abdu'l-Bahá's ministry, he visited the Holy Land, and remained there for varying periods of time. He also travelled in Egypt, India, Caucasia and Turkistán. Finally, in about 1903, he came to settle permanently in the Holy Land, where he died in Haifa on 27 December 1920.

Truly, in his long years of steadfast and uncomplaining service, Ḥájí Mírzá Ḥaydar-'Alí, the Angel of Mount Carmel, had fulfilled this injunction laid upon him by Bahá'u'lláh (*Tablets*, p. 246):

> We have brought thee into being to serve Me, to glorify
> My Word and to proclaim My Cause. Centre thine energies
> upon that wherefor thou hast been created by virtue of the Will of the
> supreme Ordainer, the Ancient of Days.

19

The Great Mujtahid

MÍRZÁ MUḤAMMAD-ḤASAN, known as Mírzáy-i-Shírází, was the greatest mujtahid of his day. He was considered the sole *Marja'u't-Taqlíd* for the entire Shí'ih world, which meant that all the Shí'ihs in every country looked to him as their spiritual leader and as their guide and exemplar in matters of application of the Holy Law of Islám.

The father of this great man was Mír Maḥmúd-i-Khushnivís, a resident of Shíráz famed for his calligraphy in the Nasta'líq style. He was a paternal cousin of the father of the Báb.

Mírzáy-i-Shírází was born on 5 May 1815 in Shíráz and received his initial education there. He was later sent to Iṣfahán which was at that time the foremost city of learning in Írán. In about 1843 he travelled to 'Iráq but at first used to return frequently to Iṣfahán, until he began to attend the classes of Shaykh Murtiḍáy-i-Anṣárí. It was then that he decided to settle in 'Iráq. Little by little he became known as the most prominent student of Shaykh Murtiḍá, who was acknowledged as the leading mujtahid of the Shí'ih world. When Shaykh Murtiḍá died in 1864, Mírzáy-i-Shírází succeeded him as teacher of his circle of students. Over the next few years, his stature among the other 'ulamá increased to the point that when Siyyid Ḥusayn-i-Turk died in 1882, Mírzáy-i-Shírází became acknowledged as the sole *Marja'u't-Taqlíd* for the Shí'ih world. He is also called *Ḥujjatu'l-Islám* (the Proof of Islám), *Áyatu'lláh* (the Sign of God) and *Mujaddid* (Renewer, i.e. of Islám) by his biographers.

In 1875, Mírzáy-i-Shírází transferred his residence from Najaf to Sámarrá and remained there until his death. In 1891–2 there occurred the famous protest against the Tobacco Régie. As a result of a *fatwa* which is said to have been issued by Mírzáy-i-Shírází, the Government of Írán and the foreign diplomatic establishment were amazed to observe an almost complete cessation of the use of tobacco in Írán. The Sháh was forced to capitulate and the tobacco concession was cancelled.

Mírzáy-i-Shírází died on 20 February 1895 and his body was carried from Sámarrá to Najaf, where it was buried.

The story of Mírzáy-i-Shírází does not end there, however. It has an interesting aspect from the point of view of the Bahá'í Faith. For, unknown to all, Mírzáy-i-Shírází had since his youth been a believer in the Báb and Bahá'u'lláh. He only chose to reveal this towards the end of his life and then only to a relative, Áqá Mírzá Áqá, Núri'd-Dín-i-Afnán, who was an Afnán on his mother's side, but whose father was a paternal cousin of Mírzáy-i-Shírází. The events leading up to this interview have been recorded by Áqá Mírzá Áqá's son, Mírzá Ḥabíbu'lláh Afnán, and the rest of this chapter is a translation of his account. (Footnotes are by the translator. Ed.)

When, in 1311 [1893–4], the mother of Áqá Siyyid Ḥusayn-i-Afnán [Ṣáḥibih-Sulṭán Bigum] with her daughter Fáṭimih Bigum, who is the mother of the late Muvaqqari'd-Dawlih,* were visiting the Holy Shrines in 'Iráq, they went to the house of Mírzá Ḥujjatu'l-Islám [Mírzáy-i-Shírází] in order to introduce themselves to him.

After the formalities, the mother said: 'I am the wife of the late Ḥájí Mírzá Abu'l-Qásim and this is my daughter. We would ask for your special blessing and favour.'

'Which Ḥájí Mírzá Abu'l-Qásim?' he asked.

'The maternal uncle of Áqá Mírzá Áqá,' she replied.

'Which Áqá Mírzá Áqá?'

'The son of the late Mírzá Zaynu'l-'Ábidín.'

Then he remembered who it was and said: 'The Áqá Mírzá Zaynu'l-'Ábidín who lived near the gate of the Masjid-i-Jámi'?'

'Yes,' she replied, and he was overjoyed.

'Where is Áqá Mírzá Áqá now?' he then asked.

'He was living in Egypt, but it appears from what he has written that he now intends to return to Shíráz.'

'Do you know whether he has already travelled and reached Shíráz or not?'

'He has still not arrived.'

'How much longer are you intending to remain at the Holy Shrines?'

'We will stay for perhaps fifteen more days and when we have completed our pilgrimage, we will return to Búshihr.'

* The father of Mr Balyuzi. (MM)

'Please remember to do the following when you return to Búshihr. If you find that Áqá Mírzá Áqá has already passed through that town and is on his way to Shíráz, then let it be. But if he arrives while you are in Búshihr, please say to him from me: "Be sure to come to the Holy Shrines and visit me, for it has been many years that I have been deprived of meeting members of my family." And if you leave Búshihr before he arrives, leave a message for him with a trustworthy person that it is necessary for me to see him.'

(The late Ḥujjatu'l-Islám had family ties with the late Áqá Mírzá Áqá, that is to say their fathers were paternal cousins and were also related to the father of the Báb. It was for this reason that he was trying to arrange this meeting.)

The days of the pilgrimage of those two ladies at the Holy Shrines drew to a close and they went to bid farewell to Ḥujjatu'l-Islám. They said to him: 'We are taking our leave today.' He urged them once more not to forget his message to Áqá Mírzá Áqá and to ensure that when he came to the Holy Shrines, he would come and see him.

After completing their pilgrimage the ladies returned to Búshihr and on the very same day the ship carrying Áqá Mírzá Áqá arrived at Búshihr. They met each other and the ladies conveyed the message of Ḥujjatu'l-Islám.

Áqá Mírzá Áqá has said: 'I was very hesitant as to whether I should go and visit or not. Eventually, I decided that I ought to go. The same ship took me on to Baṣrah and from Baṣrah I travelled to Baghdád. I sent a letter to Ḥujjatu'l-Islám saying: "In conformity with your wishes, your message has been forwarded to me [in which] you had stressed that when I reached 'Iráq I should visit you. I am now at Baghdád. Whenever you appoint a time I shall come to see you."

'I sent the letter through one of the Arab Bahá'ís and instructed him to identify himself as my messenger and then deliver it. When the letter reached him and he realized I was in Baghdád, he sent the following reply:

'"O Light of my eyes! Dear and honoured one! Your letter was received. Since at the present time there is much coming and going of pilgrims, please remain in Baghdád for fifteen days even though it may be an inconvenience to you. Then at the expiry of the fifteen days, come here so that we can meet. I am very eager to meet you. I am sending this reply with your messenger."

'After seeing this reply, I remained in Baghdád, according to the instructions, for fifteen days. At the expiry of that time, I set out to Sámarrá with a number of the Arab Bahá'ís. Upon our arrival, the Arabs found a place for us to stay and we settled in there.

'The following morning I called on His Honour and found an old man with a radiant face, sitting with pillows around him on which he was resting. The people who were being admitted to his presence would kiss his hand, sit in his presence for an hour or so, and then be dismissed. I, like the others, went forward, kissed his hand and introduced myself. He looked at me and enquired after my health. He asked: "Where are you staying?" I did not know but the Arab Bahá'ís who were with me gave the address. He did not speak to me any more nor pay any attention to me, and after sitting for more than one hour, I got up and again without paying any attention to me, he said "Farewell!"

'I was annoyed at his ignoring me and was not in a good mood. "What a thing to do," I said to myself. "I have caused myself a lot of trouble for no reason and have come here from Bú<u>sh</u>ihr to no purpose." I was very offended. I arrived at the place where I was staying and said to my companions, "Let us make preparations to leave at first light tomorrow."

'At the time of the call to prayer, which was two hours before sunrise, I was up and drinking tea, the others were busy collecting their belongings, it was just getting light and I was looking from the shutters towards the gate of the house when I saw an *á<u>kh</u>únd* [divine] coming. When he reached the door of the house, he called out to one of the Bahá'ís whose name was 'Alí. 'Alí went over to speak to him and he said, "Say that I have a message from His Honour the Mírzá, which I want to convey to Áqá Mírzá Áqá." 'Alí conveyed the message and I went over and spoke to the *á<u>kh</u>únd*. He said, "His Honour, the Ḥujjatu'l-Islám, has asked that you come to see him alone, without your companions."

'I decided to go, but my companions said: "We cannot let you go alone. Anything could happen."

'"These thoughts are wrong," I replied. "He must want to see me about something since he has specially sent for me."

'In the end my companions agreed and I set out without them. The name of the *á<u>kh</u>únd* was <u>Sh</u>ay<u>kh</u> Ḥasan and he was one of the intimates of Ḥujjatu'l-Islám. I went with him until we reached the door of the house of His Honour the Mírzá, where I had been the previous day. But he carried on round the corner.

'"The house of His Honour the Mírzá is here, O Shaykh," I said to him; "where are you going?"

'"This is the *bírúní* [outer apartments]," he replied. "He has instructed that you be taken in through the door of the *andarúní* [inner apartments] which are private."

'He went on another twenty paces and opened a door. In the corner of the hallway there was a room. He opened the door and held up the curtain. I went in and found His Honour, the Ḥujjatu'l-Islám, as on the previous day, with cushions around him, lying down.

'I greeted him and he replied. Then he said to Shaykh Ḥasan: "Go and make some tea and bring it. No one is to be permitted to come here, for it is fifty years since I have seen any of my relatives. I want one hour free from interruption to be with him. Even the children are not to be permitted."

'After giving these instructions, he said, "Also, close the door." And so Shaykh Ḥasan closed the door and left. Then he opened his arms and embraced me. He wept copiously and I felt so sorry for him that I began to weep too. He sat me down next to him and poured out expressions of affection and favour.

'"I know that you were annoyed at the way we met yesterday and were displeased. I realized that you were angered. What can I do with such people? What can I do? It was for this reason that I sent Shaykh Ḥasan to you in the early morning to bring you here so that I can meet you."

'At this moment, Shaykh Ḥasan brought in the tea.

'"Leave it and go," he said. "Áqá Mírzá Áqá will pour the tea."

'Shaykh Ḥasan put down the tray and left. I poured some tea and offered it to him. He said, "You drink it." I declined but he insisted and so I drank the tea. He ordered me to fill up the same cup again and he drank from it. Then we began speaking. He asked a few questions about where I had been during these years, what I had heard and which persons I had met. I asked: "What sort of persons?" He said: "Persons who have put forward claims and have caused controversy – that is to say, people with new ideas."

'I replied: "In 1294 [*sic*] when I travelled from Shíráz, I went to Bombay where I occupied myself trading. Here I was friendly with and associating with Iranian and foreign merchants. I met all types of people and we would discuss every kind of topic. For example, I met

Ḥájí Muḥammad-Ibráhím-i-Shírází,* who is known as Muballigh, and he spoke of many important matters. When I considered what he said and weighed his words justly, I could not refute them."

"" Where did you go after Bombay?"

"In 1305 [19 September 1887–6 September 1888], I went from Bombay to Egypt, and I remained for some time in Port Sa'íd and Cairo and was in contact with all sorts of people."

"Where did you go from there and whom did you meet?"

'It suddenly occurred to me, from his questions, that perhaps he wanted to extract a confession from me and cause me trouble. But I thought about this and seeing that there was no one present but myself and him, I thought it unlikely that he was planning anything. So I decided to answer his questions cautiously.

"For a time I went to visit my uncle, Ḥájí Mírzá Siyyid Ḥasan,† and I met there some important people from among the notables such as Áqá Muḥammad-Muṣṭafáy-i-Baghdádí‡ and others."

"What did they speak of?"

"They spoke of the new cause, and whatever they said was supported by proofs from the verses of the Qur'án and the Ḥadíth of the Prophet [Muḥammad] to such an extent that no fair-minded person could deny it. And so I wanted very much to see Your Honour so that I could ask you what my position is according to religious law and what my moral and religious duty is. Should they be accepted or rejected?"

"God, may He be exalted, has said that the parts of the body are for the use of creation that mankind may utilize each of them. Thus, for example, eyes are created for seeing, ears for hearing, the tongue for speech, hands for touching and feet for walking, but He has created the heart for knowing and understanding Him and has ordained it as the place of His effulgence. He has said: 'The heart of man is the throne of the All-Merciful.' Since it is thus, Satan has no place there. And therefore if this cause is not from God, it will have no effect on the heart and being of a man. Whatever the heart accepts and understands must, without doubt, come from God – it will not err."

'When I heard this reply of his, I became more confident and felt free to speak.

* A prominent Bahá'í teacher who was responsible for the conversion of some of the Afnán family.

† Known as Afnán-i-Kabír, a Bahá'í resident in Beirut.

‡ One of the prominent Bahá'í residents of Beirut (see chap. 20).

'"Now, my dear friend, where did you go from Beirut?" he asked.

'"I went to 'Akká."

'He smiled and asked, "And what did you find there?"

'"From what point of view do you mean?"

'"From both the material and spiritual points of view."

'"From a worldly point of view, I found such majesty, power, and authority that no king or emperor could hope to rival. And as for the spiritual realm, whatever you have heard of the previous manifestations of the power of God [i.e., the Prophets] or have seen in their books, you will find a more complete and one thousand times more mighty a demonstration of that revelation in this holy Personage. For example, from the Holy Prophet [Muḥammad] the verses of the Holy Qur'án were revealed in thirty sections [*juz'*], gradually over a period of twenty-two years. From this holy Being, that is to say, Bahá'u'lláh, in one month ten times the Holy Qur'án is revealed with the utmost correctness and eloquence for the world of humanity. And it is such that no fair-minded man can refute it nor produce the like of it."

'"It is indeed so, if one be fair-minded," he replied. "I myself have seen some of these writings and they cannot be compared with the verses of previous revelations. No, they are much more eloquent and profound."

'Then respectfully I asked, "When did you come to this conclusion?"

'He smiled and said: "Do you want to hear a confession from me then, my son?"

'"God forbid! It is only because Your Eminence is the most learned of mankind that I wanted to know so as to increase the certainty in my own heart."

'"My dear friend! Since you want to know, I will tell you. I was a young man, studying at Iṣfahán, when the Báb came to that town. I was present at a gathering with the Imám-Jum'ih and the theological students at the house of the late Mu'tamidu'd-Dawlih, Manú<u>ch</u>ihr <u>Kh</u>án. They were asking Him questions of every sort, testing His knowledge, and He was answering each one convincingly and with the utmost eloquence so that all of us fell into an astonished silence. Then one of the theological students asked a question and He began to give a full reply. That student showed himself to be unfair and recalcitrant. His answer to that person decided me and I was convinced and understood everything. Nor did I allow this understanding to wane.

Whatever of His verses and commentaries came to hand, I read and they renewed my inner, spiritual being. No doubt has since then entered my mind, and this outward glory that God has granted me is on account of the fact that I approached this matter fairly and accepted this Cause."

'After hearing these words and becoming completely reassured about that holy man, I said: "Now that this blessed Cause is manifest and proven to Your Eminence and the reins of control over millions of the Shí'ite sect are in your hands, if you consider it advisable, you could make this matter public so that the people will be saved from ignorance and error and will enter the way of right guidance."

'"What are you saying, my son? These people are not fair-minded. Is my rank higher than that of Mullá Ḥusayn-i-Bushrú'í or Áqá Mírzá Muḥammad-'Alíy-i-Bárfurúshí [Quddús] and Ákhúnd Mullá Muḥammad-'Alíy-i-Zanjání [Ḥujjat] and the others? They would have done the same with me as they did with them. The best thing was for me to conceal my belief. In the meantime, I was able to perform such services that were I to tell you of them, you yourself would testify that it was right for me to conceal the matter and help the Cause."

'"I would like to hear of the assistance that you have given," I said.

'"In 1301 [sic],* a number of the believers were arrested by Náyibu's-Salṭanih, Kámrán Mírzá, in Ṭihrán and kept in prison in harsh circumstances for two years. Every day they were interrogated and matters were made very difficult for them. I wrote to Náṣiri'd-Dín Sháh saying: 'Why have you, without any reason and without my authorization [*fatwá*], caused such harm to befall them? It has been due to you that this Faith has spread among the peoples and countries. The Apostle of God [i.e., Muḥammad] has said: "Mankind seeks after what is forbidden." Your prohibitions and persecutions have strengthened this cause. You must certainly, as soon as my letter arrives, send for the prisoners, be kind to them and set them free. And from now onwards, do not cause anyone to be killed on account of this matter.' After the arrival of my letter, Náṣiri'd-Dín Sháh summoned the prisoners, gave them one *sharafí* each and set them free. Among them was Ḥájí Mullá 'Alí-Akbar [-i-Sháhmírzádí, Ḥájí Ákhúnd], Áqá Mírzá Abu'l-Faḍl [-i-Gulpáygání], Ḥájí Amín, Mashhadí 'Alíy-i-Qazvíní and other important persons. That was one of the things that I did to serve the Cause.

* AH 1300 was the year of these arrests, AD 12 November 1882–1 November 1883.

'"And another was when Siyyid Jamálu'd-Dín-i-Asadábádí, who is known as Afghání, was planning some mischief in Istanbul. He had interpolated some material into the *Kitáb-i-Aqdas* and had inserted some rubbish of his own into that book. Among the things that he had inserted was that the mosques of Islám should be demolished and razed to the ground. Mecca should be destroyed and Medina pulled down. With some other things, he translated this into Turkish and gave it to Sulṭán'Abdu'l-Ḥamíd so that the Sulṭán might become angry and mischief might result therefrom. Sulṭán 'Abdu'l-Ḥamíd wrote an account of this book to me and asked me what should be done. I replied: 'You have no right to interfere in such matters. Whoever has done this has done so out of spite. Send all such books to me. After investigating the matter, I will decide what is to be done with them.' Sulṭán 'Abdu'l-Ḥamíd sent them and I had Shaykh Ḥasan throw them all into the river where they sank and were obliterated.

'"My son! You have no idea how often the 'ulamá of Írán have written to me and asked for *fatwás* [decrees against the Bahá'ís]. I have somehow managed to answer all their questions and have silenced them. If I were to tell you it all, it would tire you. Among them was [Mírzá Ḥasan-i-] Áshtíyání . . . from Ṭihrán; Shaykh [Muḥammad-] Báqir* and Shaykh [Muḥammad-] Taqí† from Iṣfahán; Siyyid 'Alí-Akbar [-i-Fál-Asírí] and Shaykh Ṭáhir-i-'Arab from Shíráz; Mullá 'Abdu'lláh-i-Burújirdí from Hamadán; and others from various places. Perhaps one hundred letters in all, and to each one I have given an answer and silenced its author."

'After hearing these words from the Ḥujjatu'l-Islám, I said: "Truly your help and assistance for this Cause have been inestimable and are worthy of praise." . . .

'Then he said: "When will you be leaving?"

'"My only intention was to meet you," I replied. "I have no other business here."

'"Then it is better if you go soon, since, when you arrived in Baghdád some mischief-makers came and said something to the effect that someone has come from 'Akká to Baghdád to teach. I gave them their reply saying: 'It is Áqá Mírzá Áqá, one of my cousins. I have personally invited him to visit the Holy Places and to come and meet me. Do not interfere in this matter.'"

* Stigmatized by Bahá'u'lláh as 'The Wolf'.

† Son of the last-named, also called Áqá Najafí.

'We embraced and said farewell and I left. As I left the house I found the Arab Bahá'ís gathered, worried, around the house of His Holiness. When they saw me they were relieved.

'"What are you doing?" I said.

'"We became worried because you took so long. We were thinking all sorts of things. Being distressed, we left our residence and gathered around the house of His Holiness waiting for you."

'"That was not necessary."

'I returned with my friends to our residence. The same day we left for Baghdád and Baṣrah and eventually reached Búshihr.'

The National Hotel in Poona, India, 1907, taken during the visits of four Bahá'í teachers (see footnote, p. 238): (in the back seat of the 1st carriage) *Mullá Muḥammad-Taqí, Ibn-i-Abhar and Mr Hooper Harris;* (in the back seat of the 2nd carriage) *Mr Harlan Ober and Mírzá Maḥmúd Zarqání, diarist of 'Abdu'l-Bahá's travels in the West;* (standing behind the front wheels of the 2nd carriage) *Áqá Khusraw*

20

The Apostles of Bahá'u'lláh

by Moojan Momen

BECAUSE THE AUTHOR'S intention to write biographical chapters on the nineteen Apostles of Bahá'u'lláh was thwarted by his death in 1980, it has fallen to the present writer to provide short accounts of the eleven Apostles not dealt with by Mr Balyuzi in this and the preceding volume.

The following are the nineteen persons designated as Apostles of Bahá'u'lláh by Shoghi Effendi, the Guardian of the Bahá'í Faith:*

1. Mírzá Músá, surnamed Kalím, the only true brother of Bahá'u'lláh
2. Mírzá Buzurg, surnamed Badí'
3. Siyyid Ḥasan, surnamed Sulṭánu'sh-Shuhadá' (See chap. 3.)
4. Mullá Abu'l-Ḥasan, surnamed Amín
5. Mírzá Abu'l-Faḍl (-i-Gulpáygání)
6. Mírzá 'Alí-Muḥammad, surnamed Varqá (See chap. 7.)
7. Mírzá Maḥmúd (Furúghí) (See chap. 13.)
8. Mullá 'Alí-Akbar (Ḥájí Ákhúnd)
9. Mullá Muḥammad, surnamed Nabíl-i-Akbar (See chap. 9.)
10. Ḥájí Mírzá Muḥammad-Taqí (Vakílu'd-Dawlih)
11. Mírzá Muḥammad-Taqí (Ibn-i-Abhar)
12. Mullá Muḥammad, surnamed Nabíl-i-A'ẓam
13. Shaykh Káẓim, surnamed Samandar (See chap. 16.)
14. Mírzá Muḥammad Muṣṭafá
15. Mírzá Ḥusayn, surnamed Mishkín-Qalam
16. Mírzá Ḥasan, surnamed Adíb
17. Shaykh Muḥammad-'Alí

* As mentioned in the Foreword, the first two were included in *Bahá'u'lláh, The King of Glory*, and chapters about the 3rd, 6th, 7th, 9th, 13th and 19th Apostles appear in Part I of this volume. Biographical notes for the remaining eleven Apostles form the material of this chapter.

Apostles of Bahá'u'lláh

(numbered as the list beginning on page 261)

18. Mullá Zaynu'l-'Ábidín, surnamed Zaynu'l-Muqarrabín
19. Mírzá 'Alí-Muḥammad (Ibn-i-Aṣdaq) (See chap. 14.)

Mullá Abu'l-Ḥasan, surnamed Amín

Mullá Abu'l-Ḥasan-i-Ardikání, who is known as Ḥájí Amín or Amín-i-Iláhí, was born in about the year AH 1232 (AD 21 November 1816–10 November 1817) in Ardikán, a small town near Yazd. At seventeen years of age he married into a family of Bábís of the town. He was persuaded to investigate the new religion and eventually, shortly after the martyrdom of the Báb, he declared his belief. When news of the Declaration of Bahá'u'lláh came, he accepted immediately and travelled throughout Írán meeting other Bábís and teaching them of the advent of Bahá'u'lláh. After a time he became the assistant of Ḥájí Sháh-Muḥammad Manshádí, Amínu'l-Bayán, who was the Trustee of the Ḥuqúqu'lláh.* He would travel about the country, earning his living by trading and also by acting as a writer for those who could not write. At the same time he collected the Ḥuqúqu'lláh and any letters that the believers wished to forward to Bahá'u'lláh, and also distributed Tablets of Bahá'u'lláh when these were received. He came to 'Akká while Bahá'u'lláh was still imprisoned in the citadel and succeeded in establishing contact with the exiles. He was the first Bahá'í from the outside world to be able to meet Bahá'u'lláh in 'Akká (in the Public Baths). He returned to 'Akká on several further occasions. When Ḥájí Sháh-Muḥammad Manshádí was killed in 1880, Ḥájí Abu'l-Ḥasan was appointed Trustee (Amín) of the Ḥuqúqu'lláh. In 1891 he was imprisoned with Ḥájí Ákhúnd for three years in Ṭihrán and Qazvín. In the time of 'Abdu'l-Bahá he continued his travels, visiting 'Akká and Haifa on several occasions. Towards the end of his life he resided in Ṭihrán and Ḥájí Ghulám-Riḍá, Amín-i-Amín, was appointed his assistant. He died in 1928 and was posthumously named a Hand of the Cause of God by Shoghi Effendi.

Mírzá Abu'l-Faḍl-i-Gulpáygání

Mírzá Muḥammad, who is known to Bahá'ís as Mírzá Abu'l-Faḍl or Mírzá Abu'l-Faḍá'il, was born in 1844 into a family of religious

* The 'Right of God' – a payment by believers instituted in the *Kitáb-i-Aqdas*.

Mullá Abu'l-Ḥasan-i-Ardikání, known as Ḥájí Amín, appointed posthumously a Hand of the Cause of God by Shoghi Effendi, Guardian of the Bahá'í Faith

Mírzá Abu'l-Faḍl-i-Gulpáygání 'It is a rare thing to find a person perfect from every direction, but he was such a person.' ('Abdu'l-Bahá speaking to Bahá'ís in Haifa, the night after Mírzá Abu'l-Faḍl's passing, 22 January 1914)

scholars in Gulpáygán. He studied the Islamic sciences, becoming well versed in both the traditional transmitted branches of knowledge as well as the rational philosophic branches. He studied at Karbilá, Najaf and Iṣfahán and eventually became the head of a religious college, the Madrisiy-i-Mádar-i-Sháh (the religious college of the Mother of the Sháh). The story of his introduction to the Bahá'í Faith through a humble blacksmith is well known to Bahá'ís. The confirmation of his belief came in 1876 after a period of studying the Writings of the Faith and seeing the prophecies of Bahá'u'lláh come true.

His conversion led to his dismissal from his post and imprisonment for five months. He then became the secretary of Mánakjí Ṣáḥib, the Zoroastrian agent in Ṭihrán. In December 1882 he was arrested, together with a large number of Bahá'ís of Ṭihrán, and was in prison for twenty-two months. After this he began extensive travels throughout Írán. It was principally through his writings that the

Bahá'í Faith was presented to the Jews of Írán in such a way as to bring a large number of them into the Bahá'í fold. In 1888 he travelled to 'Ishqábád and later to Samarqand and Bukhárá. In 1894 he spent ten months in the presence of 'Abdu'l-Bahá in 'Akká and then on the instructions of 'Abdu'l-Bahá proceeded to Cairo, where he settled for a number of years and was successful in converting some of the students of the foremost institution of learning of the Sunní world, al-Azhar. Between 1900 and 1904 he travelled to Paris and the United States where his talks and his writings enabled the nascent Bahá'í communities to gain a clearer understanding of the tenets of the Faith. He then lived in Beirut and Cairo until his death in the latter city on 21 January 1914.

Mullá 'Alí-Akbar (Ḥájí Ákhúnd)

Ḥají Mullá 'Alí-Akbar-i-Shahmírzádí, who is known as Ḥájí Ákhúnd, was born in Shahmírzád in about 1842. He was the son of a mullá of that village and after some preliminary studies in his own

Ḥájí Mullá 'Alí-Akbar-i-Shahmírzádí, known as Ḥájí Ákhúnd, appointed a Hand of the Cause of God by Bahá'u'lláh

village, he proceeded to Mashhad to attend the religious colleges there. In Mashhad he pursued every avenue of religious enquiry until eventually, in about 1861, he encountered the Bábís and was converted. When news of his conversion spread, the religious students rose against him and forced him to leave the town. He returned to Shahmírzád but was eventually forced to leave there as well. He settled in Ṭihrán. There, he became so well known as a Bahá'í that 'Abdu'l-Bahá relates that whenever there was an outburst against the Bahá'ís, he would wrap his 'abá around himself and sit waiting for the guards to come and arrest him. (*Memorials of the Faithful*, p. 11) He was arrested many times and is known to have been imprisoned on at least the following occasions: in 1868 on the orders of Mullá 'Alí Kaní; in 1872 for seven months by Náyibu's-Salṭanih; in 1882 for two years by Náyibu's-Salṭanih, together with many other Ṭihrán Bahá'ís; in about 1887; and in 1891 when he was imprisoned for two years with Ḥájí Amín. He visited 'Akká on three occasions, in about 1873, 1888 and 1899. He was entrusted with many important tasks, in particular the custodianship and transfer of the remains of the Báb. He was appointed by Bahá'u'lláh as one of the Hands of the Cause of God and was responsible for much of the teaching work, as well as for administering the community of the Bahá'ís of Írán. He died in Ṭihrán on 4 March 1910.

Ḥájí Mírzá Muḥammad-Taqí (Vakílu'd-Dawlih)

Ḥájí Mírzá Muḥammad-Taqí was born in Shíráz in AH 1246 (AD 22 June 1830–11 June 1831), the second son of Ḥájí Siyyid Muḥammad, the maternal uncle of the Báb. In his youth he met the Báb both in Shíráz and Búshihr. Then in about 1854 he settled in Yazd where he soon became one of the prominent merchants of the town. Here he was visited by Mullá Muḥammad-i-Qá'iní who spoke to him about the religion of the Báb. His belief in the Báb was confirmed by a journey in 1857 to Baghdád where he met Bahá'u'lláh. Because of his prominence in the town of Yazd, he was asked by the Russian Government to be their Consular Agent in the town, and hence he became known as Vakílu'd-Dawlih (Representative of the Government), but Bahá'u'lláh named him Vakílu'l-Ḥaqq (Representative of the True One, i.e. God). In those days, Iranian merchants were anxious to be consular agents of Foreign Powers, as this was one way of avoiding the arbitrary exactions of provincial governors and other government officials.

While he was still a resident of Yazd, Ḥájí Mírzá Muḥammad-Taqí purchased property in the town of 'Ishqábád in Russian Transcaspia. This town became a refuge for Bahá'ís escaping from persecution in Írán, and soon there was a large Bahá'í community there. Bahá'u'lláh had indicated that a Mashriqu'l-Adhkár should be built in the city and later, in the time of 'Abdu'l-Bahá, the Bahá'í community asked for permission to begin the building. 'Abdu'l-Bahá wrote to Ḥájí Mírzá Muḥammad-Taqí asking him to go to 'Ishqábád to supervise the work. And so in 1900 Ḥájí Mírzá Muḥammad-Taqí concluded all of his business affairs in Yazd and left for 'Ishqábád. There, he not only supervised the erection of the Mashriqu'l-Adhkár but paid for most of the building materials from his own funds. Then in 1906, with the

Ḥájí Mírzá Muḥammad-Taqí, known as Vakílu'd-Dawlih, the chief builder, in 'Ishqábád, of the first Mashriqu'l-Adhkar

Mírzá Muḥammad-Taqí, known as Ibn-i-Abhar, appointed a Hand of the Cause of God by Bahá'u'lláh

structure of the Mashriqu'l-Adhkár almost complete, Ḥájí Mírzá Muḥammad-Taqí travelled to Haifa where he was warmly received by 'Abdu'l-Bahá. He remained in Haifa until his passing in 1909, and is buried in the Bahá'í cemetery at the foot of Mount Carmel.

Mírzá Muḥammad-Taqí, Ibn-i-Abhar

Mírzá Muḥammad-Taqí was born in Abhar, a village between Qazvín and Zanján. His father, who came from a family of the leading divines of Abhar, became a believer in the Báb through reading some of His writings. Because of persecution, the family moved to Qazvín and in about 1868 became followers of Bahá'u'lláh. In 1874 his father died by poison and after this Ibn-i-Abhar moved to Zanján where he reinvigorated the Bábí community, causing most of them to enter the Bahá'í fold. His activities in Zanján, however, led to his imprisonment for fourteen months. After his release, he travelled throughout Írán and later made a trip to the Holy Land in 1886. He was appointed a Hand of the Cause of God in the same year and travelled extensively in Írán, Caucasia, Turkmenistan and India. From 1890 to 1894 he was imprisoned in a dungeon in Ṭihrán, and for a time wore the same chains as had been put on Bahá'u'lláh when a prisoner in Síyáh-Chál. After his release, he went to the Holy Land and then to 'Ishqábád. In 1897 he participated in the gathering of the Hands of the Cause which led to the formation of the Central Spiritual Assembly in Ṭihrán. Settling in Ṭihrán, he assisted in the establishment of the Tarbíyat Bahá'í School, while his wife, Munírih Khánum, the daughter of Ḥájí Ákhúnd, played a major role in the founding of the Girls' School. In 1907 he travelled through India with two American Bahá'ís, Harlan Ober and Hooper Harris, accompanied by Mírzá Maḥmúd Zarqání. His travels within Írán were extensive, and on eleven occasions he visited the Holy Land. He passed away in 1917.

Mullá Muḥammad, surnamed Nabíl-i-A'ẓam

Mullá Muḥammad was born in Zarand on 29 July 1831 of humble parents. He was a shepherd by occupation but strove hard to overcome the handicap of a meagre education. He learnt to read the Qur'án and often went with his father to Qum where he listened to the discourses of the prominent religious figures there. In 1847, while on a visit to his maternal uncle in the village of Rubáṭ-Karím, Nabíl overheard a conversation about the Báb and was immediately interested. Later, through Siyyid Ḥusayn-i-Zavári'í he was more fully informed of the Faith of the Báb and became a believer. Nabíl proceeded to Qum where Siyyid Ismá'íl-i-Zavári'í confirmed his belief, and together they tried to join the Bábís at Shaykh Ṭabarsí but found that they were too late. He took up residence in Ṭihrán in the same *madrisih* (religious college) as Mírzá Aḥmad, the transcriber of the Báb's writings, and met many of the Bábís who lived in or were passing through that town, including Bahá'u'lláh.

At the time of the execution of the Seven Martyrs of Ṭihrán in 1850, Nabíl was persuaded to return to his home village, but later he left for Qum hoping to meet Mírzá Aḥmad there. Failing to find him, Nabíl proceeded to Káshán and eventually located Mírzá Aḥmad in Kirmánsháh; he remained there until after Bahá'u'lláh's passage through that town in 1851. Bahá'u'lláh instructed them to proceed to Ṭihrán where they engaged themselves in transcribing and distributing the writings of the Báb, until the situation became too dangerous and Nabíl returned to Zarand.

There followed the attempt on the life of the Sháh in 1852 and the persecution of the Bábí community to the point of its near annihilation. During those dark days, Nabíl put forward a claim to leadership of the Bábí community stating that he was in receipt of Divine inspiration. But later, when he visited Baghdád and came to recognize Bahá'u'lláh's station, he withdrew his claim.

From Baghdád and Adrianople, Bahá'u'lláh sent Nabíl on numerous journeys to the Bábís of Írán. During the Adrianople years, his major task was to alert the Bábís to Bahá'u'lláh's claim to be 'He Whom God shall make manifest'. On one journey, he was instructed to perform the pilgrimage to the House of the Báb in Shíráz and the House of Bahá'u'lláh in Baghdád, being the first to do this according to the laws revealed by Bahá'u'lláh.

From Adrianople, Nabíl was sent by Bahá'u'lláh to Egypt on a mission which resulted in his imprisonment (see *Bahá'u'lláh, The King of Glory*, pp. 265–8). When freed Nabíl hurried to 'Akká, but being espied by the followers of Azal who had stationed themselves near the city-gate, he was ejected from the city. He wandered around the countryside, living for a time on Mount Carmel and for a time in Nazareth until he was able to enter 'Akká. He was sent by Bahá'u'lláh on yet another journey to Írán during which he confirmed the belief of many of the Bahá'ís. He then took up residence in 'Akká until the time of the passing of Bahá'u'lláh in 1892. Overwhelmed with sorrow at this event, Nabíl ended his own life by jumping into the sea. He was a great poet and, besides writing a lengthy history of the Faith, he has preserved many of the historical events of the Faith in the form of poetry which he used to send to the Bahá'ís of Írán. A complete collection of his extensive poetical writings has not yet been made.

Mírzá Muḥammad Muṣṭafá

The father of Mírzá Muḥammad Muṣṭafáy-i-Baghdádí, Shaykh Muḥammad Shibl, was a distinguished follower of the Shaykhí leader, Siyyid Káẓim-i-Rashtí, and was indeed his personal representative in Baghdád. When Mullá 'Alíy-i-Basṭámí, the Letter of the Living, was brought to Baghdád and imprisoned there (see *The Báb*, pp. 59–61), Shaykh Muḥammad Shibl visited him in prison, learnt of the claim of the Báb and became a believer. Later, that distinguished Letter of the Living, Ṭáhirih, stayed at the house of Shaykh Muḥammad Shibl in Baghdád for a period and when the time came that she was to be expelled from 'Iráq, Shaykh Muḥammad and Mírzá Muṣṭafá accompanied her to Qazvín and then travelled on to Ṭihrán, where they met Mullá Ḥusayn-i-Bushrú'í. Such were the events that filled the childhood and youth of Mírzá Muṣṭafá, who was born in Baghdád in about 1837. During the period that Bahá'u'lláh was in Baghdád, Mírzá Muṣṭafá became devoted to Him, although, of course, Bahá'u'lláh had not put forward a claim at this time. In 1874 Mírzá Muṣṭafá was arrested along with many others of the Bahá'ís of Baghdád, and after this he travelled to 'Akká and sought permission from Bahá'u'lláh to live in the vicinity of that city. Bahá'u'lláh instructed him to take up his residence in Beirut where he was frequently of service to those Bahá'ís travelling to 'Akká. After the ascension of Bahá'u'lláh, he moved to Alexandretta (Iskandarun), where he died in 1910.

Mírzá Ḥusayn, surnamed Mishkín-Qalam

Mírzá Ḥusayn, a native of Shíráz but resident in Iṣfahán, was a Ṣúfí of the Ni'matu'lláhí Order. He was a calligrapher of the first rank, a fine

Mírzá Muḥammad Muṣṭafáy-i-Baghdádí, one of the believers who assisted in the transport of the remains of the Báb to 'Akká in 1899

Áqá Ḥusayn-i-Iṣfahání, known as Mishkín-Qalam (see Bahá'u'lláh, The King of Glory, *pp. 161 and 251, for specimens of his highly-valued calligraphy)*

poet, and was also noted for his witty and subtle mind, all of these being qualities highly prized in nineteenth-century Írán. And so Mírzá Ḥusayn or Mishkín-Qalam, his artistic name by which he is usually known, was never short of wealthy patrons. However, he himself preferred to travel as a wandering dervish with few possessions. 'Abdu'l-Bahá states that he first heard of the Faith in Iṣfahán, but it was in Baghdád a few years after Bahá'u'lláh's departure from that city that Mishkín-Qalam learned more about the new religion from Zaynu'l-Muqarrabín and Nabíl-i-A'ẓam. He set out for Adrianople and after a brief sojourn in Aleppo reached the presence of Bahá'u'lláh where his belief was confirmed. After a while, he travelled to Istanbul and his talents soon brought him to the attention of the notables of that capital city. However, the Iranian ambassador plotted against him and caused his arrest. When Bahá'u'lláh and His companions were exiled to 'Akká, Mishkín-Qalam was sent with them in the same ship but was compelled to go on to Cyprus where he remained in detention and exile. He was eventually freed and came to 'Akká in 1886, taking up residence in the Khán-i-'Avámíd. After the passing of Bahá'u'lláh, he travelled to Egypt, Damascus and India (the last in 1905). 'Abdu'l-Bahá, when He heard that Mishkín-Qalam was growing old and weak in India, recalled him to the Holy Land and he remained there until his death in about 1912.

Mírzá Ḥasan, surnamed Adíb

Ḥájí Mírzá Ḥasan was born in Ṭalaqán in September 1848. His father was an eminent cleric and Ḥájí Mírzá Ḥasan underwent the usual religious education at Ṭihrán and Mashhad. From 1874 onwards he was employed by one of the Qájár princes, I'tidádu's-Salṭanih, and later by another prince, Mu'tamidu'd-Dawlih. These two princes used to publish a large number of books which were written for them by their employees but published in their own names. In this way, Mírzá Ḥasan contributed to such important works as the encyclopaedic *Námiy-i-Dánishvarán*, until his becoming known as a Bahá'í caused his dismissal from such work. He was also, for a time, Imám-Jum'ih (Friday prayer leader) and teacher at the Dáru'l-Funún, Írán's first educational establishment founded on modern lines. He was given the title Adíbu'l-'Ulamá (littérateur of the 'ulamá) and was a poet of considerable talent.

It was his close friend, the eminent cleric Shaykh Hádí Najmábádí, who pointed out to Mírzá Ḥasan the similarity between his views and those of the Bahá'ís, and this prompted the latter to investigate the Bahá'í Faith. In about 1889, after prolonged conversations with Nabíl-i-Akbar, he was converted and soon afterwards was designated by Bahá'u'lláh as one of the Hands of the Cause of God. After the passing of Bahá'u'lláh, Mírzá Ḥasan was much involved in dealing with the activities of the Covenant-breakers. In AH 1315 (AD 2 June 1897–21 May 1898), he participated in the meetings of the Hands of the Cause which evolved over several years into the Central Spiritual Assembly of Ṭihrán, the precursor of the Iranian National Spiritual Assembly. He was chairman of this body. He also played an important part in the founding of the Tarbíyat Schools in Ṭihrán and in their administration. In 1903 he travelled to Iṣfahán where he was

Mírzá Ḥasan, entitled Adíbu'l-'Ulamá and known as Adíb, one of the four Hands of the Cause of God appointed by Bahá'u'lláh

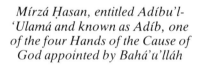

Shaykh Muḥammad-'Alíy-i-Qá'iní, nephew and close companion of Nabíl-i-Akbar

briefly imprisoned during the upheaval there. From there he proceeded to Shíráz, Bombay, and eventually to 'Akká. 'Abdu'l-Bahá instructed him to travel through India and Burma in the company of the American Bahá'í, Sidney Sprague. He eventually returned to Ṭihrán where he died on 2 September 1919.

Shaykh Muḥammad-'Alí

Shaykh Muḥammad-'Alíy-i-Qá'iní was the nephew of Nabíl-i-Akbar. He was possessed of many talents, excelling in oratory, calligraphy and music. He was born in Naw-Firist near Birjand in AH 1277 (AD 20 July 1860–8 July 1861). His parents died when he was young and he was brought up by an uncle, Mullá Áqá 'Alí. While still a young man undertaking religious studies at Mashhad, he was apprised of the

Bahá'í Faith and soon became an ardent believer. He became the close companion of his erudite uncle Nabíl-i-Akbar until the latter's death in 1892. He lived in 'Ishqábád for a while and then in Ṭihrán where he married the daughter of Nabíl-i-Akbar. In 1903, he was instructed to accompany Mírzá Ḥasan-i-Adíb to India, but while travelling there he was caught up in the upheavals against the Bahá'ís in Iṣfahán during that year. He was stripped of his possessions, severely beaten, and was fortunate to escape with his life. He had to return to Ṭihrán but later reached India and remained there for one-and-a-half years. He then travelled to Haifa. Here 'Abdu'l-Bahá asked him to go to 'Ishqábád and to take charge of the education of children there.

He established himself in 'Ishqábád and, apart from various journeys made for the service of the Faith, he lived there for the rest of his life. After the death of Mírzá Abu'l-Faḍl-i-Gulpáygání, Shaykh Muḥammad-'Alí was asked to go to Haifa to bring to completion, with the help of others, the unfinished writings of Mírzá Abu'l-Faḍl. He was in Haifa for one-and-a-half years after the First World War, leaving for 'Ishqábád shortly before 'Abdu'l-Bahá's passing. He fell ill in 'Ishqábád and after a prolonged illness died in April 1924.

Mullá Zaynu'l-'Ábidín, surnamed Zaynu'l-Muqarrabín

Mullá Zaynu'l-'Ábidín, surnamed by Bahá'u'lláh Zaynu'l-Muqarrabín (the Ornament of the Near Ones) was noted among the companions of Bahá'u'lláh for his wit and humour, his learning and calligraphy, but above all for Bahá'u'lláh's high regard for him. He was born in Rajab 1233 (May 1818) in one of the villages of Najafábád near Iṣfahán of a family of Muslim clerics. He himself underwent a religious education and was made a preacher at a mosque in Najafábád. Although he heard of the Báb's claim in 1844 while he was on pilgrimage to Karbilá, it was not until 1851 that he was taught the new religion and became a believer. Many others were converted in Najafábád and the town soon became a stronghold of the Bábí Faith. Zaynu'l-Muqarrabín decided to visit Baghdád and meet the leading Bábís who were in exile there. He failed to find Mírzá Yaḥyá who was keeping himself hidden from the believers, and Bahá'u'lláh was at this time on His two-year sojourn in the Sulaymáníyyih area. Disappointed, Zaynu'l-Muqarrabín set off for home. As he approached

Mullá Zaynu'l-'Ábidín, surnamed Jináb-i-Zaynu'l-Muqarrabín, a designation conferred upon him by Bahá'u'lláh

Najafábád, however, he learned of a violent outburst of persecution against the believers and that officials of the Governor were searching for him. He therefore retraced his steps to Baghdád and was fortunate in meeting Bahá'u'lláh on this occasion, an encounter that confirmed his faith in the new religion. Zaynu'l-Muqarrabín became one of the pillars of the Bábí community in Najafábád and Iṣfahán, and when he heard of Bahá'u'lláh's claim to be the One promised by the Báb, he unhesitatingly accepted.

A further outburst of persecution in 1864 precipitated Zaynu'l-Muqarrabín's departure from Najafábád. He settled in Baghdád and occupied himself with transcribing Tablets. In 1870 the Bahá'ís in Baghdád were rounded up and exiled to Mosul. The Bahá'ís in Mosul, under the leadership and guidance of Zaynu'l-Muqarrabín, soon became a model Bahá'í community reflecting something of the spirit of the 'Akká community. While there, it became Zaynu'l-Muqarrabín's task to transcribe the Tablets of Bahá'u'lláh that arrived from

'Akká on their way to Írán. Thus these Tablets could be distributed more widely and each of those to whom a Tablet was addressed could have a copy.

In Dhu'l-Ḥijjah 1302 (September–October 1885) Bahá'u'lláh gave permission for Zaynu'l-Muqarrabín to come to 'Akká where he took up residence in the Khán-i-'Avámíd, continuing to transcribe Tablets and frequently having the honour of being in Bahá'u'lláh's company. Following the ascension of Bahá'u'lláh, Zaynu'l-Muqarrabín remained faithful to the Covenant until his passing in 1903.

Part II

The ancestors of Bahá'u'lláh dwelt near the Caspian Sea in the famed province of Ṭabaristán (now Mázindarán). Although born in Ṭihrán, Bahá'u'lláh maintained His ties with Mázindarán which embraces Núr, the seat of His ancestral home. Three of the following chapters relate some of the history of these regions, while two chapters trace His genealogy and give some remarkable prophecies of His advent.

21

On the Shores of the Caspian Sea

THE CASPIAN SEA, on the shores of which many a generation of the ancestors of Bahá'u'lláh lived and prospered, is known in Persian as the Sea of Khazar (Daryáy-i-Khazar). Khazars were a people of Turkish origin whose haunts bordered the north of that vast inland sea. And their story is strange indeed. They, who had no connection whatsoever with the Children of Israel, voluntarily adopted the Jewish Faith. They did it in order to free themselves of tutelage to either the Muslim Arabs or the Christian Byzantines. Being Jewish in faith would liberate them from both Islám and Christianity, they reasoned. We shall examine their history in some detail anon; but the point to note, now, is their love of independence, their intense abhorrence of submission to the will and the whims of neighbours and magnates of other lands. This love of liberty which bordered almost on rebelliousness, they shared with other dwellers of the coastal regions of the Caspian Sea, particularly the people of Ṭabaristán – the home of the ancestors of Bahá'u'lláh.

When the Arab hosts conquered Írán in the middle of the seventh century and brought Islám with them to present to the vanquished, the inhabitants of the Iranian provinces adjoining the Caspian Sea, sheltered in the fastnesses of mount and forest, refused to let the Arabs in and refused to alter their religious affiliation. Moreover, they received with open arms anyone who had challenged the caliphs of Damascus and later of Baghdád, and gave them sustenance and refuge. Most of those who had taken up arms against the Umayyads and the 'Abbásids were scions of the House of the Prophet. And it was the pacific influence of those who had escaped from the clutches of the caliphs that led the recalcitrants to embrace Islám. Their Islám, however, was different from that professed by the caliphs, for it was to Shí'ism, in its various guises, that they inclined.

In the following pages we shall take a closer look into the adventures of these people who lived in the periphery of the Caspian Sea: the Sea of Khazar.

'Abda'r Raḥmán III, perhaps the greatest of all the rulers of al-Andalus (Moorish Spain), in AD 929 proclaimed himself Caliph and Amíra'l-Mu'minín (Commander of the Faithful) – a powerful rival to both the 'Abbásid caliphs of Baghdád (who were also Sunnís) and to the Ismá'ílí Shí'ih caliphs of Cairo (the Fáṭimids). 'Abda'r Raḥmán was a very remarkable man. Following the style set by the 'Abbásids, he took the title an-Náṣir li-Díni'lláh: Defender of the Faith of God. A man free of prejudice and fanaticism, he raised Ḥisdai Ibn Shapruṭ, his court physician and a Jew, to the highest position of trust in his kingdom. And Ḥisdai served him with devotion. Then it came to Ḥisdai's ears that far away, half-the-world distant to the East, there was a king, who, with his people, professed the Faith that he himself did. Ḥisdai Ibn Shapruṭ was as remarkable a man as his enlightened master. He has put it on record that he first heard of that incredible Jewish realm from merchants of Khurásán. He found it hard to believe. Then envoys from Byzantium reached Cordoba and they confirmed everything which the Khurásání merchants had related. They even could give Ḥisdai the name of the king of that Jewish Land, which happened to be Yúsuf (Joseph).

Bursting with curiosity and enthusiasm, Ḥisdai addressed a respectful letter to King Joseph of Khazaria. The letter was very long and the writer longed for more information regarding everything. He wrote:

> I feel the urge to know the truth, whether there is really a place on this earth where harassed Israel can rule itself, where it is subject to nobody. If I were to know that this is indeed the case, I would not hesitate to forsake all honours, to resign my high office, to abandon my family, and to travel over mountains and plains, over land and water, until I arrived at the place where my Lord, the King rules . . . And I also have one more request: to be informed whether you have any knowledge . . . of the Final Miracle [the coming of the Messiah] which, wandering from country to country, we are awaiting. Dishonoured and humiliated in our dispersion, we have to listen in silence to those who say: 'every nation has its own land and you alone possess not even a shadow of a country on this earth'. (Quoted in Koestler, *The Thirteenth Tribe*, p. 71)

King Joseph, in his reply to the Jewish minister of 'Abda'r-Raḥmán, made it clear that he and his people did not, at any time, claim descent from Israel. He stated unequivocally that the people of Khazaria were of the seed of Japheth (Yáfith), the third son of Noah. King Joseph went on to say that Togarma, the grandson of Japheth, was the common ancestor of all the Turkish tribes. 'We have found', he writes, 'in the family registers of our fathers, that Togarma had ten sons, and the names of their [*sic*] offspring are as follows: Uigur, Dursu, Avars, Huns, Basilii, Tarniakh, Khazars, Zagora, Bulgars, Sabir. We are the sons of Khazar, the seventh . . .' (ibid. p. 72)

King Joseph then related the story of King Bulan, and how it happened that he came to accept the Jewish Faith and gave up idolatry.

When Bulan, perhaps the first hereditary king of Khazaria [writes Salo Wittmayer Baron], adopted the monotheistic faith, he apparently embraced it only in the form of a minimal 'religion of Abraham,' which he had heard invoked by spokesmen of Christianity and Islam as well as of Judaism. He may have been attracted by a legend, current in Arab and Jewish circles, that Turks and other Mongols were descendants of Abraham's sons by Keturah. According to Ibn Fadhlan,* the Khazar kings customarily had twenty-five wives. 'Each of them is the daughter of one of the kings who confront him [the vassal princes], taken freely or by force. He also has sixty slave-girls, concubines, all of superb beauty. Each of them, concubines as well as free-born ladies, lives in a castle of her own.' The khagan [khágán] may indeed have felt that such a harem was a legitimate imitation of King Solomon's polygamous establishment and of the wise king's use thereof as an instrument of imperial policy. Hebrew books must have been extremely scarce. Certainly talmudic tractates had then only begun to be circulated in the more civilized countries. Even copies of Scripture had to be brought out of a cave, according to the Cambridge fragment . . .

Only at the end of the century did King Obadiah conform more fully with the accepted tenets and observances of official Judaism. Afterwards, King Joseph, in his letter to Ḥisdai ibn Shapruṭ to which we owe that assertion, admitted the irregularity of the Khazar calendar. When Petaḥiah arrived in that vicinity he was shocked to learn that 'in the land of Kedar [Khazar] there are no Jews, only heretics. And Rabbi Petaḥiah asked them: Why do you not believe in the words of the sages? They replied: Because our fathers did not teach them to us. On the eve of Sabbath they cut all the bread which they eat on the Sabbath. They eat in the dark, and sit the whole day on one spot. Their prayers consist only of psalms. And when Rabbi Petaḥiah imparted to them

* Ibn Fadlán: Aḥmad, son of Fadlán (son of Ráshid, son of Ḥimád), was a jurisconsult of Baghdád. In the days of al-Muqtadir, the 'Abbásid caliph (AD 908–32), he headed a mission to the king of the Bulgars. He wrote a travelogue, which has been quoted by such eminent writers and geographers as Mas'údí, Iṣṭakhrí and Yáqút. (HMB)

our ritual and prayer after meals they were pleased. They also said: We have never heard what the Talmud is.' (*A Social and Religious History of the Jews*, vol. 3, pp. 201–2)

We shall see later what eventually happened to Khazaria. Now, we ought to go back in time to the years when the people of Khazaria were still pagans and idolaters; we need not go back to the origins of the Khazars. They certainly were Turks, and certainly not Mongolians. Even in recent times certain outbursts of nationalistic and racial fervour have tended to confuse the issue. It was definitely very misplaced for the Turks of Anatolia to take pride in being of the same stock and breed as Chingíz Khán.

In the days of Chosroes I – Parvíz, the great Anúshirván the Just (reigned AD 531–79) – three gold 'guest thrones' were kept in the throne-room of his palace in Ctesiphon. They were reserved for three potentates well known in the world of those times: namely, the Emperors of China, Byzantium and Khazaria. It is not recorded that any of them ever paid a visit to Ctesiphon or ever met Chosroes, but the fact that those gold thrones were there awaiting them is a sure indication of the attractive qualities of the Sásánid monarch, and of the position which the ruler of Khazaria had attained, to be ranked with the Emperors of China and Byzantium.

The grandson of Anúshirván, Chosroes II, gained his throne with the aid of Emperor Maurice of Byzantium and overthrew a pretender, but in the year AD 602 Maurice went down before a mob and Phocas, a mere centurion, usurped his throne. Maurice, who had been forced to abdicate, was cruelly murdered, together with five sons, by a successor entirely unworthy of his rule. 'The reign of Phocas', writes Gibbon, 'afflicted Europe with ignominious peace, and Asia with desolating war . . . Every province of the empire was ripe for rebellion; and Heraclius, exarch of Africa, persisted above two years in refusing all tribute and obedience to the centurion who disgraced the throne of Constantinople.' Although urged to rescue and govern the empire, the exarch was old and called upon his son Heraclius to undertake this dangerous enterprise. Sailing with his fleet from Carthage to Constantinople, Heraclius stripped Phocas of his crown and ascended the throne of the Caesars. He had to begin rebuilding an almost shattered Roman polity. Byzantium was indeed in a parlous condition, for the troops of Chosroes, who had considered it his duty to avenge the death of his benefactor, had made deep inroads into Byzantine territory. Heraclius was faced with a formidable task, but his great advantage was the weakness of character of the Persian monarch.

In the beginning Heraclius could do nothing to stem the Persian avalanche. Antioch fell, and so did Jerusalem. The True Cross was seized and carried by the victors. Now, Heraclius sought a reliable ally, and his choice rested on the pagan king of Khazaria. Let us look at the picture, as depicted by Edward Gibbon:

> . . . To the hostile league of Chosroes with the Avars, the Roman emperor opposed the useful and honourable alliance of the Turks. At his liberal invitation, the horde of Chozars [Khazars] transported their tents from the plains of the Volga to the mountains of Georgia; Heraclius received them in the neighbourhood of Teflis [Tiflís], and the khan with his nobles dismounted from their horses, if we may credit the Greeks, and fell prostrate on the ground, to adore the purple of the Caesar. Such voluntary homage and important aid were entitled to the warmest acknowledgements; and the emperor, taking off his own diadem, placed it on the head of the Turkish prince, whom he saluted with a tender embrace and the appellation of son. After a sumptuous banquet, he presented Ziebel with the plate and ornaments, the gold, the gems, and the silk, which had been used at the Imperial table, and, with his own hand, distributed rich jewels and ear-rings to his new allies. In a secret interview, he produced the portrait of his daughter Eudocia, condescended to flatter the Barbarian with the promise of a fair and august bride, obtained an immediate succour of 40,000 horse, and negociated a strong diversion of the Turkish arms on the side of the Oxus. (chap. 46)
>
> . . . .
>
> When the ambition of Chosroes was reduced to the defence of his hereditary kingdom, the love of glory, or even the sense of shame, should have urged him to meet his rival in the field. In the battle of Nineveh, his courage might have taught the Persians to vanquish, or he might have fallen with honour by the lance of a Roman emperor. The successor of Cyrus chose rather, at a secure distance, to expect the event, to assemble the relics of the defeat, and to retire by measured steps before the march of Heraclius, till (A.D. 627. Dec. 29) he beheld with a sigh the once loved mansions of Dastagerd. Both his friends and enemies were persuaded, that it was the intention of Chosroes to bury himself under the ruins of the city and palace; and, as both might have been equally adverse to his flight, the monarch of Asia, with Sira, and three concubines, escaped through an hole in the wall nine days before the arrival of the Romans. (ibid.)

The faithless, cringing Chosroes took to his heels. He abandoned armies to their fate. All that he cared for was his own personal safety. This was the man who had straddled Byzantium. This was the man who had dared to tear up the letter of the Prophet of Arabia. His own son put him in chains and had him stabbed to death.

It is time now to break away from the sad, tragic and demeaning story of Parvíz, Chosroes II, and look forward a century to a new chapter of Khazar history.

When the Sásánian hegemony was swept away by the Arab onslaught,* the Khazar kingdom became conscious of its isolation. And as the Arabs penetrated into the Caucasus, they broke, time and again, through the mountain pass of Darband, close to the Caspian Sea, which they named 'Báb-al-Abwáb' (The Gate of Gates), to ravish the land of the Khazars. On the other hand, when the opportunity presented itself, Khazars did the same, erupted into the newly-conquered lands of Islám and caused chaos and confusion. In the year AD 730 Khazars occupied both Georgia and Armenia, annihilated an Arab army outside the city of Ardibíl (in the Persian province of Ádharbáyján, home of Shaykh Ṣafíyyi'd-Dín, the ancestor of the Ṣafavids), and rode on as far as Mosul and Díyarbakr.

The last time the Arabs made their way into Khazaria, under the command of the Umayyad Marwán (destined to be the last caliph of Damascus), the Khazars were caught unaware and suffered heavy defeat. They had to sue for peace and Marwán demanded the conversion of the Khazar king to Islám. It seems that the khágán complied and nominally became a Muslim; but with the withdrawal of Marwán, he went back to his paganism. Most likely this episode brought the khágán and his people to their final choice: to adopt a monotheistic Faith, which would give them such stamina and strength as to be able to withstand both the pressure of the Byzantine Christendom and the Islám of the Arabs. And strange enough, at about the same time that Charles Martel defeated the Muslims at Poitiers near Tours (October, AD 732) and stopped the Muslim incursion, the Khazars inflicted such a crushing defeat on the Arabs that they did not try ever again to outflank the Byzantine bastion and pour into the vast areas of Eastern Europe. As Dimitri Obolensky, Professor of Russian

* Yazdigird III, the last of this dynasty, was defeated at Nihávand near Ecbatana (present-day Hamadán) in 641. The genealogy of Bahá'u'lláh can be traced to him (see chap. 23).

and Balkan History in the University of Oxford, has stated: 'The main contribution of the Khazars to world history was their success in holding the line of the Caucasus against the northward onslaught of the Arabs.' (*The Byzantine Commonwealth*, p. 172)

The Jewish Khazaria lived for centuries. It prospered and its people remained firmly wedded to their Jewish Faith. Even St. Cyril (Constantine, 826–69), the celebrated 'Apostle of the Slavs', who visited Khazaria, could make no impression on those determined Turks, bent on preserving their independence. In recent times, much has been written and said about a 'Third Force' in world politics. It can be conjectured that the Kingdom of Khazaria was in its day, and considered itself to be, that 'Third Force', neither inclined to Christianity nor to Islám, treading a middle path, at peace with all and committed to none. Of course that idyllic condition could not be sustained for long. Fresh migrations from the hinterlands of the Euro-Asian continental block, brought the Viking to descend on Europe, and the Rus (Rhous and Rhos as well) to make life miserable for the inhabitants of the Eastern marches. In the year AD 833 the Khazar ruler sent an appeal to Emperor Theophilus of Byzantium to help him build a fortress on the River Don, to serve as a garrison post needed because of the increasing menace of the Rus. The Emperor was delighted to render assistance and the fortress of Sarkel came into being. Arthur Koestler writes:

Sarkel was built just in time; it enabled them [the Khazars] to control the movements of the Rus flotillas along the lower reaches of the Don and the Don – Volga portage (the 'Khazarian Way'). By and large it seems that during the first century of their presence on the scene,* the plundering raids of the Rus were mainly directed against Byzantium (where, obviously, richer plunder was to be had), whereas their relations with the Khazars were essentially on a trading basis, though not without friction and intermittent clashes. At any rate, the Khazars were able to control the Rus trade routes and to levy their 10 per cent tax on all cargoes passing through their country to Byzantium and to the Muslim lands.

They also exerted some cultural influence on the Northmen, who, for all their violent ways, had a naive willingness to learn from the people with whom they came into contact. The extent of this influence is indicated by the adoption of the title 'Kagan' [Khágán] by the early Rus rulers of Novgorod. This is confirmed by both Byzantine and Arab sources; for instance, Ibn Rusta, after describing the island on which Novgorod was built, states: 'They

* Very roughly, 830–930.

have a king who is called Kagan Rus.' Moreover, Ibn Fadlan reports that the Kagan Rus has a general who leads the army and represents him to the people. (*The Thirteenth Tribe*, p. 92)

Koestler, himself a Hungarian, further writes:

The Magyars had been the Khazars' allies, and apparently willing vassals, since the dawn of the Khazar Empire . . . About their origin all we know with certainty is that the Magyars were related to the Finns, and that their language belongs to the so-called Finno-Ugrian language family, together with that of the Vogul and Ostyak people living in the forest regions of the northern Urals. Thus they were originally unrelated to the Slavonic and Turkish nations of the steppes in whose midst they came to live – an ethnic curiosity, which they still are to this day. Modern Hungary, unlike other small nations, has no linguistic ties with its neighbours; the Magyars have remained an ethnic enclave in Europe, with the distant Finns as their only cousins. (ibid. p. 96)

As Koestler remarks, some time in the 'early centuries of the Christian era', the Magyars were pushed out of the Urals by other nomads. That has been the recurring theme of all the migrations along and across the Eurasian expanse: one group being forced westwards or southwards by another. For nearly 150 years, to the end of the ninth century, Magyars lived under Khazar domination; the Khazars and Magyars never fought each other. This was indeed a strange phenomenon. There existed a state of intermediate warfare between other groupings, as well as between these two and others. Indeed, such was the nature of their relationships that the Magyars acted as stewards for the Khazars to collect levies.

Koestler writes: 'The arrival of the Rus radically changed this profitable state of affairs. At about the time when Sarkel was built, there was a conspicuous movement of the Magyars across the Don to its west bank' (p. 97). The Khazars (here Koestler accepts Toynbee's explanation) placed the Magyars to the west of the Don, in order to set up a barrier against the incursions of the Slavs. Khazars did all they could to make Magyars a stable group of people, provided them with a king and even went to the extent of having a number of their clans dwell amongst the Magyars and become one with them. But by the end of the ninth century of the Christian era, Magyars once again set out westwards and settled down in the territory which we know now as Hungary. The Khazars had lost a prop. And the pressure of the Slavs continued unabated. Apart from the perils posed by the Slavs, a

Turkish tribe – the fierce Ghuzz (who within little more than a century were to defeat Sulṭán Sanjar,* the Saljúqid, and capture him) – attacked another Turkish tribe which tried to move into and settle down in Khazaria, but was driven out.

Perils abounded and the days of the Jewish Khazaria were numbered. D. M. Dunlop writes: 'By the 9th century at all events the Russians were strong enough to occupy a part of the Khazar territory in the west, including the city of Kiev.' That was the beginning of the end. When the Russians sailed into the Caspian Sea to raid Persian territory, they had the unwilling assistance of the Khazars. But the situation was getting out of hand, and around AD 960 the Khazars came to the conclusion that to allow the Russians to come down the Volga into the Caspian Sea was a dangerous game. They tried to put a stop to it. However, as Khazaria was slowly declining, the Russians were gathering more strength. The downfall and extinction of Khazaria, its date and circumstances, have all remained a matter of contention amongst historians, past and present. However, Dunlop asserts that the year 965 was 'the year in which the Russians invaded Khazaria', and that 'the Khazar kingdom in its traditional form hardly survived the Russian invasion.' (*The History of the Jewish Khazars*, pp. 238, 244, 247)

Historians have yet to settle (if it ever can be settled) the problem of the date of Khazaria's extinction. Some have been bold enough to state that it was the Mongol invasion of the early thirteenth century that destroyed Khazaria. Even if that proud land and its proud people eked out an impoverished independent existence for another two centuries, the eminent fact is that by the end of the tenth century of the Christian era the Khazaria which had defied the Arabs as well as the Byzantines had ceased to be. And the Jewish Khazars, just as the other clans and tribes and groupings had done, took the road to the West. They spread over Europe. Many of the Jews of the Diaspora in central, northern and eastern Europe are the descendants of those very brave men: the Turks who cherished a way of life, all their own, unfettered by submission and homage to Powers mightier than themselves.

* Reigned 1118–57.

22

The Story of Ṭabaristán

ṬABARISTÁN, THE RENOWNED PROVINCE lying south of the Caspian Sea, known today by the even more honoured name of Mázindarán, has ever been a land of marvels. Great men strode across its scene. The manliness of its inhabitants and their intense desire to remain self-ruled and independent have remained unsurpassed. Ṭabarí, the foremost historian of Islám, as his name indicates stepped out of this delectable corner of Írán. Even Fárs and its Persepolis of ancient splendour cannot compete with the magnificence of Mázindarán. Here dwelt the ancestors of Bahá'u'lláh.

In the preface to his abridged translation of Ibn Isfandíyár's *History of Ṭabaristán* (E. J. W. Gibb Memorial, Volume II), Edward Granville Browne, the distinguished orientalist of the University of Cambridge, wrote:

Separated from the rest of Persia by the lofty barrier of the Elburz Mountains, culminating in the great cone of Damáwand (Dunbáwand), the Caspian provinces have always possessed, to a certain extent, a history and character apart. Long after the Sásánian dynasty had fallen and the rest of Persia had been subdued by the Arabs, the Ispahbads continued to strike their Pahlawí coinage and maintain the religion of Zoroaster in the mountains and forests of Ṭabaristán; and their struggles against the Arabs were only ended about A.D. 838 by the capture and cruel execution of the gallant Mázyár, the son of Qárin, the son of Wandá-Hurmuz. Twenty-five years later was established the Shí'ite rule of the Zaydí Sayyids, which lasted till A.D. 928; and these were followed by the noble house of Ziyár, of whom Shamsu'l-Ma'álí Qábús was especially conspicuous for his literary eminence.* Even after the disastrous Mongol invasion, representatives of the ancient aristocracy of Ṭabaristán continued to wield a more or less considerable power.

Of this strange and interesting country the clearest and most ineffaceable

* This is a mistake. The author of the celebrated book: *Qábús-Námih*, was 'Unṣuru'l-Ma'álí, Kaykávús, a grandson of Shamsu'l-Ma'álí Qábús. (HMB)

MAP OF NORTHERN IRAN

(See map of Iran, page 5.)

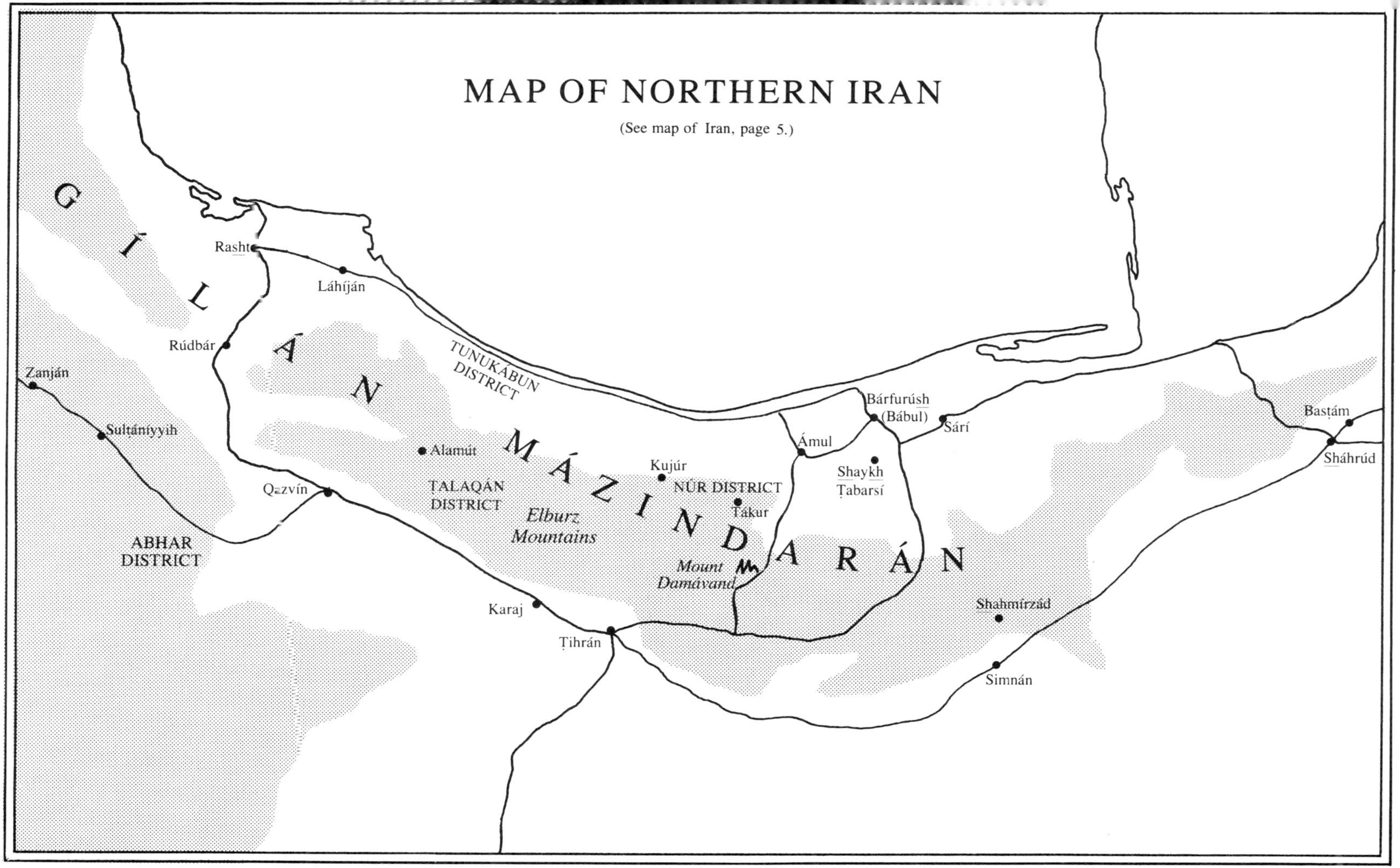

recollection must remain in the mind of every traveller who has visited it. I merely traversed it in about a week on my homeward journey from Persia in the autumn of 1888, yet of no part of that journey do I preserve a more vivid impression; the first entry, from the great stony plain of 'Iráq-i-'Ajamí into the lower hills at Ágh, with its rippling streams and almost English hedge-rows; the long winding climb to the eastern shoulder of the mighty Damáwand; the deep cañons of the Lár; the Alpine beauties of René; the gradual descent, through rock-walled valleys, into virgin forests, bright with the red blossoms of the wild pomegranate, and carpeted with ferns and mosses; the sluggish streams and stagnant pools of coast-ward fenlands; ancient Ámul, with its long slender bridge; Bárfurúsh and the swampy rice-fields of Shaykh Ṭabarsí, memorable in the history of the Bábí religion; and the sandy downs towards the Caspian Sea. (pp. x–xi)

In the following pages we shall examine the witness of Ibn Isfandíyár, whose love for Ṭabaristán glows through the pages of his book.*

On the Characteristics and Wonders of Ṭabaristán

From time immemorial, Ṭabaristán has been the refuge and the stronghold of mighty kings and magnates. Because of its natural strength and difficult mountain passes, like a storehouse where rarities and treasures are sent thereto for safekeeping, any ruler overcome by an enemy, finding it impossible to dwell anywhere else in this world, would seek security in this domain and find release from the stratagems of the foe. The land was one and the king was one; and the people of Ṭabaristán had no need of the goods of any other land. Whatever exists in the abundance of the world, needed for good living, can be procured therein. In all seasons one finds there gladsome vegetation, waters pure and luscious, all varieties of bread, good and wholesome, of wheat, rice and millet; all sorts of meat and flesh of beasts and birds, contrary to what can be found in other domains; delicious foods; bright and clear beverages, wines yellow, red and white, coloured like unto a flower and ruby and similar to rose-water, in clarity and delicacy like unto the tears of lovers: bringer of joy and exultation like achieving union with the beloved, of little nuisance like the company of men of good intent, productive of power and profit, bereft of the headache of intoxication, fragrant like pure

* The author both summarizes and translates Ibn Isfandíyár and also quotes Browne's translation; the extracts from Browne are indicated. (Ed.)

musk. The winter of Ṭabaristán is like unto the autumn of other districts, and its summer resembles the spring of other lands. All its earth is covered with groves and orchards, so that eyes meet nothing but greenery. The urban and the rural areas are joined together. Springs and water channels flow from their sources over pebbles. The mountain, the plain and the sea are together united. The air as it blows from the north is soft and equable. But due to the proximity of the sea and the plenteousness of rainfall at times, the moisture and the mist exceed those of other places.

It was related by the Qáḍí Abú 'Abdi'r-Raḥmán Muḥammad b.* al-Ḥasan b. 'Abdu'l-Ḥamíd al-Lamrásakí to Abu'l-Ḥasan 'Alí b. Muḥammad al-Yazdádí, on the authority of his father, who had it from men of ancient time, that there lived in the neighbourhood of Lamrásak a man named Shahr-Khwástán [Shahr-Khástán] the son of Zardastán, possessed of great wealth in personal and landed property and cattle, aged, experienced, and surrounded by numerous sons, cousins and kinsmen, all loyally attached to him. When Farrukhán, the great Ispahbad [Ispahbud], had completed the construction of Sárí and the great Dyke, all the people, save Shahr-Khwástán, offered him their congratulations and eulogies. The Ispahbad was vexed at this omission and despatched two horsemen to bring Shahr-Khwástán before him. When they arrived, he was holding a great banquet, at which all the local nobles and gentry were present. Ordering the two messengers to be hospitably entertained, he packed in sacks samples of all the products of Ṭabaristán, garments of wool, silk, linen and cotton, bread-stuffs of all sorts, sweetmeats,† apples, cereals, water-cresses, fresh and salted game, birds, fruits, wines, fragrant herbs, flowers, and the like, and, furnished with these, set off for Sárí, where he arrived at day-break. By chance the Ispahbad was giving a great banquet, at which he was presiding, seated on a high throne, whence, after pronouncing a *khuṭba* [ceremonial discourse] after the fashion of kings, he addressed the people as follows. 'O men of Ṭabaristán, know that ye were a people dwelling apart in a corner of the world, of whom no fame was spread abroad, and to whose country none were attracted. Ye dwelt in jungles with the wild beasts and beasts of prey, ignorant of the enjoyments of life, the ways of men, soft raiment, good horses and agreeable perfumes. It was I who introduced you to nobler aims and a richer and more desirable life; who built for you fine cities which attracted travellers and merchants from afar, so that rare and precious merchandises flowed into your country, and ye became notable and famous in the world, and your cities celebrated for their wealth and splendour. For all this I deserve your thanks.' Then all those present, except Shahr-Khwástán, rose up and applauded. The Ispahbad, observing with displeasure Shahr-Khwástán's silence, cried to him, 'What ails thee that thou art tongueless as a fish

* Ibn, or Bin: 'the son of'. (HMB)
† Edward Browne has shortened the list of all the foodstuffs and delicacies. (HMB)

and soulless as a serpent?' [The word that Browne has translated as 'soulless' is 'Píchán' in Persian, which means 'twisting'.] Said the other, 'If permission be accorded me, I will speak;' and, on receiving permission, he produced and opened the ten sacks which he had brought with him, and displayed their contents. Then he spoke as follows: 'May the Ispahbad-Ispahbadán* live long! O assembly, [lend me your ears, for an hour, and consider what I have to say.' He brought out those edibles and beverages and clothings out of the sacks for the people to see. Then he said:] 'We were in this land men independent of imports from other countries, contented with what sufficed for our needs, and enjoying ample ease and luxury. None hindered us, nor envied us, nor contended with us, nor coveted our country, nor was cognizant of its secrets.† We had need of no one; we had houses, corn-lands and hunting-grounds within the Great Dyke, and every two parasangs was stationed a head-man, captain or squire, whom all man [*sic*] readily obeyed. Now this Prince‡ [omitted in translation: 'may he prosper and triumph'] hath made all strangers and foreigners to know us and our land, [and the secrets of our domain, and tore open the veil concealing our condition and caused enemies and adversaries to appear. Whilst no creature, barred, could find a way into this province] and hath caused them to flock hither and settle here, and ere long they will pick a quarrel with us, strive to take our land, and drive forth our children as wanderers and exiles.' Then the Ispahbad and the people perceived that he spoke truly, and asked what should now be done, to which he replied, 'The thing is done, and there is now no averting it. Had you consulted with me sooner, I would have shewn you a way. Please God that by the Prince's [king's] good fortune no harm may result.' (pp. 30–32, translated by E. G. Browne and amended by the author)

'The virtue, beauty, health and excellence of the women of Ṭabaristán have been already mentioned [by Ibn Isfandíyár] in connection with the narrative of the building of Ámul by Fírúz-Sháh.' (E.G.B., p. 32)

Ibn Isfandíyár quotes Abu'l-Ḥasan-i-Yazdádí as having heard from a centenarian Khurásání that he had been all the world over, and had never found a domain like Ṭabaristán for 'enjoying life', for 'security', for 'comfort' and for 'cleanliness'. Furthermore:

You never find therein deadly snakes, scorpions, lion and tiger and beasts and insects that are injurious; like the snakes of Sajistán and Hindústán [India] and scorpions of Niṣíbín and Qáshan [Káshán], Jáshk and Múqán; locusts of 'Askar; tarantulas and fleas of Ardibíl; beasts of Arabia, crocodiles of Egypt, sharks of Baṣrah; or famine of Damascus, heat of 'Ummán and Síráf and Ahváz. And the whole world agrees that for residence a man of

* Ispahbud-i-Ispahbudán. (HMB)
† Left out by Edward Browne: 'No one had any inclination towards us'. (HMB)
‡ 'King and ruler' in the original. (HMB)

good taste cannot find a land better than Ṭabaristán. Of materials and goods permissible, such as wood and fruit, reeds and herbs, medicinal substances of the plain and the mount, mines of sulphur, copperas, collyrium stone, and many a mine of gold and silver, which bring profit and means of living to the poor and provide merchandise and goods for the use of the rich, all can be found there. All kinds of choice cloths of linen, cotton, silk and wool in varied grades of golden and woollen materials are exported to the east and the west of the world.

Yazdádí has related that in the first instance, they came to Ṭabaristán for satin and woven cloth, for the costly silk material: *'uttábí* [so named after its inventor, 'Uttáb] and all kinds of highly-priced brocades and greatly-valued scarlet cloth, and expensive wine, and camphor, the very best of its kind; and striped cloth, silken and woollen and narrow; and thick coverlets and blankets, be it Jahrumí carpets or Maḥfurí; also Baghdádí crystal glass, and 'Abbádání mats . . . They did not find anywhere else in the world goods of such excellence. Until our days the market wherein to obtain the wares of Saqsín [a country in Turkistán] and Bulghár [Bulgaria], was the city of Ámul. And the people of Ṭabaristán traded with Bulghár and Saqsín, because Saqsín is situated opposite Ámul on the other side of the sea. It is said that a ship takes three months to reach Saqsín . . . And there are women in Ṭabaristán who earn fifty dirhams a day by their handiwork . . .

It is related that a man of Ṭabaristán got married in Mecca. And as it is the way of loving one's native land, he used every day to talk lavishly of his city, until one day he said that one never finds a beggar in Ámul. The people of Mecca decided to give lie to his claim, until one day they found a man [that is, a beggar] and took him there [to meet the Ṭabarí who was making so much noise]. He [the Ṭabarí] asked the mendicant: 'Are you from Ámul? [The mendicant] answered: 'Yes, I am from Ámul, and the quarter in which I live is Ḥázmih Kúy.' The mendicant described every aspect of Ámul. The Ṭabarí then tried to confuse him, asking the names they used in Ámul for certain objects, and found his answers to be wrong. And so he told the man that he was fraudulent. Then that man admitted that he was really a native of Ray and had been taken to Ámul in his childhood by his parents. (HMB translation; see pp. 33–4.)

Edward Browne takes up the translation here:

The taxes and imposts of Ṭabaristán are light, and especially was this the case under the rule of the House of Báwand [Bávand], while the water is abundant, good, and freely accessible to all. The satraps, governors and Ispahbads of Ṭabaristán have always enjoyed a great influence, and Kisrás and Caliphs alike have sought their advice and counsel. Their doctors, scribes, physicians, astronomers and poets also include many famous names, and, from the time of Ferídún [Firaydún] and Minuchihr [Manúchihr], who have been already mentioned, many great and notable men have sought refuge there . . . (p. 34)

Ibn Isfandíyár mentions that Dárá, 'fleeing before Alexander, took refuge in Ṭabaristán, and sent a message to the invader, saying, "I grant that you have conquered the Seven Climes, but what will you do with Farshwádjar?" '* (p. 35)

Now we come to the 'wonders of Ṭabaristán': Ibn Isfandíyár first mentions Mount Damávand and says:

> 'Alí Ibn Rabban al-Káṭib mentions in his book *Firdaws al-Ḥikmat* that from the village Ask to the summit, the ascent takes two days, and that [the summit] is like a conical dome. There is permanent snow all round it except at the top, where in the space of thirty *jaríbs* snow does not settle either in the summer or in the winter. There it is all sand, into which the feet sink. When you stand on the sand at the summit all the peaks round look like hills, and the Caspian Sea can be seen right at the front. There are three† cavities at the top of this mount from which sulphurous vapours are emitted, and tremendous sounds are heard coming out of these cavities, caused by the flaming of fire; and in truth, there is fire within this mount; and because of the heavy wafting of wind no animal can stay there. It is said that the Philosopher's Stone of the alchemists can be obtained there. Yazdádí relates that in the days of Shamsu'l-Ma'álí Qábús there was a young man called the son of Amír Ká, who found there red sulphur and produced gold. When the king came to know he ran away. (HMB translation; see pp. 35–6.)

Ibn Isfandíyár mentions a number of other wonders that are found in Ṭabaristán. One of these is located in the district of Úmídvárih-Kúh. There is a well in that area, he says, which is called Cháh-i-Víjan, and cannot be fathomed. Time and again great lengths of ropes were taken there, tied together and let down into the well, but the bottom could not be touched. And when they threw stones into it the noise of their falling could be heard for a long time. He further records that in summertime a scented and cool breeze blows out from the depths of the well. There are trees around it which provide fragrant timber. Sitting on that wood during the summer affords coolness (p. 39). Ibn Isfandíyár is most keen to enumerate and describe as many as possible of the 'wonders of Ṭabaristán', some of which are trivial, such as the description of a mountain where a poisonous plant grows.

Some Rulers of Ṭabaristán

The most notable of all the rulers and kings who came out of

* An ancient name for Mázindarán and Gílán.

† Browne translates as 'thirty craters and fissures'. (Ed.)

DYNASTIES AND RULERS OF ṬABARISTÁN AND NORTHERN ÍRÁN

mentioned in this chapter

Dates are according to the Muslim (AH) calendar, followed after an oblique stroke by the Christian (AD) dates. See also the list of Dynasties and Rulers of Írán, p. 325. Bosworth, *The Islamic Dynasties*, lists and describes the dynasties in Írán after Muḥammad; many of the following dates come from this book.

BÁDÚSPÁNIDS	45–1006/665–1599
BÁWANDIDS *or* BÁVANDIDS (ISPAHBUDS)	45–750/665–1349
Sharvín (Sharwín I)	155–181/772–797
Shahríyár I	181–210/797–825
Shápúr	210–222/825–837
Rustam I	253–282/867–895
DÁBWAYHIDS (DÁBÚYIDS)	25–141/645–758
Farrukhán (Farkhán Ibn Dábwayh)	90–103/708–21
ISPAHBUDS, *see* BÁWANDIDS, *also* BÁDÚSPÁNIDS	
JASTÁNÍYÁNS (JUSTÁNIDS)	From 2nd cent.–315/c. 796–927
Vahsúdán (Wahsúdán)	uncertain
Jastán III	290–300/903–912
'Alí	300–304/912–916
MUSÁFIRIDS *or* SÁLÁRIDS *or* KANGARIDS	c. 304–c.483/c.916–c.1090
ṢAFFÁRIDS	253–c.900/867–c.1495
Ya'qúb Ibn Layth-i-Ṣaffár	253–265/867–879
'Amr Ibn Layth	265–289/879–901
SÁMÁNIDS	204–395/819–1005
Ismá'íl I	279–295/892–907
Naṣr II	301–331/914–942
Manṣúr I	350–366/961–976
Núh II	366–387/976–997
ṬÁHIRIDS	205–259/821–873
'Abdu'lláh	213–230/828–845
Muḥammad	248–259/862–873
ZAYDÍS (SIYYIDS), ṬABARISTÁN	250–316/864–928
Ḥasan Ibn Zayd (Dá'ía'l-Kabír)	250–270/864–883
Muḥammad Ibn Zayd	270–287/883–900
Ḥasan Náṣiru'l-Ḥaqq	301–304/913–916
Ḥasan Ibn Qásim	304–316/916–928
ZIYÁRIDS	315–c.483/927–c.1090
Mardávíj	315–323/927–935
Vushmagír	323–356/935–967
Bísutún	356–367/967–978
Shamsu'l-Ma'álí Qábús	367–402/978–1012
Falaku'l-Ma'álí Manúchihr	402–420/1012–1029
'Unṣuru'l-Ma'álí, Kaykávús	441–?c.483/1049–?c.1090
Gílán-Sháh	?c.483/?c.1090(rule uncertain)

Ṭabaristán were the sovereigns of Ál-i-Búyih or the Buwayhids (AD 932–1062). There were three brothers: 'Alí, Ḥasan and Aḥmad, to whom the 'Abbásid caliphs of Baghdád were compelled to assign the titles: 'Imádu'd-Dawlih (the Mainstay of the State), Ruknu'd-Dawlih (the Pillar of the State), and Mu'izzu'd-Dawlih (He Who Gives Might to the State), respectively. Aḥmad occupied Baghdád, and made the caliph his puppet. The Buwayhids were Shí'ihs of the Ithná-'Asharíyyah, or Twelver, denomination. Spiritually they did not owe allegiance to the 'Abbásids. But facing an Islamic world, preponderantly Sunní, they had to maintain the caliph on his throne. The people of Daylam and Gíl (Ṭabaristán and Gílán), having stood out for long against the encroachments of the Arab invaders, and clinging to their Zoroastrian Faith for many decades, spurned the Islám of the caliphs: Damascene or 'Iráqí, and always gave refuge to those descendants of 'Alí, who, fleeing from the tyrannies of the caliphs, sought security amongst them. And it was a descendant of 'Alí, a member of the House of Muḥammad, who led them into the Shí'ih fold.

THE FIRST EIGHT IMÁMS OF THE HOUSE OF 'ALÍ

mentioned by the author. Numerals refer to the chronological sequence of the Imáms and AD dates are given.

1.	'Alí Ibn Abí-Ṭálib	632–661
2.	Ḥasan Ibn 'Alí	661–669
3.	Ḥusayn Ibn 'Alí	669–680
4.	'Alí II, Zaynu'l-'Ábidín	680–712
5.	Muḥammad al-Báqir	712–734
6.	Ja'far aṣ-Ṣádiq	734–765
7.	Músá al-Káẓim	765–799
8.	'Alí Ibn Músa'r-Riḍá	799–818

Let us begin the story of Ṭabaristán where Ibn Isfandíyár begins, with the tragic tale of one of the most accomplished men whom one encounters in the chronicles of Islám: 'Abdu'lláh Ibna'l-Muqaffa'. This extraordinary man, although professing Islám, was in truth an enthusiastic Manichaean. By translating Pahlaví texts into Arabic, with his own embroidering and interpellation, he tried to diffuse Manichaean doctrines. Al-Muqaffa', whose real name was Dádhbih, son of Dádhjushras, fell to the fury of Manṣúr, the second of the 'Abbásid caliphs (AD 754–75), who had him put to death in a most horrific manner. For the people of Ṭabaristán, who would not submit to the Arab caliph, the work and the fate of 'Abdu'lláh Ibna'l-Muqaffa' provided both an inspiration and a warning.

THE 'ABBÁSID CALIPHS

mentioned by the author. Numerals refer to the chronological sequence of the Caliphs and AD dates are given.

2.	'Al-Manṣúr	754–775
5.	Ar-Ras͟híd	786–809
7.	Al-Ma'mún	813–833
8.	Al-Mu'taṣim	833–842
10.	Al-Mutawakkil	847–861
12.	Al-Musta'ín	862–866
18.	Al-Muqtadir	908–932
20.	Ar-Ráḍí	934–940

According to Ibn Isfandíyár, Fars͟hvád͟hgar* encloses Ṭabaristán, Daylamistán and Gílán (p. 14). Then this author of the history of Ṭabaristán gives details of the early days of city-building in that delectable area, and ascribes actions to kings and rulers and heroes of the ancient past, who, we know now, were chiefly mythical figures, but also we know that some of them were historic persons whose real names have been forgotten in the course of centuries by their fellow-countrymen, and feats have come to be ascribed to them which are figments of imagination. But this much is certain, that well-famed towns and cities of Ṭabaristán (or Mázindarán) go back to antiquity (pp. 14–30). Ibn Isfandíyár relates that the Jámi' Mosque of the town of Sárí was built by a descendant of Imám 'Alí during the reign of Hárún ar-Ras͟híd (AD 786–809), but Prince Mázyár, the son of Qáran, completed the construction (p. 17).

Having mentioned Prince Mázyár, it is well to stop here and tell his story. Even if Mázyár did, as Ibn Isfandíyár alleges, finish the work of raising a mosque at Sárí, he remained firmly wedded to his Zoroastrian Faith. He was a leader of the Mubayyaḍah (the White-Clad), deadly opposed to the other grouping, the Musawwidah, who donned black garments to indicate their attachment to the House of

* According to Arsène Darmesteter (1849–94), the celebrated French orientalist, this name is a corruption of Patas͟hk͟hwár, the name of the mountain range which separates Ṭabaristán from the rest of the Iranian Plateau.

'Abbás. Mázyár yearned with all the intensity of his soul to drive the Arabs out of the whole of Írán, and detested those of his own nation who had not only embraced the Faith of the Arabian Prophet, but were totally submissive to their conquerors and, even more, supported them. Mázyár made a pact with Afshín, who was also of royal lineage (his ancestors had ruled over Transoxania and hence Ḥaydar al-Afshín was wrongly called a Turk), to end the domination of the 'Abbásids. According to Ibn Isfandíyár, Qáran, the father of Mázyár, had gone to Baghdád at the invitation of the caliph who wished him to embrace Islám, but Qáran refused and returned home.

Mázyár was at odds with his own great uncle, Ispahbud Shahríyár, and wished to be the sole champion of Ṭabaristán. He picked a quarrel with Shahríyár, but was routed in the battle that ensued and fled to the domain of a cousin. The victor in that contest was firmly demanding that the vanquished should be handed over to him. Mázyár managed to escape and took refuge with 'Abdu'lláh Ibn Sa'íd al-Jarshí, the Caliph Ma'mún's (AD 813–33) representative in Ray, who had been well acquainted with Mázyár's father and grandfather. After a while this representative took Mázyár with him to Baghdád. There the prince of Ṭabaristán met Bizíst, the astronomer (or rather, the astrologer) to Ma'mún. This man was a native of Ámul and promised Mázyár every assistance within his capacity. His praises of Mázyár made Ma'mún eager to receive him. To make the story short, the caliph was greatly impressed by Mázyár and when the right moment came, the prince of Ṭabaristán was given the mountainous regions of Ṭabaristán to rule.

Mázyár very soon found means to rid himself of Ispahbud Shápúr, a grandson of Ispahbud Sharvín. Gradually Mázyár's excesses became hard for the people to bear. Ma'mún came to hear of their complaints and sent his astronomer to investigate. Mázyár, while giving Bizíst a most friendly reception, managed to terrify him. Consequently, when he and the qáḍís of Ámul and Rúyán reached Baghdád they declared that all was well. However, the qáḍí of Ámul could not escape the pangs of conscience and confessed that he had lied to the caliph. Ma'mún was then on the point of leaving Baghdád to levy war on Byzantium, and promised that on his return he would take action against Mázyár. In the meantime, the people of Ámul and Rúyán broke into revolt. Mázyár put down the rebellion with a heavy hand and stopped a description of the true picture reaching Baghdád, whilst continuously sending false reports to the caliph. Though himself an ardent leader and supporter of the Mubayyaḍah, in his reports to Ma'mún he laid all the blame for unrest and revolt at the door of those White-Clads and assured the caliph that he had the situation well in hand. Ma'mún, in order to satisfy himself, sent an emissary, Muḥammad Ibn Sa'íd, to find how matters stood in Ṭabaristán. He too, beguiled by Mázyár, exonerated him. Now Ma'mún took the extraordinary step of turning over the whole of Ṭabaristán to its prince. (His governance lasted two years, to AD 839. Ed.)

Well satisfied with his success, Mázyár came almost into the open. He meant to destroy the 'Abbásids, and began persecuting all who were inclined towards them. Muslims were flung into prisons and their gaolers were Mazdeans and Khurramdínís.* Ma'mún died in the year 833 and his brother, Muḥammad al-Mu'taṣim, succeeded him. 'Abdu'lláh, the Ṭáhirid emir of Khurásán and Ray, took Mázyár to task but Mázyár did not heed him. It is claimed that Bábak (a Mazdean or a Mazdakí), who was little more than an adventurer, was in league with Mázyár and Afshín, but the latter betrayed him and sent him in chains to Baghdád where Mu'taṣim put him cruelly to death. Mázyár, who knew that before long he would have to fight for his life, was turning Ṭabaristán into a well-entrenched and fortified war camp. Afshín, on the other hand, had his eyes on the vastness of Khurásán. He hoped that the Ṭáhirid emir, in any contest, would be worsted by Mázyár, and then it would fall to him to liberate Khurásán from the 'Abbásid yoke. However, Mázyár's wretched rule nullified all that Afshín had hoped. The prince of Ṭabaristán dispossessed the Bávandí Ispahbuds, in the first instance, and then, apart from one brother, Kúhyár, who had served him well, he denied his other brothers and his relatives what was theirs by right. His enormities mounted high and the people of Ṭabaristán were heartily sick of him.

At last 'Abdu'lláh, the Ṭáhirid emir, struck. Three armies converged on Ṭabaristán. Now Mázyár's relatives, even his favoured brother, Kúhyár, betrayed him. It was Kúhyár who led the enemy to his brother's lair. A present-day historian, Ismá'íl Mahjúrí, writes that the men on the trail of Mázyár went through passes and passed by forts that 'until that day no stranger's feet had trodden'. Mázyár was taken into custody and hauled before the Ṭáhirid emir, who, well

* Khurramdínís are reputed to have been followers of Mazdak, the heresiarch of the days of Ghubád and Chosroes I, Sásánian monarchs.

aware of Afshín's complicity with Mázyár, asked the chained prince of Ṭabaristán to give him the letters he had received from the prince of Transoxania. Furthermore, on the road to 'Iráq and Sámarrá, the Ṭáhirid gave Mázyár so much wine to drink that the prince's tongue was loosened, and he blurted out all the details of his secret pact with Afshín. Thus that brave man from Transoxania was also doomed. Mu'taṣim himself supervised and directed Afshín's arrest. No matter how tyrannous and devious the prince of Ṭabaristán was, no matter how many he had injudiciously sent to their death, he was a very brave man and he yearned to free his native land. Afshín, too, was brave and had motives beyond reproach. Their cruel deaths showed, once again, the hollowness of the claims of the 'Abbásids. Their rule was far from humane. The twin corpses of Mázyár and Afshín graced the gates of Mu'taṣim's capital for many years.

Mázyár was dead, but not the independent spirit of the people of Ṭabaristán. Their goal was the same as Mázyár's: to make a clean sweep of the alien rule. Now as the tyranny of the governor appointed by the Ṭáhirids pressed hard upon them, the people of Ṭabaristán turned to the scions of the House of the Prophet to extricate them from the clutches of their oppressors.

When 'Abdu'lláh al-Ma'mún, the seventh 'Abbásid caliph, named 'Alí Ibn Músá ar-Riḍá, the eighth Imám, to be his successor, many of his relatives (and he had twenty-one brothers) made their way to the great city of Ray and its neighbourhood. But those halcyon days did not last long. Under pressure from his rebellious kinsmen, Ma'mún was forced to change his decision. Shí'ihs have always maintained that at Ṭús in Khurásán, where Hárún ar-Rashíd, the father of Ma'mún, had died and was buried, the 'Abbásid caliph gave Imám Riḍá poisoned grapes, causing his death. The magnificent Shrine of Imám Riḍá at Mashhad in Khurásán is one of the holiest shrines of the Islamic world. In the shadow of the tomb is also situated the grave of Hárún ar-Rashíd, held in opprobrium by the Shí'ihs. Following the death of the eighth Imám, the descendants of 'Alí who had congregated in Írán fled to the safety of Daylamistán (soon to attain fame as the homeland of the Buwayhids) and Ṭabaristán. Some of them lost their lives, but the majority found protection afforded by the Ispahbuds of Ṭabaristán.

After the death of al-Mutawakkil (AD 847–61), the 'Abbásid caliph who was particularly hostile to the family of 'Alí, the descendants of

'Alí began to assert themselves. One of them, Yaḥyá Ibn 'Umar – a descendant of Zayd, the son of the fourth Imám – who lived in retirement in Kúfah, took steps to lead a revolt. A century before, his grandsire Zayd, driven to rebellion because the minions of the Umayyad caliph Hishám (AD 724–43) had denied him justice, had done the same and had lost his life.

Now, when it became evident that Yaḥyá Ibn 'Umar was going to challenge the 'Abbásids, the people of 'Iráq came to him with a proposition: if it was impecuniosity which had induced him to appear as a rebel, they would collect all he needed of the goods of the world and present them to him. But Yaḥyá refused to accept riches from them because his whole object, he said, was to rescue the Faith of Muḥammad from degradation. He too lost his life, fighting Muḥammad, the Ṭáhirid emir of Khurásán, whom the caliph sent against him. When Yaḥyá died, more of his kinsmen, scions of the House of 'Alí, hastened to the refuge of Daylam and Ṭabaristán.

Once the Ṭáhirids had Ṭabaristán in their power, they installed a tyrannical and brutal governor, Muḥammad Ibn Aws, who made life miserable for the people of that region. For a while they just groaned, but finally they appealed to the cowed descendants of 'Alí to come to their rescue. In the city of Rúyán there lived a descendant of Ḥasan, the second Imám, named Muḥammad Ibn Ibráhím, famed for his piety and integrity. The leaders of the people of Ṭabaristán invited him to put himself at their head, to challenge the Ṭáhirids and their 'Abbásid overlords. Muḥammad Ibn Ibráhím felt unable to shoulder the responsibility but directed these determined men to take their case to his brother-in-law, Ḥasan Ibn Zayd, who lived in Ray. As soon as the notables of Ṭabaristán made their proposal to Ḥasan Ibn Zayd, he eagerly undertook to lead them into battle. That resolute, unflinching man is known to history as Dá'ía'l-Kabír (the Great Caller). He fought many battles, and disentangled many rivalries amongst the Ispahbuds of that enclave by the Caspian Sea. His chief adversary was the Ṭáhirid Sulaymán, son of Amír 'Abdu'lláh. When worsted on every side Sulaymán hit upon a plan to win over the Daylamites, but the plan miscarried and the defeated Sulaymán escaped to Gurgán. Having abandoned his wife and children at Sárí, he wrote to the Dá'í to beg the restoration of his family, and the latter was magnanimous enough to accede to his request. That final victory over the Ṭáhirid brought great joy to the Dá'í because he felt that his fallen kinsman, Yaḥyá Ibn 'Umar, had been avenged.

Once firmly established in the governance of Ṭabaristán, the Dá'í proceeded with the establishment of the Shí'ih doctrine throughout his domain. He instructed his appointees in all the towns and cities of Ṭabaristán to follow in every detail the rulings of 'Alí Ibn Abí-Ṭálib, the first Imám, and gave them a specific line of guidance which made the Shí'ih practice the pattern for the whole province. But his brand of Shí'ism was Zaydí, neither Ismá'ílí nor Ithná-'Asharí. As for Sulaymán, he realized that the role he had played in Ṭabaristán was over, and so wended his way to Baghdád where the caliph, al-Musta'ín, gave him the constabulary of his capital.

The fame of the Dá'í reached an ever-widening circle, and large numbers of the descendants of 'Alí came pouring into Ṭabaristán. It is related that whenever Dá'í rode out, three hundred siyyids with drawn swords accompanied him. But Dá'í knew no peace. His very successes in capturing city after city outside Ṭabaristán, which included the great city of Ray, brought forces against him which he could not withstand. He became a fugitive, but had another turn of fortune which regained him much that he had lost. But once again an adversary loomed on the horizon – no less a person than Ya'qúb Ibn Layth-i-Ṣaffár. Ya'qúb himself had been an adventurer and had risen from humble beginnings to great power. He too was a Shí'ih, and a Twelver to boot. He had nothing but contempt for the 'Abbásids, and no respect for the Dá'í's pretensions. Yá'qúb came storming into Ṭabaristán, and although the Daylams scorned him he took it out of the people of other regions, particularly those of Kujúr. The Ṣaffárid intruder was not obstructed by human beings only. Elements and insects of the thick woods also combined to punish him. Forty consecutive days of lightning, thunder and rain decimated the ranks of his army. Nearly forty thousand of his soldiers perished. Flies killed most of the camels which carried his equipage. Ya'qúb was glad to leave Ṭabaristán behind him.

Next, Dá'í came up against one of the Ispahbuds of the House of Bávand. His name was Rustam, and although outwardly at peace with the Dá'í, he intended to have the whole of Ṭabaristán to himself. However, his effort remained fruitless; the ebbs and tides of the flow of fortune kept Dá'í still riding the storms. But then gout killed him. His was an amazing episode. Muḥammad, his brother, succeeded him. Ispahbud Rustam tried once again to assert himself and once again was beaten. In the end he lost his life by treachery.

Now another star had risen on the horizon of Khurásán. Amír Ismá'íl, the Sámánid, although claiming descent from the nobility of pre-Islamic Írán, was a Sunní devoted to the House of 'Abbás. He had overthrown 'Amr, the brother of Ya'qúb Ibn Layth who was a Twelver Shí'ih, at the express order of the 'Abbásid caliph. And next he turned on Muḥammad Ibn Zayd in Ṭabaristán. Muḥammad died on the battlefield, and his son Zayd was captured and taken to Bukhárá. Zayd's tragic story reached the ears of Amír Ismá'íl. Magnanimously the Sámánid ruler allowed him, should he wish, to return to Ṭabaristán. But Zayd preferred retirement in Bukhárá.

Muḥammad Ibn Zayd, who ruled over Ṭabaristán for sixteen years, was a very generous man, helping his kinsmen in Medinah and providing them with ample funds. Moreover, he rebuilt the Shrines of the Imáms in Najaf and Karbilá, which the impious hands of the 'Abbásid, al-Mutawakkil, had desecrated and destroyed.

The reign of the House of 'Alí in Ṭabaristán was over, but not their influence. Abú-Muḥammad, Ḥasan Ibn 'Alí, known as Náṣiru'l-Ḥaqq – a descendant of 'Umar al-Ashraf, son of the fourth Imám – had to flee to Daylamistán in company with many others of the descendants of the first Imám. As soon as he reached safety he began to teach the Shí'ih doctrine. Jastán III of Daylam, the son of Vahsúdán, embraced that variety of Islám which he was preaching. Until this point of time, there is every reason to believe that the rulers and the people of Daylam had tenaciously kept their old Faith. Although its identity is not very clear, it has been alleged that it may not have been Zoroastrian (Mazdean). Whatever the case, the independent spirit of the people of Daylam, evident long before the coming of Islám and the Arabs, had made these brave people the cynosure of the vastly greater number of men amongst whom they lived. But here we must once again make a diversion and go with the years, to learn a little more about the Daylamites from whose lowest ranks the glorious House of Búyih emerged.

That Caspian province, north of the Elburz range, which is known today as Gílán, was known as Daylamán in the days when Sásánians were the masters of Írán. And in that province, Siyyid Aḥmad-i-Kasravi* tells us, dwelt two tribes, one named Gíl and the other

* A brilliant but erratic Persian historian of recent years. His highly unorthodox and extravagant views led him into a court-room, on trial for heresy. Fanatics broke into the Court of Justice and murdered him.

Daylam. The first tribe had its haunts in those areas where today the cities of Rasht and Láhíján are situated, the second grouping occupied more southerly regions, where we now have the settlements of Rúdbár and Alamút.* Apparently these two tribes came from the same stock. In the course of time they separated. The Daylams were more numerous and more powerful, and were determined to reject whatever and whomsoever were alien to their land. Rebellious in pre-Islamic times, the coming of Islám and the Arabs made them even more determined not to submit. They fought the Arabs in battle after battle.

Towards the end of the second century Hejira (Hijrah), circa AD 796, one encounters the dynasty of Jastáníyán holding the reins of authority in the Daylam country. The most famous of these rulers was Jastán III. The friendly reception which he accorded to Náṣiru'l-Ḥaqq resulted in the conversion of the Daylams to the Faith of the Arabian Prophet. They became fervent Shí'ihs, totally rejecting the 'Abbásids. Jastán unhesitatingly took up the cudgels on the part of the descendants of 'Alí and fought the Sámánids. Although once defeated, he did not give up the contest. But the next episode in the history of this dynasty is indeed strange. Jastán III was murdered by his brother, 'Alí, whose name indicates that he had become a Muslim. Next we hear of 'Alí breaking away from the long tradition of his people and becoming a partisan of al-Muqtadir (908–32), the vacillating, unreliable 'Abbásid caliph. But true to his colours Muqtadir eventually dismissed 'Alí. Now the power of the Jastáníyáns was on the wane.

An event of great interest which occurred during the years of Muqtadir's caliphate was the raid of the hitherto unknown Russians on the shores of Ṭabaristán. They were uncouth pagans and robbers. Their sudden descent on Ṭabaristán caused some havoc, many were killed and homes and warehouses were pillaged; but the Russian raiders were driven out in the end.

The Sámánids did not keep Ṭabaristán for long. As soon as their official, Muḥammad-i-Bal'amí, withdrew, Náṣiru'l-Ḥaqq gathered forces from Gíl and Daylam and wrested the province from its unwanted occupiers. Further attempts to win Ṭabaristán for the Sámánids proved fruitless and Náṣiru'l-Ḥaqq remained its master to the end of his days, although he left governance to others and retired

* Alamút became the fortress of Ḥasan-i-Ṣabbáḥ, the Ismá'ílí ruler (AD 1090–1124).

from rulership, devoting his time to literature and the furtherance of knowledge and authorship. Men came from far and wide to sit at his feet and learn. Ṇásiru'l-Ḥaqq (also known as Náṣir-i-Kabír: Náṣir, the Great) died at the advanced age of ninety-five.

The rest of the story of the siyyids and their rule over Ṭabaristán is characterized by constant struggle. There were many claimants, and the Sámánids were never totally absent from the scene. One of them, Amír Naṣr, a very accomplished ruler, never took the field himself except once and that nearly ended in disaster. But now, other men of ability and ambition had arrived, men such as Mákán, the son of Kákí; Asfár, the son of S͟hírúyih; Mardávíj, the son of Ziyár. As soon as Ḥasan Ibn Qásim, the last of the siyyid potentates, was killed outside the city of Ámul in the year 928, Asfár established himself as the sole ruler of Ṭabaristán. Asfár and Mardávíj were both Daylamites, Mákán in Ray represented the Sámánids. The two Daylamites fell out between themselves, and Asfár lost. Now, Mardávíj, whom C. E. Bosworth characterizes as 'one of the fiercest of these Daylamī condottieri' (*The Islamic Dynasties*, p. 92), had the field entirely to himself and ranged as far as Iṣfahán and Hamadán.

About this time, the three brothers, 'Alí, Ḥasan and Aḥmad (see p. 296), sons of Búyih, a Daylamite who had been for years in the service of Mákán, seeing him much reduced, left him and joined Mardávíj. They were destined to found a dynasty which overpowered the 'Abbásids – the desideratum of all the Daylamites. Mardávíj, although outwardly converted to Islám, was secretly, like his brother Vus͟hmagír and Asfár, a dedicated Mazdean. He tried to revive the traditions of the Sásánians, and detested the Caliphate as heartily as any faithful man of Daylam and Gíl. At Iṣfahán (in the winter of 934–5) he suddenly ordered the observance of the rites of Sadih, the winter festival* of the Mazdeans. Soon, in that city, he met his death at the hands of his Turkish officers. Finding that they had been negligent with the preparation for the festival – lighting a huge bonfire on the banks of Záyandih-Rúd – he was enraged, and the Turks, fearing for their lives, caught him unaware in his bath and murdered him. Thus died one of the most remarkable men of Daylam, whom Bosworth stigmatizes as one of the 'condottieri'. (Mardávíj, a Ziyárid, ruled from AD 927 to 935. Ed.)

* The four great festivals of pre-Islamic Írán consisted of Naw-rúz (Spring), Tír (Summer), Mihragán (Autumn), Sadih (Winter). Mihragán – the festival of Mihr (Sun), recalled the worship of Mit͟hrá.

Strangely enough, the sons of Búyih did not remain tied to the Ál-i-Ziyár (Ziyárids), and the obvious reason can be found in the ambitions which they themselves nurtured. They were set to dominate the whole world of Islám. Of course they did not attain that zenith, but nevertheless they rose to great heights. The whole of Ṭabaristán, and not only Ṭabaristán but the whole complex of Islamic society, stretching from the vale of Oxus and the foothills of Hindú-Kush to the waters of the Atlantic, experienced many an upheaval in the opening decades of the fourth Hejira century.

Vushmagír had to contend with the Ál-i-Búyih right to the end. And when he died in a riding accident, his two sons, Bísutún, or Bihistún, and Qábús, fought over his heritage. The younger, Qábús, was soon forced to seek refuge in Bukhárá, of all places. Manṣúr, the Sámánid Amír, helped him, whereas the elder brother had been aided by 'Aḍudu'd-Dawlih, the greatest ruler of the Buwayhids. However, Bísutún died in 978 and Qábús came into full possession of Ṭabaristán. Shamsu'l-Ma'álí Qábús (reigned 978–1012) is one of the most notable princes of Ṭabaristán. He was a talented man, well versed in literature, and was also a man of great ability. But the rivalries of the Buwayhids entangled him as well. 'Aḍudu'd-Dawlih had incurred the displeasure of his father, Ruknu'd-Dawlih, because he had challenged his cousin, Izzu'd-Dawlih Bakhtiyár the son of Mu'izzu'd-Dawlih Aḥmad (one of the three brothers, founders of the Buwayhid Dynasty), and led his armies to Baghdád. But the ailing Ruknu'd-Dawlih, who died in Iṣfahán in September 976, was reconciled with his son before his death, appointing him his successor. 'Aḍudu'd-Dawlih had a full brother, Mu'ayyidu'd-Dawlih Búyih, and a half-brother Fakhru'd-Dawlih 'Alí. Now, 'Aḍudu'd-Dawlih, disregarding the injunctions of his father, sent Mu'ayyidu'd-Dawlih to fight their half-brother, who, unable to withstand the onslaught, fled to Ṭabaristán and sought the aid of Shamsu'l-Ma'álí Qábús. Mu'ayyidu'd-Dawlih demanded in rude terms the surrender of Fakhru'd-Dawlih, which infuriated a man as refined as Shamsu'l-Ma'álí. Inevitably battle was joined between them, but Qábús did not have an army strong enough to keep the Buwayhid at bay. Together with the Buwayhid prince, who had taken refuge with him, he took the road to Khurásán. There, Núḥ II, the Sámánid Amír, gave Qábús the aid he required. But treachery undid them. Once again, in Khurásán, Qábús and Fakhru'd-Dawlih found themselves hopelessly stranded, because the Sámánids, themselves rapidly in decline, could no longer aid them. The stalwart men who had come to the fore were Sabuk-takín and his son, Maḥmúd, the <u>Gh</u>aznavid, Turks and fanatically Sunní.

However, death came to the rescue of Fa<u>kh</u>ru'd-Dawlih. First, 'Aḍudu'd-Dawlih and then, within a year, Mu'ayyidu'd-Dawlih died. Fa<u>kh</u>ru'd-Dawlih came back to regain his patrimony. But he proved to be an ingrate. He gave Ṭabaristán to a general who had deserted the Sámánids. Fa<u>kh</u>ru'd-Dawlih was indeed a man of uncertain character. The great vizier, Ṣáḥib Ibn 'Abbád, had helped him to his throne and with wise guidance had enabled him to retain it, but as soon as Ṣáḥib died, Fa<u>kh</u>ru'd-Dawlih broke his word, confiscated all of Ṣáḥib's property and threw the relatives of that wonderful man into prison. Death overtook Fa<u>kh</u>ru'd-Dawlih in 997. At last, after seventeen years of exile, <u>Sh</u>amsu'l-Ma'álí returned to his beloved Ṭabaristán. Notwithstanding all his splendid attainments, <u>Sh</u>amsu'l-Ma'álí Qábús, having known bitter years of adversity, had developed a hardness and harshness of character which lost him many friends. After some years, the independent spirit of the people of Ṭabaristán could no longer tolerate his excesses. Condemning to death Ispahbud <u>Sh</u>ahríyar, the Bávandí prince, as well as Na'ím Zamán, his own chamberlain and a much loved man, brought its retribution. Qábús fled to Basṭám in <u>Kh</u>urásán. His son, Falaku'l-Ma'álí Manú<u>ch</u>ihr, stood by him and wished him to return. But Qábús knew that he could no longer rule the people of Ṭabaristán. Manú<u>ch</u>ihr placed him in a fortress for his own safety, but a number of generals made their way into the fortress and murdered him. Thus ended the life of one of the most talented and accomplished men who had ever adorned the scene of Ṭabaristán. Now the days of the Ziyárids as well as the Buwayhids were drawing to a close.

Falaku'l-Ma'álí Manú<u>ch</u>ihr had to make his submission to Maḥmúd, the <u>Gh</u>aznavid, and marry a daughter of that unbearable fanatic. The end of the Ziyárid rule is a matter of conjecture. Did Unṣuru'l-Ma'álí, Kaykávús, the author of the celebrated work, *Qábús-Námih,** and his son Gílán-<u>Sh</u>áh (for whose edification that book was composed by his learned and worldly-wise father) ever rule over Ṭabaristán? Opinions differ and diverge. But that which is certain is the fact – sad though it is – that the curtain had come down

---

* Translated into English by Reuben Levy under the title of '*A Mirror for Princes*'.

over the independence of Ṭabaristán in the days of Falaku'l-Ma'álí Manúchihr, attachment to whom made Abu'n-Najm Aḥmad, the famed poet of Dámghán, adopt Manúchihrí as his *nom de plume*.

One could relate in detail the adventures, oftentimes gripping, of the Ispahbuds, whose forebear was Kayús, a Sásánid prince, brother of the great Anúshirván, Chosroes I. Those Ispahbuds of the House of Bávand grace the history of Ṭabaristán, but they did not spring from the stock of Daylam or Gíl. We have already had glimpses of the House of Jastán which brought forth wise and just rulers. Ṭabaristán had another line of Ispahbuds, variously known as Musáfirids, Sálárids, or Kangarids, who had Daylamistán within their grasp, but only for a short time. Ádharbáyján was their main hunting-ground until the Ismá'ílís of Alamút ended their power in the middle of the eleventh century.

The story of Ṭabaristán, independent Ṭabaristán, had reached its close. The Saljúqs, who came next, rode roughshod over that dearly-cherished province by the Caspian Sea. But some flicker of its independence remained, until it was totally extinguished by the man who established Shí'ism throughout Írán: the Ṣafavid, Sháh Ismá'íl.

Ṭabaristán of ancient fame was dead. But Mázindarán (the new Ṭabaristán) lived to attain the apogee of honour and distinction. Therein dwelt, flourished and prospered the ancestors of Bahá'u'lláh – the Supreme Manifestation of the Almighty God.

23

The Ancestry of Bahá'u'lláh

THE CELEBRATED BAHÁ'Í scholar, Mírzá Abu'l-Faḍl-i-Gulpáygání, has written that at the time when he lived in Ṭihrán a controversy arose amongst some of the Bahá'ís regarding the purpose of verses composed by Shalmaghání that point to the Advent of a Manifestation of God in future years.

Abú-Ja'far Muḥammad Ibn 'Alí was a native of the village of Shalmaghán, which was situated in the region of Wásiṭ in 'Iráq. So he was known as ash-Shalmaghání. He was a Shí'ih and a close associate of Ḥusayn Ibn Rúḥ, who claimed to be the third deputy of the Hidden Imám. Ḥusayn Ibn Rúḥ was a prominent member of the House of Nawbakht, and owed his appointment to the previous deputy: Abú-Ja'far Muḥammad Ibn 'Uthmán al-'Umarí. Despite his high connections, he was thrown into gaol by the highly-capricious 'Abbásid caliph, al-Muqtadir.

Shalmaghání is greatly vilified, because during the period of Ḥusayn Ibn Rúḥ's incarceration he changed his views and denied the existence of a Hidden Imám. The Twelvers, amongst whom Shalmaghání had enjoyed prestige and leadership, then directed their efforts towards his destruction. During the caliphate of ar-Ráḍí (AD 934–40) Shalmaghání and Ibráhím Ibn Abí-'Awn, one of his ardent supporters, were both put to death and their bodies were burned.

In a Tablet addressed to Mullázádih of Ṭabríz, 'Abdu'l-Bahá points out that Shalmaghání spoke the word of truth, foretelling the rise of the Divine Luminary from the horizon of Írán, but that men devoid of truth denounced him and condemned him to death.

The following pages are from the pen of Mírzá Abu'l-Faḍl, to whom 'Abdu'l-Bahá referred Áqá Khusraw Bimán for information concerning the ancestry of Bahá'u'lláh. His reply was later published as a pamphlet in Bombay and is here translated, in part, by the present author.*

'Some considered that the poem under consideration carried the tidings of the Advent of the Primal Point. They took the word "Fársí" that appears in the poem to be the same as "Shírází". Others considered the reference to be to the Advent of the Abhá Beauty, because Shalmaghání had denied that the appearance of the Promised One would be from the House of Háshim, and had prophesied that the Light of Abhá would shine from the House of Kisrá [Chosroes]. Thus it is proved [they concluded] that the prophecy gave the tidings of the Advent of the Blessed Beauty and not of the Báb.

'Sometime previous to that I had noted these words in the *Dasatír* [a book related to the Mazdean Faith]: "Should it remain of high Heaven, I shall raise up one of your people and shall show Him the Way, and shall not take away prophethood and Lordship from thy children". And in other books of the Pársís I had observed amongst the tidings which they carry the definite statement that this bounty shall be realized after the passage of twelve hundred and some more years from the time of the inception of the Faith of Islám: that is to say, before 1300 years have come to pass from the birth of Islám that shining Luminary will appear over that delectable horizon. Briefly, for these reasons I reached the conclusion that the ancestry of the House of Núrís goes back to the ancient dynasties of Írán; and therefore Shalmaghání intended in that poem to convey the tidings of the Advent of the Abhá Beauty and not the Advent of the Primal Point.

'However, since firmly holding this conception without the support of the testimony of history was not a rational act, I went out to investigate the matter in the history of Ṭabaristán. Historians maintain that consequent to the victory of the Muslims over Írán and the extinction of the Sásánids, some princes of Írán captured Mázindarán, and several dynasties branching out from them reigned over that domain for a very long time. Such were the Bádústáníyán, who, as it is retailed in *Ḥabíbu's-Siyar* [a history by Khundmír, AD 1523], after the abandonment of the capital by Yazdigird the son of Shahriyár [Yazdigird III, the last of the Sásánids], took over Mázindarán and

* *Sharḥ-i-Shajarih Námih-i-Mubárakih* (Description of the Blessed Genealogy). See Bibliography.

protected it from domination by the Arabs. The seat of the government of the Bádústáníyán was at the city of Ámul and the city of Bárfurúsh and also other central cities of Ṭabaristán. For many a generation the governance of these cities belonged to this dynasty. And of the kings of Ṭabaristán there is also the dynasty of Ál-i-Ziyár whose first ruler was Mardávíj, the son of Ziyár, who came to power in the year AH 315 [AD 927] and within a short time brought all the cities of Ṭabaristán under his independent reign. The Ziyárids held power for nearly one-hundred-and-sixty years. Their capital was Gurgán or Jurján. They were descendants of Sásánids. The most famous of them is 'Unṣuru'l-Ma'álí Kávús the son of Vushmagír, son of Mardávíj, son of Ziyár of Daylam. To this day, his book the *Qábús-Námih*, which he wrote in a style eloquent and strong for the edification of his son, Gílán-Sháh, is well-famed and pleasing to masters of ethics.

'Again, of the kings of Ṭabaristán is the dynasty of the Sipahbudán of Mázindarán. Historians consider them to have been the real kings of Mázindarán, and trace their descent back to Anúshirván the Just. The residence and the seat of government of this dynasty was mostly in the district of Núr and Kujúr. Every ruler of this line dwelt with his family and offspring in the castles of these areas. And the people of Ṭabaristán – peasant and landlord, ruler and governor – kept their Zoroastrian Faith until the third century of the Hijrah. It was then that Dá'íy-i-Kabír, Ḥasan Ibn Zayd-i-'Alawí, conquered Ṭabaristán and the star of the 'Alawid Zaydíyyih rulership rose over Eastern lands. When that happened all the people of Ṭabaristán, young and old, rich and poor, without compulsion and dislike, guided by this great Emir, were converted to Islám and became known far and wide as faithful to the Imámate of the Zaydíyyih School. The rulership remained with this dynasty until the star of the Ṣafavids rose in turn. Ṭabaristán was then governed by the celebrated Emir, Áqá Rustam-i-Rúzafzún. He refused to acknowledge the sovereignty of Sháh Ismá'íl. Because of that the emirate of that House became extinct. All of those emirs were well known for their devotion to the Imáms, and for their patronage of knowledge and learned men. Some of the celebrated savants have penned invaluable tomes dedicated to the rulers of Gurgán and Ṭabaristán. Eminent poets have composed lambent odes in praise of the Sipahbuds of Mázindarán. One such was Manúchihrí, the well-famed poet of the fifth century AH [eleventh century AD] who praised

Falaku'l-Ma'álí Manúchihr, the son of Shamsu'l-Ma'álí Qábús, the son of Vushmagír, from whose name he adopted his sobriquet. And another was the celebrated Kháqání, who composed splendid odes in praise of the Sipahbuds of Mázindarán. Another famous poet, Ẓahír-i-Fáriyábí [twelfth century AD], although in the service and a panegyrist of Qizil-Arslán [AD 1186–91, Atábak of Ádharbáyján] and a fervent Sunní himself, addressing his patron in an ode tells him that after thirty years of service in 'Iráq, it is the King of Mázindarán who supplies the daily bread of the poet. And in another ode, equivocally he says: "Decided have I to turn towards Mázindarán. Love of Abú-Bakr and friendship for 'Umar provide not the means of living."

'In brief, when I noticed these occasions in history books I became convinced that in all probability I could find correctly the genealogy of the Abhá Beauty. Then a number of trustworthy people stated that Riḍá-Qulí Khán, entitled Amíru'sh-Shu'ará, has mentioned in his book *Nizhád-Námih* that the descent of the House of Núrís goes back to the just king, Anúshirván. This was a reliable source, because Hidáyat [Riḍá-Qulí Khán's sobriquet], although immersed in waywardness, is one of the most celebrated historians of Írán. *Rawḍatu'ṣ-Ṣafáy-i-Náṣirí* is one of his works, over which he has toiled many years and has rearranged a famous book. Secondly, Hidáyat is an enemy of the Cause of God. The nonsense which he has included and published in the Appendices to *Rawḍatu'ṣ-Ṣafá*, even overtaking the author of *Násikhu't-Taváríkh* [a history of the world in several volumes by Muḥammad-Taqí Khán-i-Sipihr of Káshán, entitled Lisánu'l-Mulk] in shameless fabrication and disparagement, provides clear proof of his enmity. Therefore it was evident that had he had any doubt regarding the descent of the House of Núrís from the just monarch, Anúshirván, he never would have put it on record and given it wide publicity.

'Fortunately, at that very time I met the late Ḥájí Mírzá Riḍá-Qulí [a half-brother of Bahá'u'lláh] at the home of one of the noblemen of Ṭihrán. The host, prompted by me, asked Ḥájí Mírzá Riḍá-Qulí to explain who the forebears were of the House of Núrís. He replied that their descent was from Yazdigird-i-Shahriyár [the last of the Sásánids]. Our host further enquired whether they had a genealogical table to indicate their descent, or was it only a matter of oral tradition and repetition passed on by the prominent personages of the House? Ḥájí Mírzá Riḍá-Qulí replied that such a genealogical table existed, in which the names, the professions, and the entitlements of every one of the forebears of this House are all recorded, right up to Yazdigird the son of Shahriyár. One could gather from what he said that there were several copies extant of that genealogical table in the possession of his cousins and the prominent members of his family.

'When these evidences were all obtained I presented a supplication to the Holy Threshold of the Abhá Beauty, stating the variety of views expressed regarding Shalmaghání's intent and the tidings related to Írán and the historical evidences that exist. In answer I was honoured with a Tablet, dated 26 Sha'bán 1299 [July 1882]. Regarding the intent of Shalmaghání in his poem, the Pen of the All-Merciful did thus inscribe in that holy Tablet: "O Abu'l-Faḍl! Verily thou hast spoken the truth and hast brought to light that which was enshrined in his words . . ." (*Sharḥ-i-Shajarih Námih-i-Mubárakih*, p. 14)

'As it happened, in those years Ustád Javánmard, the principal of the Pársí School of Yazd and a teacher of the school, who was a prominent Bahá'í of Pársí origin, wrote a supplication and enquired about the genealogy of the Blessed Perfection. In answer to that supplication the Tablet of *Shír-Mard* was revealed. In that Tablet it is said: "You had enquired about the pure-natured ancestors; Abu'l-Faḍl-i-Gulpáygání, upon whom be My Glory, has written of heavenly works on this theme that would impart information and increase perception." Since the text of the Tablet was not available, here the gist of it was quoted.

'What I have written here is also the gist of the treatise which I wrote about the holy Family. And since on 28th of Rabí'u'l-Avval 1300 [February 1883], on the orders of Kámrán Mírzá, the Náyibu's-Salṭanih, a number of friends and myself were arrested in Ṭihrán, and all my books and writings were looted, the manuscript of that treatise fell into the hands of enemies and was lost to me . . .'

24

The Testimony of Ahl-i-Ḥaqq

AHL-I-ḤAQQ – The People of Truth (the name by which they refer to themselves) – are known to the public at large as 'Alíyu'lláhí, those who assert the divinity of 'Alí: 'Alí Ibn Abí-Ṭálib, the cousin of the Prophet Muḥammad, the husband of His beloved daughter, Fáṭimah, the first to believe in Him (apart from His wife, Khadíjah), the first rightful Imám, the fourth Caliph. Their own answer to the above allegation is best summed up in this couplet:

God, we do not consider 'Alí to be,
And, in no way, separate from God is he.

It was believed and reported by so eminent a historian as Ṭabarí that 'Abdu'lláh Ibn Sabá, a Jewish convert, introduced the belief in the divinity of 'Alí into the realm of Islám, and paid with his life for that blasphemy, 'Alí himself ordering his death. This view has been contested in recent years. Whether such a person as 'Abdu'lláh Ibn Sabá existed or not, the fact remains that the belief in the divinity of 'Alí was current in Islám from early days. On occasions it found fantastic expression. There was a group called *Mukhṭi'ah* – the Errant – who maintained that the Angel Gabriel made an error by bringing the call to Prophethood to Muḥammad, because Prophethood had really been ordained for 'Alí. Even more ludicrous was the belief of a group of people called *Azdaríyyah*, who alleged that 'Alí, the father of Ḥasan and Ḥusayn (the second and third Imáms), was really a man named 'Alí al-Azdarí, while the Imám 'Alí was the Creator, and the Creator cannot possibly have progeny.

Enough has been said to indicate the nature of aberrations regarding 'Alí. Those groups and many others similar to them in the Shí'ih camp, who upheld such fantastic views, were collectively called *Ghulát* – Extremists.

But the Ahl-i-Ḥaqq of recent centuries have nothing in common with those weavers of fancy, those producers of weird and grotesque notions who flourished amazingly in early times. They are an esoteric denomination; of that there can be no doubt. But they are also people distinguished for their integrity, tolerance, amiability and charity. Although they have been much harmed by the ignorant and the fanatic, they never harm anyone. Their stronghold is the township of Kirand and the Gúrán country in western Írán, not far from the city of Kirmánsháh and the border with 'Iráq.

When Bahá'u'lláh, banished from Írán, reached Kirand on His way to 'Iráq, the notables and the generality of the inhabitants of that delectable township received Him with marked respect.

That area of western Írán is mostly peopled by ethnic minorities, chiefly the Kurds. The majority of Kurds are Sunnís, but a sizeable number of them belong to Ahl-i-Ḥaqq. Consequently almost all the literature of this esoteric group is in Kurdish, but with a modicum in Turkish. In Syria and Lebanon, the Ahl-i-Ḥaqq are known as Nuṣayrí. The Company of Yáristán is another appellation for them, Yáristán meaning the 'Abode of Friends'.

The fanatics in the Islamic world did great harm to the people of Yáristán, condemning their prominent men to death. That persecution drove them underground, and they drew an effective veil over their beliefs. As a result dissension and varied beliefs appeared among them. One of the early leaders of Yáristán, Sulṭán Isḥáq (Isaac), warned his followers against making their beliefs widely known until the advent of Khávandigár (the Lord). Sulṭán Isḥáq was truly a ruler, and his seat of government was at Huwayzih in the Persian oil-province of Khúzistán. He himself was a devotee of Siyyid Muḥammad-i-Musha'sha'. This siyyid, at the hour of death, passed his power and position to Sulṭán Isḥáq. The Ahl-i-Ḥaqq believe that because the Sulṭán had purity of heart and intent, truth was unfolded to him. But he had inveterate enemies, notably his brothers, who, although many people had chosen to follow the Sulṭán, led a mob against him. Consequently Sulṭán Isḥáq abdicated and with a number of his followers took the road to northern regions: Kirand and Gúrán and Qal'iy-i-Zanjír. When they reached the vale of Shish, enemies were at their heels. Pír-Binyámín (Benjamin) asked the Sulṭán to find a way of rescue. Sulṭán Isḥáq guided his people to climb to the top of the mount and spend the night there. The enemies stopped at the base of the mountain, awaiting dawn to rush the besieged and cut them down. Then, it is believed, the Sulṭán ordered this Pír-Binyámín or another elder, named Pír-Dávar, to take a handful of dust and throw it at the enemies, whereupon a tremendous storm arose: thunder, lightning and tempestuous winds. A few of the Sulṭán's followers then charged the enemy, who, in the dark and in the thick of the storm began fighting each other. When dawn came, only a small number of them had survived the struggle, and when they realized what had happened, they fled the field.

Now, the story goes, Pír-Binyámín begged the Sulṭán to show some particular favour towards those of his followers who had lost their lives. Sulṭán Isḥáq ordered the Company of Yáristán to fast for three days in memory of the martyrdom of those Yárs (Friends). The Kurds observe this fast, but there are differences amongst them as to the exact time and date; some consider it to be at that time of year when the Pleiades face the moon.

Once the peril was averted, Sulṭán Isḥáq and his followers went to Kirand and settled in that neighbourhood. The Sulṭán took his abode at Qal'iy-i-Zanjír. This place is considered by Ahl-i-Ḥaqq to be equivalent to the Ka'bah. It is named after Pír-Dávar. Very few ever visit it, because the pilgrimage there is conditional upon total detachment and renunciation of all earthly ties. There are two mountains in that area called Váláhú and Balábanú by Ahl-i-Ḥaqq. The latter is the mountain of Sulaymáníyyih, to which Bahá'u'lláh went. There Darvísh Ṣidq-'Alí, the attendant of the Shrine of Pír-Dávar, on meeting Him came to see in Him all the signs by which the Promised One was to be recognized.

Darvísh Ṣidq-'Alí became greatly devoted to Bahá'u'lláh. Thus did 'Abdu'l-Bahá speak of him:

> He was a dervish; a man who lived free and detached from friend and stranger alike. He belonged to the mystic element and was a man of letters . . . unlike the other Ṣúfís he did not devote his life to dusty ḥashísh . . . only searched for God, spoke of God, and followed the path of God.
>
> He had a fine poetic gift and wrote odes to sing the praises of Him Whom the world has wronged and rejected . . .
>
> That free and independent soul discovered, in Baghdád, a trace of the untraceable Beloved. He witnessed the dawning of the Daystar above the horizon of 'Iráq, and received the bounty of that sunrise. He came under the spell of Bahá'u'lláh, and was enraptured by that tender Companion. Although he was a quiet man, one who held his peace, his very limbs were like so many tongues crying out their message. When the retinue of Bahá'u'lláh was about to leave Baghdád he implored permission to go along

as a groom. All day, he walked beside the convoy, and when night came he would attend to the horses. He worked with all his heart. Only after midnight would he seek his bed and lie down to rest; the bed, however, was his mantle, and the pillow a sun-dried brick.

. . . In his high station, that of groom, he reigned like a king; indeed he gloried over the sovereigns of the earth. He was assiduous in attendance upon Bahá'u'lláh; in all things, upright and true . . .

While in the barracks, Bahá'u'lláh set apart a special night and He dedicated it to Darvísh Ṣidq-'Alí. He wrote that every year on that night the dervishes should bedeck a meeting place, which should be in a flower garden, and gather there to make mention of God . . .

This eminent dervish spent his whole life-span under the sheltering favor of God. He was completely detached from worldly things. He was attentive in service, and waited upon the believers with all his heart. He was a servant to all of them, and faithful at the Holy Threshold . . . (*Memorials of the Faithful*, pp. 36–8)

That dervish festival mentioned by 'Abdu'l-Bahá is styled 'Íd-i-Laylatu'l-Quds – the Festival of the Night of Holiness. It is said that whenever Sulṭán Isḥáq visited the mountains of Sulaymáníyyih and its environs he told his followers that He Who ruled over destinies of nations would come there and decide the issue.

Sulṭán Isḥáq was apparently a contemporary of Amír Tímúr-i-Gúrkání (Tamerlane, AD 1370–1405). He had seven sons, all of whom arose after the passing of their father to promote his teachings. Each one of them laid a foundation of belief, and that was why there came to be seven denominations within the Circle of Yáristán. Apparently all of the seven were in agreement about points of belief, differing only about fasting. The following paragraphs describe how that difference is explained.

Sháh Ibráhím, a grandson of Sulṭán Isḥáq, was established in Baghdád and the fame of his virtues spread far and wide. In Tabríz the ruler, Sháh Jahán, had an official whose son fell terribly ill and the physicians were unable to cure him. Hearing of the miraculous deeds attributed to Sháh Ibráhím, the official took his son to Baghdád where Sháh Ibráhím cured the boy. Today the book of Qúshchí-'Ughlí, the son of that official, is well regarded and treasured by Ahl-i-Ḥaqq. That book of verses, all in Turkish, has many references to the advent of the Báb and His martyrdom in Ádharbáyján, and to the advent of Bahá'u'lláh in Baghdád and His sojourn in the Holy Land. Until Qúshchí came to Baghdád the membership of Yáristán was confined to the Kurds, but after his attachment to Sháh Ibráhím an appreciable number of Turks came within its orbit.

Seven men, it is related, took the road to Baghdád, full of zeal, singing, dancing, and playing their musical instruments, but since they had not been summoned by Sháh Ibráhím and had not obtained his permission before setting out, they were endangered by a snowstorm and died in a cave where they had taken refuge. Pír-Binyámín requested Sháh Ibráhím to bestow some favour upon them, and he instituted fasting for a week in their memory. Again Pír-Binyámín intervened. Many of the members of Yáristán, he pleaded, would succumb should they refrain from eating and drinking for seven days. Then Sháh Ibráhím reduced the days of fasting to three. This is why, it is explained, the Turks of Yáristán observe the fast in memory of those who perished in the cave, while the Kurds of Yáristán do it in remembrance of the martyrs who died defending Sulṭán Isḥáq.

Khán-Átash, who was a contemporary of Nádir Sháh (1736–47), the Afshárid, put a ban on fasting. He is the last of the spiritual guides and was a descendant of Sulṭán Isḥáq. He based his pronouncement on the words of Sulṭán Isḥáq and Sháh Ibráhím, who had definitely stated that their decree of fasting would endure until the Advent of Khávandigár, and then the command would be His. Khán-Átash declared that this Advent was close at hand, and the people of Yáristán should be exceedingly happy and rejoice. Khán-Átash left no successor.

Ḥájí Mírzá 'Abdu'lláh-i-Ṣaḥíḥ-Furúsh (resident in Ṭihrán) was a prominent member of the Company of Yáristán. Having enthusiastically embraced the Bahá'í Faith and being well acquainted with all the texts of Ahl-i-Ḥaqq, he was moved to compose a book,* pointing out and proving that the prophecies contained in those texts have all been fulfilled in the Advents of the Báb and Bahá'u'lláh.

Many are the words of wisdom and of right counsel which Sulṭán Isḥáq bequeathed to the Company of Yáristán. Would to God that all the people of Írán had given a receptive ear to these words, as did the Kurds and the Turks who found their spiritual home in Yáristán: 'If thou carest for thine own Faith thou wilt not abuse the Faith of any other.'

The elders and seers of Yáristán have spoken of two Advents, in the

* The title of his book was *Istidlálíyyih Baráy-i-Ahl-i-Ḥaqq*. He died several decades ago. See Bibliography. (Ed.)

Ḥájí Mírzá 'Abdu'lláh-i-Ṣaḥíḥ-Furúsh (left), *author of a book on the Ahl-i-Ḥaqq, with Mírzá Ghulám-Ḥusayn*

fullness of time. At first, they have predicted, Binyámín (Benjamin) will step forth, to be followed by the greater Advent of Hávangár (Khávangár) or Khávandigár (the Lord). Shaykh Amír, who lived some two centuries prior to the Advent of the Báb, specified that Binyámín was to declare the nearness of the Coming of the Lord.

Siyyid Farḍí, who also lived about two hundred years before the days of the Báb, told his disciples, when his death was close at hand, that a man named Taymúr (Tímúr) would come out of the village of Bányárán (which is in the district of Gúrán), in the guise of Ayut-Húshyár. He will be, the Siyyid declared, the 'Herald of Truth'. Indeed, during the reign of Muḥammad Sháh (1834–48), a young man named Taymúr, nearly twenty years old, came from that village, love-intoxicated, and cried out: 'O Yáristán, I have tidings for you; my Lord, the generous King is here. I am Taymúr, Taymúr: Ayut-Húshyár, come to herald Mihdí of Sháh Khávangár.' Taymúr had several thousands of the people of Yáristán gathered round him. In the early part of the reign of Náṣiri'd-Dín Sháh, Taymúr was arrested and the Shí'ih divines condemned him to death.

Qúshchí-'Ughlí clearly prophesied the emergence of the company which had attained salvation from the area of Khurásán, and indeed that referred to the Bábu'l-Báb (Mullá Ḥusayn) and his companions, who took the road to Mázindarán from Khurásán.

Taymúr had, in a couplet in Kurdish, spoken of the eighteen (the exact number of the Báb's Letters of the Living) who would stand with their Commander. Láchin, another seer of Yáristán, clearly named the city of Shíráz as the place where choice gifts of the spirit would be offered.

Other seers of Yáristán, such as Naw-rúz, Karím and Rustam, specified the years that Binyámín would have to fulfil his mission, which tally with the number of years of the Ministry of the Báb; and pointed to the martyrdom of the Báb and His disciple, Anís (Mírzá Muḥammad-'Alíy-i-Zunúzí), at Tabríz. Still others foresaw the upheaval of Zanján and the exodus from Khurásán. All these prophecies are in Kurdish verse. Then we have Murád, another Kurd and a poet, who very clearly mentioned the attempt which would be made on the life of the Sháh, because he would be considered responsible for the martyrdom of the Lord of the Age. That same Murád left no doubt that Ḥusayn, the Deliverer on Whose brow rests the crown of divine sovereignty, would be put in chains during the reign of Náṣiri'd-Dín Sháh. And Láchin, already quoted, made the Advent of Ḥusayn, who is Sháh Khávandigár, the point in time marking the commencement of a trial of strength with the Qájárs and the rapid downfall of that clan. He also specified Damávand as the area from which Sháh Khavandigár would step into the arena of the world. Láchin dwelt particularly on the cruelties and the misdeeds of the Qájárs and plainly declared that their iniquities would cause lamentation, and that He Who rides the charger of Truth would quit Írán.

Moreover, Shaykh Amír foretold the retirement of Bahá'u'lláh to Sulaymáníyyih:

> He went away to a place unknown to all. The King and the Lord of Binyámín went away to a place, unknown to all. Men are looking for Him in vain. The Lord is manifest in a human temple and people know not.

Then, Naw-rúz specified the mountain Váláhú (the range of mountains on which Sulaymáníyyih is situated) as the place where

Faith would be renewed. Ḥaydar was the next seer to look into the future and see the return of the King of Truth – Bahá'u'lláh – from the mountain where He dwelt; and he commented on the bounties which He would shower on the people. Astounding, also, is Íl-Bagí's wording of his prophecy: 'The Bábís shall follow Bahá.' And once again Láchin foretold the doom of the Qájárs: 'By the roar of men, lion-hearted, and by the call of the dragon of the Lord, tremble shall the very foundation of the Qájárs.'

Shír Khán was another Kurdish seer who foretold in detail the Advent of Bahá'u'lláh in Baghdád, the Declaration of His Cause in springtime (the Riḍván period), the opposition of the divines, the frustration of their designs, and Bahá'u'lláh's journey to Istanbul: 'Baghdád and Istanbul we shall bring under our dominion'. Rustam, already quoted, foretold a good deal more of those events associated with the rise and the diffusion of the Faith of Bahá'u'lláh: 'How wonderful is the horseman [the rider] who, with sword drawn, shall conquer Najaf, Baghdád, Istanbul, Rúm [Ottoman domains], and Farang [Europe], and reach the shores of the Black Sea.' 'The King of Truth is in Shám [Syria], and the Herald at Tabríz.'

Khán Almás pointed to the Turkish Revolution (1908), the spread of the Faith in the West, the degradation of Írán, the Ministry of 'Abdu'l-Bahá, the establishment of the House of Justice.

Finally, to crown these breath-taking prophecies which are found in the texts (mainly and chiefly Kurdish) of the people of Yáristán, let us hear once again from Murád:

> The King of Glory seated on the throne of sovereignty called the peoples of the world to gather and dwell under the pavilion of unity. Murád! to thee He gave the tidings that 'We have revealed all that was hidden'. The Lord of the World, the Master of all who dwell therein, now established on the seat of Judgement. He shall judge between nations, and give the people that which they deserve.

25

The Land of Ṭá

THE LAND OF ṬÁ – the area of Ṭihrán, capital-city of Írán – was a home of ancient splendour. And it had a tryst with destiny. Its hour of incomparable honour, of crowning glory, of supernal bliss, arrived on the 12th day of November 1817. For on that never-to-be-forgotten day, Ṭihrán witnessed within its compass the birth of the Supreme Manifestation of God.

This chapter will tell the story of the environs of Ṭihrán from earliest times. Thus, in the Apocrypha – the Book of Judith:

Therefore [Nebuchadnezzar]* was very angry with all this country, and sware by his throne and kingdom, that he would surely be avenged upon all those coasts of Cilicia, and Damascus, and Syria, and that he would slay with the sword all the inhabitants of the land of Moab, and the children of Ammon, and all Judea, and all that were in Egypt, till ye come to the borders of the two seas.

Then he marched in battle array with his power against king Arphaxad in the seventeenth year, and he prevailed in his battle: for he overthrew all the power of Arphaxad, and all his horsemen, and all his chariots,

And became lord of his cities, and came unto Ecbatane, and took the towers, and spoiled the streets thereof, and turned the beauty thereof into shame. He took also Arphaxad in the mountains of Ragau and smote him through with his darts, and destroyed him utterly that day. (1: 12–15)

Ragau mentioned in the Book of Judith is the celebrated city of Ray (Rhages). The mountains of Ragau are the ranges in Shimrán, the area of a number of summer resorts at the foothills of Elburz (Alburz), which today are for the most part joined together and modern Ṭihrán has reached up to them. One of these delectable spots was Murgh-Maḥallih, much loved by Bahá'u'lláh. In ancient times the great city of Ray (or Rayy) was well to the south of the Shimrán ranges and the large village of Ṭihrán. A few of the summer resorts in the upper slopes of Elburz were (and still are) exceedingly pleasant in the summer months, but isolated oftentimes in the heart of the winter.

* Reigned 605–562 BC.

Murgh-Maḥallih, a much-loved summer residence of Bahá'u'lláh in the district of Shimrán

Avesta, the Zoroastrian scriptures, also contains reference to the area of Ray. It is described as a sacred enclave. Overlooking old Rhages (which, as we shall see, was totally destroyed centuries ago) was the mountain known as Mt. Bíbí Shahr-Bánú. On it a shrine has been erected, to which men are not admitted. Shahr-Bánú, most reliable historians agree, was a daughter of Yazdigird III, the last of the Sásánian kings who went down before the sweeping tide of Islám. Shahr-Bánú was made a prisoner and taken to Medinah. 'Umar, the second caliph, gave her to Ḥusayn, who inherited the Imámate from his brother, Ḥasan, and fell a martyr on the bank of the Euphrates. Legend has it that after the appalling slaughter of the descendants of the Prophet on the plain of Karbilá, Shahr-Bánú, to escape from the unholy hands of the minions of the Umayyad usurpers, rode Duldul – the renowned horse of her illustrious husband who was decapitated and trampled by the hooves of the steeds of a merciless foe – and fled from the battlefield. The enemy set out in pursuit. But Duldul sprouted wings and thus Shahr-Bánú made good her escape. That wonderful horse, it was believed by the credulous, carried the daughter of Yazdigird all the way to the distant Ray. There, it was maintained, a cleft in the hillside opened to swallow her, after which the gaping aperture was closed.

That is the legend which gained currency over the centuries. But the truth is quite apart. Discarding the miraculous element, the fact of the matter is that Shahr-Bánú could not have been on the bank of the Euphrates. She died, long before the terrible destruction of the House of the Prophet, at the time she gave birth to 'Alí, the fourth Imám, known as Zaynu'l-'Ábidín (the Adornment of the Devout). 'Alí, the Medial (*Awsaṭ*), as he was also known, on the day his glorious father quaffed the cup of martyrdom was a sickly boy of uncertain health, fever-ridden, and pining on his bed. Thus he remained the sole survivor of the holocaust, and the mantle of Imámate came to rest on his shoulders. And because the blood of the Sásánians ran in his veins, in the eyes of the Persians, smarting under defeat, his spiritual heritage was greatly enhanced. It was in Persia that many of his descendants found refuge and support, escaping from the tyrannies of the caliphs of Damascus and, later, of Baghdád.

On that mount of Bíbí-Shahr-Bánú, sanctified in Islamic times by a legend, once stood a temple dedicated to Náhíd:* Anáhítá. Hence the reference in Avesta to the sacredness of the area of Ray, which included then the village that has grown into a colossal capital-city: Ṭihrán – the birthplace of Bahá'u'lláh. Anáhítá was one of the supreme 'Ízids' of the Mazdean (Zoroastrian) Faith. Greeks knew Anáhítá as Aphrodite and Romans as Venus Erucina. In the area of Ṭihrán and the mountainous region to the north of it, which in early Islamic times came to be known as Qaṣrán, the worship of Anáhítá was widespread.

It is asserted that Alexander the Great set out to destroy Zoroastrianism in Írán. He demolished Mazdean temples and put their priests to death. The inhabitants of Ray and its environs, being strongly attached to their religion and even described as fanatical, suffered heavily in the days of Alexander. Niẓámí of Gandzha (now Kirovabad in Soviet Caucasia), one of the most eloquent classical poets of Persia who flourished in the twelfth century AD under the Saljúqs, graphically relates these depredations of Alexander. Apparently his successors in Írán, the Seleucids, followed the same

* Náhíd, Zuhrah in Arabic, means Venus. The Arabic name denotes the brilliance of this planet.

DYNASTIES AND RULERS OF ÍRÁN

mentioned in this book, alphabetically by dynasty.
See also the list and note on p. 295.

ACHAEMENIANS 559–330 BC	
Cyrus II, the Great	559–c.529 BC
Artaxerxes II	404–359 (358) BC
Darius III, Codomanus	336–330 BC
AFSHÁRIDS 1148–1210/1736–1795	
Nádir Sháh	1148–1160/1736–1747
ARSACIDS (PARTHIANS) 247 BC – AD 226	
Farhad V	2 BC – AD 4
BUWAYHIDS 320–454/932–1062	
Line in Kirmán	
Mu'izzu'd-Dawlih (Aḥmad)	324–338/936–949
'Aḍudu'd-Dawlih	338–372/949–983 (also in Fárs)
Line in Fárs and Khúzistán	
Imádu'd-Dawlih ('Alí)	322–338/934–949 (also in Jibál)
Line in Jibál	
Ruknu'd-Dawlih (Ḥasan)	335–366/947–976
Branch in Hamadán and Iṣfahán	
Mu'ayyidu'd-Dawlih Búyih	366–373/977–983
Branch in Ray	
Fakhru'd-Dawlih 'Alí	366–387/977–997 (also in Hamadán)
GHAZNAVIDS 366–582/977–1186	
Maḥmúd, Sulṭan	388–421/998–1030
KHÁRAZMSHÁHÍS (KHWÁRAZM-SHÁHS) c.470–628/c.1077–1231	
'Alá'u'd-Dín Muḥammad-i-Khárazmsháh	596–617/1200–1220
Jalálu'd-Dín-i-Mankubarní	617–628/1220–1231
PARTHIANS, *see* ARSACIDS	
QÁJÁRS 1193–1342/1779–1925	
Ághá Muḥammad Khán	1193–1212/1779–1797
Fatḥ-'Alí Sháh	1212–1250/1797–1834
Muḥammad Sháh	1250–1264/1834–1848
Náṣiri'd-Dín	1264–1313/1848–1896
Muẓaffari'd-Dín	1313–1324/1896–1907
Muḥammad-'Alí	1324–1327/1907–1909
ṢAFAVIDS 907–1145/1501–1732	
Sháh Ismá'íl	907–930/1501–1524
Ṭahmasb I	930–984/1524–1576
'Abbás I, the Great	996–1038/1588–1629
SALJÚQS (SELJUQS) 429–590/1038–1194	
Alp Arslán	455–465/1063–1072
Malik Sháh I	465–485/1072–1092
Muḥammad I	498–511/1105–1118
Sanjar	511–552/1118–1157
SÁSÁNIANS AD 224–641	
Ardashír I	226–241
Chosroes I (Anúshirván)	531–579
Chosroes II (Khusraw Parvíz)	590–628
Yazdigird III	632–641
SELEUCIDS 312–64 BC	
Seleucus I Nicator	312–281 BC
TÍMÚRIDS 771–912/1370–1506	
Tímúr (-i-Lang or -i-Gúrkání)	771–807/1370–1405
ZANDS 1163–1209/1750–1794	
Karím Khán	1163–1193/1750–1779
Luṭf-'Alí Khán	1203–1209/1789–1794

policy of repression in relation to the Mazdeans. Then a great earthquake hit Ray and razed it to the ground. When Seleucus Nicator came to rebuild that city of renown, he named it Europos.

The Seleucids had their day. On the whole, Írán flourished under them, but soon the onrush of the Parthians, who were of Iranian stock, swept them into limbo. The Parthian dynasty of the Arsacids (Ashkáíyán in Persian), who now held sway, made the city of Ray their spring capital. Under the Arsacids the area of Ṭihrán came to assume a central position. And the Mazdeans regained their freedom of belief. The Arsacids, although destroying the semi-Greek Seleucids, were themselves influenced by Hellenism. They did give recognition to Ahúramazdá of Zoroastrianism, but they also propagated the worship of Mithra and Anáhítá. Even more, they revered Zeus and Apollo of the Greeks. Later, Artemis also joined their Parthenon. Arsacids, with their liberal beliefs, practised complete religious toleration.

The Arsacids had, before long, to cope with the rising power of Rome. In the year 53 BC, in the vicinity of Carrhea (Ḥarrán of Islamic times) in Mesopotamia, they inflicted a crushing defeat on the Roman legions. Crassus, the Roman general, was killed. There and then the Roman expansion to the East came to a halt and ended. Octavius (Augustus, the first emperor of Rome) was an officer in the army of Crassus and was present at the battle of Carrhea.

It was during the reign of Augustus and the Arsacid Farhád V that Jesus was born, in Bethlehem. The Jews were now enslaved, once again, groaning under a foreign yoke. The glories of David and Solomon had long become memories of a dead past. Now even the brave deeds of Judas Maccabeus, who heroically defied Antiochus Epiphanes (176–164 BC), were fast receding into a dim memory. And the yoke of the Romans rested heavily on the children of Israel.

The Parthians, on the other hand, besides the tolerance which they habitually practised, were exceedingly kind and helpful to the Jews because they resented the Romans and their tyrannies. The Arsacid kings even went to the length of actively supporting the Jews to drive out Herod, who was a puppet of Rome, in the year 40 BC and helped put Antigonus, the 'last representative'* of the Maccabees, on the throne. For three years Antigonus held the Romans at bay, and died bravely when the inevitable happened: Romans triumphed and Herod was restored.

* The words quoted are from Magnus, *Outlines of Jewish History*, p. 23. (Ed.)

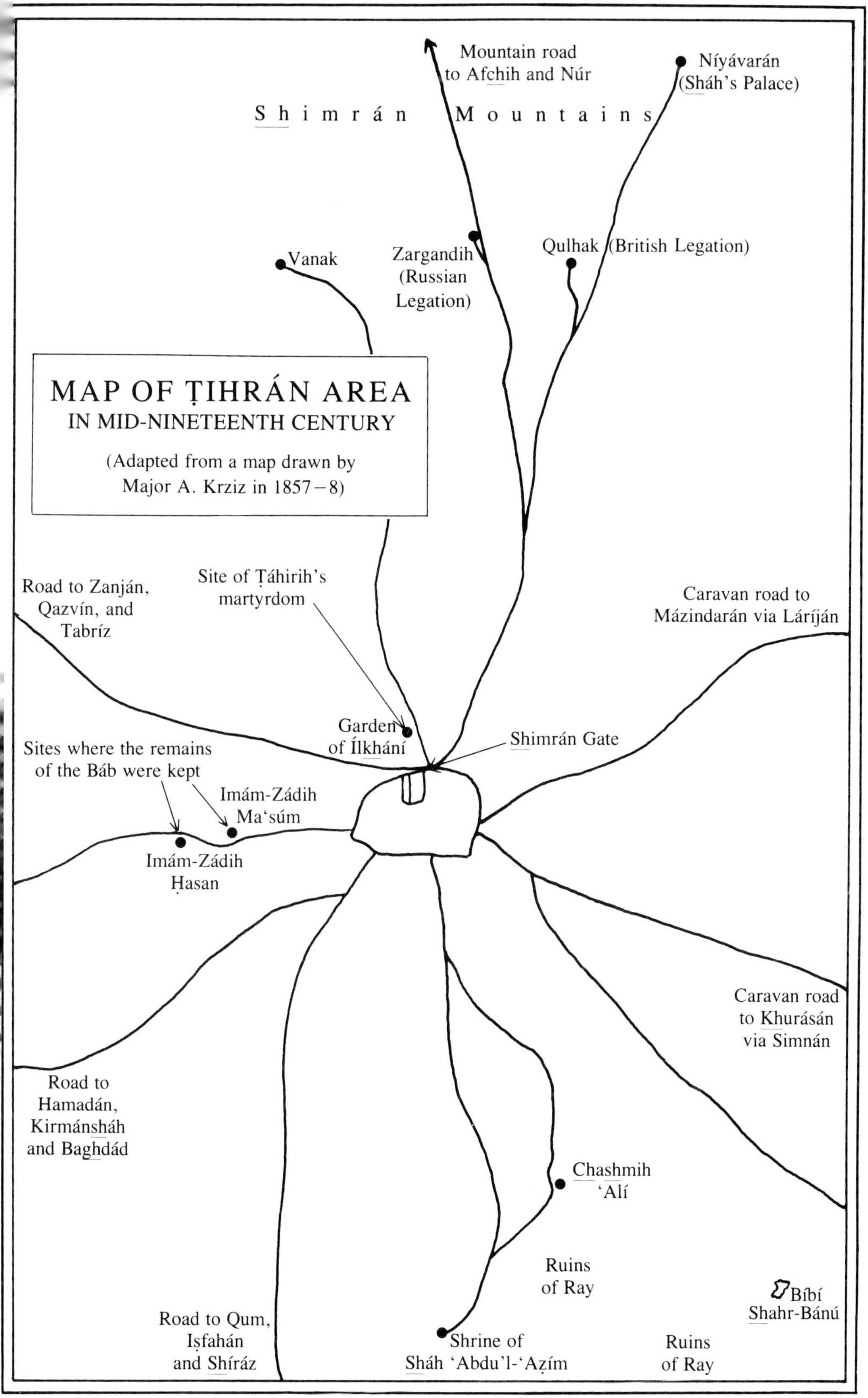

MAP OF ṬIHRÁN AREA
IN MID-NINETEENTH CENTURY
(Adapted from a map drawn by
Major A. Krziz in 1857–8)
Mountain road
to Afchih and Núr
Níyávarán
(Sháh's Palace)
Shimrán Mountains
Vanak
Zargandih
(Russian
Legation)
Qulhak (British Legation)
Road to Zanján,
Qazvín, and
Tabríz
Site of Ṭáhirih's
martyrdom
Caravan road to
Mázindarán via Láríján
Garden
of Ílkhání
Shimrán Gate
Sites where the remains
of the Báb were kept
Imám-Zádih
Ma'súm
Imám-Zádih
Ḥasan
Caravan road
to Khurásán
via Simnán
Road to
Hamadán,
Kirmánsháh
and Baghdád
Chashmih
'Alí
Ruins
of Ray
Bíbí
Shahr-Bánú
Road to Qum,
Iṣfahán
and Shíráz
Shrine of
Sháh 'Abdu'l-'Aẓím
Ruins
of Ray

But now to go back to the story of Ray and Ṭihrán: Ray, as we have seen, was chosen by the Arsacid kings to be their spring resort, and that city became known by their name, 'Arshak' (Ashk).

In the year AD 226, after a reign of nearly five centuries, the Arsacids lost their throne to Ardashír,* who ruled in the province of Fárs. Ardashír was the grandson of Sásán, a priest of a temple in the city of Istakhr, dedicated to Anáhítá. When Ardashír overthrew the Parthians he claimed descent from the Achaemenians, and set out to restore the Mazdean Faith to its pristine purity. Now the religion of Zoroaster was beset with the problem of Zervanism. The most authoritative work in English on Zervanism is that of the late R. C. Zaehner (Spalding Professor of Eastern Religions and Ethics in the University of Oxford). In his introduction to that voluminous and exceedingly readable and informative tome, *Zurvan, A Zoroastrian Dilemma*, Prof. Zaehner wrote:

Both the Zoroastrians in Sassanian times and the Shī'ah Muslims in the Safavī period proved to be exceptionally intolerant of other religions – largely, one suspects, to emphasize their difference from the neighbouring states. (p. 3)

He goes on to say:

. . . Zoroastrianism was uncompromisingly dualist. Nor was its dualism the classic dualism between spirit and matter which would have provided a common meeting-ground with the Indian Jains . . . , with the Gnostics to the West, and with the Manichaeans in Īrān itself. It was a dualism of spirit, postulating two principles at the origin of the Universe — the Spirit of Good or Ohrmazd, and the Spirit of Evil or Ahriman. This extremely original idea dates back to Zoroaster himself, and it is his basic contribution to the philosophy of religion . . .

Though it was no doubt Zoroaster himself who sowed the seed of spiritual dualism, it was left to his epigones in later times to systematize it . . .

It can be readily understood that so fundamental a dualism might well produce a reaction, since the history of religion proves that the nature of man seems to demand a unified godhead. This reaction duly appeared: it is what we call Zervanism. As might be expected in a heterodox sect, in Zervanism we do appear to find traces of alien ideas which were so rigorously excluded from the Zoroastrian orthodoxy . . .

. . . The Zervanites tried to re-establish the unity of the godhead by positing a principle prior and superior to Ohrmazd and Ahriman, thereby doing away

* Ardashír (or Ardishír) is the same as Artaxerxes in Greek. In his day his name had this form in Middle Persian: Artakhishatr. In the Achaemenian times it was pronounced thus: Artakhishatra.

with that essential dualism which is the hub of the Zoroastrian position . . . (pp. 3–5)

Here is not the place to counter the belief that the Faith of Zoroaster was not essentially monotheist, although duality is apparent in its own guise. This is not the place either to present a detailed account of Zervanism, its arguments, its duels with the revived Mazdeanism under the Sásánians. But before leaving the subject it ought to be said that Zervanism, despite suppression, endured throughout the Sásánian period, sometimes even in the ascendant.

In the days of the Sásánians, the governance of Ray resided with the family of Mihrán. This powerful family took its name from a village of that name and had arisen to prominence in the whole area of Ṭihrán. In the present-day Ṭihrán there is a large garden called Mihrán, situated in the road until recently known as Avenue Kúru<u>sh</u>-i-Kabír (Cyrus the Great). That is the site of the old village. Bahrám-i-<u>Ch</u>úbin, who rebelled against Chosroes II – <u>Kh</u>usraw Parvíz – and even occupied the throne for a while at Ctesiphon, was an outstanding member of the family of Mihrán. At the end Chosroes defeated him and Bahrám fled to Turkistán. His grandson, Siyáva<u>kh</u><u>sh</u>, was the Governor of Ray and the area of Ṭihrán when the armies of Islám invaded Írán.

Throughout the reign of the Sásánians, the area of Ṭihrán maintained its supremacy in the domain of religion. Two great fire-temples sprang up: one to the north of Ṭihrán, within the environ of Qaṣrán on the heights of Mt. Tú<u>ch</u>ál; the other, to the south, in the vicinity of the present-day Shrine of <u>Sh</u>áh 'Abdu'l-'Aẓím. The worship of Náhíd (Anáhítá) also held its ground firmly right to the end.

Írán and Byzantium ruined themselves with their constant warfare. Chosroes II, at first scoring victory after victory over the Byzantines, even overrunning Jerusalem and carrying away what was believed to be the true cross, wilted under brilliant and desperate counter-attacks by Heraclius. He, who had defied the summons of the Arabian Prophet, fled miserably from the battlefield, Byzantine armies penetrated deep into Persian territory, and the disgraced and crestfallen Chosroes was deposed by his son, <u>Sh</u>írúyih, and murdered in his prison-cell. How awesome sound those prophetic verses of the Qur'án which foreshadowed the victory of the Byzantines and the abasement of the overbearing Parvíz:

Rúm [the Byzantines] were defeated in the near land. They, after their defeat, shall be victorious, in a few years. Command belongs to God, before and after; and on that day the believers shall rejoice in God's aid. God will aid whomsoever He willeth. And He is the All-Mighty, the Merciful. The promise of God: God faileth not to fulfil His promise, but most men do not know it. (30: 1–5)

Very soon after the débâcle of Chosroes II, the triumphant armies of Islám poured into Írán and Yazdigird III, the last of the Sásánians, suffered the same fate as Darius III, Codomanus, the last of the Achaemenians. He was treacherously murdered.

Writing of the ancestors of Bahá'u'lláh, the Guardian of the Bahá'í Faith states:

He derived His descent, on the one hand, from Abraham (the Father of the Faithful) through his wife Katurah, and on the other from Zoroaster, as well as from Yazdigird, the last king of the Sásáníyán dynasty. He was moreover a descendant of Jesse, and belonged, through His father, Mírzá 'Abbás, better known as Mírzá Buzurg – a nobleman closely associated with the ministerial circles of the Court of Fatḥ-'Alí Sháh – to one of the most ancient and renowned families of Mázindarán (*God Passes By*, p. 94).

The extinction of the Sásánian dynasty occurred in the year AD 641, at the Battle of Nihávand. After that battle, which the Arab historians came to call Fatḥ-al-Futúḥ – Victory of Victories – Yazdigird was a fugitive, and was murdered ten years later, in the vicinity of Marv in Khurásán.

The coming of Islám made no appreciable difference to the way of life in the area of Ray and Ṭihrán. According to the great historian at-Ṭabarí (whose name indicates that he was a man of Ṭabaristán), in the year AH 22 (AD 644) Zínabí,* a general in the service of Siyávakhsh, the hereditary governor of Ray, betrayed his master because of a grudge against him, and opened the gates of the city to the Arab commander. Later he strove hard to make peace between the conquerors and the people of Ray. The Mazdeans agreed to pay *jizyah* (poll-tax), like other *dhimmís* (people of the Book). However, they proved insubordinate and turbulent. With the passage of time, the number of the Mazdeans decreased; but bending knees to the caliphs of Damascus and later of Baghdád was abhorrent even to the newly converted. And before long Shí'ism spread throughout the area. A number of the prominent disciples of the fifth and the sixth

* Originally Zínbudí: the head of the armoury.

Imáms – Muḥammad al-Báqir and Ja'far aṣ-Ṣádiq – were men of Ray, such as Yaḥyá Ibn Abi'l-'Alá, 'Aṭíyyah Ibn Najíḥ Abú-Mutahhar, 'Abdu'r-Raḥím Ibn Sulaymán, and 'Isá Ibn Máhán.

Sh͟áh 'Abdu'l-'Aẓím, whose shrine in the area of Ray has for centuries been a place of pilgrimage, died there in the year AH 250. He led a secluded life while residing in Ray, and used to visit from time to time a grave in the neighbourhood, claiming that Ḥamzih, a son of Imám Músá al-Káẓim, the seventh Imám, was buried there. The Shrine of Imám-Zádih Ḥamzih, himself a scion of the House of Muḥammad, now stands, in its magnificence, next to that of Sh͟ah 'Abdu'l-'Azím.

Next, we hear that several villages in the area of Ray and Ṭihrán, such as Vanak, had rallied to the Zaydí sect. This development was due to the fact that on the other side of the Elburz range, in the Caspian province of Ṭabaristán, descendants of 'Alí Ibn Abí-Ṭálib, following the Zaydí rite, had come to power. Zayd was a son of the fourth Imám – 'Alí, known as Zaynu'l-'Ábidín, whom the tyrannies of the Umayyads drove into open revolt; despite the advice of his nephew, Imám Ja'far aṣ-Ṣádiq, he gathered a force to wage war on the caliph at Damascus. The result was a foregone conclusion. Zayd suffered defeat and martyrdom. Eventually a sect grew up bearing his name, although he himself had never made a particular claim to a position of spiritual authority.

In the days when the 'Abbásids – the scions of 'Abbás, the uncle of the Prophet – rose up in the name of the House of Muḥammad to overthrow the Umayyads, Abú-Muslim of K͟hurásán became the engineer of their victory over the ungodly, as they said. But very soon the 'Abbásids went the way of the Umayyads, and Abú-Ja'far al-Manṣúr treacherously put Abú-Muslim to death in 755. Before long a sect sprang up claiming that Abú-Muslim was not dead, but lived in hiding in the mountains of Ray. These are the mountains which rise up from the plain of Ṭihrán and overlook it; they afforded in those early centuries many places of refuge. As time went on these Muslimíyyahs (so they were called) changed their tune. Abú-Muslim, they asserted, would emerge in the fullness of time to vanquish the ingrates and the unfaithful. But it was still in the caves of Elburz where they located their hero, who had chosen to withdraw for the time being from the world. 'Withdrawal and Return' was fast becoming the pattern of dissident beliefs.

The Khurram-Dínán (or Khurramíyyah) were another group of innovators and recalcitrants, both strong and troublesome, in the area of Ray and Ṭihrán. They were the ones who cherished the memory of Mazdak, the heresiarch who was put to death, with a large number of his followers, by Chosroes I in 528.

As centuries rolled on, Ray became the most populous city of Asia, and the Ṭihrán area flourished accordingly. An amazing development was the congregation of the descendants of 'Alí, the first Imám, in these environs. The large number of shrines harbouring the remains of the sons and grandsons of the Imám that one encounters in the plain and running up to the heights of the Elburz range and even beyond onto those heights themselves, are evidences of that remarkable turn of events in the first centuries of the Muslim Era. A modern writer of Írán, Dr Ḥusayn Karímán, divides the descendants of 'Alí, who made their way to the northern limits of that land, into four categories. First, there were those who suffered by the tyrannies of the Umayyads, and particularly by the enormities of their despicable agent, Ḥajjáj Ibn Yúsuf. Next came the group who had been heartened by the fact that 'Abdu'lláh al-Ma'mún had named, in the year 815, the eighth Imám, 'Alí Ibn Músa'r-Riḍá, as his successor. But before long, under pressure from the dispossessed 'Abbásids, Ma'mún changed his mind and secretly, it is claimed, encompassed the death of Imám Riḍá by poisoning. The 'Alawíyyín, noting the treachery, had hastily to seek places of refuge. The third category consisted of those descendants of 'Alí who had rallied to the support of their kinsmen, in rebellion against the caliphs. Once their leaders were destroyed they had to find routes of escape. The fourth group were those 'Alawíyyín who flocked to Mázindarán (Ṭabaristán) when their relatives found power and authority in that region. And it must be said at once that the dwellers of both sides of the Elburz range, discontented as they were with the caliphs, received the descendants of 'Alí with joy.

We have already described how Ḥasan Ibn Zayd, then living in Ray, accepted the rulership of Ṭabaristán (see pp. 301–2), where he established the Shí'ih doctrine throughout his domain. Within a few years he was master not only of Ṭabaristán, but of the whole area of Damávand and Ray and Ṭihrán as well, where he was firmly established by the year 867. Ḥasan was succeeded by his brother Muḥammad, who, although unable to retain Ray, did succeed in building shrines over the graves of the descendants of 'Alí in those northern regions. Centuries later some of them, such as the shrines of Imám-Zádih Ḥasan, Imám-Zádih Ma'ṣúm and Imám-Zádih Zayd, were to harbour for a while the remains of the Báb – the Qá'im of the House of Muḥammad.

The Sámánids, who came to power in Transoxania and Khurásán and ruled from Bukhárá (819–1005), had their origins in the Mihrán family of the area of Ṭihrán. (See p. 329.) When Amír Ismá'íl was presented with the domain of Ray, he declined to annex it to his kingdom. 'This is a city of ill omen,' he declared. In contrast, for the sake of obtaining the governorship of Ray, 'Umar Ibn Sa'd and Shimr had consented to take up arms against the grandson of the Prophet and encompass his martyrdom on the banks of the Euphrates.

The coming of the Buwayhids (932–1062) out of the Daylam country on the shores of the Caspian, and their establishment particularly in Ray where Ḥasan (entitled Ruknu'd-Dawlih) ruled,* made Shí'ism of Ithná-'Asharíyyah (Twelvers) the dominant force in the whole area of Ray and Ṭihrán. Sulṭán Maḥmúd (998–1030), the Ghaznavid centred on the land that is now Afghánistán, followed the Buwayhids to power. He was fanatically and intolerantly Sunní in his religious profession, took Islám with the sword to India, and inflicted great hardships on the Shí'ih population of the area of Ṭihrán. His actions were indeed shameful, particularly so as they came in the wake of the benevolent rule of the Buwayhids. He set up two hundred gallows and hanged as many prominent and outstanding Shí'ites as he could catch in his net. He accused them of being Qirmaṭí (Carmathian). Not only the Shí'ihs, but the Mu'tazilites as well suffered at the hands of Maḥmúd. The great library of Ṣáḥib – the wise and learned vizier of the Buwayhids – was raided and despoiled. Ibn Athír, the celebrated Arab historian, amply testifies to the depredations of the agent of Sulṭán Maḥmúd in that well-stocked library. But once he was in his grave and the Ghaznavid domination had ended, the Shí'ite supremacy was restored in that area.

Then came the Saljúqids (1038–1194). They too were Sunní, but like the Shí'ite Buwayhids they lorded it over the 'Abbásid caliphs, who were reduced to impotence. Indeed, gone were the might and dominance of Hárún and Ma'mún. The 'Abbásids had become puppets in the hands of both Shí'ihs and Sunnís.

The changes that took place in the fortunes of the Shí'ihs of Ray and

* He was one of the three brothers who were the builders of Buwayhid power. (Ed.)

Ṭihrán, under the Saljúqid kings, were truly spectacular. Learning, in whatever quarter it was found, was greatly respected. And Ṭihrán came to be noticed more and more. In the *Fárs-Námih* of Ibn Balkhí, dedicated to Sulṭán Muḥammad – the Saljúqid monarch (1105–18), son of the well-famed Malik-Sháh (1072–92) – particular mention is made of the pomegranates of Ṭihrán, whose excellence is compared to the goodness of the pomegranates of the district of Kavár in Fárs.

In the days of Niẓámu'l-Mulk – the celebrated vizier of the Saljúqids Alp-Arslán and his son Malik-Sháh – who was a staunch Sunní of the Sháfi'ite school, the village of Ṭarasht in the area of Ṭihrán had become a Shí'ih stronghold where regular conferences and seminars were held to discuss matters of text and tradition. The learned man who directed these circles was a well-known Shí'ih theologian: Khájih Ja'far Ibn Muḥammad, author of several books. The Saljúqid vizier, as already stated, was a Sunní of very decided views; moreover, he was not altogether well-intentioned towards those who believed in the Imámate. But he made it a point to go from Ray, every week, to that Shí'ih village, and sit at the feet of the Shí'ih theologian.

The Saljúqids were succeeded by the Khárazmsháhís who were also Sunnís and exerted pressure on the Shí'ihs of the area of Ray and Ṭihrán. But it was of no avail and Shí'ism became deeply rooted.

We come now to the catastrophe of the Mongol invasion which shook the whole Realm of Islám to its foundations and left the great city of Ray for ever desolate. It happened in the reign of 'Alá'u'd-Dín Muḥammad-i-Khárazmsháh (1200–20). Sulṭán Muḥammad was a foolish king. His overbearing haughtiness, the veniality and greed of his chief frontiersman, the senseless execution of the emissaries of the Mongol overlord (who, incidentally, were Muslims) directed the wrath and the fury of Chingíz Khán (whose intentions, at the very beginning, were thoroughly peaceful and neighbourly) to the vast Empire of the Khárazmsháh. Even worse, 'Alá'u'd-Dín Muḥammad proved a bad planner, a bad general and a cringing coward. While scores of flourishing districts and cities, homes of culture and beauty, were burned and devastated, while thousands perished and thousands more took to the wilderness, the hapless 'Alá'u'd-Dín Muḥammad died, an abandoned fugitive, in the forlorn island of Ábaskún off the coast of Ṭabaristán. His very brave son, Jalálu'd-Dín-i-Mankubarní, faced the Mongol hordes with the utmost courage, but the enemy was far too strong. Furthermore, fellow-Muslims betrayed him and he was murdered by a demented Kurd on a lone hilltop.

Now that Ray was in ruins, and was never to rise again, the area of Ṭihrán became of prime importance. Its people, as we have seen, had been staunch Shí'ihs for a long time. They were regarded jealously by their Sunní neighbours who began concocting fables about them, and some of these fables are strangely reflected in such authoritative works as *Mu'jama'l-Buldán* of Yáqut al-Ḥamaví.

In the succeeding centuries which saw the rise and the downfall of the descendants of Chingíz, the appearance of many petty kingdoms, the scourge of Amír Tímúr (Tamerlane), the civilizing influence of his progeny (which stood in amazing contrast to Tímúr's own destructiveness), the ruined Ray and the flourishing Ṭihrán were crossed and re-crossed, visited and re-visited by many a magnate. The Ál-i-Bádúspán of Rúyán in the western part of Ṭabaristán, towards the middle of the fourteenth century captured the whole area of Ṭihrán and Ray. These Ispahbuds also had Núr and Kujúr within their domains. They are known as Rustamdáríyáns as well, because they were centred in Rustamdár. Their rule endured in that area of Ṭabaristán well into the reign of Sháh 'Abbás the Great, the Ṣafaví ruler.

Ruy Gonzalez de Clavijo, who led an embassy from the court of Henry III, King of Castile, to the court of Tamerlane, gives a good account of Ṭihrán, where he stayed for a couple of days in the best house of the town; Tamerlane himself had lodged there.

In our narrative we have now reached the days of the Ṣafavids. With them Írán is made new. Ismá'íl, a scion of Shaykh Ṣafíyyi'd-Dín of Ardibíl, at the age of thirteen came out of the forests of Gílán by the Caspian Sea to avenge the death of his father and his grandfather. He claimed that he was a descendant of Imám Músá al-Káẓim, the seventh Imám. It is now proved, beyond any measure of doubt, that he was not a siyyid. Of a certainty he was of Kurdish origin, and had Turkish blood as well as Greek. Despina, a daughter of Kalo Ioannes, the last Greek emperor of Trebizond, was the mother of his mother. Habitually he spoke and wrote in Turkish, and composed poems in Turkish. He dragged an Írán mostly Sunní into the Twelver Shí'ih fold. Írán lacked enough Shí'ih divines. He brought those whom he needed from Jabal 'Ámil in Syria. And there is no question that Shaykh Ṣafíyyi'd-Dín, whose name was given to the dynasty which Ismá'íl founded, was a Kurd, a Sunní and the head of a Ṣúfí fraternity.

It is with the advent of Sháh Ṭahmásb I, son of the founder of the dynasty and its second monarch, that Ṭihrán rises to eminence. In the first place Ṭahmásb had his capital in Qazvín, which is within a short distance from Ṭihrán. Secondly, Ṭahmásb was a pious man, narrow-minded even with his piety, as evidenced by his treatment of Anthony Jenkinson, a traveller from England in search of trade. He spent time and money liberally to restore and beautify the Shrine of Sháh 'Abdu'l-'Aẓím. Visiting that shrine, Sháh Ṭahmásb had to pass through Ṭihrán. The trees and verdure, and the plenteousness of water there, pleased him, and he decided to have it surrounded by a moat and give it battlements and four gates. Towers to the number of the súrihs of the Qur'án – one hundred and fourteen – were placed in the battlements, and within each tower one of the súrihs was entombed.

Pietro della Valle, the 'Roman patrician' who sojourned for seven years in Persia during the reign of Sháh 'Abbás the Great, became well acquainted with 'Abbás. During one of his peregrinations, waiting on the Sháh, he visited Ṭihrán with his Nestorian Christian wife, Ma'ání, whom he had married in Baghdád. Pietro liked Ṭihrán and was enchanted by the stately plane trees which he found adorning its thoroughfares. Apparently, unlike his grandfather, 'Abbás was not fond of Ṭihrán. He had no palace of his own within the city, and was forced to live in tents outside. Moreover, on one occasion the people of Ṭihrán had insulted him by seeming indifference.

During the Afghán invasion, which resulted in the virtual extinction of Ṣafavid rule, Ṭihrán, for long a stronghold of Shí'ism, suffered greatly at the invaders' hands. For a while, they took a defensive position in Ṭihrán and added to its fortifications. Nothing of importance happened in Ṭihrán or to Ṭihrán in the succeeding decades. Occasionally, Nádir Sháh, the Afshárid, passed through it; and once he encamped there for a fairly long time.

In the wake of the assassination of Nádir Sháh in the year 1747, a period of total anarchy ensued. There were three chief contenders for power: an Afghán named Ázád Khán; Muḥammad-Ḥasan Khán, the chieftain of the Qájárs (who occupied a good part of the area that was Ṭabaristán); and Karím Khán-i-Zand, a Lur and in no way Turkish.

Karím Khán was in Ṭihrán when his stubborn rival, the Qájár chief, was treacherously murdered and decapitated in his haunts by the Caspian Sea. The murderer carried the trophy triumphantly to Ṭihrán, hoping for high reward. But the wretch had thoroughly misjudged the Zand Khán. As soon as Karím set eyes on the head of his rival, sorrow seized his heart and his tears flowed. He ordered the execution of the murderer, and the head of Muḥammad-Ḥasan Khán was respectfully interred in the precincts of the Shrine of Sháh 'Abdu'l-'Aẓím. Such a man was Karím Khán-i-Zand.

Karím Khán ascended the throne in Ṭihrán, but refused to assume the designation of 'Sháh'. He was only Vakílu'r-Ru'áyá, he said, 'the Deputy of the People'. Then he had a fresh moat dug round Ṭihrán, added to its fortifications and battlements and ordered the construction of a number of mansions and government buildings. He intended to make Ṭihrán his capital-city. But soon he changed his mind and went to Shíráz – the immortal Shíráz of the glorious Báb, as it would become – and established his capital there.

We have now almost reached the end of our story of Ṭihrán, which the Qájárs made their capital-city. And Ṭihrán in the nineteenth century witnessed many infamies, great and small, the handiwork of the Qájár usurpers. Ághá Muḥammad Khán, the eunuch-king and first of the Qájárs, who inaugurated a dynasty which ruled from 1779 to 1925, began his blood-stained reign in the foothills of the Elburz range by ordering an odious deed – foul to commit and foul to relate – the dastardly treatment meted to the last of the Zands: the brave, the generous, and immensurably high-minded Luṭf-'Alí Khán.

And what then of the Land of Ṭá? At a time when the New Age was foreshadowed by Shaykh Aḥmad and Siyyid Káẓim; when its Herald Prophet the Báb was preparing the way for 'Him Whom God shall make manifest', and was martyred; when that glorious, expected One, Bahá'u'lláh, the 'Lord of Hosts' and the 'Master of the Day of Judgement', received in a dungeon in Ṭihrán an intimation of His Mission and was exiled to live and die in Ottoman domains – the Land of Ṭá was the scene of much tyranny and degradation, and its suffering and eclipse are still evident. Yet its true station, destined to be perceived and understood by all mankind, was promised and extolled by Bahá'u'lláh in these glowing words:

> *Let nothing grieve thee, O Land of Ṭá, for God hath chosen thee to be the source of joy to all mankind . . . Rejoice with great joy, for God hath made thee 'the Day Spring of His light' inasmuch as within thee was born the Manifestation of His Glory.*

Appendix

The Village of Qúch-Ḥiṣár

QÚ<u>CH</u>-ḤIṢÁR IS ONE OF THE several villages of the rural district of <u>Gh</u>ár, in the vicinity of Ṭihrán. <u>Gh</u>ár forms part of the larger district of Ray which includes the precincts of the Shrine of <u>Sh</u>áh-Zádih 'Abdu'l-'Aẓím. Qú<u>ch</u>-Ḥiṣár belonged to Bahá'u'lláh, and Ḥájí Mírzá Áqásí, the wily Ṣadr-i-A'ẓam of Muḥammad <u>Sh</u>áh and the Antichrist of the Bábí Revelation, had had his covetous eyes on this excellent property.

We know there were strong ties of friendship between Mírzá Buzurg, the Vazír-i-Núrí, father of Bahá'u'lláh, and Mírzá Abu'l-Qásim, Qá'im-Maqám the Second, the high-minded vazír of Muḥammad <u>Sh</u>áh. We also know that it was the statesmanship, the effort and endeavour of this Qá'im-Maqám that secured the throne for Muḥammad <u>Sh</u>áh. He had pledged his word to the late Náyibu's-Salṭanih, stood by his word, and, in the teeth of strong opposition by a number of royal pretenders, brought the son of his late master from far-off Tabríz and had him crowned. Qá'im-Maqám had been faithful, but not so the ingrate who now occupied the imperial seat. Muḥammad <u>Sh</u>áh listened to the promptings of the Antichrist, and destroyed his benefactor.

One of the first acts of Qá'im-Maqám, on gaining Ṭihrán, was to appoint Mírzá Buzurg, the Vazír-i-Núrí to a post in Luristán. He was given the administration of Burújird and a considerable area of the Ba<u>kh</u>tíyárí country which had suffered from unrest. A royal rescript issued by Muḥammad-<u>Sh</u>áh is extant, dated August 1835, in appreciation of the services rendered by Mírzá Buzurg in Burújird and its environs.

But very soon, too soon, those halcyon days came to an end. Ḥájí Mírzá Áqásí triumphed, Qá'im-Maqám was treacherously murdered,* and the friends of Qá'im-Maqám found themselves in dire straits. Mírzá Buzurg was recalled from Burújird, deprived of all posts and positions, even of his stipend, and forced into the seclusion of his home. He had a large family to support, and before long he ran into financial difficulties. From then to the end of his days, life was a continuous struggle against impoverishment. And Qúch-Ḥiṣár was a property mortgaged time and again.

At the time of his affluence, Mírzá Buzurg had gradually bought two-thirds of the village of Qúch-Ḥiṣár. The rest he held on lease and was successfully farming the whole of the property. And at the time of adversity, Qúch-Ḥiṣár proved invaluable as a security to borrow money for day-to-day expenses. That inevitable oft-repeated borrowing by Mírzá Buzurg began in Dhu'l-Ḥijjah, the closing month of the year AH 1251 (April 1836). Ḥájí Mullá 'Abbás-'Alíy-i-Núrí, a trusted confidant of Mírzá Buzurg, mortgaged a third of Qúch-Ḥiṣár on his behalf. Áqá Bahrám, a well-known eunuch of the royal household, provided the money. It was a short-term arrangement, and on the last day of Muḥarram, the first month of 1252, Mírzá Buzurg raised money from some other source and redeemed this debt. Immediately, on the following day (the 1st day of Ṣafar), the same Ḥájí Mullá 'Abbás-'Alíy-i-Núrí mortgaged the same section of the property on behalf of the Vazír, and borrowed 700 *túmáns* for him from Mírzá Muḥammad-Taqíy-i-Áshtíyání. When six months had expired and Mírzá Buzurg had been unable to settle the debt, the Áshtíyání lender almost foreclosed the mortgage. However, the Vazír negotiated a fresh agreement with that creditor to last for another six months. Apart from the property at Qúch-Ḥiṣár, Mírzá Buzurg was, perforce, using the houses in which he and his large family lived in Ṭihrán as securities to raise further loans. That was the state to which the malevolence of Ḥájí Mírzá Áqásí had reduced him.

In April 1837, Mírzá Buzurg paid his debt to that Áshtíyání in full. Next, in June 1838, one-sixth of Qúch-Ḥiṣár was mortgaged to Karbilá'í Muḥammad-Hádí Astarábádí for one year for the sum of 670 *túmáns*. The condition was that if the sum was not repaid within the set time together with an additional 74 *túmáns*, the property would revert to Karbilá'í Muḥammad-Hádí. Fortunately, within forty days,

* He was strangled because Muḥammad Sháh had pledged his word to his father never to be privy to the spilling of the blood of that good man and accomplished vazír. See index references to Qá'im-Maqám in *Bahá'u'lláh, The King of Glory*, *The Báb* and *'Abdu'l-Bahá* for further information on him.

Mírzá Buzurg was able to borrow 251 *túmáns* and this together with a silk robe was sufficient to repay the mortgage. But so difficult was Mírzá Buzurg's position that in July 1838 we find him mortgaging the property again, this time to the daughter of the deceased Ḥájí Muḥsin for the sum of 375 *túmáns*. This debt must also have been paid off after a short while although no documentary evidence exists as to when and how.

The strain of his financial predicament took its toll on Mírzá Buzurg and in the middle of 1839 (the beginning of AH 1255), he passed away.

Mírzá Buzurg had named Shaykh Muḥammad-Taqí of Núr as his trustee and his own brother, Mullá (or Shaykh) 'Azízu'lláh, the supervisor for the disposition of his inheritance. This arrangement, however, had been entirely verbal and there was no written document to support it. Therefore Bahá'u'lláh drew up such a document, and asked the people who knew of His father's wishes to affix their seals and signatures to it. Ḥájí Mullá 'Abbás-'Alíy-i-Núrí, Mullá Mírzá Bábá, Mullá Qásim and Mírzá 'Alí-Riḍáy-i-Sunjí witnessed this document. Mírzá Buzurg had also stated that whatever of his property he had distributed amongst his offspring in his own lifetime was entirely their concern and no longer his, and that which was his own to leave behind comprised the sheep in Tákur and the village of Qúch-Ḥiṣár. He had specified, as well, that his debts amounted to 1,200 *túmáns*. He had charged his trustee to clear his debts, divide two-thirds of whatever was left amongst his inheritors, in accordance with the law of the Qur'án, and use the remaining third in any way the trustee himself deemed advisable.

Once these preliminaries were completed and implemented, Mullá 'Azízu'lláh, on behalf of Shaykh Muḥammad-Taqí of Núr and the minors amongst the children of Mírzá Buzurg (Mírzá Yaḥyá, Mírzá Muḥammad-Qulí, Fáṭimih-Sulṭán Khánum, Nisá' Khánum and others), acting together with Mírzá Mihdí (a full older brother of Bahá'u'lláh)* and Mírzá Muḥammad-Ḥasan (His half-brother), mortgaged one-sixth of Qúch-Ḥiṣár and borrowed 200 *túmáns* from Mírzá Aḥmad, Mustawfíy-i-Núrí. It was a short-term loan for two months only. It is strange that this debt was not paid in time and Mírzá Aḥmad-i-Mustawfí foreclosed the mortgage and took the land into his own possession. Mírzá 'Alí-Riḍáy-i-Sunjí then bought it from Mírzá Aḥmad. It is interesting to note that one of the witnesses of that

* Mírzá Mihdí was already dead, but this refers, presumably, to his estate. (Ed.)

mortgage which resulted in the loss of one-sixth of Qúch-Ḥiṣár was Mullá 'Abdu'l-Fattáḥ, one of the victims of the holocaust of 1852. Another witness was Ḥájí Mullá 'Abbás-'Alí, the confidant of Mírzá Buzurg, who had acted in previous years on his behalf. A third witness was Mullá Mírzá Bábá, another martyr of future years.

A letter, written by Shaykh Muḥammad-Taqíy-i-Núrí to Ḥájí Mullá 'Abbás-'Alí is extant, in which he states that in order to clear Mírzá Buzurg's debts, he himself gave half of the village of Qúch-Ḥiṣár to Mírzá Ḥusayn-'Alí (Bahá'u'lláh), took from Him 80 *túmáns* in cash, and passed on to Him 700 *túmáns* of His father's debts. He also questions the validity of Mírzá 'Alí-Riḍá's transaction. The same mujtahid of Núr wrote to Mírzá 'Alí-Riḍá, directing him to cancel the sale and take back his money, which he apparently did. Shaykh Muḥammad-Taqí claimed that as Mírzá Buzurg's trustee, he should have been consulted, and his consent obtained. Thus with the help of the mujtahid of Núr, that one-sixth of the property also passed into the possession of Bahá'u'lláh. And since He was the holder of two-thirds of Qúch-Ḥiṣár, the whole estate was placed under His management, and other owners whose holdings were small received their annual dues from Him.

In the year 1844 some officials, casting their eyes on this prosperous and profitable property, laid an unjust claim to it, stating that Qúch-Ḥiṣár had, in reality, been part of Crown lands. Bahá'u'lláh took the case to Muḥammad-Sháh. Now the chief witness was Mustawfíyu'l-Mamálik, and he testified most definitely that the village of Qúch-Ḥiṣár had never been part of Crown lands in the rural district of Ghár and Fasháfúyih. The royal rescript, accordingly, directed the high-handed officials to cease interfering in the affairs of that village. It seems that Ḥájí Mírzá Áqásí had penned the royal edict, which was issued in June 1844. This peril over, the next centred in the very person of Ḥájí Mírzá Áqásí, and made itself felt within three years.

Let the inimitable pen of Nabíl-i-A'ẓam relate the rest of the story of Qúch-Ḥiṣár:

> Ḥájí Mírzá Áqásí, the Grand Vazír of Muḥammad Sháh, though completely alienated from Bahá'u'lláh's father, showed his Son every mark of consideration and favour. So great was the esteem which the Ḥájí professed for Him, that Mírzá Áqá Khán-i-Núrí, the I'timádu'd-Dawlih, who afterwards succeeded Ḥájí Mírzá Áqásí,* felt envious. He resented the superiority

* Not immediately; in between them came Mírzá Taqí Khán, the Amír-Niẓám and Amír Kabír, who was responsible for ordering the execution of the Báb.

Ḥájí Mírzá Áqásí, the Grand Vizier of Muḥammad Sháh

which Bahá'u'lláh, as a mere youth, was accorded over him. The seeds of jealousy were, from that time, implanted in his breast. Though still a youth, and while His father is yet alive, he thought, He is given precedence in the presence of the Grand Vazír. What will happen to me, I wonder, when this young man shall have succeeded His father?

After the death of the Vazír [Mírzá Buzurg], Ḥájí Mírzá Áqásí continued to show the utmost consideration to Bahá'u'lláh. He would visit Him in His home, and would address Him as though He were his own son. The sincerity of his devotion, however, was very soon put to the test. One day, as he was passing through the village of Qúch-Ḥiṣár, which belonged to Bahá'u'lláh, he was so impressed by the charm and beauty of that place and the abundance of its water that he conceived the idea of becoming its owner. Bahá'u'lláh, Whom he had summoned to effect the immediate purchase of that village, observed: 'Had this property been exclusively my own, I would willingly have complied with your desire. This transitory life, with all its sordid posessions, is worthy of no attachment in my eyes, how much less this small and insignificant estate. As a number of other people, both rich and poor, some of full age and some still minors, share with me the ownership of this property, I would request you to refer this matter to them, and to seek their consent.' Unsatisfied with this reply, Ḥájí Mírzá Áqásí sought to achieve his ends through fraudulent means. As soon as Bahá'u'lláh was informed of his evil designs, He, with the consent of all concerned, immediately transferred the title of the property to the name of the sister of Muḥammad S͟háh, who had repeatedly expressed the desire to become its owner. The Ḥájí, furious at this transaction, ordered that the estate should be forcibly seized, claiming that he already had purchased it from its original possessor. The representatives of Ḥájí Mírzá Áqásí were severely rebuked by the agents of the sister of the S͟háh, and were requested to inform their master of the determination of that lady to assert her rights. The Ḥájí referred the case to Muḥammad S͟háh, and complained of the unjust treatment to which he had been subjected. That very night, the S͟háh's sister had acquainted him with the nature of the transaction. 'Many a time', she said to her brother, 'Your Imperial Majesty has graciously signified your desire that I should dispose of the jewels with which I am wont to adorn myself in your presence, and with the proceeds purchase some property. I have at last succeeded in fulfilling your desire. Ḥájí Mírzá Áqásí, however, is now fully determined to seize it forcibly from me.' The S͟háh reassured his sister, and commanded the Ḥájí to forgo his claim. The latter, in his despair, summoned Bahá'u'lláh to his presence and, by every artifice, strove to discredit His name. To the charges he brought against Him, Bahá'u'lláh vigorously replied, and succeeded in establishing His innocence. In his impotent rage, the Grand Vazír exclaimed: 'What is the purpose of all this feasting and banqueting in which you seem to delight? I, who am the Prime Minister of the S͟háhans͟háh of Persia, never receive the number and variety of guests that crowd around your table every night. Why all this extravagance and vanity? You surely must be meditating a plot against me.' 'Gracious God!' Bahá'u'lláh replied. 'Is the man who, out of the abundance of his heart, shares his bread with his fellow-men, to be accused of harbouring criminal intentions?' Ḥájí Mírzá Áqásí was utterly confounded. He dared not reply. Though supported by the combined ecclesiastical and civil powers of Persia, he eventually found himself, in every contest he ventured against Bahá'u'lláh, completely defeated. (Unpublished)

Needless to say, prior to the sale of Qúc͟h-Ḥiṣár to the sister of Muḥammad S͟háh, Ḥájí Mírzá Áqásí had used every means, fair and foul, to prevent it. He had incited a number of the heirs of Mírzá Buzurg to appeal to Siyyid Abu'l-Qásim, the Imám-Jum'ih of Ṭihrán, with the plea that Bahá'u'lláh had deprived them of their patrimony. The Imám-Jum'ih, being a just man, had investigated the case put to him most thoroughly and assiduously, and found that the plea was false. He had given a clear verdict accordingly. S͟hayk͟h Muḥammad-Taqí, the mujtahid of Núr, had lent his support to Bahá'u'lláh.

Having failed miserably to achieve his purpose in an ecclesiastical court, Ḥájí Mírzá Áqásí had next tried to utilize the power and influence of Maḥmúd Khán, the notorious Kalántar of Ṭihrán. He had induced Mírzá Muḥammad-Taqí,* a younger son of the Vazír-i-Núrí, to draw up a statement pledging himself not to enter any transaction, regarding any part of the village of Qúch-Ḥiṣár, without the knowledge and consent of the Kalántar. Mírzá Riḍá-Qulí, the brother of Mírzá Muḥammad-Taqí, and their mother, Kulthúm Khánum, had also certified this document and affixed their seals to it. But, in truth, they were not entitled to the ownership of any part or section of that village. When Bahá'u'lláh was apprised of this curious stratagem of Ḥájí Mírzá Áqásí, He personally bought the one-twelfth of the property which belonged to His nephews – Mírzá Muḥammad-Báqir and Mírzá Maḥmúd, sons of Mírzá Muḥammad-'Alí – and then, with the full consent of other smallholders, sold the property of Qúch-Ḥiṣár to the sister of Muḥammad Sháh. Within a few months, Muḥammad Sháh was dead and Ḥájí Mírzá Áqásí had fallen from power. Thus ended the saga of Qúch-Ḥiṣár.

* He was a poet with the sobriquet of 'Paríshán'. In later years, he satirized Bahá'u'lláh. He died relatively young.

Bibliography

'ABDU'L-BAHÁ. *Memorials of the Faithful*. Translated and annotated by Marzieh Gail. Wilmette, Illinois: Bahá'í Publishing Trust, 1971.

'ABDU'LLÁH-I-ṢAḤÍḤ-FURÚSH. *Istidláliyyih Baráy-i-Ahl-i-Ḥaqq*. Ṭihrán: Bahá'í Publishing Trust, BE 123/AD 1966.

ABU'L-FAḌL, MÍRZÁ. *Kitábu'l-Fará'id*. Cairo: undated. Written in AH 1315/ AD 1897.

—— *Sharḥ-i-Shajarih Námih-i-Mubárakih* (Description of the Blessed Genealogy). Bombay: Muṣṭáfá'i, AH 1321/AD 1905.

BAHÁ'U'LLÁH. *Epistle to the Son of the Wolf*. Trans. by Shoghi Effendi. Wilmette, Illinois: Bahá'í Publishing Trust, rev. edn 1976.

—— *Gleanings from the Writings of Bahá'u'lláh*. Trans. by Shoghi Effendi. Wilmette, Illinois: Bahá'í Publishing Trust, rev. edn 1978.

—— *Tablets of Bahá'u'lláh revealed after the Kitáb-i-Aqdas*. Trans. by Habib Taherzadeh with the assistance of a Committee at the Bahá'í World Centre. Haifa: Bahá'í World Centre, 1978.

BARON, SALO WITTMAYER. *A Social and Religious History of the Jews*. Vol. III. New York: Columbia University Press, 1957.

BOSWORTH, C. E. *The Islamic Dynasties*. Edinburgh: Edinburgh University Press, Paperback edn (rev.), 1980.

BROWNE, E. G. *An Abridged Translation of the History of Ṭabaristán*, by Muḥammad B. Al-Ḥasan B. Isfandiyár, compiled about AH 613 (AD 1216). An abridged translation. Leyden: E. J. Brill. London: Bernard Quaritch, 1905.

—— *Materials for the Study of the Bábí Religion*. Cambridge University Press, 1918.

—— (ed.) *A Traveller's Narrative written to illustrate the Episode of the Báb*. Vol. II. Cambridge University Press, 1891.

—— *A Year Amongst the Persians*. Cambridge University Press, 2nd edn 1926.

CURZON, G. N. *Persia and the Persian Question*. 2 vols. London: Longmans, Green and Co., 1892.

DIEULAFOY, JANE. *La Perse, La Chaldée et la Susiane*. Paris: Librairie Hachette et Cie, 1887.

DUNLOP, D. M. *The History of the Jewish Khazars*. Princeton Oriental Studies, Vol. 16. Princeton University Press, 1954.

Fayḍí, Muḥammad-'Alí. *Khánadán-i-Afnán*. Ṭihrán, BE 128/AD 1971.

Gibbon, Edward. *The Decline and Fall of the Roman Empire*. Vol. 2, Chap. XLVI. (repr. of last edn revised by the author). London: Alex. Murray & Son, 1870.

Gonzalez de Clavijo, Ruy. *Narrative of his embassy to the court of Timour, at Samarcand, AD 1403–6*. Trans. by Clements R. Markham. London: for the Hakluyt Society, 1859.

Ḥaydar-'Alí, Ḥájí Mírzá. *Bihjatu'ṣ-Ṣudúr*. Bombay: 1913.

Ishráq-i-Khávarí, 'Abdu'l-Ḥamíd. *Kitáb-i-Núrayn-i-Nayyirayn*. Ṭihrán: Bahá'í Publishing Trust, BE 123/AD 1966.

—— *Risáliy-i-Ayyám-i-Tis'ih*. Ṭihrán: Bahá'í Publishing Trust, BE 103/AD 1946.

Journal of the Royal Asiatic Society. Vol. 21 (NS). London: 1889.

Karímán, Dr Ḥusayn. *Ṭihrán dar gudhashtih va ḥál*. Ṭihrán: Intishárát-i-Dánishgáh-i-Millí. Sháhansháhí 2535/AD 1976.

Kirmání, Aḥmad Majdu'l-Islám. *Táríkh-i-Inḥilál-i-Majlis*. (ed. Maḥmúd Khalílpúr). Iṣfahán: Intishárát-i-Dánishgáh-i-Iṣfahán, SH 1351/AD 1972–3.

Koestler, Arthur. *The Thirteenth Tribe: The Khazar Empire and its Heritage*. London: Hutchinson & Co (Publishers) Ltd, 1976.

Levy, Reuben. *A Mirror for Princes*. The Qábús Náma by Kai-Ká'ús Ibn Iskandar, Prince of Gurgán. Trans. from the Persian. London: The Cresset Press, 1951.

Magnus, Lady. *Outlines of Jewish History*. London: Vallentine, Mitchell, rev. edn 1958.

Má'idiy-i-Ásmání. A compilation of Bahá'í Writings. Compiled by 'Abdu'l-Ḥamíd Ishráq-i-Khávarí. Vol. 8. Ṭihrán: Bahá'í Publishing Trust, BE 129/AD 1972.

Malik-Khusraví Núrí, Muḥammad-'Alí. "Milk-i-Haḍrat-i-Bahá'u'lláh: Qariyyih Qúch-Ḥiṣar". *Áhang-i-Badí'*, year 26, nos. 4–5. Ṭihrán: National Bahá'í Youth Committee, BE 128/AD 1971.

Momen, Moojan. *The Bábí and Bahá'í Religions, 1844–1944*. Oxford: George Ronald, 1981.

Nabíl-i-A'ẓam (Muḥammad-i-Zarandí). *The Dawn-Breakers*. Nabíl's Narrative of the Early Days of the Bahá'í Revelation. Wilmette, Illinois: Bahá'í Publishing Trust, 1932.

Obolensky, Dimitri. *The Byzantine Commonwealth – Eastern Europe, 500–1453*. London: Weidenfeld & Nicolson, 1971.

Samandar, Shaykh Káẓim. *Táríkh-i-Samandar*. Ṭihrán: Bahá'í Publishing Trust, BE 131/AD 1974.

Shoghi Effendi. *The Advent of Divine Justice*. Wilmette, Illinois: Bahá'í Publishing Trust, rev. edn 1969.

—— *God Passes By*. Wilmette, Illinois: Bahá'í Publishing Trust, 7th ptg 1974.

—— *The World Order of Bahá'u'lláh*. Wilmette, Illinois: Bahá'í Publishing Trust, rev. edn 1955.

SULAYMÁNÍ, 'AZÍZU'LLÁH. *Maṣábiḥ-i-Hidáyat*. 8 vols. Ṭihrán: Bahá'í Publishing Trust, Vol. 1, BE 104/AD 1947; Vol. 3, BE 123/AD 1966; Vol. 7, BE 129/AD 1972.

VALLE, PIETRO DELLA. *The travels of Signor Pietro della Valle, a noble Roman, into East-India and Arabia Deserta*. London, 1665.

ZAEHNER, R. C. *Zurvan, A Zoroastrian Dilemma*. Oxford: Clarendon Press, 1955.

Glossary

'Abá Outer cloak or mantle.
Ájúdán-Báshí Chief Adjutant.
Ákhúnd See *Mullá*.
Alláhu-Abhá 'God is All-Glorious'.
Amír Kabír Title of Mírzá Taqí Khán-i-Faráhání, who became Grand Vizier.
Azalí Follower of Mírzá Yaḥyá, Ṣubḥ-i-Azal.
Bábí Follower of the Báb.
Bahá'í Follower of Bahá'u'lláh.
Bírúní Outer or men's quarters.
Darvísh Dervish. A Ṣúfí vowed to poverty.
Farmán Order or royal decree.
Farrásh Footman, lictor or attendant.
Farrásh-Báshí Head footman or chamberlain.
Farsang (Farsakh) A distance of approximately 3 miles, or 6–7 kilometres.
Fatwá (Fatvá) Sentence or judgment by a Muslim Muftí.
Ḥájí Muslim who has performed the pilgrimage to Mecca, or *Ḥajj*.
Ḥuqúqu'lláh 'Right of God'; payment by believers instituted in the *Kitáb-i-Aqdas*.
Ijtihád The power of the Shí'ih divine to issue *ex cathedra* decrees and judgments.
Imám Applied particularly by Shí'ihs to one of the twelve Apostolic successors of Muḥammad. An *imám* is also one who leads a congregation in prayer.
Imám-Jum'ih Member of the 'ulamá who leads the Friday prayers.
Jaríb 10,000 square metres.
Ka'bah (Ka'bih) Most Holy Shrine of Islám, in Mecca.
Kajávih A kind of pannier, howdah, or litter.
Kalántar Mayor.
Khán Prince or chieftain. A khán is also an inn.
Kisrás Caesars.
Madrisih School or religious college.
Masjid Mosque.
Mírzá Prince when after a name, or simply 'mister' when prefixed to a name.

Most Exalted Pen A designation of Bahá'u'lláh.
Mu'adhdhin Muezzin, one who sounds the call to prayer.
Mujtahid Doctor of Law.
Mullá One who has had a theological education.
Murshid Ṣúfí spiritual guide.
Mutaṣarrif Governor, under the Válí.
Nargileh See *Qalyán*.
Parasang See *Farsang*.
Páshá Honorary title given to provincial governors, ministers and military officers of high rank in Turkey.
Qáḍí (Cadi) A religious judge.
Qá'im 'He Who shall arise'; the Promised One of Shí'ih Islám.
Qalyán A pipe for smoking through water.
Qiblih 'Point of Adoration', towards which people turn in prayer (i.e., Mecca for Muslims, the Shrine of Bahá'u'lláh at Bahjí for Bahá'ís).
Ṣadr-i-A'ẓam Grand Vizier, Prime Minister.
Sardár Sirdar, military commander.
Shaykh Elder, teacher, master of a dervish order, etc.
Shaykhí Member of the school founded by Shaykh Aḥmad-i-Aḥsá'í.
Shí'ih(s) Followers of the first Imám, 'Alí, cousin and son-in-law of Muḥammad, and of his eleven hereditary successors; in contrast to the more numerous Sunnís, who uphold the line of elected Caliphs beginning with Abú-Bakr.
Siyyid Descendant of Muḥammad, entitled to wear the green turban.
Ṣúfí Muslim mystic.
Súrih (Sura) Chapter of the Qur'án; also a Tablet of Bahá'u'lláh.
Táj 'Crown'; a felt head-dress.
Túmán Unit of Iranian currency.
'Ulamá 'Those who know'; persons learned in Islamic law.
Válí Governor-General, governor of a Turkish province.
Vazír (Vizir) Vizier, minister of state.

INDEX

I. GENERAL INDEX

A Traveller's Narrative (ed. E.G. Browne), Browne's note re death of Áqá Mírzá Ashraf, 32; Jadhdháb tells authorship to Browne, 185

A Year Amongst the Persians (E.G. Browne), extracts describing Iṣfahán and graves of King and Beloved of Martyrs, 40–43; extract describing discourse of 'Andalíb, 60–61; referred to, 28n

'Abbás I (the Great), Ṣafavid ruler, 325; mentioned 7, 33, 40, 335, 336

'Abbás-'Alíy-i-Núrí, Ḥájí Mullá, trusted confidant of Mírzá Buzurg, 340–42 *passim*

'Abbás-Qulí Khán, illustration, 231

'Abbásids (AD 750–1258), 113, list of caliphs (in Baghdád) mentioned by author, 297; mentioned, 113, 279, 280, 299, 301, 304, 324, 331, 333

'Abda'r Raḥmán III, ruler of Andalus, 280

'Abdu'l-'Azíz, Sulṭán (reigned 1861–76), Istanbul described on night of deposition, 183; mentioned, 208

'Abdu'l-Bahá (Servant of Bahá), the Centre of the Covenant, illustration, 65; Most Great Branch, 72–3; 'Mystery of God', 72; *Suriy-i-Ghuṣn* reveals powers, quoted, 52–3; Bahá'u'lláh explains His power, 81–2; poems in praise of, by 'Andalíb, 73, by Varqá, 73, 75, 76, 84; refers to Mírzá Abu'l-Faḍl about ancestry of Bahá'u'lláh, 309; Covenant-breakers conspire against, 73, 161–3, 189; keeps Jamál Effendi in teaching field, 124; chooses him for mission to Amínu's-Sulṭán, 124, 126; describes attainments of Nabíl-i-Akbar and designates as Hand of the Cause, 112, 115; meets and advises Shaykhu'r-Ra'ís, 148; instructs Ibn-i-Abhar on eminent Bahá'ís, 150; Mírzá Abu'l-Faḍl ten months with, 265; advises Varqá to move his Bahá'í archives, 85; desires first-hand account of martyrdoms of Varqá and Rúḥu'lláh, 108; sends Vakílu'd-Dawlih to supervise building of 'Ishqábád Temple, 267; advises Samandar to leave daughter in Bahjí, 210–11; arranges restoration of House of the Báb, 236; silent concerning activities of Shaykhu'r-Ra'ís, 153–4; travels in Europe and America, 64; sends Furúghí to announce return to Haifa, 169; sends Rafsanjání to London, 140n; praises Mullá Muḥammad-Riḍá, 104; lauds Mírzá Abu'l-Faḍl, 104; sends Samandar and Ḥakím-Báshí to meet Ṭihrán Assembly, 213–14; presents Treatise on Politics to Sháh and notables, 176; addresses Tablet to the Hague (1919), 176; arranges refutation of *Kitáb-i-Nuqṭatu'l-Káf*, 213; stops circulation of *Kashfu'l-Ghiṭa'*, 213n; confirms truth of ash-Shalmagháni's verses on advent of future Manifestation, 309, 313; explains action of the Báb at martyrdom, 211. **Tablets and Writings** quoted to or concerning: Abu'l-Faḍl, 313; 'Andalíb, 74; Darvísh Ṣidq-'Alí, 316–17; Furúghí, 157; Ḥájí Mullá Mihdí, 75–6; Ḥusayn-i-Zanjání, 108; Jamál Effendi, 120, 126; Muḥammad-Ṣádiq Khán, 28; Nabíl-i-Akbar, 112, 115; Ṣádiq-i-Muqaddas, 23; Shalmagháni, 313; Shaykhu'r-Ra'ís, 155; mentioned, 3, 33, 87, 237, 242, 274, 321

'Abdu'l-Hamíd II, Sulṭán (reigned 1876–1909), receives Shaykhu'r-Ra'ís, 148; consults Mírzáy-i-Shírází on interpolations in *Kitáb-i-Aqdas*, 259

'Abdu'l-Ḥusayn Na'ímí, son of Na'ím, 141

'Abdu'l-Ḥusayn-i-Ṭihrání, Shaykh, 29; plans against Bahá'u'lláh, 112

'Abdu'l-Javád, Mírzá, divine of Iṣfahán, 38

II. INDEX OF PLACE NAMES